Asset Management

Tools and Issues

Asset Management
Tools and Issues

Frank J. Fabozzi
EDHEC Business School, France
Francesco A. Fabozzi
Stevens Institute of Technology, USA
Marcos López de Prado
Cornell University, USA
Stoyan V. Stoyanov

World Scientific
NEW JERSEY • LONDON • SINGAPORE • BEIJING • SHANGHAI • HONG KONG • TAIPEI • CHENNAI

Published by

World Scientific Publishing Co. Pte. Ltd.
5 Toh Tuck Link, Singapore 596224
USA office: 27 Warren Street, Suite 401-402, Hackensack, NJ 07601
UK office: 57 Shelton Street, Covent Garden, London WC2H 9HE

Library of Congress Cataloging-in-Publication Data
Names: Fabozzi, Frank J., author. | Fabozzi, Francesco A., author. | López de Prado, Marcos, author. | Stoyanov, Stoyan V., author.
Title: Asset management : tools and issues / Frank J. Fabozzi, EDHEC Business School, France, Francesco A. Fabozzi, Stevens Institute of Technology, USA, Marcos López de Prado, Cornell University, USA, Stoyan V. Stoyanov.
Description: Singapore ; Hackensack, NJ : World Scientific, [2021] | Includes bibliographical references and index.
Identifiers: LCCN 2020035412 | ISBN 9789811222931 (hardcover) | ISBN 9789811225758 (ebook) | ISBN 9789811225765 (ebook other)
Subjects: LCSH: Institutional investments--Management. | Asset allocation. | Portfolio management.
Classification: LCC HG4521 .F257 2021 | DDC 332.67/253--dc23
LC record available at https://lccn.loc.gov/2020035412

British Library Cataloguing-in-Publication Data
A catalogue record for this book is available from the British Library.

For any available supplementary material, please visit
https://www.worldscientific.com/worldscibooks/10.1142/11901#t=suppl

Desk Editors: Ramya Gangadharan/Lum Pui Yee

Typeset by Stallion Press
Email: enquiries@stallionpress.com

Frank J. Fabozzi

To the memory of sister, Lucy Fabozzi.

Francesco A. Fabozzi

To my father the man I aspire to be and to my sisters, Patricia and Karly.

Marcos López de Prado

To my brilliant engineering students: You are our hope for a better future.

Stoyan V. Stoyanov

To my wife Petya and my children Ava and Nia.

Contents

Preface

This book provides a description of the tools used in asset management as well as a more in-depth explanation of specialized topics and issues covered in the companion book, *Fundamentals of Institutional Asset Management*. Here we provide a brief description of each chapter in the current book and the reason based on our experience in the industry and in teaching undergraduate and graduate students why we decided to cover the topics in this book.

The first chapter describes asset management companies. We describe the characteristics of asset management companies and differentiate them from wealth management companies, and how traditional asset management companies differ from hedge funds. The governing document between a client and an asset management company is the investment management agreement. The basic terms of this agreement are described in the chapter and the appendix to the chapter is a sample investment management agreement. In the chapter, we also describe what clients are looking for from their asset manager, how the industry is changing, and what is needed to build the asset management company of the future.

Understanding the fundamentals of accounting is needed by those seeking to be a security analysts. To analyze a company, an equity analyst uses traditional financial statement analysis coupled with an investigation of a company's management and an economic analysis of a company's position in an industry. But an understanding of financial statements is also necessary for those who are quantitative analysts. This is because a company's fundamental factors are constructed from its financial statements.

Yet, blindly accepting numbers from a company's financial statement without realizing that alternative accounting treatments may be possible and the discretion given to management in making financial performance more attractive, could distort the recommendation of an equity analyst or the use of incorrectly computed factors incorporated into a quantitative model. In Chapter 2, the key financial statements are reviewed, and the assumptions made in preparing financial statements are explained. There is no explanation of the mechanics of preparing financial statements (i.e., no debit and credit mechanics). This chapter provides a good review for those who have not had a course in financial accounting.

The largest non-government sector of the investment-grade bond market is the residential mortgage-backed securities sector. So, any bond portfolio manager should be familiar with the products in this sector: mortgage pass-through securities, collateralized mortgage obligations, and stripped mortgage-backed securities. In Chapter 3, we describe these securitized products and explain how and why they are created. The mechanics for creating these products, referred to as structuring a pool of assets or loans or securitizing a pool of assets, is also used in creating asset-backed securities.

Statistical and operations research tools commonly used in quantitative asset management are covered in the Chapters 3 through 7. Chapter 4 covers financial econometrics: regression analysis, principal component analysis, and time-series models for volatility (ARCH and GARCH).

In asset management, the performance of a portfolio or investment strategy will often depend on the outcome of many random variables with changes in every variable impacting performance proceeding along a substantial number of possible paths. Because these eventualities make it impractical to evaluate all possible combinations of outcomes in order to assess the risks, Monte Carlo simulation is employed. In Chapter 5, we explain the basics of Monte Carlo simulation, describing the steps in a simulation and then providing several asset management applications.

An optimization model prescribes the best course of action to be pursued in order to achieve an objective. The optimization models used in most asset management applications such as asset allocation, portfolio construction, and portfolio rebalancing are mathematical programming models. The various types of mathematical programming models used for optimization in asset management and several applications are described in Chapter 6.

Asset managers have relied on financial econometric tools described in Chapter 4 to identify patterns in data. Machine learning offers researchers new tools for identifying patterns using nonlinear and high-dimensional techniques. After explaining how machine learning differs from financial econometrics in Chapter 7, we describe machine learning, provide a brief overview of machine learning tools, and describe the various applications to asset management. We also explain how to develop machine learning strategies. Formulating such strategies is non-trivial, and their misuse can lead to disappointing results.

In the classical asset allocation problem (more popularly referred to as modern portfolio theory as formulated by Harry Markowitz), variance is used as a proxy for risk. However, the variance penalizes symmetrically both positive and negative returns. In Chapter 8, we describe extensions of mean–variance analysis capturing asymmetry of risk by means of a risk measure or an asymmetric measure of dispersion focusing on the features which are most relevant for asset allocation decision-making. These features include the capacity to capture the skewness and kurtosis present in the observed asset returns, the dependence which is most relevant for extreme losses, and most importantly, consistency with the principle of diversification. Because it is common to use alternative risk measures in conjunction with a distributional assumption for asset returns, in Chapter 8 we review the most popular distributional hypotheses, focusing on what makes the extended frameworks different from mean–variance analysis. Every extension of mean–variance analysis is consistent with a risk–reward ratio which can be used as a measure of risk-adjusted performance.

In describing various theories in finance and explaining the implementation of various strategies, short selling and leveraging are key. The ability to borrow securities in the market when short selling, financing a position to create leverage, and using a portfolio of holdings as collateral to generate incremental returns falls into the area of securities finance and collateral management. Chapter 9 discusses securities lending and other vehicles used in securities finance and collateral management. The focus is on equities in Chapter 9. Repurchase agreements, commonly used to fund positions in the bond market, are the subject of Chapter 10.

Chapters 11–14 delve into quantitative equity strategies. The issues in implementing quantitative research are discussed in Chapter 11. In that chapter, we describe the process of performing quantitative research, how to convert research into implementable trading strategies, the issues associated with the quantitative approach to asset management, the common objective of a quantitative research process, and issues in selecting a sample and methodology for estimating a model.

The wide range of quantitative equity strategies is then discussed in Chapter 12. We begin the chapter by describing the differences between the fundamental and quantitative approaches to asset management. Then we set forth a taxonomy of quantitative equity strategies and describe multi-factor strategies, asset allocation strategies, factors strategies, event-based strategies, statistical arbitrage strategies, textual strategies, and alternative data strategies. After describing these strategies, we explain how to develop quantitative strategies and describe the five properties of a good quantitative investment model and strategy.

The challenges in implementing equity factor investing are the subject of Chapter 13, where we begin with a description of the current state of factor research. Equity transaction and trading costs are described in Chapter 14. Although we briefly described these costs in Chapter 13 of the companion book, the discussion in this book is much more comprehensive.

As explained in Chapter 13 of the companion book, there are two types of factor models: return forecast factor models and risk forecast factor models. Chapters 15 and 16 show how risk forecast factor models are used for equity and bond portfolio management, respectively.

In the last two chapters of the book, we explain the issues and methodologies for backtesting investment strategies. Chapter 17 describes the biases associated with backtesting and provides an overview of the three commonly used methodologies and their advantages and disadvantages. The focus is on the walk-forward method. Also described in Chapter 17 is the information that should be disclosed to clients regarding the results of backtesting a proposed investment strategy. In Chapter 18, the focus is on the use of the Monte Carlo method for backtesting and its advantages over other methods for backtesting an investment strategy.

Each chapter begins with the chapter's learning objectives. At the end of each chapter, there is a comprehensive list of the key points covered in the chapter.

The Companion Book

The companion book, *Fundamentals of Institutional Asset Management*, has 19 chapters grouped into six parts. Each chapter begins with learning objectives.

Part One provides an explanation of the key activities involved in asset management (Chapter 1) and the various forms of risk (Chapter 2). The four chapters in Part Two describe the investment vehicles and asset classes: equities (Chapter 3), debt instruments (Chapter 4), collective investment vehicles and alternative assets (Chapter 5), and financial derivatives (Chapter 6).

Part Three covers theories about portfolio selection and asset pricing. The fundamentals of measuring return and risk are the subject of Chapter 7. Chapter 8 covers what is popularly known as *modern portfolio theory* despite being introduced almost 70 years ago by Professor Harry Markowitz, the 1990 co-recipient of the Nobel Memorial Prize in Economic Sciences. This theory, also referred to as mean–variance analysis, provides a framework for the construction of efficient portfolios — portfolios that offer the maximum expected return for a given level of risk. The implementation of mean–variance analysis is not straightforward. There are issues associated with the estimation of the inputs required in the optimization model that must be employed to obtain efficient portfolios. These implementation issues are also explained in Chapter 8. In Chapter 9, the fundamentals of asset pricing models — models that describe the relationship between some measure of risk and expected return — are explained. The two most well-known asset pricing models — the capital asset pricing model and the arbitrage pricing theory model — are both covered in the chapter, as well as a brief introduction to other factor models.

The five chapters in Part Four cover common stock analysis and portfolio management. Stock analysts rely on financial analysis in evaluating a company's operating performance and financial condition. The tools of financial analysis are covered in Chapter 10. Methods for valuing a company's stock based on discounted cash flow models and relative valuation models are explained in Chapter 11. The wide range of common stock strategies are covered in Chapters 12 and 13. In Chapter 12, we discuss the concept of market efficiency and its implications for investment strategies. The remainder of the chapter covers investment strategies when investors believe that the market is price-efficient. These strategies are referred to as beta strategies. Active equity strategies, also referred to as alpha strategies, are the subject of Chapter 13. In that chapter, we also describe the reasons why an asset manager generated the realized return (return attribution analysis), the capacity issue associated with investment strategies, and the fundamentals of backtesting an investment strategy. How equity derivatives are used to control the risk of common stock portfolios is the subject of Chapter 14.

Four chapters are the subject of Part Five, which is devoted to bond analytics and portfolio management. Chapter 14 explains how bonds are priced and the various yield measures. The measures for quantifying interest rate risk are the subject of Chapter 15. In addition, in that chapter we discuss various credit risk measures. Bond portfolio strategies, indexing and active, are explained in Chapter 16. Unlike indexing in the equity market, indexing in a bond portfolio is challenging. To control a bond portfolio's interest rate and credit risk, derivatives are used. The instruments and how they are used to control risk are explained and illustrated in Chapter 17.

There has been considerable growth in multi-asset funds — funds where the asset manager invests in not only equities and bonds, but also alternative assets. The strategies used in managing multi-asset portfolios are the subject of Chapter 18, the one chapter comprising Part Six.

About the Authors

Frank J. Fabozzi is editor of *The Journal of Portfolio Management* and co-editor/co-founder of *The Journal of Financial Data Science.* He is Professor of Finance at EDHEC Business School. Over the past 35 years, he has held professorial positions at MIT, Yale, Princeton, and New York University. He is a trustee of the BlackRock closed-end fund complex. He has authored more than 120 books and more than 200 articles in peer-reviewed journals. He is the CFA Institute's 2007 recipient of the C. Stewart Sheppard Award and the CFA Institute's 2015 recipient of the James R. Vertin Award. He was inducted into the Fixed Income Analysts Society Hall of Fame in November 2002. He earned the designations of Chartered Financial Analyst (CFA) and Certified Public Accountant (CPA). He received his BA and MA in economics in 1970 from The City College of New York where he was elected to Phi Beta Kappa, and received a PhD in economics in 1972 from the City University of New York. In 1994 he was awarded an Honorary Doctorate of Humane Letters from Nova Southwestern University.

Francesco A. Fabozzi is a doctoral student in data science at the Stevens Institute of Technology. He is the managing editor of *The Journal of Financial Data Science.* He has worked as a research associate at NYU's Courant Institute in the Department of Mathematical Finance. He is on the Curriculum Board of the Financial Data Professionals Institute (FDP Institute). He interned at AQR in the firm's machine learning group. Francesco has published in the *Journal of Financial Econometrics* and assisted in the authoring of *Global Financial Markets.* He earned a BA in economics in 2018 from Princeton University and an MS in financial analytics in 2019 from the Stevens Institute of Technology.

Marcos López de Prado is the CIO of True Positive Technologies (TPT), and Professor of Practice at Cornell University's School of Engineering. Marcos launched TPT after he sold some of his patents to AQR Capital Management, where he was a principal and AQR's first head of machine learning. Concurrently with the management of investments, since 2011 Marcos has been a research fellow at Lawrence Berkeley National Laboratory (US Department of Energy, Office of Science). He is the author of several graduate textbooks, including *Advances in Financial Machine Learning* (Wiley, 2018) and *Machine Learning for Asset Managers* (Cambridge University Press, 2020). Marcos is the co-founder and co-editor of *The Journal of Financial Data Science.* He earned a PhD in financial economics (2003), a second PhD in mathematical finance (2011) from Universidad Complutense de Madrid. In 2019, he received the "Quant of the Year Award" from *The Journal of Portfolio Management.*

Stoyan V. Stoyanov is Equity Research Director at a prominent financial services firm. Prior to this role, he was a research professor of finance in the Center for Finance and the College of Business at Stony Brook University. He has held professorial positions at EDHEC Business School and EDHEC Risk Institute–Asia. He has published over 40 articles in leading academic and practitioner-oriented scientific journals, contributed to many professional handbooks, and coauthored several books on probability and stochastics, financial risk assessment, and portfolio optimization. He earned his BA in economics and MS in applied probability and statistics from Sofia University in 2002 and a PhD in mathematical finance in 2005 from Karlsruhe Institute of Technology.

Acknowledgments

We would like to acknowledge the assistance of the following individuals in the writing of this book:

- Chapter 3 is coauthored with Anand K. Bhattacharya, Professor of Finance Practice in the Department of Finance, W.P. Carey School of Business, and the faculty director for the MS Finance program, and Bill Berliner, Managing Director, Fixed Income Research and Investor Relations, PennyMac.
- Chapters 9 and 10 are coauthored with Steven Mann, Distinguished Professor Emeritus at the University of South Carolina.
- Chapter 11 is coauthored with Sergio M. Focardi, professor and researcher at the Finance Group of the Pole Universitaire De Vinci in Paris, and a founding partner of The Intertek Group, and K.C. Ma, the Mary Ball Washington/Switzer Bros. Endowed Professor of Finance at The University of West Florida.
- Chapters 12–14 are coauthored with Joseph Cerniglia, an adjunct professor at the Courant Institute of Mathematics at New York University and visiting scholar at the University of Pennsylvania, and Petter N. Kolm, Clinical Professor of Mathematics and Director of the Mathematics in Finance M.S. Program at New York University's Courant Institute.

Chapter 1

Asset Management Companies

Learning Objectives

After reading this chapter, you will understand:

- the categories of professionally managed assets: collective investment funds and discretionary mandates;
- the differences between asset management and wealth management;
- the differences between traditional asset management companies and hedge funds;
- important characteristics of asset management firms;
- the basic terms of an investment management agreement;
- what clients are looking for from their asset managers;
- how the asset management business is changing and strategies to deal with the changes; and
- how to build the asset management company of the future.

Introduction

In this chapter, we describe the asset management industry, the characteristics of firms in this industry, the challenges that they face, and how to create the asset management company of the future.

Categories of Professionally Managed Assets

There are two categories of professionally managed funds: collective investment funds and discretionary mandate assets.

Collective Investment Funds

With *collective investment funds*, investors will purchase and redeem shares for an interest in a pool of assets managed by an asset management company. The basis for the purchase price and the redemption price is the net asset value (NAV), which is equal to the market value of the assets minus the fund's liabilities divided by the number of shares outstanding. Collective investment funds are set up according to a country's securities laws. For example, in the United States, the regulating entity is the Securities and Exchange Commission (SEC) established by the Securities Act of 1933.

The advantage of a collective investment fund from the investor's perspective is twofold. First, it allows investors to obtain diversification, which would not be possible to obtain with limited funds to invest. For example, in the absence of a collective investment fund, an investor who has $25,000 to invest will find it difficult to obtain diversification. Yet, by purchasing shares in collective investment funds where the fund's investment strategy is to invest in different asset classes, diversification can be achieved. Second, collective investment funds are professionally managed so that the investor benefits from the knowledge of professional investors, for which the investor pays a management fee.

Discretionary Mandates

Discretionary mandates give the asset management company the right to execute trades and construct portfolios on behalf of clients. The client, the owner of the assets or beneficial owners, does not grant the asset managers the right to do whatever they see fit. Rather, the client will impose guidelines that must be followed by the asset manager as set forth in the investment management agreement. For example, there will be an agreed upon investment strategy which the asset manager is permitted to pursue and the allocation among asset classes in which the asset manager may invest. There are other parameters that are typically imposed as well as the benchmark index and the risk-profile of the portfolio. In the case of an equity portfolio, the risk profile could be expressed in terms of how much the portfolio's beta may deviate from 1 and the acceptable range for the tracking error; for a bond portfolio, the risk-profile can be set in terms of how much the portfolio's duration can deviate from the benchmark's duration or the acceptable range for the tracking error.

Asset Management versus Wealth Management

Asset management companies can be viewed as a subset of wealth management companies, in that asset management is one of the several activities performed on behalf of a client. Whereas an asset management company will manage a portion of a client's assets where the client has invested in a collective investment or in a discretionary mandate, wealth management deals with all financial aspects of a client. That is, the activities performed by a wealth manager go beyond that of asset management and include asset allocation of all of client's wealth, tax advising, estate planning, retirement planning, insurance, and the selection of investment vehicles. A wealth manager will advise on the selection of collective investment vehicles that may be managed by the firm's asset management team or a third-party asset management team.

There are three ways in which the two differ. First, for the amount of funds allocated to an asset management company via a collective investment or a discretionary mandate, the asset manager seeks to maximize the return on those funds subject to any imposed constraints as set forth in the investment management agreement, which will be described shortly. A wealth manager is responsible for offering solutions to a multitude of financial issues faced by a client, including providing guidelines for diversification. Second, asset management companies use their in-house expertise to create products based on market conditions that investors may select to invest in and which wealth managers will recommend to their clients. Wealth managers do not solely rely on expertise in the range of investment vehicles, but also call upon the skills of tax accountants, estate planning attorneys, and insurance agents in putting together a financial plan on behalf of a client. The third way that the two differ is in what they charge clients for the cost of their service. An asset management company charges a fee based on the amount of assets under management (AUM) in a collective investment vehicle or a discretionary mandate. In some arrangements, there may be an incentive fee based on performance. The cost charged by a wealth manager is a retainer fee and may also include a fee based on AUM.

Traditional Asset Management versus Hedge Funds

Asset management companies include traditional asset management firms and hedge funds. Both types of asset management companies use the same strategies that we describe throughout this book and the companion book. However, there are five differences between these two types of asset management firms.

First, a hedge fund will take greater investment risks (i.e., make much larger bets) than a traditional asset management company. That is, a hedge fund will use a high-risk version of an investment strategy that may be used by a traditional asset management company. This is done through the use of leverage and derivatives.

The second difference is the management fee charged by the two. For a traditional asset management company, the management fee is typically based solely on AUM but may involve a modest performance fee. In contrast, the typical fee structure for a hedge fund is "2 and 20". This means that the hedge fund manager receives 2% of AUM each year and 20% of the positive return generated.

The third difference between the two is the use of a benchmark. Performance for a traditional asset management company is typically some benchmark such as an equity index or a bond index. That is, performance is gauged based on a relative basis. For example, in 2000, 2001, and 2002 the annual return on the S&P 500 was −9.1%, −11.9%, and −22.1%, respectively. If a traditional asset manager's performance for those three years had been −5%, −8%, and −15%, the asset manager had consistently outperformed the benchmark despite the fund returns being negative. For hedge funds, on the other hand, there is typically no benchmark. Instead, performance is evaluated on an absolute return basis. This means that if the fund's returns in the same three years were the same as that of a traditional asset manager, the hedge fund manager failed to deliver the return expected by the fund's investors.

The fourth difference relates to those who may invest in a hedge fund. The individuals permitted to invest in a hedge fund are restricted by the SEC to *accredited investors*. An accredited investor, also referred to as a sophisticated investor, has a special status under US securities law, in that they are permitted to invest in unregistered securities. As explained shortly, a hedge fund is an unregistered security. The definition of an accredited investor is based on threshold income and net worth as defined in Rule 501 of Regulation D of the Securities Act of 1933.[1]

[1]The income and net worth thresholds are subject to change by the SEC. Proposed changes have been released in December 2019 (SEC Release 33-10734). As of this writing, to qualify an accredited investor, an individual must have: (1) an individual or a joint

The last difference between traditional asset management companies and hedge funds involves government regulation. In the United States, although all asset management companies have the same anti-fraud provisions and have a fiduciary duty to their clients, there is less government regulation for hedge funds in terms of disclosure. Moreover, since hedge funds are unregistered securities, under federal securities law, they are prohibited from advertising. Consequently, hedge funds cannot market their products like traditional asset managers.

Characteristics of Asset Management Companies

The following are the four important characteristics of asset management companies:

- Fiduciaries on behalf of clients;
- Investment decisions guided by clients;
- Compliance with legal and regulatory guidelines;
- No use of leverage on its own behalf.

Fiduciaries on Behalf of Clients

The funds invested by an asset management firm are from the clients, not the asset management firm. The assets in which the asset management firm invests are not held by the firm but by a *custodian*. Prior to the 1929 stock market crash, the method for safekeeping of the financial instruments purchased by an investor was self-custody. That is, the investor was responsible for the physical certificates that showed their claim. Following the 1930s, trust companies took over the custodial function. However, trading volume in the stock market made the transferring of stock certificates from one of the seller's financial institution to the buyer's financial institution difficult. That has changed. Today, the safekeeping of the financial assets purchased by an asset manager on behalf of a client is done by a qualified financial custodian. The four largest custodians are banks: BNY Mellon, JPMorgan, State Street, and Citigroup. The global assets under custody of just these four banks are worth \$114 trillion.[2]

net worth of at least \$1 million or (2) either a \$200,000 or \$300,000 joint annual income over the last 2 years, with an expectation of earning the same in the future.

[2]A brief history of custody in the United States is provided in Fidelity [2018].

The asset management firm may not commingle the firm's assets with those of the client. It cannot guarantee return performance. For a collective investment vehicle, the gains after all fees are distributed only to the fund's shareholders. For a separate account, any gain after fees is distributed to the individual investors. Finally, in its management of a client's funds, the portfolio manager may not be a counterparty to trades that it does on behalf of its clients nor be the counterparty in an over-the-counter derivatives transaction.

Investment Decisions Guided by Clients

While the portfolio management team makes the decisions about the securities in which to invest given an investment strategy, it is the client who provides the guidelines by selecting the asset classes in which to invest and the strategy to be pursued. In the case of registered investment companies (i.e., mutual funds and closed-end funds), an investor selects a fund based on the investment strategy described in the prospectus, along with the types of securities in which the fund invests and the constraints (e.g., no short selling or concentration limits).

Compliance with Legal and Regulatory Guidelines

The asset management industry operates within a highly regulated environment where the complex rules are constantly changing. There is typically not one regulatory entity involved. For example, in the United States if an asset management firm is managing funds on behalf of an insurance company in addition to collective funds, the manager must comply with the regulations of the insurance industry as well as the rules mandated by the SEC. When managing funds for a pension fund, the manager is subject to regulations under the Employee Retirement Income Security Act (ERISA) under the supervision of the US Department of Labor.

Larger asset management companies that manage funds in several countries must be aware of the rules formulated by the regulatory authorities in each foreign country where they operate, as well as their domestic regulatory authority.

No Use of Leverage on its Own Behalf

Unlike a bank and bank-related financial institutions, an asset management company's balance sheet is quite simple. Typically, it uses no leverage except on behalf of its client when permitted to do so and the same for the use of derivatives. When a portfolio manager seeks funding, it is on behalf of its clients.

The Investment Management Agreement

When an asset management company agrees to provide services to an individual or an organization, the legal document that sets forth the terms of the service is the *Investment Management Agreement* (IMA). The appendix to this chapter provides a template for an IMA for a separate account and which we will refer to in describing an IMA's basic terms:

- Use of pooled vehicles and other managers;
- Reporting;
- Brokerage;
- Voting;
- Compliance;
- Adviser liability;
- Termination.

An IMA begins with the *Appointment* of the asset manager (see Section 1 of the sample IMA). The *Authority of Manager* section (Section 2 of the sample IMA) sets forth what the asset manager is authorized to do without the approval of the client. Notice in the sample IMA that the asset manager is not allowed to accept delivery of cash or securities or establish any custodial arrangement. It is the client that selects the custodian.

The *Guidelines and Instructions* section (Section 3 of the sample IMA) describes the client's investment objectives and any investment restrictions. Typically, the details are described in an exhibit that is included in the IMA. If the asset manager wants to modify the investment guidelines, the IMA specifies the approval process that the manager must go through to make the change.

The section describing *Fees* (Section 4 in the sample IMA) indicates how the fees that the client must pay the asset manager are determined. Often, there is a schedule in the form of an exhibit that provides the fee arrangement in more detail. Other issues regarding the fee arrangement are explained such as when the fee payments are to be made (typically quarterly) and compensation if the assets are managed for less than a year (either due to short initial period or the termination of the manager).

How the asset manager trades the assets in the account is described in the *Brokerage* section (see Section 8 of the sample IMA) and what the asset manager is allowed to consider in selecting a broker to execute trades. An asset manager who is managing multiple separate accounts as well as multiple collective investment vehicles will often execute a trade for all of these accounts simultaneously (referred to as aggregation or "bunching" of orders). After the trade is executed, the asset manager must allocate the trade among all of the accounts. The Brokerage section sets forth that the allocation should not favor any account over the other accounts. Moreover, if the trade is executed at different prices, this section explains how the prices are to be determined for each account.

The asset manager must provide written reports to the client. The *Reports* section (Section 10 of the sample IMA) explains the frequency of the reports and the timeliness of the reports. Typically, the reports are provided frequently.

In reporting to clients, the value of the assets in the account must be provided. How the value of the assets in the account are to be determined is described in the *Valuation* section (Section 11 in the sample IMA). If for some reason there is difficulty in determining a value for some assets, the Valuation section will mandate that the asset manager must act in good faith in determining the fair market value.

When the holdings in an account include common stock, there is an issue as to how the voting rights associated with the stock should be cast. The *Proxies and Other Legal Notices* section (Section 12 of the sample IMA) sets forth what the asset manager may or may not do. Other actions such as how the asset manager should handle the bankruptcy of a creditor in the account's holdings are also explained in this section.

The *Termination* section (Section 14, labeled *Termination; Survival*) covers the actions that a client may take to terminate the agreement (i.e., fire the asset manager) or that the asset manager may take in no longer wanting to manage the client's assets. This can be done on short notice in writing by either party (typically 30 days).

What Clients are Looking for from their Asset Managers

Several research studies have looked at what clients are looking for when their assets are being managed by asset management companies as well as wealth management companies. Based on a survey of investors, a study by PwC [2019], "Asset Management Revolution: Investor's Perspectives", looked at this question. There are three findings of this study. First, investors are looking for a better way to interact with the firms that manage their capital, embracing digital technology to do so. Second, investors are increasingly interested in social responsibility and other non-financial aspects of investing. These first two findings suggest that investors may no longer be focusing solely on just financial performance in isolation from other factors. Third, there is recognition by investors of the higher level of competitiveness in the industry so that now they are paying more attention to management fees and a firm's operations.

To assess the priorities and satisfaction of investors, PwC conducted a survey with respect to six key areas of concern to investors: (1) risk-return, (2) fees, (3) environmental, social, and governance (ESG), (4) relationships, (5) operational strength, and (6) macroeconomic and political environment. The survey participants included 750 institutional investors and 10,000 retail investors around the world. From the participant responses, PwC created an "Investor Alignment Index". The index measures the gap between how satisfied investors are with their asset managers' performance in each of the six key areas compared to how important that area is to them based on a scale of 1–10. The sign of the index had the following meaning. A positive score indicated that the investors in the survey did feel that asset managers meet the needs of investors, while a negative score indicated that the needs of the investors were not satisfied. A value of zero indicates that there is no gap.

The PwC survey found that the most important of the six key areas was macroeconomic and political environment. This area was particularly important for the retail investors in the survey. Generally, retail investors are most vulnerable to an economic downturn. The PwC survey also found that retail investors placed high priority on relationships. PwC notes that one of the major reasons retail investors found relationships to be important is likely due to the need of retail investors to receive communication and an explanation so that they can be reassured that managers are well-aware of the risks when there are difficult market conditions.

How the Fundamentals of the Asset Management Industry are Changing

Several market commentators and reports by brokerage firms and consulting firms have sought to identify the reasons why there will be major changes in the asset management industry and wealth management industry. The way in which firms in these industries respond to these changes will determine their success.

The complex regulatory environment has been identified by many market commentators as a major challenge that will change the industry. But there are other factors influencing the industry, including how the behaviors of investors have changed and technological advancements. There are numerous white papers and industry studies that have discussed the challenges that will change the industry. One such study is by Tikam, Vij, and Pal [2016] of WNS Global Services. The authors argue that there are three trends that will impact the industry. In addition to discussing these three trends, the authors explain how asset management companies can capitalize on them.

Structural Changes in Business Models Resulting from Digital Technology Disruption

The first trend is that digital disruption is causing structural changes to the current business models of asset management companies. The financial technology (FinTech) industry has disrupted all of the sectors of the financial management services industry and caused incumbents to respond to them. FinTech companies have attracted investors because of their simplified and lower fee structure, transparency, and more enjoyable user experience.

With respect to changes in consumer behavior, a study by Salesforce cited by Tikam, Vij, and Pal identified two insights. First, in making investment decision, Millennials (18–24) rely less on the advice provided by financial advisers than on online reviews and peer recommendations. In contrast, Baby Boomers (age 55 and greater) in making investment decisions rely on a combination of both financial advisers and online reviews. Second, Millennials are not interested in the traditional fee structure used by wealth managers.

Tikam, Vij, and Pal suggest three response strategies that asset management companies can use to respond to this first trend: (1) raise awareness, (2) segment clients and serve their needs, and (3) re-align business models. Raising awareness involves the leaders of asset management companies identifying potential disruptive technologies and formulating innovative strategies to deal with them.

With respect to the second response strategy, to improve customer satisfaction, asset management companies should identify the needs of the different segments of their client base. One segmentation approach is to divide customers into those who require personal attention and those who prefer self-service. The Salesforce study provides insights as to how different generations prefer personal attention and self-service. The study found that greater independence in making investment decisions is preferred by individuals from age 18 to 54 (i.e., Millennials, age 18–34, and Generation Xers, age 35–54). That is, these generations provide a self-service model. When the group elects to make decisions based on financial advisers, they want it to be a collaborative effort. Preference for relying primarily on financial advisers in making investment decisions is preferred by Baby Boomers. Moreover, the Salesforce study also indicates that the type of model used by clients also explains the type of investments they prefer. For example, individuals who prefer the self-service model are likely to do their own investment research and tend to like inexpensive funds that track an index such as ETFs and yet are likely to be interested in alternative assets. Moreover, this group tends to be less likely to favor a given asset manager and spread their business to multiple companies.

For the third response strategy, re-aligning business models and business relationships, leaders of asset management companies must have proactive policies for responding to the disruptive changes by FinTech companies. Tikam, Vij, and Pal suggest that this can be done in two ways. First, given the mistrust of some segments of the population to the investment advice of financial advisers and the greater trust in technology, asset management companies should develop technology that blends with human advise. Second, asset management firms can partner with startup FinTech companies.

Complex and Frequent Regulatory Changes

An asset management firm that operates globally is subject to the securities laws of each country in which it operates. Regulations in countries are frequently revised, requiring that the compliance group of an asset management company be aware of these changes. For example, Tikam, Vij, and Pal note a study where it was found that on an average day there were 155 regulatory updates issued by regulators throughout the world. On an annual basis, this meant that the compliance group of an asset management company that operates globally could potentially have to deal with 40,603 updates in just one year. This action is just for regulatory updates. It does not include major regulatory changes that lead to a significant revision of models used by compliance groups for monitoring the company's many funds and for preparing regulatory reports. The revision of these models is not a matter of changing one line of computer code, but can cut deeply into the profitability of asset management companies. Moreover, it increases operational risk and could result in significant penalties imposed by regulators.

The three strategies suggested by Tikam, Vij, and Pal for responding to this second trend are (1) initiate smart regulatory tracking, (2) implement centralized regulatory coordination, and (3) outsourcing part or all of the regulatory compliance activities to a third party. The first two response strategies involve establishing a tracking system of daily regulatory announcements and storing those updates on a centralized database. Today, there are several FinTech firms that specialize in software for compliance reporting for regulatory purposes. These FinTech firms are referred to as RegTech (regulatory technology) companies.

Increasing Pressure on Profit Margins

The rising cost of compliance and cyber security costs, the increased volatility of the equity market, competition from low-cost distributors, and the change in investor preferences to low-cost investment vehicles, in particular indexed products such as ETFs, will put pressure on an asset management company's profit margins. A decline in the equity market impacts revenues, in that it reduces AUM. With a management fee that is fixed as a percentage of AUM, a decline in equity values reduces revenues.

The four response strategies suggested by Tikam, Vij, and Pal are (1) conduct an as-is assessment of the impact of regulatory changes on profit margins, (2) implement automation to increase efficiency and reduce resource costs, (3) develop an innovative strategy, and (4) outsource operations that are not part of the core business. An as-is assessment analysis will allow asset management companies to identify how regulatory change impacts all segments of its business and then formulate a strategy for each segment should regulations change.

The second response strategy requires that each segment of the business be analyzed to determine how automation can be used. For example, for the investment advisory business, the use of robo-advisory services is appealing to Millennial investors. The growth of robo-advisory services is apparent from the acquisition of FinTech companies specializing in this area by asset management and wealth management companies, and the development of robo-advising internally by banks.

Another area where automation can reduce costs is in transaction processing. Technology is available to reduce the processing of transactions. The development of an innovative product strategy that provides solutions to clients, complies with regulations, and is justified on a risk-return basis can generate revenue to enhance profits. ETFs are a good example of what can be done. It is not that ETFs are new vehicles. Rather, there are various ETF investment strategies that appeal to investors. While these are low-fee products, they are scalable. To attract clients, asset management companies can utilize social media channels to share their investment insights.

As for the fourth response strategy, non-core operations include settlement, reconciliation, monitoring of fund performance, and data management. These non-core operations can be outsourced and will enhance profits if this can be done more efficiently by third-party vendors.

Building the Asset Management Company of the Future

We conclude this chapter with how the asset management company of the future should be built. To do so, we draw from a December 2019 blog coauthored by Seth P. Bernstein, President and Chief Executive Officer of Alliance Bernstein, and Kate Burke, the Chief Administrative Officer of Alliance Bernstein [Bernstein and Burke, 2019]. They list the following as what it will take to build the asset management company of the future:

- Culture;
- Raising the bar for FinTech innovation;
- Building solutions that deliver differentiated alpha;
- Responding to the demand for responsible investing strategies;
- Developing new ways to partner with investors.

Bernstein and Burke emphasize the critical role of an asset management company's culture, which is the constant amid persistent change. Culture is important not only for the company for opening diverse perspectives for everyone in the firm (the investment management team, research group, and client service group), it also instills trust in clients. To emphasize the importance of culture, in summarizing the blog, Seth Bernstein states:

> In our view, culture is the one constant that runs through all of these initiatives and helps us connect today to tomorrow ... But none of it can be achieved without exceptional talent and creating an environment in which employees can thrive.

FinTech generally refers to the application of new technology in providing financial solutions to individuals and firms. This trend that has arisen since the Global Financial Crisis — a trend that is referred to as the "FinTech Revolution" — is that technology firms have moved in and begun to offer services that were always offered by traditional financial institutions such as asset management firms [see Imerman, Fabozzi, and Jain, 2021]. Bernstein and Burke point out how innovations provided by FinTech companies can amplify the impact of an asset management company's human talent. These innovations do so by providing far more effective ways for performing asset management activities, from investment management and portfolio construction to servicing clients. The role of data science (Big Data, artificial intelligence, and machine learning)[3] in developing and analyzing information is critical for developing investment strategies, analyzing data, and understanding the experiences of clients. However, as Bernstein and Burke note, the use of data science by asset management companies is in its early stages. They state that

> Like all firms, we're still refining the formula for applying data science, because it's a field that continues to evolve ... But there's so much promise. In addition to enhancing the quality of our analysts' information, we're also using data science to enhance our investment processes and platforms — and to better understand what our clients need.

Investors are looking for innovative investment strategies that can generate excess returns, or alpha. Therefore, asset management companies must be able to build solutions for clients so that they can develop investment strategies to deliver alpha. This can be done internally or by acquiring capabilities to do so.

Clients are now demanding more transparency about where their money is being invested. They want asset management companies to develop responsible strategies/solutions in which they can invest, as well as expecting the firm to integrate those principles in other solutions that are offered. These strategies include ESG investing, ethical investing, and green investing.[4] Asset management companies must be capable of developing such solutions that are increasingly being demanded by clients.

Finally, asset management companies must have the ability to build deeper partnerships with clients that are beyond the traditional relationship between a client and an asset management company. This involves providing dialogues that offer investment insights so that clients better understand drivers of returns, the latest analytical tools and how they can be used, and new markets and the opportunities they offer, among other

[3]Chapter 7 covers machine learning.

[4]These issues are discussed in Chapter 13 in the companion book.

things. This can be done by asset management companies providing white papers/insights on their websites and periodic Podcasts.

Bernstein and Burke summarize their view on how to build the asset management company of the future as follows:

> Managing core businesses. Serving clients effectively. Making thoughtful cost reductions. Rethinking processes and approaches. Investing in strategic initiatives including talent, technology, and innovation as well as product development.

Key Points

- The two categories of professionally managed funds include: collective investment funds and discretionary mandate assets.
- Asset management companies can be viewed as a subset of wealth management companies, in that asset management is one of the several activities performed on behalf of a client.
- An asset management company will manage a portion of a client's assets where the client has invested in a collective investment or in a discretionary mandate.
- Wealth management involves all financial aspects that a client has: asset allocation, tax advising, estate planning, retirement planning, insurance, and the selection of investment vehicles.
- Three ways in which asset management and wealth management companies differ: (1) the asset manager seeks to maximize the return on those funds subject to any imposed constraints as set forth in the investment management agreement, while a wealth manager is responsible for offering solutions to a multitude of financial issues faced by a client, including providing for diversification, (2) asset management companies create products that investors may select to invest in, while wealth managers will not rely solely on their investment expertise in the range of investment vehicles but also call upon the skills of tax accountants, estate planning attorneys, and insurance agents in putting together a financial plan on behalf of a client, and (3) an asset management company charges a fee based on the AUM and possibly an incentive fee based on performance, while a wealth manager charges a retainer fee and may also include a fee based on AUM.
- Five differences between traditional asset management companies and hedge funds are (1) a hedge fund will take greater investment risks than a traditional asset management company, (2) the management fee for a traditional asset management company is typically based solely on AUM

while for a hedge fund it is a "2 and 20" structure, (3) the performance for a traditional asset management company is typically some benchmark but for a hedge fund performance is evaluated based on an absolute return basis, (4) only accredited investors may invest in hedge funds, and (5) hedge funds are unregistered securities and cannot market their product like traditional asset managers.

- Important features of asset management companies are that they are fiduciaries, they invest based on guidelines provided by clients, they must comply with legal and regulatory guidelines, and they do not employ leverage on their own behalf.
- When an asset management company agrees to provide services to an individual or an organization, the legal document that sets forth the terms of the service is the Investment Management Agreement (IMA).
- Three trends that will impact the asset management industry are (1) digital disruption causing structural changes to the current business models of asset management companies, (2) complex and frequent regulatory changes, and (3) increasing pressure on profit margins.
- The following are what has been suggested to build the asset management company of the future: culture, raising the bar for FinTech innovation, building solutions that deliver differentiated alpha, responding to demand for responsible investing strategies, and developing new ways to partner with investors.

References

Bernstein, S.P., and K. Burke, 2019. "Building the asset management firm of the future," Blog AllianceBernstein. Available at https://www.alliancebernstein.com/library/building-the-asset-management-firm-of-the-future.htm.

Fidelity, 2018. "Custody in the age of digital assets." Available at https://www.fidelitydigitalassets.com/bin-public/060_www_fidelity_com/documents/FDAS/custody-in-the-age-of-digital-assets.pdf.

Imerman, M., F. J. Fabozzi, and N. Jain, 2021. *The Economics of FinTech*. Cambridge, MA: MIT Press.

PwC, 2019. "Asset management revolution: Investor's perspectives." Available at https://www.pwc.com/gx/en/industries/financial-services/assets/pwc-awm-revolution-screen.pdf.

Tikam, J., A. Vij, and N. Pal, 2016. "Three trends shaping the asset management industry, and how to capitalise on them." WNS Global Services. Available at https://www.wns.com/Portals/0/Documents/Whitepapers/PDFFiles/651/34/WNS_Whitepaper_Three_Trends_Shaping_the_Asset_Management_Industry_and_How_to_Capitalise_on_Them.pdf.

Appendix: Sample Investment Management Agreement[5]

This Agreement is made this __ day of ____, 200[ ] (the "Agreement"), by and between [Name of Adviser] (the "Manager"), a [______] company, and ______ (the "Client").

1. Appointment. Client hereby appoints Manager as an investment manager to manage such of Client's assets as Client shall from time to time assign to it, the proceeds from the sale of such assets, and the income attributable to such assets (the "Account"). Client shall promptly notify Manager in writing of any increase or reduction in the amount of the Account's assets subject to Manager's investment direction.
2. Authority of Manager. Manager is authorized to supervise and direct the investment and reinvestment of the assets in the Account, subject to such limitations as are contained in the Guidelines described in Section 3 of this Agreement, as they may be from time to time amended, and subject to Client's right to direct the investment of the Account by means of Instructions as described in Section 3 of this Agreement. Manager, as Client's agent and attorney-in-fact with respect to the Account, when it deems appropriate and without prior consultation with Client, may: (a) buy, sell, exchange, convert and otherwise invest or trade in any stocks, bonds, options, units and other securities, including money market instruments, whether the issuer is organized in the United States or outside the United States, at such times and in such manner as Manager determines; (b) place orders for the execution of such securities transactions with or through such brokers, dealers or issuers as Manager may select, which brokers or dealers are entitled to receive compensation out of the Account for their services; (c) execute any documentation as the Account's agent and attorney-in-fact as Manager may deem necessary to facilitate any such investment or reinvestment; and (d) purchase, sell, exchange or convert foreign currency in the spot or forward markets as agent or principal, at the market rate, as determined by Manager in its sole discretion. Manager, as Client's agent and attorney-in-fact with respect to the Account, when it deems appropriate and without prior consultation with Client, may engage external legal counsel to review trade-related documentation for bank loans and other over-the-counter instruments, and charge the Account

[5]Reproduced from https://www.sec.gov/Archives/edgar/data/38777/000119312509241304/dex1012.htm.

for such costs. Manager may give a copy of this Agreement to any broker, dealer or other party to a transaction, as evidence of its authority to act on the Account's behalf.

Manager is not authorized to accept delivery of cash or securities for the Account or to establish or maintain custodial arrangements for the Account. Client shall choose a custodian (the "Custodian") to hold physical custody of the Account. Client shall direct the Custodian to segregate the assets in the Account and to invest and reinvest them in accordance with the directions transmitted by Manager and received by the Custodian. Such directions shall be given in writing, or given orally and confirmed in writing promptly thereafter. Client shall not change the Custodian without giving Manager reasonable advance written notice of its intention to do so, together with the name and other relevant information with respect to the new Custodian. Manager shall not be liable for any act or omission of the Custodian.

3. Guidelines and Instructions. Attached hereto as Exhibit A is a statement of the investment objectives of Client together with a statement of any and all specific investment restrictions applicable to the investment of the Account (the "Guidelines"). Client shall have the right at all times to modify the Guidelines or to give Manager instructions ("Instructions") to buy, sell or retain any investment, but no modification of the Guidelines and no Instructions or modifications of Instructions shall be binding upon Manager unless Manager has received written notice of them from an Authorized Person (as defined in Section 5(d)). Manager shall have a reasonable period to bring the Account into compliance with any changes to the Guidelines. Manager shall be under no duty to make any investigation or inquiry as to any statement contained in any written Guidelines or Instruction given and, unless and until specifically advised otherwise, Manager may accept the same as conclusive evidence of the truth and accuracy of the statements contained therein. The Guidelines and all Instructions, unless they expressly provide otherwise, shall continue to be effective until duly canceled by subsequent modifications duly communicated to Manager in writing.
4. Fees. As full compensation for its services under this Agreement, Manager shall be paid quarterly a fee equal to one-fourth of the annual rates specified in Exhibit B, based on the asset value of the Account as of the last day of each calendar quarter on which the New York Stock Exchange is open for trading (the "Valuation Date"). The initial billing period will begin when this Agreement is signed by Client

and accepted by Manager, and initial funding has been received by the Custodian (the "Inception Date"). The initial fee will be pro-rated to cover the period from the Inception Date through the Valuation Date for that calendar quarter and will be based on the valuation as of that Valuation Date. Future quarterly fees will be calculated similarly in arrears. If Manager shall serve for less than the whole of any quarter, its compensation shall be determined as provided above on the basis of the value of the assets in the Account as of the end of the date of termination and shall be payable on a pro rata basis for the period of the quarter for which it served as Manager hereunder. Client shall direct the Custodian automatically to charge to the Account and pay directly to Manager all of Manager's fees upon the Custodian's receipt of an invoice from Manager.

5. Representations and Warranties. Client hereby acknowledges, represents and warrants to, and agrees with Manager, as follows:
   (a) Client Assets. Client is the sole owner of all assets in the Account and (i) there are no restrictions on the transfer, sale or public distribution of any such assets and (ii) no option, lien, charge, security or encumbrance exists over such assets, except as disclosed to Manager in writing.
   (b) Authority. The Client has full authority and power to engage Manager under the terms and conditions of this Agreement, and such engagement does not violate Client's constituent documents, any other material agreement, order or judgment of any court or governmental authority, or any law applicable to Client. Client further represents that all investments permitted herein are within its power to enter into and have been duly authorized.
   (c) Form ADV. Client acknowledges receipt of Part II of Manager's Form ADV. Not with standing anything to the contrary herein, if Client did not receive a copy of the Form ADV at least forty-eight (48) hours prior to execution of this Agreement, Client shall have the right to terminate this Agreement without penalty within five (5) business days of the execution of this Agreement; provided, however, that Client shall be at risk for any market fluctuations in the Account up to the time of such termination.
   (d) Authorized Persons. Any individual whose signature is affixed to this Agreement on Client's behalf has full authority and power to execute this Agreement on Client's behalf. Client represents that the officer specified on the attached Certification of Authorized Persons (Exhibit C) is authorized to act for Client and to certify to

Manager from time to time, by listing on, and delivering to Manager Exhibit C or a substantially similar form, those other persons who also are so authorized to act on Client's behalf ("Authorized Persons"). The Client shall promptly notify Manager in writing of any event that could reasonably be anticipated to affect any such individual's authority under this Agreement.

(e) Notice of Certain Events. Client will promptly notify Manager in writing of any occurrence that results, or threatens to result, in any representations by Client contained in this Agreement becoming inaccurate, false, misleading or incomplete.

6. Non-Exclusive Agreement. Nothing in this Agreement shall be deemed to limit or restrict Manager's right, or the right of any of its officers, directors or employees, to engage in any other business or to devote time and attention to the management or other aspects of any business, whether of a similar or dissimilar nature, or to render investment advisory services or services of any kind to any other corporation, firm, association or individual. Client understands that Manager provides investment advisory services to numerous other clients and accounts. Client also understands that Manager may give advice and take action with respect to any of its other clients or for its own account which may differ from the timing or nature of action taken by Manager with respect to the Account.

   Nothing in this Agreement shall impose upon Manager any obligation to purchase or sell or to recommend for purchase or sale, with respect to the Account, any security (including long and short positions) which Manager, or its affiliates, or its or their shareholders, directors, officers or employees may purchase or sell for its or their own account(s) or for the account of any other client. Client acknowledges that Manager's ability and that of its affiliates to effect or recommend transactions may be restricted by applicable regulatory requirements in the United States and elsewhere or its or their internal policies designed to comply with such requirements. Consequently, there may be periods when Manager may not initiate or recommend certain types of transactions in certain investments when Manager or its affiliates are performing services or when aggregated position limits have been reached, and Client will not be advised of that fact.

7. Liability of Manager. Except as may otherwise be provided by law, Client specifically agrees that Manager shall not be liable for: (a) any loss that Client may suffer by reason of any investment decision made

or other action taken or omitted in good faith and with that degree of care, skill, prudence and diligence under the circumstances then prevailing that a prudent person acting in a like capacity would use in the conduct of an enterprise of a like character and with like aims; (b) any loss, expense or other liability (including but not limited to attorneys' fees) incurred by Client or Manager arising from or in connection with Manager's compliance with the Guidelines or Instructions believed by Manager to be accurate; (c) any act or failure to act by any broker or other person with whom Manager or Client may deal in connection with the subject matter of this Agreement; or (d) any loss or failure or delay in performance of any obligation under this Agreement arising out of or caused, directly or indirectly, by circumstances beyond Manager's reasonable control, including, without limitation, acts of God, earthquakes, fires, floods, wars, terrorism, civil or military disturbances, sabotage, epidemics, riots, interruptions, loss or malfunctions of utility, computer software or hardware, transportation or communication service, accidents, labor disputes, acts of civil or military authority, governmental actions and inability to obtain labor, material, equipment or transportation.

8. Brokerage. Where Manager places orders, or directs the placement of orders, for the purchase or sale of portfolio securities for the Account, in selecting brokers or dealers to execute such orders, Manager is expressly authorized to consider, among other factors, the fact that a broker or dealer has furnished statistical, research or other information or services which enhance Manager's investment research and portfolio management capability generally. It is further understood in accordance with Section 28(e) of the Securities Exchange Act of 1934, as amended, that Manager may negotiate with and assign to a broker a commission which may exceed the commission which another broker would have charged for effecting the transaction if Manager determines in good faith that the amount of commission charged was reasonable in relation to the value of brokerage and research services (as defined in Section 28(e)) provided by such broker, viewed in terms either of the Account or Manager's overall responsibilities to Manager's discretionary accounts.

Nothing herein shall preclude the aggregation or "bunching" of orders for the sale or purchase of portfolio securities in the Account with other accounts managed by Manager. With respect to the allocation of trades, Manager shall not favor any account over any other and purchase or sale orders executed contemporaneously shall be allocated in a manner it deems equitable among the accounts involved. In some cases, prevailing trading activity may cause Manager to receive various execution prices on the entire volume of any security sold for the accounts of its clients. In such cases, Manager may, but shall not be obligated to, average the various prices and charge or credit the Account with the average price, even though the effect of this aggregation of price may sometimes work to the disadvantage of the Account. Client understands and acknowledges that Manager or its affiliates may, based upon such factors as Manager deems to be important, such as Manager's or its affiliates' respective trading strategies or their respective accounts' relative sizes or investment objectives or investment restrictions, restrict to certain accounts purchases and sales of securities acquired in initial public offerings, including those that trade or are expected to trade at a premium in the secondary market.

In no event shall Manager be obligated to effect or place an order for any transaction for Client which Manager believes would violate any applicable state or federal law, rule, or regulation, or of the regulations of any regulatory or self-regulatory body to which Manager or any of its affiliates is subject to at the time of the proposed transaction.

9. Confidential Relationship. Each party agrees that all non-public confidential information concerning the other party which may become available to such party in connection with services, transactions or relationships contemplated in this Agreement shall at all times be treated in strictest confidence and shall not be disclosed to third persons except as (a) may be required by law or regulatory authority, including but not limited to any subpoena, administrative, regulatory or judicial demand or court order, (b) as otherwise set forth in this Agreement, or (c) upon the prior written approval of the other party to this Agreement. Client authorizes Manager (i) to include Client's name in a representative or sample client list prepared by Manager, provided Manager shall not disclose Client contact information or any information about Client's holdings, and (ii) to use Manager's investment experience with respect to the Account, or the Account's performance, in composite performance presentations, marketing materials, attribution analysis, statistical compilations, or other similar compilations or presentations, provided such use does not disclose Client's identity except to the extent permitted by Client.

10. Reports. Manager shall send to Client a written report of the Account as of the Valuation Date of each calendar quarter. Such reports shall be submitted within a reasonable period following such Valuation Date. For the purposes of all reports made by Manager to Client, foreign securities denominated in foreign currencies will be valued in United States dollars, unless otherwise agreed by Manager and Client. Client shall examine promptly each such report and any other report provided by Manager. To the extent permissible under applicable law, upon the expiration of the sixty (60) day period immediately following the date of such report, or the termination of this Agreement as provided herein, if earlier, Manager shall be forever released and discharged from all liability and accountability to anyone with respect to each such report, including, without limitation, all acts and omissions of Manager shown or reflected in each such report, except with respect to any acts or omissions as to which Client shall have filed written objections with Manager within such sixty (60) day period. Nothing herein shall impair the right of Manager to a judicial settlement of any report rendered by it.
11. Valuation. In computing the asset value of the Account, if market quotations are readily available for securities listed on a securities exchange or on the NASDAQ National Market or NASDAQ Small Cap Market, Manager shall value those securities at the last quoted sales price or the official closing price, respectively, on the Valuation Date, or, if there is no reported sale, within the range of the most recently quoted bid and ask prices. Manager shall value over-the-counter securities within the range of the most recent bid and ask prices. If securities trade both in the over-the-counter market and on a stock exchange, Manager shall value them according to the broadest and most representative market as determined by Manager. Any security for which a current market quotation cannot be established or a market event occurs that calls into question the reliability of current market quotations, or any other security or asset, shall be valued in a manner determined in good faith by Manager to reflect its fair market value.
12. Proxies and Other Legal Notices. Decisions on proxy voting will be made by Manager unless such decisions are expressly reserved by Client. Manager's obligation to vote proxies shall be contingent upon (i) receipt of proxies from the Custodian or Client in a timely manner, and (ii) the lack of any legal encumbrance to voting, including any securities lending or similar program. Manager shall not be expected or required to

take any action with respect to lawsuits involving securities presently or formerly held in the Account, or the issuers thereof. However, Manager will use commercially reasonable efforts to file proofs of claim on behalf of the Account in class-action lawsuits involving securities presently or formerly held in the Account and, in that regard, Manager may, without prior permission or consent, disclose information about the Account whether by including such information in any such proofs of claim or otherwise disclosing such information in any matter related thereto. Manager may, at any time, terminate this service of filing proofs of claim by giving notice of such termination to Client, and such service shall, if not sooner terminated, automatically terminate upon the termination of this Agreement. Client acknowledges that by filing a proof of claim on Client's behalf, Manager may waive Client's right to pursue separate litigation against the issuer with respect to the subject matter of the lawsuit.

Client also acknowledges that Manager or its affiliates may, from time to time, recommend litigation against an issuer (whether by opting out of any existing class action lawsuit or otherwise) on behalf of one or more of the registered investment companies or other pooled investment vehicles advised by Manager or its affiliates. In such cases, Manager will not provide Client with notice of, or the opportunity to participate in, such litigation. Client agrees to hold Manager harmless for not including the Account in any such litigation.

With respect to bankruptcies involving issuers of securities on behalf of one or more of the registered investment companies or other pooled investment vehicles advised by Manager or its affiliates, Client also acknowledges that Manager may, in its sole discretion, participate in bankruptcy proceedings and join creditors' committees on behalf of one or more of the registered investment companies or other pooled investment vehicles advised by Manager or its affiliates. Unless otherwise agreed, Manager will not be expected or required to file proofs of claim with respect to securities held in the portfolio of the Client that may be the subject of bankruptcy proceedings. Manager will not be responsible for any failures to make such filings or, if Manager is acting under the authority granted to it, determines in its sole discretion to make such filings, for any failure to make such filings in a timely manner.

13. Acknowledgment of Investment Risk. Notwithstanding any provision herein to the contrary, Client understands that the value of investments

made for the Account may go down as well as up and is not guaranteed. Client agrees that Manager has not made and is not making any guarantees, including without limitation a guarantee as to any specific level of performance of the Account. Client further understands and acknowledges that investment decisions made on behalf of Client's Account by Manager are subject to various market, currency, economic, and business risks as well as the risk that those investment decision will not always be profitable. Client acknowledges that past performance results achieved by accounts supervised or managed by Manager are not indicative of the future performance of the Account. Client understands that securities, mutual funds and other non-deposit investments are not deposits or other obligations of, or guaranteed by, Manager or any affiliate, are not insured by the Federal Deposit Insurance Corporation ("FDIC") or any other government agency, and are subject to investment risk, including possible loss of principal amounts invested.

14. Termination; Survival. This Agreement may be terminated by either party upon thirty (30) days' written notice to the other party. Such termination will not, however, affect the liabilities or obligations of the parties under this Agreement arising from transactions initiated prior to such termination. Sections 4, 7, 9, 10, 17, and 18 shall survive the termination of this Agreement. Upon any termination of this Agreement, Manager shall have no further obligations hereunder, provided that: (a) any liability under this Agreement of one party to the other shall survive and remain in full force and effect, notwithstanding such termination, with respect to any claim or matter on which either of the parties has given the other written notice prior to such termination (except that Manager may render to Client a statement of fees due Manager through the date of termination after such date), until such liability has been finally settled; (b) Manager retains the right to complete any transactions open as of the termination date and to retain amounts in the Account sufficient to effect such completion; and (c) Manager shall be entitled to its fees and expenses, pro rated to the date of termination. Upon termination, it shall be Client's exclusive responsibility to issue instructions in writing regarding any assets in the Account.

15. Assignment. This Agreement may not be assigned (within the meaning of the Investment Advisers Act of 1940, as amended), in whole or in part, by Manager without the prior written consent of Client. Subject

to the preceding sentence, Manager may delegate all or part of its duties under this Agreement to any affiliate.

16. Communications. All reports and other communications required hereunder to be in writing shall be delivered in person or sent by first-class mail postage prepaid, overnight courier, or confirmed facsimile with original to follow.

    If to Client:

    Attention: ____________

    If to Manager:

    Attention: ____________

    Either party to this Agreement may, by written notice given at any time, designate a different address for the receipt of reports and other communications due hereunder.

17. Governing Law; Venue. This Agreement shall be governed by and construed and enforced in accordance with the laws of the United States and with the laws of the State of [California] [New York] without giving effect to the choice of law or conflict of law provisions thereof. The parties hereby consent to jurisdiction and venue in the federal and state courts located in [the State of California] [New York County of the State of New York].
18. Entire Agreement; Modification. This Agreement: (a) sets forth the entire understanding of the parties with respect to the subject matter hereof; (b) supercedes any and all previous agreements, understandings and communications, oral or written, regarding this subject matter; and (c) may not be modified, amended, or waived except by a specific written instrument duly executed by the party against whom such modification, amendment, or waiver is sought to be enforced. In the event of any conflict or inconsistency with this Agreement and any instructions or investment guidelines that are not made part of this Agreement or any investment policy statement, this Agreement will control.
19. Headings. The headings of the sections of this Agreement are for convenience of reference only and will not affect the meaning or operation of this Agreement. As used herein, references in the singular shall, as and if appropriate, include the plural.
20. Counterparts. This Agreement may be executed in any number of counterparts, each of which will be deemed an original, but all of which together will constitute one and the same instrument.

21. Severability. In the event that any provision of this Agreement is deemed to be void, voidable, illegal, or invalid for any reason, such provision will be of no force and effect only to the extent that it is so declared void, voidable, illegal, or invalid. All of the provisions of this Agreement not specifically found to be so deficient will remain in full force and effect.

IN WITNESS WHEREOF, the parties hereto have caused this Agreement to be duly executed by their duly authorized officers to be effective as of the date first written above.

[NAME OF CLIENT]

By: ____________________
Name: [Authorized officer]
Title:

[NAME OF ADVISER]

By: ____________________
Name:
Title:

EXHIBIT A

Statement of Investment Objectives

[To be provided by Client]

Statement of Client Account Restrictions

[To be provided by Client]

Exhibit A

EXHIBIT B

FEE SCHEDULE

As compensation for managing the Account, Manager shall be paid as follows:

Exhibit B

EXHIBIT C

CERTIFICATION OF AUTHORIZED PERSONS

I certify, as the ____________ (*specify title; e.g., general partner [of a partnership]; president, secretary [of a corporation]*) that the following persons are "Authorized Persons" under the Agreement:

NAME	TITLE	SPECIMEN SIGNATURE
____________	____________	____________
____________	____________	____________
____________	____________	____________
____________	____________	____________
____________	____________	____________
____________	____________	____________
____________	____________	____________
____________	____________	____________

____
Name of Legal Entity (Please Print)

By: ________________________
Signature

____
Name and Title (Please Print)

Date: ____________

Exhibit C

Chapter 2

Fundamentals of Financial Statements

Learning Objectives

After reading this chapter, you will understand:

- the purpose of financial statements;
- the five financial statements: statement of income, statement of comprehensive income, balance sheet, statement of cash flows, and statement of shareholders' equity;
- what is meant by generally accepted accounting principles (GAAP);
- the assumptions made in preparing financial statements using GAAP;
- the principles underlying GAAP;
- common ways in which income smoothing has been used to manipulate income;
- the role of the independent auditor;
- the different possible auditor opinions;
- how the earnings per share of a company is calculated;
- the difference between basic earnings per share and diluted earnings per share; and
- the activities of the statement of cash flow.

Introduction

A company's financial statements provide an investor with a summary of the operating, financing, and investing activities of a business. There are at least five financial statements: statement of income, statement of comprehensive income, balance sheet, statement of cash flows, and statement of shareholders' equity.

With a basic understanding of financial statements, we will see how financial statements are analyzed to provide the information sought about the performance of a company[1] and how the information can be used to estimate the fair value of a company's stock. That is, just looking at the raw numbers reported in the financial statements will not be sufficient to assess the performance of a company; rather, it is the combining of the raw data from the basic financial statements that is necessary to do so. This task is referred to as financial statement analysis.

In explaining financial statements in this chapter, we will use Procter & Gamble Co. as an example. This company is a US manufacturer of consumer goods whose products are sold in more than 180 countries. The company has five segments: Beauty, Grooming, Heath Care, Fabric & Home Care, and Baby, Feminine & Family Care. The company's stock is traded on the New York Stock Exchange with the ticker symbol "PG" and its stock is included in the Dow Jones Industrial Average.

The financial statements for publicly traded companies are distributed to shareholders via the annual report that such companies are required to distribute under the US securities law. Moreover, the financial statements become part of the periodic filing with the SEC, the Form 10-K, which contains much more information than contained in the annual report.

Overview of the Five Financial Statements

In this section, we begin with an overview of the five financial statements and then move on to explain the assumptions and principles in constructing financial statements under GAAP.

Income Statement

The *income statement* is a summary of the company's operating performance over a period of time (e.g., a fiscal quarter or a fiscal year). Other terms used for the income statement are the *statement of earnings*, the *statement of operations*, and the *profit and loss statement*. This financial statement begins with the company's net sales or equivalently its revenue. That item seems to be fairly simple to understand. However, that is not

[1]See Chapter 10 in the companion book.

always the case for the reasons we explain later in this chapter when we discuss the accounting rules as to when a company is permitted to recognize revenue so as to include it in the income statement. The last line, the "bottom line", is the company's *net income* or *net earnings*, which is also shown in terms of how much was earned per share of stock, referred to as its *earnings per share.*

Table 1 shows the statement of earnings of Procter & Gamble for three fiscal years: 2015, 2016, and 2017. Note that its fiscal year ends on June 30. Its 2017 net earnings were $15.411 billion. Following the net earnings on the income statement are two values shown for the company's earnings per share: $5.80 and $5.59. We'll explain the reason for two numbers later in the chapter.

Statement of comprehensive income

The comprehensive income of a company includes all income and expenses recognized by a company during the fiscal year. It is a much broader measure of income or loss than a company's net income, including values not represented in the income statement. We will describe comprehensive income later in this chapter. The financial statement that shows this broader measure of income is called the *statement of comprehensive income.*

Balance Sheet

A *balance sheet*, also called the *statement of financial condition*, shows the amount of a company's assets, liabilities, and equity as of the last day of the company's fiscal year in the case of an annual balance sheet and on the last day of the fiscal quarter in the case of a quarterly balance sheet. The assets of the company are the resources that management has to operate the firm by. How were the assets financed? That is where the liabilities and equity come into play because they indicate how the assets were used and where the funds were obtained. The liabilities represent the amount that the company borrowed. Equities represent the amount of the company assets financed by the owners of the firm (i.e., the stockholders in the case of a corporation). Since a company can only be financed from debt and equity, there is the well-known accounting identity: assets = liabilities + equity.

Table 2 shows the 2017 and 2016 balance sheet of Procter & Gamble. For 2017, the total assets were $120.406 billion. For that year, the liabilities and equity (shown as shareholders' equity on the balance sheet) were $64.628

TABLE 1: Procter & Gamble Statement of Earnings: 2017 and 2016

Amounts in millions except per share amounts; Years ended June 30	2017	2016
NET SALES	$ 65,058	$ 65,299
Cost of product sold	32,535	32,909
Selling, general and administrative expense	18,568	18,949
Venezuela deconsolidation charge	–	–
OPERATING INCOME	13,955	13,441
Interest expense	465	579
Interest income	171	182
Other non-operating income/(expense), net	(404)	325
EARNINGS FROM CONTINUING OPERATIONS BEFORE INCOME TAXES	13,257	13,369
Income taxes on continuing operations	3,063	3,342
NET EARNINGS FROM CONTINUING OPERATIONS	10,194	10,027
NET EARNINGS/(LOSS) FROM DISCONTINUED OPERATIONS	5,217	577
NET EARNINGS	15,411	10,604
Less: Net earnings attributable to non-controlling interests	85	96
NET EARNINGS ATTRIBUTABLE TO PROCTER & GAMBLE	$ 15,326	$ 10,508
BASIC NET EARNINGS PER COMMON SHARE:		
Earnings from continuing operations	$ 3.79	$ 3.59
Earnings/(loss) from discontinued operations	2.01	0.21
BASIC NET EARNINGS PER COMMON SHARE	$ 5.80	$ 3.80
DILUTED NET EARNINGS PER COMMON SHARE: (1)		
Earnings from continuing operations	$ 3.69	$ 3.49
Earnings/(loss) from discontinued operations	1.90	0.20
DILUTED NET EARNINGS PER COMMON SHARE	$ 5.59	$ 3.69
DIVIDENDS PER COMMON SHARE	$ 2.70	$ 2.66

TABLE 2: Procter & Gamble Statement of Comprehensive Income: 2017 and 2016

Consolidated Statements of Comprehensive Income Amounts in millions; Years ended June 30	**2017**	**2016**
NET EARNINGS	**$ 15,411**	$ 10,604
OTHER COMPREHENSIVE INCOME/(LOSS), NET OF TAX		
Financial statement translation	**239**	(1,679)
Unrealized gains/(losses) on hedges (net of $(186), $5 and $739 tax, respectively)	**(306)**	1
Unrealized gains/(losses) on investment securities (net of $(6), $7 and $0 tax, respectively)	**(59)**	28
Unrealized gains/(losses) on defined benefit retirement plans (net of $551, $(621) and $328 tax, respectively)	**1,401**	(1,477)
TOTAL OTHER COMPREHENSIVE INCOME/(LOSS), NET OF TAX	**1,275**	(3,127)
TOTAL COMPREHENSIVE INCOME	**16,686**	7,477
Less: Total comprehensive income attributable to non-controlling interests	**85**	96
TOTAL COMPREHENSIVE INCOME ATTRIBUTABLE TO PROCTER & GAMBLE	**$ 16,601**	$ 7,381

billion and $55.778 billion, respectively. As can be seen, the sum of the liabilities and equity is equal to the assets.

Now for what might seem to be a simple question. If Procter & Gamble wanted, for whatever reason, to sell off all of its assets, approximately how much would it obtain? Look at the balance sheet: the assets are shown as having a book value of $120.406 billion.

Unfortunately, that is not the answer. The reason is that the interpretation of the total assets shown on the balance sheet depends on the accounting rules used in constructing the financial statements. By this it is meant that there are certain accounting principles we will discuss that are applied in preparing financial statements. We'll discuss these accounting rules later in the chapter and will then be able to understand what $120.406 billion means.

Here is another question that may seem to be straightforward. By checking the balance sheet, can you determine what the market value of the common stock of Procter & Gamble was on June 30, 2017, the last day of its fiscal year? The stockholders' equity on the balance sheet shows that value to be $55.778 billion. In fact, around June 30, 2017, Procter & Gamble's stock was selling for around $87 per share and there were approximately 4.009 billion shares outstanding. The approximate market value of the stock outstanding (referred to as its *market capitalization*) on June 30, 2017, was $348.783 billion ($87 per share multiplied by 4.009 billion shares). Thus, the market value of the stock far exceeded the stockholders' equity as reported on the balance sheet. The reason for this is once again the accounting rules for computing stockholders' equity.

Statement of Cash Flows

The cash flow of a company is critical for a variety of reasons. We will provide a formal definition of what cash flow means later. The *statement of cash flows* is a summary of a company's cash flows that contains information about where the company received and utilized its cash. More specifically, the statement of cash flows has three components: the cash flow from operations, the cash flow from investment activities, and the cash flow from financing activities.

Statement of Shareholders' Equity

The *statement of shareholders' equity* provides a summary of the changes in the stockholders' equity. In addition, it includes information regarding actions taken that have altered the number of shares outstanding. Such actions include the repurchasing of any stock by the company and the exercise of any stock options granted by the company over time, and the sale of treasury stock.[2] The basic structure of this financial statement is to provide a reconciliation of the amount reported in each component of stockholders' equity from the beginning of the fiscal year to the end of the fiscal year.

Generally Accepted Accounting Principles

To be useful to users of financial statements, the information contained in financial statements should provide relevant information, provide reliable information, and be prepared in a consistent manner so that investors can

[2]Treasury stock will be explained later in this chapter.

make an informed decision about the investment merits of a company as an equity investment or creditworthiness as a borrower of funds.

Generally Accepted Accounting Principles (GAAP) are a framework of accounting standards, rules, and practices that have been authoritatively established by recognized accounting bodies in the United States. In the United States, publicly traded companies must report on a GAAP basis as set forth by the Financial Accounting Standards Board (FASB) and the accounting standards promulgated through its Statement of Financial Accounting Standards (SFAS). The FASB is an independent organization that the Securities and Exchange Commission (SEC) has designated to develop accounting standards.[3]

Outside the United States, the *International Accounting Standards Board* (IASB) sets GAAP. The IASB's accounting standards are called *International Financial Reporting Standards* (IFRS), which is referred to as non-US GAAP. The United States is transitioning to IFRS. Fortunately, generally there are more similarities than differences between US GAAP and non-US GAAP (IFRS) because for most types of transactions, non-US GAAP follows the same basic principles and conceptual framework as US GAAP.

GAAP Assumptions

In the recording of financial transactions and the final generation of financial statements, there are assumptions that are made and principles that must be followed. These assumptions and principles are important because they affect the way that users of financial statements interpret the reported numbers. The following three assumptions are made in preparing financial statements in accordance with GAAP: (1) monetary unit assumption, (2) time period assumption, and (3) going concern assumption.

Monetary unit assumption

In the United States, the monetary unit in which financial statements are prepared is the US dollar. The impact of inflation together with a principle discussed below, whereby assets must be recorded at their historical cost, may cause problems in using and interpreting these values in an inflationary environment.

[3]Despite these rules there is ample room for manipulating financial statements. See, for example, Mulford and Comiskey [2002] and Schilit, Perler, and Engelhart [2018].

Time period assumption

Annual financial statements are constructed so as to cover operations over any consecutive 12-month time period selected by the company and referred to as the fiscal year. The three months covered by the four quarterly financial statements follow from the fiscal year selected. Many businesses are highly cyclical. Typically, a company will select its fiscal year so as to coincide with the low point of activity in its business cycle.

Going-concern assumption

The going-concern assumption is critical in applying the GAAP discussed in the next section. To assume that a company will continue its business operations is to say that in the normal course of business (1) the company anticipates realizing what it has paid for its assets at the amount recorded on its balance sheet and (2) to satisfy its liabilities to creditors. If the going-concern assumption is unwarranted for a company, then the amount, as well as the classification of assets and liabilities in the balance sheet as explained later in this chapter, may need to be adjusted. This adjustment will have consequences for the reporting of revenues, expenses, and equity. Later we will see that within the balance sheet there is a time classification of assets and liabilities referred to as current and non-current items. This time classification has to do with a timeframe of one year and more than one year. For that time classification to be meaningful, the going-concern assumption must be justified. Similarly, the GAAP of historical cost, revenue recognition, and matching are meaningful only within the context of the going-concern assumption.

GAAP

The six GAAP are (1) full disclosure principle, (2) conservatism principle, (3) revenue recognition principle, (4) cost principle, (5) matching principle, and (6) materiality principle. These assumptions are briefly explained as follows:

Full disclosure principle

This full disclosure principle means that for the accounting numbers of such accounting items as revenues, expenses, and assets, there should be narrative and additional numerical disclosures provided in the notes accompanying the financial statements. In the absence of this full disclosure, an analysis of financial statements would not be complete.

Conservatism principle

There are certain transactions where it is necessary to make an estimate when recording a transaction. For example, when a company purchases equipment, an estimate must be made of its economic life in order to determine how the cost of the equipment will be spread out over time. The periodic cost allocated to future fiscal periods is called depreciation. The conservatism principle means that when an accountant is preparing financial statements with estimates provided by the company's management that are equally likely to occur, the least optimistic estimate must be used.

Revenue recognition principle

Revenue recognition seems to something that everyone in a business organization understands and should not be confused about. Holding aside fraudulent acts, let's look at why revenue recognition is not as straightforward as one might expect. To do so, let's use an illustration.

Suppose that a company agrees to provide a customer with services for one year for $2.4 million. The company signs an agreement for the delivery of the services with the customer on December 1, 2020, and on the date of the signing the company receives a payment of $2.4 million. The company provides the service for the full month of December 2020. In preparing the financial statements for the full year of 2020 (i.e., the time period for the financial statements for its fiscal year beginning on January 1, 2020 and ending on December 31, 2020), the $2.4 million is not treated as earned in 2020. Instead, the company only performed services for one month, not for the 12-month length of the contract. Thus, the company only earned $200,000 ($2.4 divided by 12) of the $2.4 million. The financial accounting treatment would then show revenue of $200,000 for the company's 2020 fiscal year. The revenue is shown as part of the company's income statement. The amount that the company did not earn in 2020 ($2.2 million) becomes a liability of the company.

Let's change the illustration slightly. Suppose that upon the signing of the agreement, the company agreed to invoice the customer next year but still provide the agreed upon services for December. In that case, although no cash was received, the company might record revenue of $200,000 on its income statement (thereby recognizing the revenue earned in December) and the $200,000 would be shown on its balance sheet as part of accounts receivable. However, to get this accounting treatment under GAAP, revenue is recognized if the following two conditions are satisfied: (1) the revenue is realized or realizable and (2) the revenue is earned. The first condition is satisfied if cash is received (i.e., revenue is realized in this case). The first condition can still be met if certain criteria described shortly are satisfied. Except in fraudulent transactions, it is typically clear whether the service is performed.

Returning to our illustration, in the case where the $2.4 million was received at the contract signing, the recognition of the $200,000 of revenue for the 2020 fiscal year is the appropriate GAAP treatment: cash was received and the services (by assumption) were performed. The case is not so clear when no cash is received at the signing of the agreement but will be invoiced in the next fiscal year (2021). The first three criteria listed above are satisfied. However, there is insufficient information regarding the customer to determine the collectability of the $200,000. For example, suppose that the customer is a company that is strapped for cash and is in a weak financial condition. Then there would be a question as to whether the $200,000 should be recognized. Worse yet, one can imagine a fraudulent act wherein a company enters into sham transactions with an entity that it knows cannot satisfy the payment terms of a service agreement and uses those sham transactions to inflate its revenue.

Consequently, rules for revenue recognition may seem straightforward under GAAP but complicated transactions may leave room for interpretation on whether revenue has been recognized.

Cost principle

The information in the balance sheet will identify assets that are purchased by a firm. The amount that the firm paid for the assets will be initially shown on the balance sheet. The amount on the balance sheet will change over time, but there will not be an upward adjustment due to an increase in the fair value of the asset. The downward adjustment occurs for two reasons. First, an adjustment is made for certain types of assets due to what is called depreciation or amortization, which will reduce the amount on the balance sheet below the amount paid for an asset. Even the depreciation or amortization does not reflect the true amount by which an asset declines: it is determined by the accountant by applying a set of rules as explained later in this chapter. The second reason for a downward adjustment is when it becomes evident that a value on a balance sheet has been impaired and thereby requires a reduction of that asset's carry value on the balance sheet to its fair value. GAAP specifies how to test for the impairment of an asset.

Consequently, in reviewing the balance sheet, the amount shown reflects only historical costs adjusted downward for depreciation, amortization, and any impairment. So, a company that purchases a patent from another company for $5 million, and the patent eventually has an estimated market value of $200 million, will show the amount on the balance sheet as $5 million and then reduce based on amortization.

Matching principle

For the income statement to be meaningful, the revenues and expenses must be properly matched for the period covered by the statement. That is, revenues are properly recognized (recall the revenue recognition principle) in the period in which they are earned and the expenses associated with the generation of revenues are correctly matched with those revenues.

What is important to understand is that in seeking to create an income statement that reflects a company's operations in generating income, looking at when cash is spent to generate a company's offerings (goods and services) and when it pays cash to purchase the inputs needed to generate revenue will be misleading. That is, the revenues and expenses for GAAP do not necessarily correspond with the inflow and outflow of cash.

In our discussion of the revenue recognition principle, we used an illustration of a company generating $2.4 million in cash for consulting services on December 1 of its calendar year for services to be provided for 12 months. It was clear that under GAAP, only $200,000 would be treated as revenue for the company's income statement. Suppose that the company in its previous calendar year purchased equipment costing $24 million and that equipment was used in servicing of the $2.4 million contract. To fairly represent this company's income for the calendar year, it is necessary to determine how much of that equipment was used in the generation of this calendar year's revenue. This is not done arbitrarily. As will be explained later in this chapter where we provide more details about the income statement and the balance sheet, we will see the GAAP rules for determining this amount based on accounting depreciation.

To implement the matching principle requires that the accounting be done on what is called an *accrual basis.* Under the accrual basis of accounting, revenue is recognized as we explained earlier: when it is earned and realized (or realizable) and the expenses are recognized in the period in which revenue is recognized.

When an asset is acquired that has expected benefits that are greater than one year, at the time the asset is acquired the price paid is recorded on the balance sheet as an appropriately titled asset. For example, it could be "Equipment". When the accountant creates an asset at the time of purchase, the accountant is said to be *capitalizing* the asset, as opposed to expensing the asset. Over time, the asset that has been capitalized will follow GAAP rules for the periodic reduction in its value depending on the type of asset as explained shortly: depreciation, amortization, or impairment.

Because of the matching principle, there are often *timing differences* that result from revenue and expense recognition by using the accrual basis of accounting. The timing differences that occur lead to "accruals" and "deferred" items on the balance sheet. There are four types of timing differences: accrued revenues, accrued expenses, deferred revenues, and deferred expenses.

Accrued revenue occurs when revenue is recognized prior to cash being received. This was illustrated earlier when service was performed in the month of December for $240,000, but the invoicing of this amount was in the next calendar year. *Accrued expense* occurs when an expense is recognized before cash is paid. As for deferrals, *deferred revenue* is revenue recognized after cash is received, while *deferred expense* is an expense whose recognition is realized after cash is paid.

Because the accrual basis of accounting relies on a company's discretion in determining the timing of revenue and expense recognition, there is the potential for manipulation of income. In our discussion of revenue recognition, we described how manipulation of when revenue is recognized is one of the major reasons for accounting fraud. A similar fraudulent outcome can occur if the timing of expenses is manipulated. The manipulation of income is not always to increase income. It could be done by a company to smooth income or revenue in order to meet investor expectations.

The three most common ways in which income smoothing has been used to manipulate income are channel stuffing, pull-in sales, and cookie-jar reserves.

1. ***Channel stuffing*[4]:** Channel stuffing is a scheme that accelerates revenues and income in the current fiscal period at the expense of revenues and income in a future fiscal period. The practice involves a

[4]Lai, Debo, and Nan [2011] investigate how the short-term interest of a manager in the firm's market value may motivate channel stuffing. For a further discussion and case study, see Prem, Rao, and Martin [2019].

company that is in a strong enough position to coerce companies in its distribution channel to order more of its offerings than they expect to sell. The order is shipped at the end of the fiscal quarter with the coercing company agreeing to accept the return of the shipment and provide full credit to the purchase company. The result is that the coercing company has a greater revenue and therefore a higher income for the fiscal period.

2. ***Pull-in sales***: Another practice for earnings and revenue management that companies have used is *pull-in sales*. With this practice, there are existing orders that are scheduled to ship to customers in a future fiscal quarter. Instead of shipping the order as scheduled and recognizing the revenue in the future fiscal quarter when it was supposed to be shipped, the order is shipped early and booked in the current fiscal quarter.
3. ***Cookie jar reserves***: Finally, there is the use of what is referred to as "cookie jar" reserves. In a typical cookie jar scheme, a company makes inappropriate assumptions about some expense, overstating them in a fiscal period when earnings are good (i.e., greater than investors might have anticipated, earnings years). For example, warranty expenses might be overstated and the difference between the amount recognized as an expense in the current fiscal period and the lower amount that should have been charged is placed in a "cookie jar". In a future fiscal period when earnings are not as good as anticipated by investors, the company dips into the cookie jar and does not charge the true expense for the fiscal period.

A company that incurs restructuring expenses has considerable discretion in deciding in what future fiscal period to recognize those expenses. For a publicly traded company, there might be the recognition of a substantial portion of restructuring expenses because the company is willing to take a big hit to its income in the current fiscal period in order to look more profitable in a future fiscal period. This is referred to as "big bath charges".[5]

Materiality principle

GAAP accounting recognizes that in the implementation of any of the above accounting principles there will be transactions or instances where there is

[5]To see how management big-bath accounting practices impact investor perceptions of financial statements, see Hope and Wang [2018].

no relevance for users of the financial information contained in the financial statements. In such cases, the materiality principle allows the accountant to ignore the strict adherence to a principle. However, there is no definitive answer to the question of how much a transaction or an accounting item would have to be in order to be viewed as immaterial. The accounting profession would argue that the accountant must use judgment. One would expect that the size of the transaction relative to the company's size would be an important factor used by an accountant in determining whether it is material.

The Independent Auditor and the Auditor's Report

A company's management is responsible for the preparation and integrity of the financial information presented in the financial statements. It is management that is responsible for making sure that certain estimates and judgments mandated by GAAP are done properly. Within the company, this function is performed by the internal auditors.

Users of financial statements are not likely to accept the financial statements as being unbiased if there was no independent analysis performed to attest to the fact that the financial statements were prepared in conformity with GAAP. This independent analysis is performed by an independent accounting firm that has employees who are certified public accountants (CPAs). These firms are retained by the audit committee of the board of directors to audit the financial statements and provide an opinion or a report, the different types of opinions will be discussed shortly. The independent auditor (or external auditor) works together with the internal auditor and the board's audit committee to gather information needed to form an opinion about the conformity to GAAP of management's financial statement. That is, while an auditor provides an opinion or report about the financial statements, the financial statements are still those of the company's management.

One of the following four possible auditor opinions can be given as a result of an auditor's review of the company's financial statements:

1. **Unqualified opinion:** Also referred to as a "clean opinion", an unqualified opinion means that it is the belief of the auditor that the financial statements are presented fairly in conformity with GAAP.
2. **Qualified opinion:** When the auditor believes that the financial statements present the company's financial position, results of operations,

and cash flows in conformity with GAAP, except for some matter that remains qualified, a *qualified opinion* is issued. The qualification that was the cause of the qualified opinion will be identified and explained in the auditor's opinion. The qualification will be due to either a departure from GAAP, doubt about the company continuing as a going concern, or the scope of the audit.

3. **Adverse opinion:** This opinion is issued when in the opinion of the auditor the financial statements do not present the company's financial position, results of operations, and cash flows in conformity with GAAP. This opinion is issued when there are significant departures from GAAP.
4. **Disclaimer of opinion:** This opinion is issued when an auditor is unable to formulate an opinion regarding the financial statements.

Statement of Income

The statement of income (or simply income statement) summarizes the operating performance of a company over a period (a fiscal quarter or a fiscal year). In this section, we explain the income statement and its components.

Although the presentation of the income statement varies from company to company, we'll use Procter & Gamble's income statement as shown in Table 1. We'll detail all the components of the income statement in this section.

Revenue/Sales

The proceeds received or to be received from the sale of a company's offerings are referred to as sales or revenue. The term used by Procter & Gamble as shown in Table 1 is net revenue. We explained the revenue recognition and the matching principle earlier.

Although not applicable to Procter & Gamble, there are many companies that generate revenue from long-term contracts. For example, Curtiss-Wright Corporation derives a substantial portion of its revenue from long-term contracts. For such contracts, the revenue and gross profit span more than one accounting year. We briefly describe the method for revenue recognition in such cases.

The GAAP methods for accounting for long-term contracts are (1) completed contract method and (2) percentage-of-completion method. The *completed contract method* only recognizes all the revenue and therefore income that arises from a project under a long-term contract after the obligations of the contract are fulfilled. This accounting treatment clearly violates the matching principle. However, it is justified by management if at least one of the following circumstances exist: management cannot provide reliable estimates about the percentage of completion of a project; there are inherent hazards that may interfere with completion of a project; or the project is of a short-term nature so that the impact on reported income under the completed contract method and the percentage of completion method would not vary materially.

The *percentage-of-completion method* requires that revenues for the contract be recognized each period based upon the progress of the construction (i.e., the percentage of completion). The major problem in implementing this method is that reasonably accurate estimates of completion may not be that simple to measure. GAAP requires the use of this method when estimates of progress toward completion, revenues, and costs are reasonably dependable and all of the following conditions exist: (1) the contract clearly specifies the enforceable rights regarding goods or services to be provided and received by the parties, the consideration to be exchanged, and the manner and terms of settlement; (2) the buyer can be expected to satisfy all obligations under the contract, and; (3) the company performing the contracted service can be expected to perform the contractual obligations.

Operating Costs and Operating Income

From revenue/sales are subtracted *operating costs.* The resulting measure is called the *operating income.* There are three types of operating costs: (1) cost of goods sold, (2) selling, general, and administrative expenses, and (3) research and development costs. Note that research and development expenses are expenses in the period in which they are incurred. That is they are expensed on the income statement and not capitalized as an asset.

In the income statement for Procter & Gamble in Table 1, the term operating costs does not appear. Two of the three types of operating costs appear. Note that Procter & Gamble uses the term cost of products sold rather than cost of goods sold.

Cost of goods sold

The calculation of the cost of goods sold (COGS) (or cost of products sold) is as follows:

Cost of inventory at the beginning of the accounting period
+ Cost of inventory purchased/manufacturing during the accounting period
– Cost of inventory at the end of the accounting period
= Cost of goods sold.

Or equivalently,

Cost of inventory available for sale during the accounting period
– Cost of inventory at the end of the accounting period
= Cost of goods sold.

Inventory includes raw materials inventory, work-in-process inventory, and finished goods inventory. As of its 2017 fiscal year, the following was reported in the Procter & Gamble's balance sheet (see Table 3) for inventory:

Raw materials	\$1.308 billion
Work in process	\$0.529 billion
Finished goods	\$2.787 billion

As can be seen, calculating the COGS depends on the costs of inventory at the beginning and the end of the accounting period and the cost of creating/purchasing inventory during the period. Determining the cost of inventory is referred to as *inventory valuation* or *inventory costing*. Fundamentally, the process involves the allocation of the costs of inventory available for sale between the ending inventory and the COGS.

Inventory valuation/costing

Under GAAP a company has considerable discretion in selecting the accounting method for determining the cost of inventory. We will keep the discussion brief when describing the alternative methods, what is included in the cost of inventory, and how the method adopted affects a company's net income. It should be noted that there are high-tech companies that may not have any inventory.

GAAP requires that the following costs go into the costing of inventory:

- *Parts and raw materials cost*
- *Direct labor costs*: Direct labor costs are work-related wages and fringe benefits that can be attributed to the direct production of a product or a service.

- *Manufacturing overhead costs*: Also referred to as factory overhead, factory burden, and manufacturing support costs, manufacturing overhead costs are the indirect manufacturing-related costs associated with manufacturing a product. Three examples of manufacturing overhead costs are depreciation of the fixed assets used in the production process, labor other than direct labor (referred to as indirect labor) involved in the production process (e.g., material handlers, maintenance personnel, equipment maintenance personnel, and product inspectors), and utilities used to operate the manufacturing plant and the equipment.

Using one of the following four inventory costing methods, the company determines how costs are allocated to cost of goods sold and ending inventory[6]: (1) specific identification, (2) first-in, first-out (FIFO), (3) last-in, first-out (LIFO), and (4) average cost. Once a company selects a method, it cannot simply change methods because this would make financial statements between two accounting periods difficult to fairly compare with one another.

When the specific identification method is used for inventory costing, the cost of each item sold is individually identified and recorded as cost of goods sold. The method tends to be impractical to use when a company sells large quantities of similar items. However, the method is suitable for when a company sells items that are unique from one another and each item has a high cost.

The other three methods of inventory costing — FIFO, LIFO, and average cost — determine inventory cost based on an inventory cost flow assumption. More specifically, the inventory cost flow assumptions are as follows:

- **FIFO:** Assumes that the first units in are the first units sold.
- **LIFO:** Assumes that the last units in are the first units sold.
- **Average cost:** Uses the average cost per unit to value the cost of those items sold.

The most commonly used method is FIFO.

The selection of the inventory costing method will have an impact on net income. During an inflationary period or a period where prices are rising

[6]There are other methods but they are less frequently used.

within the sector, FIFO will produce a higher net income than LIFO or average cost.

There is one more aspect of inventory valuation that is important. The historical cost principle states that an asset should be reported at historical cost. Consequently, fixed assets whose market value exceeds historical cost are not restated at the higher market value. In the case of inventory, there is revaluation of inventory when the market value declines because the inventory may become obsolete or it is simply not salable. The rule for inventory valuation is that inventory is reported at the *lower of cost or market* (LCM). Inventory revaluation is not uncommon for high-tech industries where there are different "generations" of a product.

The following is the accounting policy for inventory valuation as stated in the notes to the financial statements for Procter & Gamble:

> Inventories are valued at the lower of cost or market value. Product-related inventories are maintained on the first-in, first-out method. The cost of spare part inventories is maintained using the average-cost method.

Earnings from Continuing Operations

As the name indicates, operating income is the income derived solely from the firm's operations in selling its products and services. A company may have other expenses in running its business that are not directly related to the products and services that generate revenue. An example is expenses associated with how much it costs to borrow funds to run its business. Interest expense is the cost of borrowing funds. In the United States, interest expense is a cost of doing business and is deducted from operating income. Note that dividends paid to stockholders represent a distribution of income and is not a tax-deductible expense.

There are also other sources of income that are not generated through operations. For example, a company may use its excess cash to invest in the debt obligations of other companies or the debt of the US Treasury. The income received from such investments is interest income.

By adding non-operating income to operating income and subtracting non-operating expenses from operating income results in *earnings from continuing operations before income taxes*. By reducing this item by the *income taxes on continuing operations*, we obtain *net earnings from continuing operations*.

For Procter & Gamble for 2017, there was non-operating income in the form of interest income of $171 million. There were two non-operating expenses, interest expenses of $465 million and what is labeled as other non-operating expenses of $404 million. The label for other non-operating expenses says that it is "net". What this means is that there were other non-operating income and non-operating expenses and the difference between the two was an expense of $404 million. The notes to the financial statements tell us that it "primarily includes net acquisition and divestiture gains, investment income and other non-operating items".

This results in earnings from continuing operations before income taxes $13.257 billion. The income taxes on continuing operations were $3.063 billion. Subtracting $3.063 billion from $13.257 billion gives net earnings from continuing operations.

There is one further item that must be accounted for in order to derive a company's net earnings. A company may discontinue operations of parts of its business segments. The costs associated with discontinuing operations can be spread out over several fiscal years. The annual cost appears in the income statement as earnings or loss from discontinued operations.

For Procter & Gamble, there were earnings resulting from discontinued operations of $5.217 billion in 2017. Note 13 of the financial statement indicates there were several product categories that were discontinued. For example, in 2016 Procter & Gamble divested itself of a number of it "beauty brands", discontinued its pet care business, and its battery business. The earnings of more than $5 billion was due to a gain on the sale of several of the products it sold, primarily from the sale of its beauty brands.

Net Income Available to Common Stockholders

The net income reported is the amount earned for all stockholders: preferred stockholders (if any) and common stockholders. Common stockholders, however, are interested in the amount earned and available for them which is *net income available to common stockholders.*

Given the earnings from continuing operations and discontinued operations, adding both gives the *net income* or *net earnings* of the company. For Procter & Gamble, net earnings of $15.411 billion is the sum of the net earnings from operations of $10.194 billion plus net earnings from discontinued operations of $5.217 billion.

Two adjustments must be made to get net income available to common stockholders. First, dividends paid to preferred stockholders must be deducted. The second is to reduce earnings by what is referred to as *net income attributable to non-controlling interests* or *net earnings attributable to non-controlling interests*. This item is the portion of the company's net income and equity in consolidated subsidiaries that is owned by others.

In the case of Procter & Gamble, for 2017, net earnings attributable to non-controlling interests were $85 million and therefore net income available to stockholders was $15.326 billion ($15.411 billion – $85 million). Notice that Procter & Gamble does not label this item as net income available to stockholders but instead refers to it as "net earnings attributable to Procter & Gamble". However, this is not the net income available to common stockholders because it does not consider the dividends paid to preferred stockholders. Looking at the income statement in Table 1, the dividends paid to preferred stockholders are not shown, yet there was such payment made. Looking at note 6 of the financial statements one finds that dividends of $247 million were paid. Subtracting $247 million from net earnings attributable to P&G gives $15.079 billion which Procter & Gamble refers to as "net earnings attributable to P&G available to common shareholders", which is more generally referred to as net income available to common stockholders.

Earnings Per Common Share

Companies in their financial statements report the *earnings per common share* (EPS). This is a measure shows how much was earned for each share of common stock. It is calculated as follows:

$$\text{EPS} = \frac{\text{Net income available to common stockholders}}{\text{Number of common shares outstanding}}.$$

The numerator uses only the amount earned for common stockholders by removing the dividend payments made to preferred stockholders.

The number of common shares to use in the denominator must be calculated. The reason is that EPS is for an accounting period, but the number of common shares may change over that period. That is, it is not necessarily the case that the same number of common shares are outstanding for the entire accounting period. For this reason, the accountant calculates the weighted average number of shares outstanding.

In addition, GAAP requires that companies report two EPS measures: basic EPS and diluted EPS. *Basic earnings per share* is precisely what is in the equation above for the calculation of EPS.

The basic EPS for Procter & Gamble for 2017 was \$5.80 in its income statement. Let's see how that was computed. As explained earlier, note 6 in the company's financial statement that net earnings attributable to P&G available to common shareholders is \$15.079 billion. This is equal to net income available to common stockholders that should be used in the numerator of the EPS formula. What is the denominator of the EPS formula? That is, what is the number of shares that should be used in the EPS formula? The answer is also found in note 6. For the basic EPS calculation, the number of common shares outstanding for the calculation is 2.598 billion. The

$$\text{Basic EPS} = \frac{\$15.079 \text{ billion}}{2.598 \text{ billion}} = \$5.80.$$

This is the basic EPS value shown in Table 1.

Diluted EPS

Diluted earnings per share takes into account the potential for the conversion of securities into common stock such as securities that allow the holder to exchange it for a specified number of common stock shares and options issued by the company that grant to certain parties the right to exercise an option to obtain a specified number of shares. An example of the former is a convertible security such as convertible preferred stock or convertible debt. Collectively, all of the financial arrangements made by the company that allow a third party to potentially acquire the company's common stock shares are referred to as *dilutive securities*. Diluted EPS allows the user of the financial statements to see the potential impact on basic EPS if holders of dilutive securities actually exercised their right to obtain shares.

The formula for calculating diluted EPS is

$$\text{Diluted EPS} = \frac{\begin{array}{c}\text{Net income available to common stockholders adjusted}\\ \text{for exercise of dilutive securities}\end{array}}{\begin{array}{c}\text{Number of common shares if dilutive securities}\\ \text{are exercised}\end{array}}.$$

The reason for the adjustment in the numerator is that the net income must be adjusted for what would happen to this measure if a dilutive security is exercised. For example, think about a convertible debt. Interest is paid on that debt. If the debt holders converted to common stock, interest expense would be reduced by the amount paid to the convertible debt holders. The same is true with convertible preferred stock, but in this case, it would be the amount of dividends paid to that class of stockholders.

There is a restriction as to what dilutive securities can be included in the calculation. Any dilutive securities that can potentially make diluted EPS exceed basic EPS are excluded from the calculation of diluted EPS. Such dilutive securities are referred to as antidilutive securities.

Let's use Procter & Gamble's financial statements for 2017 to illustrate the diluted EPS calculation. The company reported the following in note 6 of its financial statement:

$$\begin{aligned}&\text{Net earnings/(loss) attributable to P\&G (diluted)} = \$15.326 \text{ billion},\\&\text{Diluted weighted average common shares outstanding} = 2.740 \text{ billion}.\end{aligned}$$

Net earnings/(loss) attributable to P&G (Diluted) is the equivalent of what is in the numerator of the diluted EPS formula. Therefore,

$$\text{Diluted EPS} = \frac{\$15.326 \text{ billion}}{2.740 \text{ billion}} = \$5.59.$$

This amount is shown in Table 1.

Statement of Comprehensive Income

Net income that is not distributed to stockholders as dividends is retained by the company and increases stockholders' equity. So, one would expect that if a company's net income was $10 million for the fiscal year and its shareholders' equity was $80 million at the beginning of the fiscal year, then stockholders' equity at the end of the fiscal year would be $90 million assuming that no dividends were distributed to stockholders'. However, at one time, there were transactions that adversely impacted stockholders' equity, but they were not shown in the income statement. In our example, suppose that the stockholders' equity at the end of the fiscal year was $75 million instead of $90 million. What happened to the missing $15 million in stockholders' equity? Companies would basically bury a transaction or series of transactions that adversely impacted stockholders' equity in the statement of stockholders' equity. That is, it would be expected that anything that impacts stockholders' equity would be identified in the income statement but that was not the case.

Because of this abuse, GAAP dealt with this issue by requiring a company report what it refers to as "comprehensive income" and "other comprehensive income". GAAP defines *comprehensive income* as

> the change in equity [net assets] of a business enterprise during a period from transactions and other events and circumstances from non-owner sources. It includes all changes in equity during a period except those resulting from investments by owners and distributions to owners.

Thus, comprehensive income includes net income. The part of comprehensive income that is added to net income to obtain comprehensive income is called *other comprehensive income* (OCI) and is defined as revenue, expenses, gains, and losses that under GAAP are recorded as part of shareholders' equity on the balance sheet but are excluded from net income. Therefore,

$$\text{Comprehensive income} = \text{Net income} + \text{OCI}.$$

Three examples of an OCI are (1) adjustments made in foreign currency from foreign subsidiaries that do not use as their functional foreign currency the US dollar, (2) in attempting to hedge its position using certain financial derivatives (swaps, futures, forwards), a loss is realized on the derivative instruments, and (3) a gain or loss on the sale of marketable securities.

Table 2 shows that statement of comprehensive income for Procter & Gamble. In 2017, its net earnings (before adjusting for non-controlling interests) were \$15.411 billion. There were four OCI items (net of taxes) totaling \$1.275 billion. This gives total other comprehensive income of \$16.686 billion (\$15.411 billion + \$1.275 billion). Reducing this amount by the amount attributable to non-controlling interest of \$85 million gives total comprehensive income attributable to common stockholders (or as Procter & Gamble labels it, "total comprehensive income attributable to Procter & Gamble") of \$16.601 billion.

Balance Sheet

Assets are what the company owns, and liabilities and equity indicate how the company financed those assets.

We will use as our illustration the 2017 balance sheet of Procter & Gamble Corporation shown in Table 3.

TABLE 3: Procter & Gamble Balance Sheet: 2017 and 2016

Amounts in millions; As of June 30		**2017**		**2016**
Assets				
CURRENT ASSETS				
Cash and cash equivalents	**$**	**5,569**	$	7,102
Available-for-sale investment securities		**9,568**		6,246
Accounts receivable		**4,594**		4,373
INVENTORIES				
Materials and supplies		**1,308**		1,188
Work in process		**529**		563
Finished goods		**2,787**		2,965
Total inventories		**4,624**		4,716
Deferred income taxes		–		1,507
Prepaid expenses and other current assets		**2,139**		2,653
Current assets held for sale		–		7,185
TOTAL CURRENT ASSETS		**26,494**		33,782
PROPERTY, PLANT, AND EQUIPMENT, NET		**19,893**		19,385
GOODWILL		**44,699**		44,350
TRADEMARKS AND OTHER INTANGIBLE ASSETS, NET		**24,187**		24,527
OTHER NON-CURRENT ASSETS		**5,133**		5,092
TOTAL ASSETS	**$**	**120,406**	$	127,136
Liabilities and Shareholders' Equity				
CURRENT LIABILITIES				
Accounts payable	**$**	**9,632**	$	9,325
Accrued and other liabilities		**7,024**		7,449
Current liabilities held for sale		–		2,343
Debt due within 1 year		**13,554**		11,653
TOTAL CURRENT LIABILITIES		**30,210**		30,770
LONG-TERM DEBT		**18,038**		18,945
DEFERRED INCOME TAXES		**8,126**		9,113
OTHER NON-CURRENT LIABILITIES		**8,254**		10,325
TOTAL LIABILITIES		**64,628**		69,153

TABLE 3: (*Continued*)

Amounts in millions; As of June 30		2017		2016
SHARE HOLDERS' EQUITY				
Convertible Class A preferred stock, stated value $ 1 per share (600 shares authorized)		**1,006**		1,038
Non-Voting Class B preferred stock, stated value $1 per share (200 shares authorized)		–		–
Common stock, stated value $1 per share (10,000 shares authorized; shares issued: 2017-4, 009.2, 2016-4,009.2)		**4,009**		4,009
Additional paid-in capital		**63,641**		63,714
Reserve for ESOP debt retirement		**(1,249)**		(1,290)
Accumulated other comprehensive income/(loss)		**(14,632)**		(15,907)
Treasury stock, at cost (shares held: 2017-1, 455.9, 2016-1,341.2)		**(93,715)**		(82,176)
Retained earnings		**96,124**		87,953
Non-controlling interest		**594**		642
TOTAL SHAREHOLDERS' EQUITY		**55,778**		57,983
TOTAL LIABILITIES AND SHAREHOLDERS' EQUITY	**$**	**120,406**	$	127,136

Assets

The assets of the company are its resources. There are different ways to classify assets. One way is based on how long it would take to convert the asset into cash. When an asset can be converted into cash within one year or one operating cycle, then it is said to be a *current asset*. A company's *operating cycle* is the length of time it takes to convert an investment of cash in inventory back into cash through the collections of sales. The operating cycle for most companies does not exceed one year. *A non-current asset* or a *long-term asset* is an asset that does not satisfy the criterion to be classified as a current asset.

Current assets

In the presentation of the assets on the balance sheet, current assets appear first and then non-current assets. The reason for this is that the order of listing is typically reported in the balance sheet in the order of liquidity, with the most liquid asset listed first and the least liquid listed last. Current assets include cash and cash equivalents, accounts receivable, inventories, prepaid expenses, short-term investment, and deferred income taxes.

The "cash equivalent" component of "cash and cash equivalent" is defined by GAAP as "short-term, highly liquid investments that are readily convertible to known amounts of cash and that are so near their maturity that they present insignificant risk of changes in value because of changes in interest rates".[7] A money market fund is given as an example of a cash equivalent. Cash equivalents are reported at historical cost based on the historical cost principle.

Short-term investments differ from the investment classified as cash equivalents. Debt securities that have a remaining maturity greater than three months but less than one year are classified as short-term investments. The reporting of this current asset is at fair market value, not at historical cost, an exception to the historical cost principle.

For Procter & Gamble, its 2017 balance sheet breaks down each category of current assets.

Non-current assets

There are two types of non-current assets: physical and intangible.

(1) *Physical assets*: Physical assets, also referred to as fixed assets, include property, plant, and equipment and are typically identified on the balance sheet as just *property and equipment.* When a fixed asset is purchased, it is recorded at the cost paid to acquire it and referred to as *gross property and equipment.* As explained earlier in this chapter, this process of creating an asset is referred to as capitalizing the asset. Each year property and equipment is depreciated based on some permissible accounting policy for depreciation. *Depreciation* is the allocation of the historical cost of a physical asset over its useful life (or economic life). It is required by the matching principle. The amount of the depreciation for the year is treated as an expense and appears on the income statement that we discussed along with the different accounting methods for depreciating a physical asset.

The company has a choice of the method used to allocate the cost of the fixed asset over the asset's expected life. That allocation is what is referred to as depreciation. The two alternatives are straight-line method or accelerated method. Using the *straight-line depreciation method*, the cost of the fixed asset (less the amount of its expected salvage value) is charged as an expense in a uniform manner over the asset's expected life. When an

[7] *Financial Accounting Standards Board Accounting Standards Codification* paragraph 305-10-20.

accelerated depreciation method is used, larger annual depreciation charges are taken in the earlier years. If the company elects to use an accelerated depreciation method, then it has a choice between two methods: declining balance method and sum-of-the-years' digits method. For our purposes, there is no need to explain these methods in any further detail. What is important is that with straight-line depreciation, the same amount is taken as depreciation each year of the asset's expected life, while with one of the accelerated depreciation methods, depreciation is higher in the earlier years of the asset's expected life and less over the later years.

What appears on the balance sheet is "plant and equipment, net" and is referred to as the "book value" or "carrying value". It is not the fair market value because of the historical cost principle. The amount of the net property and equipment is the difference between the gross amount and accumulated depreciation from the initial acquisitions. That is, *accumulated depreciation* for a physical asset is the sum of the depreciation taken each year. As explained earlier, the amount is reduced further by any impairments that are identified for some of the fixed assets.

In 2017, Procter & Gamble reported "property, plant and equipment, net" of $19.893 billion. In note 3 of its financial statement, we see that the total property, plant, and equipment was $40.148 billion, which is the gross amount. The accumulated depreciation was $20.255 billion. The net amount is what is shown on the income statement.

In note 1 to its financial statements, Procter & Gamble states the following about its accounting policy with respect to property, plant, and equipment:

> Property, plant and equipment is recorded at cost reduced by accumulated depreciation. Depreciation expense is recognized over the assets' estimated useful lives using the straight-line method. Machinery and equipment includes office furniture and fixtures (15-year life), computer equipment and capitalized software (3- to 5-year lives) and manufacturing equipment (3- to 20-year lives). Buildings are depreciated over an estimated useful life of 40 years. Estimated useful lives are periodically reviewed and, when appropriate, changes are made prospectively. When certain events or changes in operating conditions occur, asset lives may be adjusted and an impairment assessment may be performed on the recoverability of the carrying amounts.

(2) *Intangible assets*: US GAAP defines *intangible assets* as non-physical assets that entitle a company to generate rights, privileges, and other

economic benefits for the owner. GAAP defines an intangible asset as "an asset (not including a financial asset) that lacks physical substance". The GAAP definition excludes something that is thought of as an intangible asset called "goodwill", which we discuss shortly. In fact, the footnotes in financial statements refer to "goodwill and intangible assets" or "goodwill and other intangible assets" treating goodwill separately.

Intangibles assets can be classified as (1) marketing related, (2) customer related, (3) artistic related, (4) contract based, and (5) technology. Some types of intangible assets appear on the balance sheet, while others do not.

Intangible assets are classified under GAAP based on how they were acquired and their economic life. With respect to acquisition, intangible assets are classified as *internally created* (or *self-created*) *intangible assets* and *purchased intangible assets*. With respect to the latter, this occurs through the direct acquisition of an intangible asset or as a result of some business combination such as an acquisition of or merger with another company. Under GAAP, when a business combination occurs, a determination is made of identifiable intangible assets. An expert is called upon at that time to assess the fair market value of each identifiable intangible asset. So, for example, we now see that an intangible asset can arise due to (1) self-creation by the company, (2) purchase of individual intangible assets from other companies, and (3) purchased via a business combination that results in one or more identifiable intangible assets.

Purchased intangible assets: Some companies report in their balance sheet a large amount of purchased intangible assets. As with physical assets, the matching principle requires that a company allocate the acquisition cost over the asset's expected life (i.e., number of years where economic benefits are expected). In the case of a physical asset, the cost allocated and then shown as an expense on the income statement is called depreciation. For an intangible asset, it is called *amortization*. For purposes of amortization, GAAP distinguishes between an intangible asset that has an indefinite life and one that has a definite life. An intangible asset that has been acquired is classified as having an *indefinite life* if there is no foreseeable limit to the period over which it is projected to generate cash benefits for the company. For purchased intangible assets that have an indefinite life, no amortization is taken. In contrast, a purchased intangible asset with a finite life — which is defined by GAAP as having a limited number of periods over which cash benefits are expected by the company — must be amortized.

Internally generated intangible assets: Thus far we have discussed the treatment of purchased intangible assets. How are internally created intangible assets treated? This is important because high-technology companies typically create such assets. This often falls under the category of what is referred to as "research and development (R&D)". The treatment in this case is that, while there are exceptions, US GAAP requires that no intangible asset be reported in the balance sheet. Instead, US GAAP requires that R&D costs be expensed (i.e., taken as an expense on the income statement in the fiscal period when the cost is incurred).

As in the case of a tangible asset, an intangible asset that must be amortized is subject to impairment tests. If there are changes in circumstances or an occurrence of certain events, referred to as "trigger events", a determination of the impairment must be made and the intangible asset carrying value reduced or written off totally if it is determined that the impairment is not recoverable. The reduction in the carrying value on the balance sheet due to impairment results in a corresponding expense amount on the income statement.

Procter & Gamble reports trademarks and other intangible assets (net) of $24.187 billion.

Goodwill

Goodwill is an intangible asset that arises when one company acquires another company. Goodwill is measured by the difference between the price paid for the acquired company and the fair value of the net assets acquired. The fair value of the net assets is equal to the following: fair value of all identifiable tangible and intangible assets reduced by the fair value of any liabilities that the acquiring company assumed on behalf of the acquired company. On the acquiring company's balance sheet, the amount of goodwill is shown as an asset. That is, goodwill is capitalized on the balance sheet.

Goodwill is treated as an intangible asset with an infinite life. Consequently, there is no amortization of goodwill. However, goodwill like other intangible assets is subject to impairment tests that can reduce its value on the balance sheet.

In Procter & Gamble's 2017 financial statement, goodwill was reported as $44.699 billion. Note 4 of the financial statements shows how much goodwill is associated with each of its line of businesses.

Other non-current assets

Other non-current assets (or simply *other assets*) may include investments, advances to and receivables from subsidiaries, receivables from officers and employees, cash surrender value of life insurance on officers, and the cost of buildings in the process of construction.

Liabilities

The liabilities of a company represent the amount of funds that it has borrowed to finance the purchase of the assets that appear on the balance sheet. The terms "liabilities" and "debt" are used interchangeably.

On the balance sheet, the liabilities are listed in the order of their due date. Typically, they appear in two categories: current liabilities and long-term liabilities. Liabilities that are due within one year or one operating cycle (whichever is longer) are classified as *current liabilities. Long-term liabilities* are obligations that are due beyond one year.

Current liabilities

At the end of its 2017 fiscal year, Procter & Gamble reported the following for its total current liabilitics of $30.210 billion:

Accounts payable	$9.532 billion
Accrued and other liabilities	$7.024 billion
Debt due within one year	$13.554 billion

Accounts payable represents the amount owed to suppliers for purchases on credit. Accrued expenses are expenses that have been realized but not paid out.

In note 3 of the financial statement there is an explanation of what is included for the second item, accrued and other liabilities. They include marketing and promotion expenses, compensation expenses, restructuring expenses, taxes, legal and environmental expenses, and other expenses.

The third item above relates to the company's debt obligation. Companies have short-term debt obligations and long-term debt obligations. It's short-term debt obligations are those that mature within one year. Although long-term obligations may not mature until after one year, there may be part of the long-term obligation that is due within one year.

For example, a company may have issued a 20-year bond but agreed to repay the principal evenly over the next 20 years. In that case, 1/20th of the bond's debt would be considered due within one year.

For Procter & Gamble, note 10 indicates that debt due within one year consists of two items. The first is the current portion of long-term debt, which in 2017 was $1.676 billion. The second is the amount borrowed of commercial papers issued. Commercial paper is a common borrowing instrument to raise short-term funds. For 2017, it was $11.705 billion. The total of these two items and another item referred to as "Other" is equal to the $13.544 billion reported on the balance sheet.

Long-term liabilities

Examples of typical long-term liabilities are borrowings from notes and bonds issued, capital leases, and deferred taxes. "Capital leases" are lease obligations that represent long-term commitments of lease payments. The topic of leasing is not a simple one. "Deferred taxes" are taxes that may have to be paid in the future, but they are currently not due. Although for financial reporting purposes they are expensed (in accordance with the matching principle), they are due or may not be due in the future. *Deferred income taxes* are the net tax effects of temporary differences between the carrying amounts of assets and liabilities as computed for financial reporting purposes (GAAP) and the amounts computed for income tax purposes. Also included are contingent liabilities which we discuss later.

For Procter & Gamble, in 2017 there were three items reported for long-term liabilities: long-term debt, deferred income taxes, and other non-current liabilities. Note 10 of the financial statement provides a breakdown of the components of long-term liabilities. The bond debt outstanding by Procter & Gamble was $15.281 billion. It consisted of 17 bond issues denominated in US dollars, euros, and Japanese yen. Of that amount, $1.676 billion was the current portion of long-term debt. Thus, the net long-term bond debt was $13.605 billion. Capital lease obligations were $1.676 billion, and all other long-term debt was $4.382 billion. Adding these three items gives the long-term debt of $18.038 billion reported on the balance sheet.

Deferred income taxes reported for 2017 were $8.126 billion. Other non-current liabilities were $8.254 billion. Procter & Gamble did not have contingent liabilities. We'll take a closer look at other non-current liabilities and contingency liabilities shortly. Long-term liabilities were therefore:

Long-term debt	$18.038 billion
Deferred income taxes	$8.126 billion
Other non-current liabilities	$8.254 billion
Long-term liabilities	$34.418 billion

Note that Procter & Gamble did not have a heading for long-term liabilities. Instead, the three items are listed after total current liabilities. Adding the total current liabilities ($30.210 billion) to the total long-term liabilities ($34.418 billion) gives the total liabilities of $64.628 billion.

Other non-current liabilities

Let's look at the items making up other current liabilities for Procter & Gamble. According to note 3 of the financial statements, other non-current liabilities of $8.254 billion for 2017 included

Pension benefits	$5.487 billion
Other postretirement benefits	$1.333 billion
Uncertain tax positions	$0.564 billion
Other	$0.870 billion

Pension benefits reflect the present value of future retirement benefits when a company has a defined benefit pension plan. In a defined benefit pension plan, actuaries project the future payments to those who will retire and discount those future benefits at an appropriate discount rate. The resulting value is then the legal obligation of the company. In contrast to a defined benefit pension plan is a defined contribution plan. For this type of plan, a company makes payments to employees each period and the company has no further obligations. It is the responsibility of the employees to generate a return on the funds received for their retirement income.

Note 8 of the financial statements indicates that Procter & Gamble has both types of pension plans. Its defined benefit pension plan is primarily for employees outside of the United States and for plans that it acquired because of acquisitions of other companies for US employees.

Other postretirement benefits are retiree benefits for primarily health care and life insurance for mostly US employees who become eligible for these benefits when they meet a minimum age and satisfy service requirements.

Contingent liabilities

Another item included within long-term liabilities is a *contingent liability*. This liability is a potential cost that a company might incur. Under GAAP, a contingency liability is accounted for based on the probability of that cost occurring. There are three categories of contingent liabilities and for each category there is a mandated accounting treatment as per GAAP. The three categories are based on the likelihood of the contingency liability occurring: probable, reasonably possible, and remote. The accounting treatment also depends on the ability to estimate (measure) the amount of the liability that would be incurred.[8] Of course, over time, the classification of a contingent liability may change.

Stockholders' Equity

The ownership interest of a company is represented by equity. *Stockholders' equity*, also referred to as *shareholders' equity*, is the book value (carrying value) of equity. It is the book value because as we have explained, the value of the assets and the liabilities follow GAAP rules and do not reflect market values (with some exceptions). We'll explain how stockholders' equity is computed later.

---

[8]The GAAP rules are as follows:

- If a contingent liability is both probable and the company can reasonably estimate the amount of the loss that would occur, then the amount must be shown on the (1) balance sheet as part of long-term liabilities and (2) income statement as an expense.
- If the company cannot reasonably estimate the amount of the loss that would occur, then there is a disclosure about the contingency, but no amount shown on the balance sheet. (For example, litigation for patent infringement is typically shown as a contingent liability.)
- If the amount is reasonably possible, the treatment is the same as if the contingent liability cannot be estimated: note disclosure only.
- If a contingent liability is viewed to be remote, it does not appear on the balance sheet and need not be disclosed in the notes to the financial statements.

Preferred stock and common stock

A corporation has two types of stockholders: common and preferred. *Preferred stockholders* have a preference over common stockholders with respect to the distribution of dividends and in the case of a liquidation of the company. That is, common stockholders cannot receive dividends until the preferred stockholders receive their specified dividends. For preferred stockholders, the dividends may be a fixed dollar amount or an amount that varies based on some formula. In the liquidation of a company, preferred stockholders have priority over common stockholders with respect to the distribution of assets. In exchange for this preference with respect to dividends and asset distribution in the case of a liquidation, preferred stockholders give up the appreciation potential for the price of their shares compared to common stockholders. Under special circumstances, preferred stockholders are permitted special voting rights.

Looking at the balance sheet of Procter & Gamble (see Table 3), we see that the company had two types of preferred stocks that it is authorized to issue. The first is Convertible Class A preferred stock. This form of preferred stock allows the owner of the stock to convert it into common stock. It is this preferred stock that may be a dilutive security and the reason for calculating the dilutive earnings per share. The second type of preferred stock is the Non-Voting Class B preferred stock.

The common stockholders, in contrast, are the residual owners of the company. Dividends are paid to common stockholders after all debt holders have had their obligations fulfilled by the company and after preferred stockholders have received their dividends.

Classification of common stock

We have just discussed the classification of common stock based on voting rights. Now we will describe how stocks are classified in terms of authorized shares, issued shares, unissued shares, outstanding shares, and treasury stock.

When a corporation is formed, its charter will state the total number of shares that may be sold. This is referred to as the *authorized shares*. Authorized shares are then classified as *issued shares* (the number of authorized shares sold to investors) and *unissued shares* (the number of authorized shares that has not been sold to the investors).

Outstanding shares are the number of shares sold to investors. It would seem that the number of outstanding shares should be the same as the number of issued shares. This need not be the case because a company may repurchase shares from investors. Shares that are repurchased are referred to as *treasury stock*. Therefore, the number of outstanding shares plus the number of treasury shares is equal to the number of issued shares.

This information for the three types of stocks authorized by Procter & Gamble are shown in Table 2, where the total number of authorized shares for each type is shown. Note that there are no Non-Voting Class B preferred stock shares outstanding.

Par value of common stock

All financial instruments have a par value. In the case of debt obligations, par value is a meaningful concept because it (1) indicates how much the issuer must repay the bondholder prior to the maturity date and (2) coupled with the coupon rate it indicates the amount of interest rate that will be paid annually. So, a bond with a par value of $1,000 and a 4% coupon rate will pay the bondholder $40 annually in interest.

For preferred stock, the par value has a similar meaning. First, if the preferred stock is to be redeemed, then the company must repay the par value. If there is a liquidation, this is the maximum amount to which the preferred stockholders are entitled. Preferred stock has a dividend rate and the dollar amount is the product of the par value and the dividend rate.

When we get to common stock, the par value is often a meaningless value in terms of its relationship to the market value of the stock. The state in which a firm incorporates will require either par value or a stated value. As with par value, the stated value too has no relationship to the market value. The par value or stated value is important only for legal reasons. Specifically, the number of issued shares multiplied by the par or stated value establishes the company's minimum legal capital. This minimum legal capital imposes a constraint on the company with respect to the payment of dividends and the repurchasing of stock. Neither action can be taken if it results in falling below the minimum legal capital. The company's board of directors sets the par value or stated value and it is typically $1 or less so as to avoid the problem of falling below the minimum legal capital and providing flexibility for dividend and stock repurchase decisions.

For Procter & Gamble, the stated value for each type of stock is $1 per share.

Book value of shareholders' equity

The book value (or carrying value) of shareholders' equity is determined as follows:

Equity shares issued based on par value or stated value

plus	Additional paid-in-capital
plus	Retained earnings
plus	Accumulated other comprehensive income (or minus for loss)
minus	Treasury stock at cost
plus	Non-controlling interest
equals	Shareholders' equity

Note that shareholders' equity is total equity that includes both preferred and common stockholders.

Let's describe each of these components of shareholders' equity. The first component is just the legal capital based on the par value or stated value for issued shares for both preferred stock and common stock. For Procter & Gamble, the preferred stock issued at stated value is $1.006 billion and the common stock at stated value is $4.009 billion.

The second component is a result of selling the common stock at an amount in excess of its par value or stated value and is referred to as *additional paid-in-capital*. For Procter & Gamble in 2017, additional paid-in-capital was $63.641 billion.

The third component is the amount in the current fiscal period that was not distributed to shareholders since the inception of the company. For Procter & Gamble for 2017, retained earnings were $96.124 billion.

The next item, accumulated other comprehensive income, was explained earlier in this chapter. Basically, it includes unrealized gains and losses on certain investments and the amount reported in the stockholders' equity is the accumulated amount since the company's inception. This amount for Procter & Gamble for 2017 was a loss of $14.632 billion.

Shareholders' equity is then reduced by the issued shares that were repurchased by the company, which we stated earlier is treasury stock. The reduction is equal to the amount paid for the treasury stock. For Procter & Gamble, it was $93.715 billion for 2017. Non-controlling interest was $594 million.

There was one item for Procter & Gamble that is not included in the format for the stockholders' equity shown above. It is a reserve for ESOP debt retirement of $1.249 billion that is a reduction in the calculation of stockholders' equity.

Shareholders' equity for Procter & Gamble was reported as $55.778 billion in 2017.

Book value of common stockholders' equity

The book value of shareholders' equity includes all equity: preferred stock and common stock. The book value of common stockholders' equity excludes any amount of preferred stock issued (assuming that all preferred stock was issued at par and therefore nothing is included in additional paid in capital).

In the case of Procter & Gamble, the shareholders' equity of $55.778 billion in 2017 was reduced by $1.006 billion of preferred stock issued to get common stockholders' equity. Note that on the balance sheet, there is no mention of this value.

Limitations of the Balance Sheet

While the balance sheet obviously contains helpful information in assessing the value of a company, it does have limitations. There are three major limitations. The first limitation is that the balance sheet is constructed based on historical costs and therefore reflects only the book value of assets. The second limitation is that there are items in the balance sheet that are based on estimates. Finally, an important limitation is what is not included in the balance sheet. There are intangible assets that add value to a company that are not reflected on the balance sheet. These include brand loyalty, trademarks, employee loyalty, and the like.

The Statement of Cash Flows

The *statement of cash flows* provides a summary of a company's cash flows. The summary presentation is in terms of

- cash flow from operations;
- cash flow from investment activities;
- cash flow from financing activities.

From each of these three components of the statement of cash flows, the following will be obtained:

- net cash flows from operating activities;
- net cash flows from investing activities;
- net cash flows from financing activities.

The sum of the above is called the *net change in cash*. By adding the cash (including cash equivalents) on the balance sheet at the beginning of the fiscal year (i.e., end of previous fiscal year) to the net change in cash, the result is the cash (including cash equivalents) on the balance sheet at the end of the fiscal year. That is,

$$\text{Net change in cash} + \text{Cash at the beginning of the year}$$
$$= \text{Cash at end of year.}$$

Basically, the statement of cash flows reconciles the beginning of the year cash on the balance sheet with the end of year cash on the balance sheet, detailing the different sources and uses of cash that caused the change.

A great deal can be learned about a company's economic prospects by examining the sources of a company's cash flows. For example, a company that is financially strong tends to consistently generate positive cash flows from operations and invests such that it has negative cash flows from investing. A company in order to remain competitive and attractive to investors must be able to generate cash flows from its operations and to grow the company must continually make capital investments.

We will use the Procter & Gamble statement of cash flows reproduced in Table 4 for 2017 and 2016 as an example.

Cash Flow from Operating Activities

Cash flow from operating activities is the cash flow from day-to-day operating activities and is basically net income adjusted for (1) non-cash expenditures and income and (2) changes in current assets and current liabilities.

Non-cash expenditures and income for Procter & Gamble for 2017 were the seven items listed after net earnings. Among the items that are added to net earnings are depreciation and amortization and loss on early extinguishment of debt. Deferred income taxes and loss on sale of assets are deducted from net earnings.

The four items that show changes in current assets and current liabilities on the balance sheet are either added or subtracted from net earnings. By "change" it is meant the change from the prior accounting period to the current accounting period. The reason that it is necessary to adjust net income for the latter is because of the use of accrual accounting used under GAAP. The procedure is as follows:

TABLE 4: Procter & Gamble Statement of Cash Flows: 2017 and 2016

CASH AND CASH EQUIVALENTS, END OF YEAR	**$ 5,569**	$ **7,102**	$ 6,836
Amounts in millions; Years ended June 30	**2017**	**2016**	**2015**
CASH AND CASH EQUIVALENTS, BEGINNING OF YEAR	**$ 7,102**	$ 6,836	$ 8,548
OPERATING ACTIVITIES			
Net earnings	**15,411**	10,604	7,144
Depreciation and amortization	**2,820**	3,078	3,134
Loss on early extinguishment of debt	**543**	–	–
Share-based compensation expense	**351**	335	337
Deferred income taxes	**(601)**	(815)	(803)
Gain on sale of assets	**(5,490)**	(41)	(766)
Venezuela deconsolidation charge	–	–	2,028
Goodwill and intangible asset impairment charges	–	450	2,174
Change in accounts receivable	**(322)**	35	349
Change in inventories	**71**	116	313
Change in accounts payable, accrued and other liabilities	**(149)**	1,285	928
Change in other operating assets and liabilities	**(43)**	204	(976)
Other	**162**	184	746
TOTAL OPERATING ACTIVITIES	**12,753**	15,435	14,608
INVESTING ACTIVITIES			
Capital expenditures	**(3,384)**	(3,314)	(3,736)
Proceeds from asset sales	**571**	432	4,498
Cash related to deconsolidated Venezuela operations	–	–	(908)
Acquisitions, net of cash acquired	**(16)**	(186)	(137)
Purchases of short-term investments	**(4,843)**	(2,815)	(3,647)
Proceeds from sales and maturities of short-term investments	**1,488**	1,354	1,203
Pre-divestiture addition of restricted cash related to the Beauty Brands divestiture	**(874)**	(996)	–
Cash transferred at closing related to the Beauty Brands divestiture	**(475)**	–	–
Release of restricted cash upon closing of the Beauty Brands divestiture	**1,870**	–	–

TABLE 4: (*Continued*)

Amounts in millions; Years ended June 30		**2017**		**2016**		**2015**
CASH AND CASH EQUIVALENTS, END OF YEAR	$	**5,569**	**$**	**7,102**	$	6,836
Cash transferred in Batteries divestiture		–		(143)		–
Change in other investments		**(26)**		93		(163)
TOTAL INVESTING ACTIVITIES		**(5,689)**		(5,575)		(2,890)
FINANCING ACTIVITIES						
Dividends to shareholders		**(7,236)**		(7,436)		(7,287)
Change in short-term debt		**2,727**		(418)		(2,580)
Additions to long-term debt		**3,603**		3,916		2,138
Reductions of long-term debt		**(4,931)**[(1)]		(2,213)		(3,512)
Treasury stock purchases		**(5,204)**		(4,004)		(4,604)
Treasury stock from cash infused in Batteries divestiture		–		(1,730)		–
Impact of stock options and other		**2,473**		2,672		2,826
TOTAL FINANCING ACTIVITIES		**(8,568)**		(9,213)		(13,019)
EFFECT OF EXCHANGE RATE CHANGES ON CASH AND CASH EQUIVALENTS		**(29)**		(381)		(411)
CHANGE IN CASH AND CASH EQUIVALENTS		**(1,533)**		266		(1,712)
SUPPLEMENTAL DISCLOSURE						
Cash payments for interest	**$**	**518**	$	569	$	678
Cash payment for income taxes		**3,714**		3,730		4,558

Adjustment to net income to obtain cash flow	Current assets	Current liabilities
Add to net income	increase	decrease
Subtract from net income	decrease	increase

For Procter & Gamble, cash flow from operations (labeled "total operating activities") was $12.753 billion in 2017.

Cash Flow from Investing Activities

The *cash flow from investing activities* is the cash flows that are related to the acquisition of fixed assets (property, plant and equipment), intangible assets, and companies; offsetting this amount are the proceeds from the disposal of such assets.

For Procter & Gamble, cash flow from investing — called in the cash flow statement "total investing activities" — was negative \$5.689 billion.

Cash Flow from Financing Activities

Cash flow from financing activities is the cash flow from activities related to the sources of capital funds. Examples of how cash flow is used include repurchasing common stock, paying off maturing debt, and paying of dividends to stockholders. Note that interest paid for debt is part of net income, so it is not included here. Examples of how cash flow is obtained include selling of common stock, selling of bonds, and exercising options to purchase common stock.

Labeled "total financing activities", the cash flow from financing activities for Procter & Gamble for 2017 was negative \$8.569 billion.

Other Adjustments

In the case of Procter & Gamble, there was one other adjustment. It was an adjustment of a negative \$0.029 billion for the effect of exchange rate changes on cash and cash equivalents.

Net change in cash

The net change in cash is the sum of the cash flows from the following three activities:

- cash flow from operating activities;
- cash flow from investing activities;
- cash flow from financing activities.

The following table summarizes for Procter & Gamble for 2017 the net change in cash as well as how the end of period cash is determined:

Cash flow from operating activities	\$12.753 billion
Cash flow from investing activities	–\$5.689 billion
Cash flow from financing activities	–\$8.568 billion
Effect of exchange rate changes on cash and cash equivalents	–\$0.029 billion
Net change in cash	–\$1.533 billion

This means that there was a decline in cash (and cash equivalents) of $1.533 billion in 2017. This agrees with what actually happened to cash (and cash equivalents) for Procter & Gamble. The end of the year cash (and cash equivalent) at the end of the company's 2017 fiscal year was $5.569 billion. The amount at the beginning of the 2017 fiscal year (which is just the amount at the end of the 2016 fiscal year) was $7.102 billion. The difference is a decline of $1.533 billion.

Statement of Shareholders' Equity

The changes in stockholders' equity between two years is shown in the *statement of shareholders' equity.* When there is no preferred stock, this financial statement is referred to as the *statement of common stockholders' equity.* Basically, this statement reconciles the balance of each component of shareholders' equity (stock, paid-in-capital, retained earnings, accumulated comprehensive income) from the beginning of the fiscal year (i.e., end of the prior fiscal year) to the end of the current fiscal year. For each component of shareholders' equity, the statement begins with the balance at the beginning of the fiscal year. From there, the adjustments that are made to obtain the balance at the end of the fiscal year are shown.

Table 5 illustrates this for the statement of shareholders' equity for 2017 for Procter & Gamble. The last column in the first line shows the beginning period balance at the end of 2016 ($57.983 billion). The value is from the 2016 fiscal year balance sheet and the last line is the ending balance. The last column of the last row shows the ending shareholders' equity for 2017 ($55.778 billion) which is from the 2017 fiscal year balance sheet. This means that shareholders' equity declined by $2.305 billion. The purpose of the statement of shareholders' equity is to explain that decline as well as the purchase of treasury stock.

The line between the first and last row shows the reason why the shareholders' equity changed. Let's just look at a few of them. Net earnings of course causes shareholders' equity to increase. Dividends reduce shareholders' equity and as can be seen, for Procter & Gamble, dividends to common stockholders and preferred stockholders were $6.989 billion and $247 billion, respectively. Looking at the line labeled "Treasury stock" it can be seen that it decreased by $14.625 billion.

TABLE 5: Procter & Gamble Statement of Shareholders' Equity: 2017 Fiscal Year

BALANCE JUNE 30, 2016	2,668,074	$4,009	$1,038	$63,714	($1,290)	($15,907)	($82,176)	$87,953	$642	$57,983
Net earnings								**15,326**	**85**	**15,411**
Other comprehensive loss						**1,275**				**1,275**
Dividends to shareholders:										
Common								**(6,989)**		**(6,989)**
Preferred, net of tax benefits								**(247)**		**(247)**
Treasury purchases (2)	**(164,866)**						**(14,625)**			**(14,625)**
Employee plan issuances	**45,848**			**(77)**			**3,058**			**2,981**
Preferred stock conversions	**4,241**		**(32)**	**4**			**28**			–
ESOP debt impacts					**41**			**81**		**122**
Non-controlling interest, net									**(133)**	**(133)**
BALANCE JUNE 30,2017	**2,553,297**	**$4,009**	**$1,006**	**$63,641**	**($1,249)**	**($14,632)**	**($93,715)**	**$96,124**	**$594**	**$55,778**

Key Points

- A company's financial statements provide an investor with a summary of the operating, financing, and investment activities of a business.
- There are at least five financial statements: statement of income, statement of comprehensive income, balance sheet, statement of cash flows, and statement of shareholders' equity.
- The income statement is a summary of the company's operating performance over a period of time (e.g., a fiscal quarter or a fiscal year) and is also called the statement of earnings, the statement of operations, and the profit and loss statement.
- The "bottom line" is the company's net income or net earnings, which is also shown in terms of how much was earned per share of stock, referred to as its earnings per share.
- The comprehensive income of a company includes all income and expenses recognized by a company during the fiscal year and is a much broader measure of income or loss than a company's net income, including values not represented in the income statement.
- A balance sheet, also called the statement of financial condition, shows the amount of a company's assets, liabilities, and equity as of the last day of the company's fiscal year in the case of an annual balance sheet and on the last day of the fiscal quarter in the case of a quarterly balance sheet.
- The statement of cash flows is a summary of company's cash flows that contains information about where the company received and utilized its cash.
- The statement of shareholders' equity provides a summary of the changes in the stockholders' equity; that is, it is to provide a reconciliation of the amount reported in each component of stockholders' equity from the beginning of the fiscal year to the end of the fiscal year.
- GAAP is a framework of accounting standards, rules, and practices that have been authoritatively established by recognized accounting bodies in the United States.
- There are three assumptions made in preparing financial statements in accordance with GAAP: (1) monetary unit assumption, (2) time period assumption, and (3) going-concern assumption.
- The six GAAP are (1) full disclosure principle, (2)conservatism principle, (3) revenue recognition principle, (4) cost principle, (5) matching principle, and (6) materiality principle.

- The three most common ways in which income smoothing has been used to manipulate income: channel stuffing, pull-in sales, and cookie-jar reserves.
- A company's management is responsible for the preparation and integrity of the financial information presented in the financial statements.
- It is management that is responsible for making sure that certain estimates and judgments mandated by GAAP are done properly and within the company, a function that is performed by the company's internal auditors.
- The four possible auditor opinions that can be given as a result of an auditor's review of the company's financial statements are (1) unqualified opinion, (2) qualified opinion, (3) adverse opinion, and (4) disclaimer of opinion.
- The net income reported is the amount earned for all stockholders: preferred stockholders (if any) and common stockholders.
- Common stockholders are interested in the amount earned and available for them, which is net income available to common stockholders.
- The earnings per common share (EPS) is a measure that shows how much was earned for each share of common stock and calculated by dividing the net income available to common stockholders by the number of common shares outstanding.
- GAAP requires that two EPS measures be reported: basic EPS and diluted EPS.
- Diluted earnings per share takes into account the potential for the conversion of securities into common stock such as securities that allow the holder to exchange it for a specified number of common stock shares and options issued by the company that grant to certain parties the right to exercise an option to obtain a specified number of shares.
- The balance sheet is a report of a company's assets, liabilities, and equity, presented generally at the end of a fiscal quarter or fiscal year.
- The assets of the company are its resources and include current assets and non-current assets (physical asset and intangible assets).
- The liabilities of a company represent the amount of funds that it has borrowed to finance the purchase of the assets that appear on the balance sheet.
- Liabilities due within one year or one operating cycle (whichever is longer) are classified as current liabilities; long-term liabilities are obligations that are due beyond one year.

- Stockholders' equity, also referred to as shareholders' equity, is the book value (carrying value) of equity.
- The statement of cash flows provides a summary of a company's cash flows in terms of cash flow from operations, cash flow from investment activities, and cash flow from financing activities.

References

Hope, O-K., and J. Wang, 2018. "Management deception, big-bath accounting, and information asymmetry: Evidence from linguistic analysis," *Accounting, Organizations and Society*, 70: 33–51.

Lai, G., L. Debo, and L. Nan, 2011. "Channel stuffing with short-term interest in market value," *Management Science*, 57 (2): 332–346.

Mulford, C.W., and E.E., Comiskey, 2002. *The Financial Numbers Game: Dectecting Creative Accounting Practices.* Hoboken, NJ: John Wiley & Sons.

Prem, W., A. Rao, and C. Martin, 2019. "Channel-stuff or sales with a right to return?" *Journal of the International Academy for Case Studies*, 25 (1): 1–11.

Schilit, H., J. Perler, and Y Engelhart, 2018. *Financial Shenanigans: How to Detect Accounting Gimmicks and Fraud in Financial Reports 4th Edition.* NY, NY: McGraw-Hill.

Chapter 3

Securitization and the Creation of Residential Mortgage-Related Securities*

Learning Objectives

After reading this chapter, you will understand:

- the relative size of the residential mortgage-related securities market;
- the characteristics of a residential mortgage loan;
- the fundamental characteristics of a mortgage-backed security (MBS);
- how securitization transforms a heterogeneous group of disparate loans into sizable and homogeneous securities that trade in a liquid market;
- what an agency mortgage-backed security (MBS) is;
- the three types of agency MBS: pass-through securities, collateralized mortgage obligations (CMOs), and stripped MBSs;
- what a private-label or non-agency MBS is;
- the cash flow components of a mortgage loan;
- what a prepayment is and how it creates uncertainty about a loan's cash flow;
- the reasons why prepayments occur;
- how prepayment rates are measured;
- how the cash flow of an agency pass-through security is calculated;
- how an agency stripped MBS is created;

*This chapter is coauthored with Anand K. Bhattacharya, Professor of Finance Practice in the Department of Finance, W.P. Carey School of Business, and the faculty director for the MS Finance program, and Bill Berliner, Managing Director, Fixed Income Research and Investor Relations, PennyMac.

- how an agency CMO is created;
- the different types of CMOs;
- what a private-label CMO is; and
- why credit enhancement is needed for a private-label CMO.

Introduction

In the United States, the total face value of one-to-four family residential mortgage debt outstanding was $11 trillion as of the end of 2019. Originators of residential mortgage loans can either retain the loans in their portfolio or pool them and use them as collateral for the issuance of residential mortgage-related securities. Of the $11 trillion of mortgage debt outstanding, $8 trillion has been securitized (i.e., have become collateral for a mortgage-related security). Consider that the US investment-grade corporate bond market (issues rated BBB and higher) is roughly $6.5 trillion and that the US Treasury notes and bonds outstanding is roughly $12 trillion. Thus, the market for residential mortgage-related securities is a major component of investment-grade bonds available to asset managers.

Unlike corporate bonds and US Treasury notes and bonds, the evaluation of residential mortgage-related securities is far more complex. Before performing any analysis of these securities, it is necessary to understand how they are created. The process of creating these securities is called *securitization*. In this chapter, we explain how residential mortgage-related securities are created. We explain agency residential mortgage-backed securities and how from these securities agency CMOs and agency mortgage strips are created. Then we explain private-label residential mortgage-backed securities.

Agency Residential Mortgage-Backed Securities

A mortgage is a loan secured by the collateral of some specified real estate property that obliges the borrower to make a predetermined series of payments. The mortgage gives the lender (*mortgagee*) the right, if the borrower (the *mortgagor*) defaults (i.e., fails to make the contractual payments), to foreclose on the loan and seize the property in order to ensure that the debt is paid off. The interest rate on the mortgage loan is called the *note rate*. Our focus is on residential mortgage loans.

The fundamental unit in an MBS is the pool. At its lowest common denominator, mortgage-backed pools are aggregations of large numbers of mortgage loans with similar (but not identical) characteristics. Loans with a commonality of attributes such as note rate, term to maturity, credit quality, loan balance, and type of mortgage design are combined using a variety of legal mechanisms to create relatively fungible investment vehicles. With the creation of MBS, mortgage loans are transformed from a heterogeneous group of disparate assets into sizable and homogeneous securities that trade in a liquid market.

The transformation of groups of mortgage loans with common attributes into MBSs occurs using one of two mechanisms. Loans that meet the underwriting guidelines of three entities — Ginnie Mae, Fannie Mae, and Freddie Mac — are securitized as an *agency pool.* While Ginnie Mae (Government National Mortgage Association) is an agency of the US government, carrying the full faith and credit of the US government, Fannie Mae and Freddie Mac are government-sponsored enterprises. Despite this distinction, the MBSs issued by these three entities are referred to as an *agency MBS* and we review the different types in this section. There are three types of agency MBSs: pass-through securities, CMOs, and stripped MBSs.

Loans that do not qualify for agency pools are securitized in non-agency or "private-label" transactions. These types of securities do not have an agency guaranty, and must therefore be issued under the registration entity or "shelf" of the issuer.

Cash Flow Characteristics of Residential Mortgage Loan

Although a mortgagor may select from many types of mortgage loans, because our purpose here is to understand the basic cash flow characteristics of a mortgage loan, we will use the most common mortgage design: the level payment, fixed-rate mortgage. The basic idea behind the design of the level-payment, fixed-rate mortgage, or simply level-payment mortgage, is that the borrower pays interest and repays principal in equal installments over an agreed-upon period of time, called the maturity or term of the mortgage. Thus, at the end of the term, the loan has been fully amortized.

For a level-payment mortgage, each monthly mortgage payment is due on the first of each month and consists of (1) interest of 1/12 of the fixed annual note rate times the amount of the outstanding mortgage balance at the beginning of the previous month and (2) a repayment of a portion of the outstanding mortgage balance (principal).

The difference between the monthly mortgage payment and the portion of the payment that represents interest equals the amount that is applied to reduce the outstanding mortgage balance. The monthly mortgage payment is designed so that after the last scheduled monthly payment of the loan is made, the amount of the outstanding mortgage balance is zero (i.e., the mortgage is fully repaid). Thus, the portion of the monthly mortgage payment applied to interest declines each month, and the portion applied to reducing the mortgage balance increases.

The reason for this is that because the mortgage balance is reduced with each monthly mortgage payment, the interest owed on the mortgage balance declines. Since the monthly mortgage payment is fixed, an increasingly larger portion of the monthly mortgage payment is applied to reduce the principal in each subsequent month.

For the mortgagee, the cash flow from the mortgage loan is not the same as what the mortgagor pays. This is because of a servicing fee and other guarantee fee that must be paid. Every mortgage loan must be serviced.

The monthly cash flow from a mortgage loan, regardless of the mortgage design, can, therefore, be divided into three parts: (1) the servicing fee and guarantee fee, (2) the interest payment net of the servicing fee and guarantee fee, and (3) the scheduled principal repayment (referred to as *amortization*).

Prepayments and Cash Flow Uncertainty

One cannot assume that the mortgagor would not pay off any portion of the mortgage balance prior to the scheduled due date. Payments made ahead of the scheduled principal repayment dates are called prepayments. *Prepayments* occur for a variety of reasons. First, borrowers prepay the entire mortgage balance when they sell their homes. Second, borrowers may be economically motivated to pay off the loan as market rates fall below the loan's note rate. This reason for prepaying a mortgage loan is referred to as refinancing. Third, in the case of borrowers who cannot meet their mortgage obligations, the property is repossessed and sold. The proceeds from the sale are used to pay off the mortgage loan. Finally, if property is destroyed by fire or if another insured catastrophe occurs, the insurance proceeds are used to pay off the mortgage loan.

The effect of prepayments is that the cash flow from a mortgage is not known with certainty — by this we mean that the amount and the timing of the cash flow are uncertain. Consequently, ignoring defaults, the mortgagor knows that as long as the loan is outstanding, interest will be received and the principal will be repaid at the scheduled date each month. On the maturity date of the mortgage loan, the investor would recover the amount lent. What the mortgagee does not know — the uncertainty — is for how long the mortgage loan will be outstanding and, therefore, the timing of the principal payments.

Residential Agency Mortgage Pass-Through Securities

In a mortgage pass-through security, or simply a pass-through, the monthly cash flow from the pool of mortgage loans is distributed on a pro rata basis to the certificate holders. The monthly cash flow that may be distributed to the certificate holders consists of three components: (1) interest net of the servicing fee and guarantee fee, (2) regularly scheduled principal payments (amortization), and (3) prepayments.

As just noted, the difficulty for a certificate holder in estimating the cash flow is due to prepayments. This risk is called *prepayment risk*.

Prepayments and prepayment conventions

In the residential mortgage-backed securities (RMBSs) market, several conventions have been used as a benchmark for prepayment rates. Today the benchmarks used are the conditional prepayment rate and the Public Securities Association (PSA) prepayment benchmark.

The *conditional prepayment rate* (CPR) as a measure of the speed of prepayments assumes that some fraction of the remaining principal in the mortgage pool is prepaid each month for the remaining term of the collateral. The CPR used for a particular deal is based on the characteristics of the collateral (including its historical prepayment experience) and the current and expected future economic environment.

The CPR is an annual prepayment rate. To estimate monthly prepayments, the CPR must be converted into a monthly prepayment rate, commonly referred to as the *single monthly mortality* (SMM) rate. The following formula is used to determine the SMM for a given CPR:

$$\text{SMM} = 1 - [(1 - \text{CPR})^{1/12}].$$

An SMM of w percent means that approximately w percent of the remaining mortgage balance at the beginning of the month, less the scheduled principal payment, will prepay that month. That is,

$$\begin{aligned}\text{Prepayment for month } t &= \text{SMM}\\ &\times (\text{Beginning mortgage balance for month}\\ &t - \text{Scheduled principal payment for month } t).\end{aligned}$$

One problem with using the CPR is that it assumes a constant prepayment rate from the very outset of the origination of the loans. For example, it is not likely that prepayments might be the largest in dollar amount shortly after loans are originated than later on after loans have seasoned. Yet using a constant CPR makes that assumption. For residential mortgage loans, the PSA prepayment benchmark deals with this problem.[1] The PSA prepayment benchmark is expressed as a monthly series of annual prepayment rates. The basic PSA benchmark model assumes that prepayment rates are low for newly originated loans, and then will speed up as the mortgages become seasoned, and then reach a plateau and remain at that level.

The PSA standard benchmark assumes the following prepayment rates for 30-year residential mortgage loans:

- A CPR of 0.2% for the first month, increased by 0.2% per year per month for the next 29 months when it reaches 6% per year.
- A 6% CPR for the remaining years.

All months above are counted with reference to origination of the pool.

This benchmark is referred to as 100% PSA. Mathematically, 100 PSA can be expressed as follows:

If $t \leq 30$ months, then CPR $= 6\%\ (t/30)$.
If $t > 30$ months, then CPR $= 6\%$.

where t is the number of months since the mortgages originated.

Slower or faster speeds are then referred to as some percentage of PSA. For example, 50% PSA means one-half the CPR of the PSA benchmark prepayment rate and 165% PSA means 1.65 times the CPR of the PSA benchmark prepayment rate. A prepayment rate of 0% PSA means that no prepayments are assumed.

The PSA benchmark is commonly referred to as a prepayment model, suggesting that it can be used to estimate prepayments. However, it is important to note that characterizing this market convention for prepayments as a prepayment model is wrong.

Cash flow for a mortgage pass-through security

With this background on prepayment conventions, we can now discuss the structuring of agency deals. To illustrate structuring and how it is used to

[1]The PSA and the CPR approaches are not mutually exclusive alternatives but are mostly used together — the PSA explains the ramp-up of the expected CPR over the initial months of seasoning. Thereafter, the pool undergoes a constant CPR.

create bonds with different exposure to interest rate and prepayment risk via tranching, we will use a hypothetical pass-through security that will be the collateral for our illustrations. Let us look at the monthly cash flow for a hypothetical pass-through given a PSA assumption. We will assume the following for the underlying mortgages:

- type: fixed-rate, level-payment mortgages,
- weighted average coupon (WAC) rate: 6.0%,
- weighted average maturity (WAM): 358 months,
- servicing fee: 0.5% (for simplicity will ignore the guarantee fee),
- outstanding balance: $660 million.

The pass-through security has a coupon rate of 5.5% (WAC of 6% minus the servicing fee of 0.5%).

This first step in structuring requires a projection of the cash flow of the mortgage pool. The cash flow is decomposed into three components:

1. interest (based on WAC of 6% and pass-through rate of 5.5%),
2. amortization (regularly scheduled principal),
3. prepayments based on some prepayment assumption.

To generate the cash flow for the hypothetical pass-through security we will assume a prepayment speed of 165% PSA. The cash flow is shown in Table 1.

Column 2 shows the outstanding mortgage balance at the beginning of the month (i.e., outstanding balance at the beginning of the previous month reduced by the total principal payment in the previous month). Column 3 gives the SMM for 165% PSA.[2] The aggregate monthly mortgage payment is reported in column 4. Notice that the total monthly mortgage payment declines over time, as prepayments reduce the mortgage balance outstanding.[3] Column 5 shows the monthly interest that is determined by multiplying the outstanding mortgage balance at the beginning of the month by the pass-through rate of 5.5% and dividing by 12. The regularly scheduled principal repayment (amortization), shown in column 6, is the difference between the total monthly mortgage payment (column 4) and the gross

[2]Note that for month 1, the SMM shown in Table 1 is for a pass-through security that has been seasoned two months. This is because the WAM is 358 months.

[3]In the absence of prepayments, this amount would be constant over the life of the pass-through security. The formula for calculating the total monthly mortgage payment can be found in Fabozzi [2006, Chapter 22].

TABLE 1: Monthly Cash Flow for a $660 Million Pass-Through Security with a 5.5% Pass-Through Rate, a WAC of 6.0%, and a WAM of 358 Months, Assuming 165% PSA

(1)	(2)	(3)	(4)	(5)	(6)	(7)	(8)	(9)
Month	**Outstanding Balance**	**SMM**	**Mortgage Payment**	**Net Interest**	**Scheduled Principal**	**Prepayments**	**Total Principal**	**Cash Flow**
1	660,000,000	0.00083	3,964,947	3,025,000	664,947	546,435	1,211,383	4,236,383
2	658,788,617	0.00111	3,961,661	3,019,448	667,718	728,350	1,396,068	4,415,516
3	657,392,549	0.00139	3,957,277	3,013,049	670,314	909,895	1,580,209	4,593,258
4	655,812,340	0.00167	3,951,794	3,005,807	672,732	1,090,916	1,763,649	4,769,455
5	654,048,691	0.00195	3,945,214	2,997,723	674,970	1,271,261	1,946,231	4,943,954
6	652,102,460	0.00223	3,937,538	2,988,803	677,025	1,450,775	2,127,800	5,116,603
7	649,974,660	0.00251	3,928,768	2,979,051	678,895	1,629,307	2,308,202	5,287,252
8	647,666,458	0.00279	3,918,910	2,968,471	680,578	1,806,703	2,487,281	5,455,752
9	645,179,177	0.00308	3,907,966	2,957,071	682,070	1,982,813	2,664,883	5,621,955
10	642,514,294	0.00336	3,895,943	2,944,857	683,372	2,157,486	2,840,858	5,785,715
11	639,673,436	0.00365	3,882,847	2,931,837	684,480	2,330,573	3,015,053	5,946,890
12	636,658,383	0.00393	3,868,685	2,918,018	685,394	2,501,927	3,187,320	6,105,338
13	633,471,062	0.00422	3,853,466	2,903,409	686,111	2,671,401	3,357,511	6,260,921
14	630,113,551	0.00451	3,837,198	2,888,020	686,630	2,838,851	3,525,482	6,413,502
15	626,588,069	0.00480	3,819,891	2,871,862	686,951	3,004,137	3,691,088	6,562,950
16	622,896,981	0.00509	3,801,557	2,854,944	687,072	3,167,117	3,854,189	6,709,134
17	619,042,792	0.00538	3,782,207	2,837,279	686,993	3,327,655	4,014,648	6,851,928
18	615,028,144	0.00567	3,761,853	2,818,879	686,712	3,485,618	4,172,330	6,991,209
19	610,855,814	0.00597	3,740,509	2,799,756	686,230	3,640,872	4,327,102	7,126,858
20	606,528,712	0.00626	3,718,190	2,779,923	685,546	3,793,290	4,478,836	7,258,760

21	602,049,876	0.00656	3,694,909	2,759,395	684,660	3,942,748	4,627,408	7,386,803
22	597,422,468	0.00685	3,670,684	2,738,186	683,572	4,089,123	4,772,695	7,510,881
23	592,649,773	0.00715	3,645,531	2,716,311	682,282	4,232,298	4,914,580	7,630,892
24	587,735,193	0.00745	3,619,467	2,693,786	680,791	4,372,159	5,052,950	7,746,736
25	582,682,243	0.00775	3,592,511	2,670,627	679,100	4,508,595	5,187,695	7,858,322
26	577,494,549	0.00805	3,564,681	2,646,850	677,208	4,641,501	5,318,709	7,965,560
27	572,175,839	0.00835	3,535,997	2,622,473	675,117	4,770,776	5,445,894	8,068,367
28	566,729,945	0.00865	3,506,479	2,597,512	672,829	4,896,323	5,569,152	8,166,664
29	561,160,793	0.00865	3,476,148	2,571,987	670,344	4,848,172	5,518,516	8,090,503
30	555,642,277	0.00865	3,446,080	2,546,694	667,869	4,800,459	5,468,328	8,015,021
100	272,093,325	0.00865	1,875,944	1,247,094	515,478	2,349,114	2,864,592	4,111,686
101	269,228,733	0.00865	1,859,718	1,233,965	513,574	2,324,352	2,837,926	4,071,891
102	266,390,806	0.00865	1,843,631	1,220,958	511,677	2,299,821	2,811,498	4,032,456
103	263,579,308	0.00865	1,827,684	1,208,072	509,788	2,275,518	2,785,306	3,993,378
104	260,794,002	0.00865	1,811,875	1,195,306	507,905	2,251,442	2,759,347	3,954,653
105	258,034,655	0.00865	1,796,203	1,182,659	506,029	2,227,590	2,733,620	3,916,278
200	86,170,616	0.00865	786,913	394,949	356,060	742,285	1,098,345	1,493,293
201	85,072,271	0.00865	780,106	389,915	354,745	732,796	1,087,541	1,477,455
202	83,984,730	0.00865	773,358	384,930	353,435	723,400	1,076,835	1,461,765
203	82,907,896	0.00865	766,669	379,995	352,129	714,097	1,066,226	1,446,221
204	81,841,669	0.00865	760,037	375,108	350,829	704,886	1,055,714	1,430,822
205	80,785,955	0.00865	753,463	370,269	349,533	695,765	1,045,298	1,415,567

(*Continued*)

TABLE 1: (*Continued*)

(1) Month	(2) Outstanding Balance	(3) SMM	(4) Mortgage Payment	(5) Net Interest	(6) Scheduled Principal	(7) Prepayments	(8) Total Principal	(9) Cash Flow
300	16,829,401	0.00865	330,091	77,135	245,944	143,445	389,388	466,523
301	16,440,012	0.00865	327,235	75,350	245,035	140,085	385,120	460,470
302	16,054,892	0.00865	324,405	73,585	244,130	136,761	380,891	454,476
303	15,674,001	0.00865	321,599	71,839	243,229	133,474	376,703	448,542
304	15,297,298	0.00865	318,817	70,113	242,330	130,224	372,554	442,667
305	14,924,744	0.00865	316,059	68,405	241,436	127,009	368,444	436,849
350	1,876,871	0.00865	213,790	8,602	204,405	14,467	218,872	227,474
351	1,657,999	0.00865	211,940	7,599	203,650	12,580	216,230	223,829
352	1,441,769	0.00865	210,107	6,608	202,898	10,716	213,614	220,222
353	1,228,154	0.00865	208,290	5,629	202,149	8,875	211,024	216,653
354	1,017,131	0.00865	206,488	4,662	201,402	7,056	208,458	213,120
355	808,672	0.00865	204,702	3,706	200,659	5,259	205,918	209,624
356	602,755	0.00865	202,931	2,763	199,917	3,484	203,402	206,165
357	399,353	0.00865	201,176	1,830	199,179	1,731	200,911	202,741
358	198,442	0.00865	199,436	910	198,444	0	198,444	199,353

coupon interest for the month (6.0% multiplied by the outstanding mortgage balance at the beginning of the month, then divided by 12). The prepayment for the month is reported in column 7 and is found by using Equation (3.1).

The sum of the regularly scheduled principal and the prepayment is the total principal payment and is shown in column 8. The projected monthly cash flow is then the sum of the monthly interest plus the total principal payment as shown in the last column of Table 1.

At 165% PSA, the average life for this pass-through security is 8.6 years. The average life is a weighted average of the principal cash flows divided by the par value where the weight is the month when the projected principal is expected to be received.

Agency Stripped Mortgage-Backed Securities

A mortgage pass-through distributes the cash flow from the underlying pool of mortgages on a pro rata basis to the security holders. A *stripped MBS* is created by altering that distribution of principal and interest from a pro rata distribution to an unequal distribution.

In the most common type of stripped MBS, all of the interest is allocated to one class — the interest-only class — and the entire principal to the other class — the principal-only class.

Principal-only securities

A *principal-only security*, also called a PO or a principal-only mortgage strip, represents the principal component of a pool of underlying mortgages or (in the case of agency-name strips) MBS pools underlying the deal. POs are typically purchased at a substantial discount from par value. The return realized by an investor on a PO is strongly influenced by the prepayment rate of the underlying loans or pools; the faster the prepayment rate (or speed), the greater the return on the investment. If prepayment speeds increase from those assumed at the time of purchase, the investor receives principal (paid at par value) sooner than expected; since this principal was purchased at a discount, the investor's returns are enhanced. Conversely, principal is returned more slowly than expected if prepayment speeds are slow, lowering realized returns. This behavior is analogous to that of a zero-coupon bullet-maturity bond. If a 5-year zero-coupon bond is called immediately after being purchased at a deep discount, the investor's returns are boosted by the immediate return of principal. Alternatively, if the bond's maturity was somehow extended, the investor's returns would be adversely affected.

Let's look at how the price of the PO would be expected to change as mortgage rates in the market change. When mortgage rates decline below the note rate for the loans in the mortgage pool, prepayments are expected to speed up, accelerating payments to the PO holder. Thus, the cash flow of a PO improves (in the sense that principal repayments are received earlier than expected). The cash flow will also be discounted at a lower interest rate because the mortgage rate in the market has declined. The result is that the PO price will often increase significantly when mortgage rates decline. When mortgage rates rise above the note rate for the loans in the mortgage pool, prepayments are expected to slow down. The cash flow deteriorates (in the sense that it takes longer than expected to recover principal repayments). Couple this with a higher discount rate, the price of a PO will normally fall sharply when mortgage rates rise.

Interest-only securities

An *interest-only class*, also called an IO or an *interest-only mortgage strip*, has no economic par value. It represents the interest stream generated by the underlying principal, and the investor receives interest only on the amount of principal that remains outstanding. As they are akin to an annuity, their value is increased if prepayment speeds decline, as the interest stream remains outstanding longer. Conversely, their value is reduced by faster prepayments, as the amount of principal generating interest cash flows are more rapidly reduced. In fact, the IO investor may not recover the initial investment in an IO security if prepayments increased significantly, even if the security is held to maturity.

Let's look at the expected price response of an IO to changes in mortgage rates. If mortgage rates decline below the note rate for the loans in the mortgage pool, prepayments are expected to accelerate. This would result in a deterioration of the expected cash flow for an IO. While the cash flow will be discounted at a lower rate, the net effect typically is a decline in the price of an IO. If mortgage rates rise above the note rate for the loans in the mortgage pool, the expected cash flow improves, but the cash flow is discounted at a higher interest rate. The net effect may be either an increase or a decline in the IO's price.

Thus, we see an interesting characteristic of an IO: Its price tends to move in the same direction as the change in mortgage rates (1) when mortgage rates fall below the note rate for the loans in the mortgage pool and (2) for some range of mortgage rates above the note rate. (This runs contrary to the normal behavior of bond prices, which usually move opposite the change in interest rates.) Note that while both IOs and POs can have substantial price variability, the combined price changes of the IO and PO must be equal to the price change of the underlying pass-through from which they were created.

Agency Collateralized Mortgage Obligations

A *CMO* is a security backed by a pool of mortgage pass-through securities. CMOs are structured so that there are several classes of bondholders with varying average lives. The different *bond classes* are also called *tranches.* The principal payments from the underlying pool of pass-through securities are used to retire the bonds on a priority basis as specified in the prospectus.

Although we will not explain the wide range of bond classes or tranches created in a CMO structure, we will provide a few for the purpose of showing how they are created (structured) and how they alter the investment characteristics relative to the mortgage pass-through securities from which they were created: sequential-pay bonds, planned amortization class bonds, and support bonds.[4]

Sequential-pay structures

The simplest type of CMO structure is the *sequential-pay structure.* To illustrate this structure, we will use the $660 million, 5.5% pass-through security (which comprises residential mortgage loans that conform to the underwriting standards of Ginnie Mae, Fannie Mae, and Freddie Mac) to

[4]For a more detailed description of the different types of CMO bond classes, see Fabozzi, Bhattacharya, and Berliner [2011].

create a simple structure. The following structure is given and we refer to this structure as "Structure 1":

Bond Class	Par Amount ($)	Coupon Rate
A	320,925,000	5.5%
B	59,400,000	5.5%
C	159,225,000	5.5%
D	120,450,000	5.5%

In structuring an agency deal, there are only rules specified for the distribution of principal and interest. There are no rules for deals with defaults and delinquencies because payments are guaranteed by the issuer. In Structure 1, we will use the following rules:

- *Interest*: The monthly interest is distributed to each bond class on the basis of the amount of principal outstanding at the beginning of the month.
- *Principal*: All monthly principal payments (i.e., regularly scheduled principal payments and prepayments) are distributed first to bond class A until it is completely paid off. After bond class A is completely paid off its par amount, all monthly principal payments are made to bond class B until it is completely paid off. After bond class B is completely paid off its par amount, all monthly principal payments are made to bond class C until it is completely paid off its par amount. Finally, after bond C is completely paid off, all monthly principal payments are made to bond class D.

Based on these rules for the distribution of interest and principal, Table 2 shows the cash flows for each bond class assuming one prepayment speed, 165% PSA. Note that bond class A is fully paid off in month 78 and in that month principal payments begin for bond class B, which is fully paid off in month 98. Bond class C starts receiving principal payments in month 98.

Before explaining what has been accomplished in Structure 1, a few comments are in order. First, the total par value of the four bond classes in the structure is equal to $660 million, which is equal to the par value of the collateral (the pass-through security). Second, we have simplified the illustration by assuming that all bond classes have the same coupon rate. In actual deals, the coupon rate would be determined by prevailing market conditions (i.e., the yield curve) and would not necessarily be equal for each bond class.

TABLE 2: Monthly Cash Flows for Selected Months for Structure 1 Assuming 165% PSA

	Tranche A			Tranche B		
Month	**Beginning Balance**	**Principal**	**Interest**	**Beginning Balance**	**Principal**	**Interest**
1	320,925,000	1,211,383	1,470,906	59,400,000	0	272,250
2	319,713,617	1,396,068	1,465,354	59,400,000	0	272,250
3	318,317,549	1,580,209	1,458,955	59,400,000	0	272,250
4	316,737,340	1,763,649	1,451,713	59,400,000	0	272,250
5	314,973,691	1,946,231	1,443,629	59,400,000	0	272,250
6	313,027,460	2,127,800	1,434,709	59,400,000	0	272,250
7	310,899,660	2,308,202	1,424,957	59,400,000	0	272,250
8	308,591,458	2,487,281	1,414,378	59,400,000	0	272,250
9	306,104,177	2,664,883	1,402,977	59,400,000	0	272,250
10	303,439,294	2,840,858	1,390,763	59,400,000	0	272,250
11	300,598,436	3,015,053	1,377,743	59,400,000	0	272,250
12	297,583,383	3,187,320	1,363,924	59,400,000	0	272,250
75	14,039,361	3,614,938	64,347	59,400,000	0	272,250
76	10,424,423	3,581,599	47,779	59,400,000	0	272,250
77	6,842,824	3,548,556	31,363	59,400,000	0	272,250
78	3,294,268	3,294,268	15,099	59,400,000	221,539	272,250
79	0	0	0	59,178,461	3,483,348	271,235
80	0	0	0	55,695,114	3,451,178	255,269
81	0	0	0	52,243,936	3,419,293	239,451
82	0	0	0	48,824,643	3,387,692	223,780
83	0	0	0	45,436,951	3,356,372	208,253
84	0	0	0	42,080,579	3,325,330	192,869
85	0	0	0	38,755,249	3,294,564	177,628
95	0	0	0	7,149,734	3,001,559	32,770
96	0	0	0	4,148,175	2,973,673	19,012
97	0	0	0	1,174,502	1,174,502	5,383
98	0	0	0	0	0	0

	Tranche C			Tranche D		
Month	**Beginning Balance**	**Principal**	**Interest**	**Beginning Balance**	**Principal**	**Interest**
1	96,500,000	0	442,292	73,000,000	0	334,583
2	96,500,000	0	442,292	73,000,000	0	334,583
3	96,500,000	0	442,292	73,000,000	0	334,583
4	96,500,000	0	442,292	73,000,000	0	334,583
5	96,500,000	0	442,292	73,000,000	0	334,583
6	96,500,000	0	442,292	73,000,000	0	334,583

TABLE 2: (*Continued*)

	Tranche C			Tranche D		
Month	Beginning Balance	Principal	Interest	Beginning Balance	Principal	Interest
7	96,500,000	0	442,292	73,000,000	0	334,583
8	96,500,000	0	442,292	73,000,000	0	334,583
9	96,500,000	0	442,292	73,000,000	0	334,583
10	96,500,000	0	442,292	73,000,000	0	334,583
11	96,500,000	0	442,292	73,000,000	0	334,583
12	96,500,000	0	442,292	73,000,000	0	334,583
95	96,500,000	0	442,292	73,000,000	0	334,583
96	96,500,000	0	442,292	73,000,000	0	334,583
97	96,500,000	1,073,657	442,292	73,000,000	0	334,583
98	95,426,343	1,768,876	437,371	73,000,000	0	334,583
99	93,657,468	1,752,423	429,263	73,000,000	0	334,583
100	91,905,045	1,736,116	421,231	73,000,000	0	334,583
101	90,168,928	1,719,955	413,274	73,000,000	0	334,583
102	88,448,973	1,703,938	405,391	73,000,000	0	334,583
103	86,745,035	1,688,064	397,581	73,000,000	0	334,583
104	85,056,970	1,672,332	389,844	73,000,000	0	334,583
105	83,384,639	1,656,739	382,180	73,000,000	0	334,583
175				71,179,833	850,356	326,241
176				70,329,478	842,134	322,343
177				69,487,344	833,986	318,484
178				68,653,358	825,912	314,661
179				67,827,446	817,911	310,876
180				67,009,535	809,982	307,127
181				66,199,553	802,125	303,415
182				65,397,428	794,339	299,738
183				64,603,089	786,624	296,097
184				63,816,465	778,978	292,492
185				63,037,487	771,402	288,922
350				1,137,498	132,650	5,214
351				1,004,849	131,049	4,606
352				873,800	129,463	4,005
353				744,337	127,893	3,412
354				616,444	126,338	2,825
355				490,105	124,799	2,246
356				365,307	123,274	1,674
357				242,033	121,764	1,109
358				120,269	120,269	551

A condition that must be satisfied is that the total interest to be paid to all the bond classes in a month may not exceed the interest from the collateral otherwise an interest shortfall will occur. Equivalently, the weighted average coupon rate for the bond classes in the structure may not exceed the coupon rate for the collateral (6% in our illustration). Finally, although the payment rules for the distribution of the principal payments are known, the exact amount of monthly principal is not. The monthly principal will depend on the principal cash flows generated by the collateral, which in turn depends on the actual payment rate of the collateral. Thus, in order to project monthly cash flows, a prepayment assumption must be made.

Now let us look at what was accomplished by Structure 1. To see what has been accomplished, a summary of the average life (in years) of the collateral and the four bond classes under a range of prepayment assumptions is shown:

	100%	125%	165%	250%	400%	500%
Collateral	11.2	10.1	8.6	6.4	4.5	3.7
Bond class						
A	4.7	4.1	3.4	2.7	2.0	1.8
B	10.4	8.9	7.3	5.3	3.8	3.2
C	15.1	13.2	10.9	7.9	5.3	4.4
D	24.0	22.4	19.8	15.2	10.3	8.4

Note the substantial variance of the average life for the collateral. Is this a short-term security that would fit the needs of an institutional investor such as a bank or an intermediate-term security that might be suitable for an insurance company? Look at the average life of the four bond classes. They have average lives that are both shorter and longer than the collateral, thereby attracting institutional investors who have a preference for an average life different from that of the collateral. For example, a depository institution interested in shorter-term investments and concerned with extension risk (i.e., the investment becoming longer than expected) would find bond class A more appealing than the collateral because within a reasonable range of prepayment speeds, bond class A's average life will be less than five years under slow prepayment speeds while the collateral's average life can extend to a little more than 11 years.[5] At the other end of the maturity preference spectrum, consider a defined benefit pension plan that is seeking longer-term investments and is concerned with contraction risk (i.e., the investment becoming shorter than expected). That institutional investor would prefer bond class D to the collateral.

While bond class D has considerable variance in its average life, the concern of contraction risk is greater for the collateral than for bond class D. To see that, notice in the table above that at the fastest prepayment speed shown in the table (500 PSA) the average life of the collateral can contract to 3.7 years but bond class D's to only 8.3 years.

Consequently, we can see that the rules for distribution of principal among the bond classes in this structure, referred to as a sequential-pay structure, have redistributed the prepayment risk (i.e., exposure to extension and contraction risk) of the collateral among the bond classes. As a result, an unattractive asset or collateral from the perspective of institutional investors can be used to create securities that better match the needs of those investors, a point that we have stated but not demonstrated until now.

Planned amortization class bonds and support bonds

There are institutional investors who seek securities (bond classes) that have even greater protection against prepayment risk. Investment bankers have created a product for such investors. To understand how this was done by structurers for investment banking firms, look at Table 3. The table shows the total principal payment for selected months for our \$660 million, with 5.5% collateral assuming a prepayment speed of 100% PSA (column 2) and 250% PSA (column 3). The last column in Table 3 shows the minimum total principal payment for each month. That is, if the prepayment speed is constant over the life of the collateral and that the constant prepayment speed is between 100% PSA and 250% PSA, then the monthly total principal will be as shown in the last column. If the total of the principal in the last column is summed, it is equal to \$470,224,580.

The amounts in the last column allow a structurer to create a bond class, referred to as a *planned amortization class bond* (more popularly

[5]Note that the average life is not the expected maturity. Assuming 100% PSA, for example, while bond class A's average life is 4.7 years, it might still take roughly 10 years for bond class A to be completely repaid.

TABLE 3: Total Principal Payments at 100% PSA and 250% PSA and Creation of PAC Schedule for Selected Months

Month	100% PSA	250% PSA	PAC Schedule
1	995,525	1,494,837	995,525
2	1,108,446	1,774,008	1,108,446
3	1,221,042	2,052,351	1,221,042
4	1,333,255	2,329,510	1,333,255
5	1,445,026	2,605,129	1,445,026
6	1,556,298	2,878,852	1,556,298
7	1,667,013	3,150,323	1,667,013
8	1,777,113	3,419,190	1,777,113
9	1,886,540	3,685,100	1,886,540
10	1,995,237	3,947,708	1,995,237
11	2,103,149	4,206,667	2,103,149
12	2,210,219	4,461,641	2,210,219
13	2,316,391	4,712,295	2,316,391
14	2,421,610	4,958,303	2,421,610
15	2,525,823	5,199,344	2,525,823
16	2,628,975	5,435,106	2,628,975
17	2,731,013	5,665,285	2,731,013
18	2,831,885	5,889,586	2,831,885
101	2,577,230	2,709,199	2,577,230
102	2,563,858	2,669,922	2,563,858
103	2,550,555	2,631,198	2,550,555
104	2,537,320	2,593,019	2,537,320
105	2,524,154	2,555,377	2,524,154
211	1,451,822	516,114	516,114
212	1,444,240	508,066	508,066
213	1,436,697	500,136	500,136
346	712,694	48,340	48,340
347	708,916	47,342	47,342
348	705,158	46,360	46,360
349	701,419	45,394	45,394
350	697,699	44,444	44,444
351	693,998	43,509	43,509
352	690,317	42,591	42,591
353	686,654	41,687	41,687
354	683,010	40,798	40,798
355	679,385	39,924	39,924
356	675,779	39,065	39,065
357	672,191	38,220	38,220
358	668,622	37,388	37,388

referred to as a *PAC bond*), which has priority over all other bond classes in the structure with respect to receiving the scheduled principal repayment. For example, for our hypothetical $660 million, with a 5.5% pass-through security, using a lower prepayment speed of 100% PSA and an upper speed of 250% PSA, the PAC schedule would be as shown in the last column. The upper and lower prepayment speeds are referred to as the structuring speeds and the range of 100% to 250% PSA is referred to as the *structuring bands*. The non-PAC bond classes in the structure are referred to as the *support bonds* or *companion bonds*, a name given because of their function in the structure as will be explained shortly.

The key in this structure is that the support bonds accept the contraction risk if actual prepayment speeds are fast and accept the extension risk if actual prepayment are slow. Hence, unlike in the sequential-pay structure illustrated by Structure 1, where the bond classes are afforded some protection against extension risk or contraction risk but not both, PAC bonds offer prepayment protection against both extension risk and contraction risk.

The prepayment protection in a PAC structure comes from the support bonds. It is the support bonds that receive any excess principal payments beyond the scheduled amount to be paid to the PAC bond classes and must wait to receive principal if there is a principal shortfall — hence, the term support bonds to describe this bond class.

To understand the rules for distribution in a PAC structure, consider the following hypothetical structure below that we identify as "Structure 2":

Bond Class	Bond Type	Par Amount	Coupon Rate
P	PAC	$470,224,580	5.5%
S	Support	$189,775,420	5.5%

Note that the par amount in Structure 2 is the total for a PAC created with a structuring band of 100% to 250% PSA.

Table 3 shows how this is done. Columns 2 and 3 show the monthly principal payments based on prepayment speeds of 100% and 250%, respectively. The last column shows the minimum principal payment for each month. The last column is the schedule of payments to the PAC bond class. It is this schedule, referred to as the *PAC schedule*, which would be shown in the prospectus.

To understand how the principal payment rules work for a PAC bond class, look at month 12. The PAC schedule indicates that for that month the payment to be made to the PAC bond class is $2,210,219. Suppose that actual principal payments for that month are $3,200,000. Then $2,210,219 is paid to the PAC bond class (P) and the balance, $989,781, is distributed to the support bond (S).

The following table shows the average life at the time of issuance of the two bond classes:

	PSA Speed					
	50	**75**	**100**	**165**	**250**	**400**
P	10.21	8.62	7.71	7.71	7.71	5.52
S	24.85	22.71	20.00	10.67	3.28	1.86
Collateral	14.42	12.68	11.24	8.56	6.44	4.47

Note that the average life is unchanged for the PAC bond class prepayment speeds from 100% to 250% PSA, the structuring band. Also notice the considerable variation in the average life of the support bond class. Its variability is much greater than that of the collateral for the prepayments' speeds shown. This is to be expected because the support bond class provides prepayment protection for the PAC bond class.

In practice, a typical structure may have more than one class of PAC bonds. That is, there may be a series of PAC bonds. For example, consider the following structure that we will refer to as "Structure 3":

Bond Class	**Par Amount ($)**
P-A	38,308,710
P-B	153,808,875
P-C	36,116,850
P-D	73,544,130
P-E	107,941,020
P-F	60,505,005
S	189,775,410

The first six bond classes are PAC bonds and their total par value is $470,224,580, the same as the single PAC bond in Structure 2. The rules for the distribution of principal payments are in sequence as follows:

- Pay principal payments received from the collateral to P–A up to its scheduled amount and if there is any excess principal payments, then, if such excess principal payments do not exceed expected principal payments at 250 PSA, distribute them to S or else distribute them to P–A.

- After P–A is fully paid off, pay principal payments received from the collateral to P–B up to its scheduled amount and if there is any excess principal payments, then, if such excess principal payments do not exceed expected principal payments at 250 PSA, distribute them to S, or else, distribute them to P–B.
- After P–B is fully paid off, pay principal payments received from the collateral to P–C up to its scheduled amount and if there is any excess principal payments, then, if such excess principal payments do not exceed expected principal payments at 250 PSA, distribute them to S or else distribute them to P–C.
- And so on.

The average life for each PAC bond assuming various prepayment speeds is as follows:

	PSA Speed					
	50%	**75%**	**100%**	**165%**	**250%**	**400%**
P–A	1.3	1.1	1.0	1.0	1.0	1.0
P–B	5.1	4.1	3.5	3.5	3.5	3.1
P–C	8.8	7.1	5.9	5.9	5.9	4.3
P–D	11.1	9.0	7.5	7.5	7.5	5.2
P–E	15.1	12.5	10.9	10.9	10.9	7.3
P–F	19.9	18.5	18.3	18.3	18.3	12.5

Note that the average life is stable for the structuring band for all PAC bonds. This is as expected. But note further that the shorter-term PAC bonds such as P–A and P–B have stability over a wider range of prepayment speeds. The reason has to do with the support bonds. In Structure 2, there is \$189,775,410 par value of support bonds protecting \$470,224,580 par value of a single PAC bond. In Structure 3, since P–A has first priority on the principal payments, this means that from the perspective of P–A, there is \$189,775,410 par value of support bonds protecting only \$38,308,710 par value of P–A. Hence, there is greater prepayment protection beyond the structuring band. Similarly, for P–B, there is \$189,775,410 par value of support bonds protecting only \$192,117,585 (sum of par value of P–A and P–B). While the prepayment protection of P–B is provided for a wider range of prepayment speeds compared to the structuring bands, that range is less than for P–A, but greater than for P–C and P–D.

Because of their role in providing protection for PAC bond classes in a structure, support bonds have the greatest prepayment risk in a structure. Investors must be particularly careful in assessing the cash flow characteristics of support bonds to reduce the likelihood of adverse portfolio consequences due to prepayments. Unfortunately, in the early years of the CMO markets, too often buyers of these types of bond classes were not aware of their investment characteristics and were attracted to them because of their high yield based on some specified prepayment assumption rather than analyzing them on an option-adjusted basis.

In the PAC-support structure given by Structure 2, there is only one support bond. In actual deals, the support bonds are often divided into different bond classes. For example, a structurer can create support bonds that pay off in sequence. To provide some support bonds with greater prepayment protection than the other support bonds in a structure, a structurer can even carve up the support bonds to create support bonds with a schedule of principal repayments. That is, support bonds that are PAC support bonds can be created. In a structure with a PAC bond and a support bond with a PAC schedule of principal repayments, the former is called a PAC I bond or Level I PAC bond and the latter a PAC II bond or Level II PAC bond. While PAC II bonds have greater prepayment protection than the support bonds without a schedule of principal repayments, the prepayment protection is less than that provided PAC I bonds.

Private-Label Residential MBS

The private-label CMO market encompasses a variety of product and structuring variations. Technically, any deal that is not securitized under an agency or GSE shelf (i.e., Ginnie Mae, Freddie Mac, or Fannie Mae) can be considered a private label as the issuing entity has no connection to the US government (either explicit or implicit). Such deals must have some form of credit enhancement in order to create large amounts of investment-grade bonds. Today, the convention in the market, however, is to limit the private-label sector to the securitization of prime, first-lien fixed- and adjustable-rate loans.

Aside from the presence of credit enhancement, private-label deals share many features and structuring techniques with agency CMOs. There are some important differences, however, due to the nature of the loans collateralizing the deal as well as legal and regulatory issues associated with the different shelves. First, private-label deals can be structured such that derivatives, such as interest rate swaps and caps, can be inserted into the structures as risk mitigators. The GSEs, by contrast, do not allow for their inclusion in deals. Second, the loans collateralizing private-label deals are generally assumed to prepay faster than those in agency pools. The convention in the agency market is to structure deals using a base-case prepayment speed consistent with median prepayment speeds reported by Bloomberg.

Private-label deals, by contrast, are structured either to a market convention (i.e., PSA speeds ranging from 250–300%) or a predefined ramp (i.e., 6–18% CPR ramping over 12 months). The ramp is defined in the prospectus and it is typically called the *prospectus prepayment curve*, or PPC (100% PPC is simply the base ramp defined at the time of pricing). Finally, private-label deals typically have cleanup calls. These are inserted into deals to relieve the trustees from the burden of having to oversee deals with very small remaining balances. The calls are triggered when the current face of the deal and/or collateral group declines below a predetermined level.

In this section, we briefly review the mechanisms involved in creating the internal credit enhancement typically utilized in private-label deals. Note that while the focus in this section is on the structuring of fixed-rate mortgage loans, as we analyzed for the agency deals earlier in this chapter, other mortgage designs can be structured in a similar fashion.

Private-Label Credit Enhancement

The first step in structuring the credit enhancement for a private-label deal is to split the face value of the loans into senior and subordinated interests. The senior bonds have higher priority with respect to both the receipt of interest and principal and the allocation of realized losses, and are generally created with enough subordination to be rated AAA by the credit rating agencies. In most cases, the subordinate interests are subdivided (or tranched) into a series of bonds that decline sequentially in priority. The subordinate classes normally range from AA in rating to an unrated first-loss piece. These securities are often referenced as the six-pack, since there are six broad rating grades generally issued by the rating agencies. In the investment-grade category, bonds range from AA to BBB; non-investment grade ratings decline from BB to the unrated first-loss piece. The structure (or "splits") of a hypothetical deal is shown in panels A and B of Table 4, while a schematic showing how losses are allocated within the structure is contained in Figure 1.

TABLE 4: Measuring Subordination by Percentage of Deal Size and Credit Support for a Hypothetical $400 million Deal with 3.5% Initial Subordination

	Face Value ($)	**Percent of Deal (%)**
A. Tranche Size as a Percentage of the Total Deal		
AAA	386,000,000	96.50
AA	6,000,000	1.50
A	2,600,000	0.65
BBB	1,800,000	0.45
BB	1,200,000	0.30
B	1,200,000	0.30
First Loss (Non-rated)	1,200,000	0.30
Total Subordination	14,000,000	3.50
	Face Value ($)	**Credit Support (%)[a]**
B. Tranche Size Measured by Percentage of Subordination for Each Rating Level (i.e., credit support)		
AAA	386,000,000	3.50
AA	6,000,000	2.00
A	2,600,000	1.35
BBB	1,800,000	0.90
BB	1,200,000	0.60
B	1,200,000	0.30
First Loss (Non-rated)	1,200,000	0.00

Notes: [a]Calculated by summing the deal percentages of all tranches junior in priority. As an example, if cumulative losses on the deal were 0.40%, the First Loss and rated B tranches would be fully exhausted, but the tranches rated BB and above would not be affected.

Internal credit enhancement requires two complimentary mechanisms. The cash flows for deals are allocated through the mechanism of a waterfall, which dictates the allocation of principal and interest payments to tranches with different degrees of seniority. At the same time, the allocation of realized losses is also governed by a separate prioritization schedule, with the subordinates typically being impacted in reverse order of priority.

While the original subordination levels are set at the time of issuance (or, more precisely, at the time the attributes of the deal's collateral are finalized), deals with internal credit enhancement are designed such that the amount of credit enhancement grows over time. Private-label structures generally use a so-called *shifting interest mechanism*, in which the subordinate classes do not receive principal prepayments for a period of time after issuance, generally five years for fixed-rate deals. After the lockout period

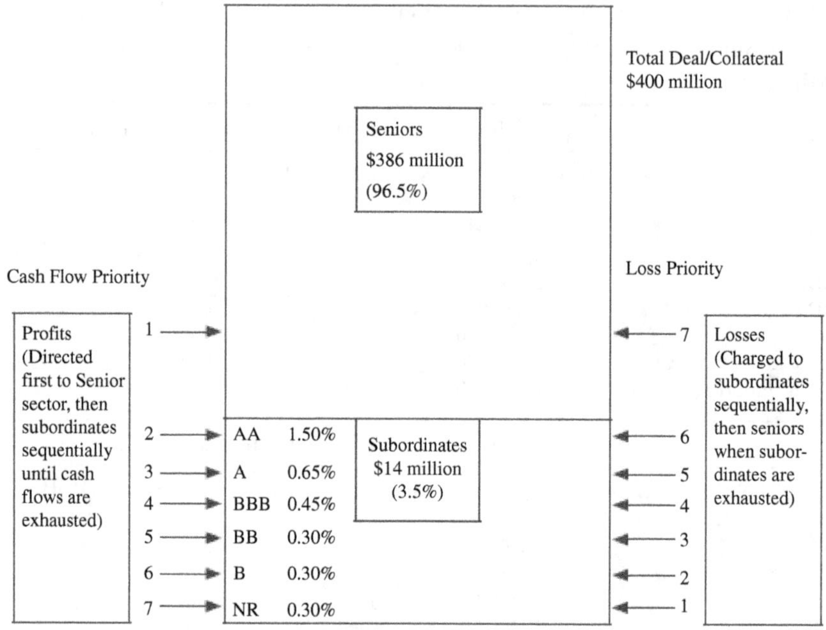

FIGURE 1: Schematic representation of a Hypothetical Structure with Cash Flow and Loss Allocations

TABLE 5: Shifting Interest Example for Subordinates on a Fixed-Rate Prime Deal

Months 1–60	Subs completely locked out from prepayments (receive amortization only)
Months 61–72	Subs receive 30% of pro rata share of prepayments
Months 73–84	Subs receive 40% of pro rata share of prepayments
Months 85–96	Subs receive 60% of pro rata share of prepayments
Months 97–108	Subs receive 80% of pro rata share of prepayments
Month 109+	Subs receive 100% of pro rata share of prepayments

expires, the subordinated classes begin to receive prepayments on an escalating basis. It is only after 10 years that the subordinated classes receive a pro rata allocation of prepayments. Locking out the subordinate bonds means that as the collateral experiences prepayments, the face value of the subordinate classes grows in proportion relative to the senior classes; the senior classes receive all the collateral prepayments during the lockout period and hence decline proportionately over time. A typical shifting interest schedule, along with notes on the effect of the principal reallocation, is shown in Table 5.

The effects of shifting interest structure are as follows: (1) senior bonds paydown faster than subordinated bonds, (2) senior bonds make up proportionately less of the deal, (3) subordination grows, providing senior bonds more protection, and (4) subordinate bonds have to protect fewer senior bonds (deleveraging).

Key Points

- A mortgage is a loan secured by the collateral of some specified real estate property that obliges the borrower (mortgagor) to make a predetermined series of payments and grants the lender (mortgagee) the right, if the borrower defaults (i.e., fails to make the contractual payments), to foreclose on the loan and seize the property in order to ensure that the debt is paid off.
- The interest rate on the mortgage loan is called the note rate.
- The fundamental unit in a mortgage-related security is the pool which is an aggregation of large numbers of mortgage loans with similar (but not identical) characteristics.
- Loans with a commonality of attributes such as note rate, term to maturity, credit quality, loan balance, and type of mortgage design are combined using a variety of legal mechanisms to create relatively fungible investment vehicles.
- By creating a residential MBS, mortgage loans are effectively transformed from a heterogeneous group of disparate assets into sizable and homogeneous securities that trade in a liquid market.
- Loans that meet the underwriting guidelines of three entities — Ginnie Mae, Fannie Mae, and Freddie Mac — are securitized as an agency pool.
- There are three types of agency MBSs: pass-through securities, CMOs, and stripped MBSs.
- Loans that do not qualify for agency pools are securitized in non-agency or "private-label" transactions.
- Private-label MBSs do not have an agency guaranty.
- For a level-payment mortgage, each monthly mortgage payment is due on the first of each month and consists of (1) interest of 1/12 of the fixed annual note rate times the amount of the outstanding mortgage balance at the beginning of the previous month and (2) a repayment of a portion of the outstanding mortgage balance (principal).

- The monthly cash flow from a mortgage loan, regardless of the mortgage design, can be divided into three parts: (1) the servicing fee and guarantee fee, (2) the interest payment net of the servicing fee and guarantee fee, and (3) the scheduled principal repayment (or amortization).
- A prepayment is a payment made in excess of the scheduled principal repayment.
- Prepayments occur because (1) borrowers sell their home, (2) borrowers become incentivized to pay off their loan as market rates fall below the loan's note rate, (3) borrowers cannot meet their mortgage obligations, so the lender repossesses the property and sells it, and (4) if property is destroyed by fire or if another insured catastrophe occurs, the insurance proceeds are used to pay off the mortgage loan.
- The effect of prepayments is that the cash flow from a mortgage loan is not known with certainty (i.e., the amount and the timing of the cash flow are uncertain).
- Investors in RMBS are exposed to prepayment risk.
- In a mortgage pass-through security, the monthly cash flow from the pool of mortgage loans is distributed on a pro rata basis to the certificate holders and includes (1) monthly interest net of the servicing fee and guarantee fee, (2) regularly scheduled principal payments (amortization) for the month, and (3) prepayments for the month.
- The two conventions used to measure prepayment rates are the conditional prepayment rate and the PSA prepayment benchmark.
- An agency stripped MBS is created by altering the distribution of principal and interest from a pro rata distribution to an unequal distribution.
- In the most common type of stripped MBS, all of the interest is allocated to one class (the interest only class) and the entire principal to the other class (the principal-only class).
- An agency CMO is a security backed by a pool of mortgage pass-through securities and is structured so that there are several bond classes (called tranches) with varying average lives.
- In an agency CMO, the principal payments from the underlying pool of pass-through securities are used to retire the bonds on a priority basis as specified in the prospectus.
- Three common agency CMOs are sequential-pay bonds, planned amortization class bonds, and support bonds.
- The private-label CMO market encompasses a variety of product and structuring variations.

- Aside from the presence of credit enhancement, private-label deals share many features and structuring techniques with agency CMOs.
- The first step in structuring the credit enhancement for a private-label deal is to split the face value of the loans into senior and subordinated interests.
- Senior bonds have higher priority with respect to both the receipt of interest and principal and the allocation of realized losses, and are generally created with enough subordination to be rated AAA by the credit rating agencies.
- In most cases, the subordinate interests are subdivided (or tranched) into a series of bonds that decline sequentially in priority and normally range from AA in rating to an unrated first-loss piece.

References

Fabozzi, F. J. 2006. *Fixed Income Mathematics: Analytical and Statistical Techniques*. New York: McGraw-Hill.

Fabozzi, F. J., A. K. Bhattacharya, and W. S. Berliner, 2011. *Mortgage-Backed Securities: Products, Structuring, and Analytical Techniques: Second Edition*. Hoboken, NJ: John Wiley & Sons.

Chapter 4

Financial Econometrics Tools for Asset Management

Learning Objectives

After reading this chapter, you will understand:

- linear regression with a single dependent variable;
- multiple linear regression;
- principal component analysis;
- estimation of factors explaining the cross-section of stock returns;
- econometric models for volatility: ARCH and GARCH.

Introduction

In general, econometric models are used to resolve two types of problems that we face on a daily basis. On the one hand, we want to have an explanation of what we observe. For example, we can ask questions about the sensitivity of the return of a given portfolio to the returns of a major market index in a given time period, is the sensitivity changing over time, or is there another factor affecting the portfolio returns that we should be worried about? Or, for example, if our portfolio outperformed a given benchmark, then what is the source of the outperformance?

On the other hand, we are concerned about the future because it is uncertain. We would like to forecast how our portfolio is likely to behave under certain conditions. These conditions may describe a different policy regime or a likely future scenario. Even though this question concerns forecasting rather than explanation, there is a connection. For instance, what would be the impact of a possible shift of the Treasury bond yields on a multi-asset class portfolio?

This chapter describes the standard econometric tools used to provide answers for such questions. We consider applications in asset pricing and risk management.

Linear Regression

Regression analysis studies the relationship between a variable called the dependent variable and one or several other variables called explanatory, or independent, variables. When the relationship is linear, then the regression analysis is called linear as well. In this section, we present different variations which have important applications in the field of asset management. We start with the simple case of a single explanatory variable because it is easier to understand, which is followed by the general case of many explanatory variables. Finally, we distinguish between a time-series regression, when the variables are observed across time, and a cross-sectional regression, when the observations concern many variables observed at a single point in time.

Single Explanatory Variable

The simplest example of a linear regression is when we consider only one explanatory variable. Denote by Y the dependent variable and by X the explanatory variable. For example, the dependent variable can be the monthly return of a given stock and the explanatory variable can be the monthly return of the S&P 500 index. We are interested in finding out how the stock return responds to changes in the market. Mathematically, the relationship is expressed as

$$Y_t = \alpha + \beta X_t + u_t,$$

where α is called the intercept, β denotes the slope coefficient, and u is referred to as a residual, which captures the error in the linear relationship and is therefore also referred to as the *error term*. Any regression model should be viewed as a statistical model rather than a causal connection between the two variables. For example, it would be incorrect to say that the return of the market as proxied by the S&P 500 index causes the stock returns. Rather, the model describes the behavior of Y in relation to X.

The linear regression model makes several assumptions:

1. **The model is linear:** This assumption implies that we hypothesize a linear relationship between the two variables.
2. **Homoscedasticity:** The variance of the error term is the same for any value of the independent variable.
3. **Independence:** The observations are independent of each other.
4. **Zero conditional mean:** The mean of the error term is zero for any value of the independent variable.

Even though some of these assumptions can be relaxed to weaker ones, the ones listed here are classical (see, for example, Fabozzi, Focardi, Rachev, and Arshanapalli [2014]).

The linear regression as given in the equation represents a statistical model which we hypothesize. Given data for the dependent and the independent variable, our objective is to estimate the model parameters α and β and use the estimated equation to carry out certain analyses. For example, we may be interested in how much the stock price is expected to drop in the event of a market decline or to test if the slope coefficient is negligible and so that the stock is said to be market neutral.

In practice, regression models are estimated by following the method of ordinary least squares (OLS). According to the OLS method, we estimate the model parameters by finding the values that minimize the errors between what is predicted by the regression model and what is observed. Denote the observed samples by $Y_1, Y_2, \ldots, Y_n$ and $X_1, X_2, \ldots, X_n$. The least squares principle is observed by solving the following problem:

$$\min_{\alpha,\beta} \sum_{t=1}^{n} (Y_t - \alpha - \beta X_t)^2,$$

where $u_t = Y_t - \alpha - \beta X_t$ represents the errors. The solution to this optimization problem is provided by the following equations:

$$\hat{\alpha} = \bar{Y} - \hat{\beta}\bar{X},$$
$$\hat{\beta} = \frac{\Sigma(X_t - \bar{X})(Y_t - \bar{Y})}{\Sigma(X_t - \bar{X})^2},$$

in which $\bar{X}$ and $\bar{Y}$ denote the sample averages. In practice, we use software tools and do not work with these equations manually, but what the equations show is that the estimators of the intercept and the slope can be easily calculated from the sample data.

Even though the choice of the least squares method to estimate parameters may seem *ad-hoc*, the estimator has nice properties. For example, the regression coefficients estimated in this way are known to be unbiased, which means that on average they coincide with the true values. Furthermore, the OLS estimator has the least variance among all linear estimators, which means that the regression parameters are estimated most accurately.

How well does the statistical model fit the data? This is a critical question for any model. In the case of the linear regression, we can measure the goodness of fit in a simple way using a metric called the coefficient of determination denoted by r^2. The idea is to take the sum of the squared errors after the parameters have been estimated and to see what the proportion of that sum of the total variation of the dependent variable is. For example, if it turns out that there is no statistical relationship between X and Y and the slope coefficient is estimated to be zero, $\beta = 0$, then the errors equal the observations of Y with the mean subtracted, $u_i = Y_i - \bar{Y}$. In the opposite direction, if the statistical model is an exact linear equation with no residual, then the sum of the squared errors will be equal to zero.

As a consequence, computing the ratio of the sum of squared errors and the total variation of the dependent variable indicates a goodness of fit. The formula for the coefficient of determination is

$$r^2 = 1 - \frac{\sum u_t^2}{\sum (Y_t - \bar{Y})^2}.$$

According to the discussion above, $r^2 = 1$ indicates a perfect fit, while $r^2 = 0$ indicates no relationship between X and Y. In general, $0 \leq r^2 \leq 1$.

In the following examples, we provide illustrations of the linear regression with a single explanatory variable and also an interpretation of the coefficient of determination in terms of systematic and non-systematic risks.[1]

Estimating the market beta of a company

According to the Nobel-prize winning capital asset pricing model (CAPM), stock returns are affected by two types of factors: the market factor and company-specific factors. The market factor aggregates risks that most companies are exposed to, such as inflation, recessions, high interest rates, wars,

[1]Rachev, Mittnik, Fabozzi, Focardi, and Jasic [2007, Chapter 5] provide several other applications in asset management: evaluating management performance using the Jensen measure, benchmark selection using Sharpe benchmarks, return-based style analysis for hedge fund survival, hedge fund survival, and measuring empirical duration for bond portfolios. For an application on factor modeling, see Engle, Focardi, and Fabozzi [2016].

etc. In contrast, company-specific risks are caused by random events unique to the particular company, such as lawsuits, strikes, successful or unsuccessful business decisions, etc. In practice, the market factor is typically proxied by a portfolio of all the stocks traded on the stock exchange in which the weight of each company is proportional to its size measured by the so-called market capitalization.

The CAPM theory is consistent with the following regression model for the stock returns of a single company,

$$R_t - r_f = \beta(R_{m,t} - r_f) + u_t,$$

where R_t denotes the time series of the stock returns, r_f denotes the risk-free rate proxied by a US Treasury bill rate, $R_{m,t}$ denotes the time series of the market portfolio return, and u_t is a residual aggregating all company-specific risks. The return differences $R_t - r_f$ and $R_{m,t} - r_f$ are sometimes referred to as *excess returns*. The regression coefficient β is company specific and captures the exposure to the market risks. It is also known as the market beta of the company and represents a measure of risk which affects, among other things, the cost at which the company can raise capital. Market betas of companies are calculated by financial analysts on a regular basis and can change through time as a company's business evolves.

In this example, we estimate the market beta of Apple Inc. making common choices for the data for the dependent and the independent variables. We work with monthly returns for both the stock and the market portfolio[2] and we use five years of data — 60 monthly returns from January 2013 to December 2017. The risk-free rate is the return of the one-month Treasury bill. The data are shown in Table 1.

Even though the regression model has no intercept, practitioners estimate the regression with an intercept, which is sometimes referred to as the market model. The estimated regression is:

$$\hat{Y}_t = 0.0078 + 1.2139X_t.$$

A visual illustration is provided in Figure 1. The estimated intercept is indeed very small and has no significant impact. The slope coefficient suggests that if the market increases by 1%, the stock price of Apple Inc. will increase by approximately 1.21%; that is, it magnifies the positive but

[2]The market portfolio is a value-weighted portfolio of all companies incorporated in the US and listed on the NYSE, AMEX, or NASDAQ. The data for the market portfolio returns and the risk-free rate are available on the website of Kenneth French: http://mba.tuck.dartmouth.edu/pages/faculty/ken.french/data_library.html.

TABLE 1: Monthly Data for Calculating the Market Beta for Apple Inc.: January 2013 to December 2017

Month	$R_{m,t} - r_f$	$R_t - r_f$	Month	$R_{m,t} - r_f$	$R_t - r_f$
Jan-2013	0.0129	−0.0309	Jul-2015	−0.0604	−0.0691
Feb-2013	0.0403	0.0452	Aug-2015	−0.0308	−0.0188
Mar-2013	0.0155	0.0003	Sep-2015	0.0775	0.0834
Apr-2013	0.028	0.0157	Oct-2015	0.0056	−0.0100
May-2013	−0.012	−0.0758	Nov-2015	−0.0217	−0.1065
Jun-2013	0.0565	0.1412	Dec-2015	−0.0577	−0.0753
Jul-2013	−0.0271	0.0767	Jan-2016	−0.0007	−0.0069
Aug-2013	0.0377	0.0256	Feb-2016	0.0696	0.1331
Sep-2013	0.0418	0.0964	Mar-2016	0.0092	−0.1400
Oct-2013	0.0312	0.0638	Apr-2016	0.0178	0.0652
Nov-2013	0.0281	0.0516	May-2016	−0.0005	−0.0370
Dec-2013	−0.0332	−0.1077	Jun-2016	0.0395	0.0899
Jan-2014	0.0465	0.0512	Jul-2016	0.005	0.0179
Feb-2014	0.0043	0.0643	Aug-2016	0.0025	0.0711
Mar-2014	−0.0019	0.0994	Sep-2016	−0.0202	0.0041
Apr-2014	0.0206	0.0727	Oct-2016	0.0486	−0.0267
May-2014	0.0261	0.0692	Nov-2016	0.0182	0.0530
Jun-2014	−0.0204	0.0287	Dec-2016	0.0194	0.0473
Jul-2014	0.0424	0.0722	Jan-2017	0.0357	0.1285
Aug-2014	−0.0197	−0.0122	Feb-2017	0.0017	0.0529
Sep-2014	0.0252	0.0720	Mar-2017	0.0109	−0.0006
Oct-2014	0.0255	0.1012	Apr-2017	0.0106	0.0628
Nov-2014	−0.0006	−0.0679	May-2017	0.0078	−0.0539
Dec-2014	−0.0311	0.0614	Jun-2017	0.0187	0.0320
Jan-2015	0.0613	0.0964	Jul-2017	0.0016	0.1018
Feb-2015	−0.0112	−0.0275	Aug-2017	0.0251	−0.0575
Mar-2015	0.0059	0.0058	Sep-2017	0.0225	0.0959
Apr-2015	0.0136	0.0410	Oct-2017	0.0312	0.0158
May-2015	−0.0153	−0.0332	Nov-2017	0.0106	−0.0126
Jun-2015	0.0154	−0.0329	Dec-2017	0.0557	−0.0117

Note: $R_{m,t} - r_f$ = Market portfolio return minus the Treasury bill rate (excess return).
$R_t - r_f$ = Apple return minus the Treasury bill rate (excess return).

also the negative market returns. As a result, as of December 2017 the company appears riskier than the overall market as represented by the market portfolio.

The r^2 value of 0.29 indicates that about 29% of the total risk of the company is explained by the market factor and the remaining 71%

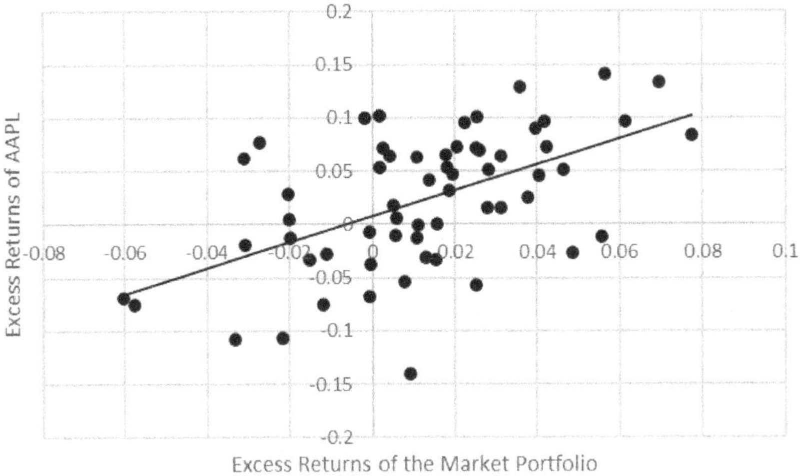

FIGURE 1: Estimated Regression for Apple Inc

Note: The monthly excess returns of the market portfolio and the excess returns of Apple Inc. are plotted on the horizontal and the vertical axis, respectively.

is company-specific risk. Such a decomposition is common for single stocks.

Why investors construct portfolios

The analysis in the previous example can be conducted for any risky asset, including any portfolio of stocks which itself can be viewed as a risky asset. If we invest a certain amount in a set of N stocks by allocating a certain weight of the initial capital to a given stock, then the portfolio return over a predefined period of time equals the weighted average of the single stock returns. If all weights are equal (to $1/N$ of the initial capital), then the portfolio is called equally weighted.

Suppose that the CAPM regression model holds for all of the single stocks,

$$R_{t,i} - r_f = \beta_i(R_{m,t} - r_f) + u_{t,i},$$

where $i = 1, 2, \ldots, N$ denotes the index of the corresponding stock in the set. The residual $u_{t,i}$ aggregates the stock-specific risks for the corresponding company and for any fixed t, the residuals corresponding to different companies are assumed to be independent random variables. Then, for the portfolio we can write

$$\frac{1}{N}\sum_{i=1}^{N} R_{t,i} - r_f = (R_{m,t} - r_f)\frac{1}{N}\sum_{i=1}^{N}\beta_i + \frac{1}{N}\sum_{i=1}^{N} u_{t,i},$$

$$R_{t,p} - r_f = \beta_p(R_{m,t} - r_f) + u_{t,p},$$

in which $R_{t,p}$ denotes the portfolio return time series, β_p denotes the portfolio market beta, and $u_{t,p}$ is the residual aggregating the companies' specific risks. The portfolio return is the average of the single stock returns in that period, the portfolio market beta is the average of the companies' betas, and the residual equals the average of the single stocks' residuals. Because the single stocks' residuals are assumed to be independent, the variance σ_p^2 of $u_{t,p}$ equals $\sigma_p^2 = \frac{1}{N^2}\sum_{i=1}^{N}\sigma_i^2$. For large portfolios, when N is large, this quantity converges to zero if we further assume that stock specific risk is bounded. Thus, by building portfolios investors can reduce stock-specific risks which is known as risk diversification. Unfortunately, the systematic risks cannot be reduced in this way — the equally weighted portfolio beta is expected to be a positive number regardless of the number of stocks included in the portfolio.

To illustrate the notion of diversification empirically, we build a portfolio of the largest 10% of all stocks incorporated in the US and listed on the US stock exchanges.[3] Consistent with the previous example, we use the 60 monthly excess returns of that portfolio from January 2013 to December 2017 and the same data for the market portfolio is used to show how to calculate a company's market beta. The input data are provided in Table 2.

The estimated regression is

$$\hat{Y}_t = -8.1 \times 10^{-6} + 0.9935X_t,$$

with $r^2 = 0.98$ and the regression line is plotted together with the data in Figure 2. The effect of diversification is illustrated by the high r^2 — stock-specific risks have been almost completely eliminated. The most significant risk is the systematic exposure to the market portfolio. As a matter of fact, because some risks can be diversified away, asset pricing theories in finance conclude that only systematic risks are rewarded — investors should not expect to earn money by taking company-specific risks. From the standpoint

[3]The measure of size is the market capitalization of the company which equals the stock price multiplied by the number of shares the company has issued. We use the data for portfolios ranked by size on the website of Kenneth French: http://mba.tuck.dartmouth.edu/pages/faculty/ken.french/data_library.html.

TABLE 2: Monthly Data for Calculating the Market Beta for an Equally Weighted Portfolio Invested in the Largest 10% of the Stocks Incorporated in the US and Listed on the US Stock Exchanges: January 2013 to December 2017

Month	$R_{m,t} - r_f$	$R_{t,p} - r_f$	Month	$R_{m,t} - r_f$	$R_{t,p} - r_f$
Jan-2013	0.0129	0.0095	Jul-2015	−0.0604	−0.0624
Feb-2013	0.0403	0.0465	Aug-2015	−0.0308	−0.034
Mar-2013	0.0155	0.0167	Sep-2015	0.0775	0.0786
Apr-2013	0.028	0.0265	Oct-2015	0.0056	0.0041
May-2013	−0.012	−0.0117	Nov-2015	−0.0217	−0.018
Jun-2013	0.0565	0.0575	Dec-2015	−0.0577	−0.0606
Jul-2013	−0.0271	−0.0241	Jan-2016	−0.0007	0.0031
Aug-2013	0.0377	0.0393	Feb-2016	0.0696	0.0618
Sep-2013	0.0418	0.0462	Mar-2016	0.0092	0.0137
Oct-2013	0.0312	0.0305	Apr-2016	0.0178	0.0137
Nov-2013	0.0281	0.0285	May-2016	−0.0005	−0.0074
Dec-2013	−0.0332	−0.0343	Jun-2016	0.0395	0.0352
Jan-2014	0.0465	0.0466	Jul-2016	0.0050	0.0024
Feb-2014	0.0043	0.0091	Aug-2016	0.0025	−0.0011
Mar-2014	−0.0019	0.0061	Sep-2016	−0.0202	−0.0139
Apr-2014	0.0206	0.0267	Oct-2016	0.0486	0.0432
May-2014	0.0261	0.0215	Nov-2016	0.0182	0.0139
Jun-2014	−0.0204	−0.0198	Dec-2016	0.0194	0.0210
Jul-2014	0.0424	0.0375	Jan-2017	0.0357	0.0378
Aug-2014	−0.0197	−0.0149	Feb-2017	0.0017	−0.0005
Sep-2014	0.0252	0.0202	Mar-2017	0.0109	0.0119
Oct-2014	0.0255	0.0256	Apr-2017	0.0106	0.0139
Nov-2014	−0.0006	−0.0006	May-2017	0.0078	0.0113
Dec-2014	−0.0311	−0.0371	Jun-2017	0.0187	0.0184
Jan-2015	0.0613	0.0611	Jul-2017	0.0016	0.0042
Feb-2015	−0.0112	−0.0146	Aug-2017	0.0251	0.0261
Mar-2015	0.0059	0.0159	Sep-2017	0.0225	0.0153
Apr-2015	0.0136	0.0075	Oct-2017	0.0312	0.0311
May-2015	−0.0153	−0.0189	Nov-2017	0.0106	0.0097
Jun-2015	0.0154	0.0205	Dec-2017	0.0557	0.0579

Note: $R_{m,t} - r_f$ = Market portfolio return minus the Treasury bill rate (excess return). $R_{t,p} - r_f$ = Portfolio return minus the Treasury bill rate (excess return).

of the regression analysis, this means that the intercept in the regression is expected to be a very small, economically insignificant number.

Hypotheses testing

The regression parameters are estimated using the least-squares principle. For instance, using the sample in the example, we found that the company's

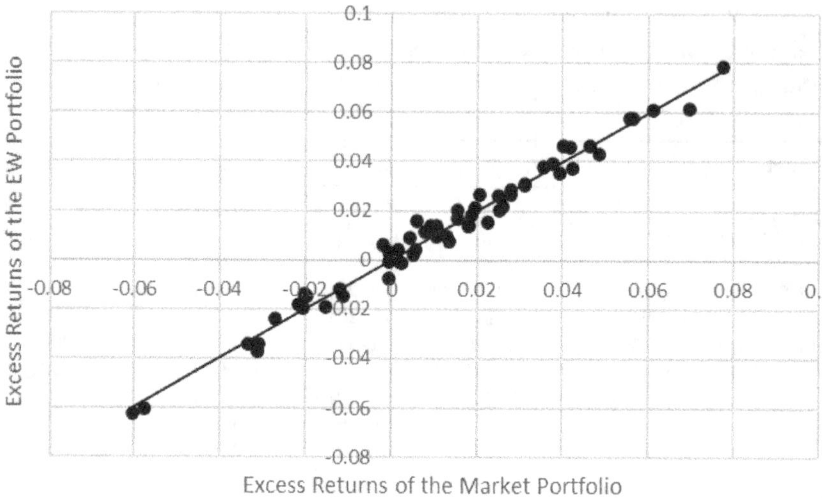

FIGURE 2: Estimated Regression for the Equally Weighted Portfolio of the Largest 10% of US Stocks

beta is estimated to equal 1.21. The next question that arises is to what degree we can trust the number? If the beta is equal to zero, then the implication is that there is no relationship between the dependent variable and the independent variable. With real data, the estimated beta is extremely unlikely to be exactly equal to zero even if there is indeed no relationship between the two variables. As a consequence, we need to employ additional analysis to be able to conclude that no relationship is likely (i.e., if the slope coefficient is likely to equal zero).

In statistics, this is known as hypothesis testing. Conceptually, the parameter estimator is a function of the sample. This is evident from the expressions of $\hat{\alpha}$ and $\hat{\beta}$. If we take different samples generated from the two variables and re-estimate the coefficients for each sample, then the estimates will vary. These variations can be described by means of their distributions; that is, we treat the parameter estimator as a random variable. Testing a hypothesis for a particular parameter value reduces to checking how likely it is for that value to be the true parameter value given the distribution of the estimator.

To find the distribution of the estimator, however, it is common to make additional assumptions, which we will not discuss here. It is sufficient to know that under fairly general assumptions about the distributions of the stochastic variables in the regression equation, we can find approximately the distribution of the estimators for samples that are relatively large. To test hypotheses, it is common to employ a statistic of the following type:

$$t = \frac{\text{estimator} - \text{value}}{\text{standard error}},$$

where *value* means the hypothesized value that we are testing for and *standard error* means the standard deviation of the estimator. Such statistics are also known as t-statistics because they have a Student t distribution with degrees of freedom parameter equal to $n-2$ where n denotes the sample size and the number two denotes the number of coefficients that are estimated — in this case an intercept and a slope coefficient.

In practice, software packages calculate the t-statistic by plugging in the estimated value for *estimator,* subtract the hypothesized value, and then divide by the standard error of the estimator, which is also estimated from the data. Then, they calculate the p-value of the t-statistic using the Student t distribution. If the p-value is very small (it is common to consider 0.01 or 0.05 as reference values), then we conclude that the estimated number is statistically significant. Otherwise, we conclude that the estimated number is insignificant and we cannot reject the hypothesis that the regression coefficient equals the hypothesized value.

For example, if we want to test the hypothesis that there exists a statistically significant relationship between the two variables as modeled by the linear regression, then more formally the estimator is $\hat{\beta}$ and the hypothesized value is zero. If the p-value of the statistic is below 0.05, we say that we cannot reject the hypothesis that there is no relationship at the 5% level of significance.

The next example provides a more detailed illustration of the output of a linear regression together with further comments on hypothesis testing.

The low-volatility anomaly

The CAPM is tested empirically, first, by estimating the one-factor market model which includes an intercept and, second, by testing if the intercept is statistically insignificant. If it is not, then the expected excess return of the risky asset equals

$$E(R_t - r_f) = \alpha + \beta E(R_{m,t} - r_f),$$

in which the presence of α indicates that the expected return of the left-hand side cannot be entirely explained by the term $\beta E(R_{m,t} - r_f)$. Thus,

α represents abnormal performance which can be positive or negative and is referred to as "alpha", which is consistent with our notation.

From the standpoint of asset pricing theory, availability of assets with a statistically significant intercept may indicate that the CAPM theory is incomplete. At the same time, investors in general, and hedge funds in particular, are quite interested in finding such assets because, at least in principle, such assets can be used to construct a portfolio with a riskless profit. However, whether this profit materializes out of sample is a separate question.

Consider the following simple portfolio strategy which we will refer to as a low-volatility strategy. At the end of any given month, we calculate the volatilities of the stocks of all companies incorporated in the US and traded on the US stock markets using the most recent 60 daily returns. Then, we rank the stocks by the calculated volatilities in decreasing order and build an equally weighted portfolio from the 10% of the least volatile of them (bottom 10%). This portfolio is held unchanged until the end of the next month when the process is repeated. We calculate the monthly return of this investment strategy every month.

If we had started this strategy in August 1963, we would have collected 655 monthly returns by the end of December 2017.[4] Using this sample, we estimate a regression in which the dependent variable is the time series of the excess returns of the strategy and the explanatory variable is the time series of the monthly excess returns of the market portfolio. The risk-free rate is the monthly return on the 1-month US Treasury bill.

The estimated regression line is plotted in Figure 3 and is described by the following equation:

$$\hat{Y}_t = 0.004431 + 0.5194X_t,$$

with additional information provided in Table 3.

Both the intercept and the slope coefficients are highly significant because their p-values are negligible. To put it differently, the intercept estimate is 0.004431, which is a small number close to zero, but the standard error of the estimator is an order of magnitude smaller. As a result, even though the intercept is tiny, it is very unlikely that the real value of the parameter is zero. The same interpretation follows for the slope coefficient.

From a finance point of view, the interpretation of this regression is as follows. Although not provided in the table, the average monthly excess

[4]We use the data for portfolios ranked by variance on the website of Kenneth French: http://mba.tuck.dartmouth.edu/pages/faculty/ken.french/data_library.html.

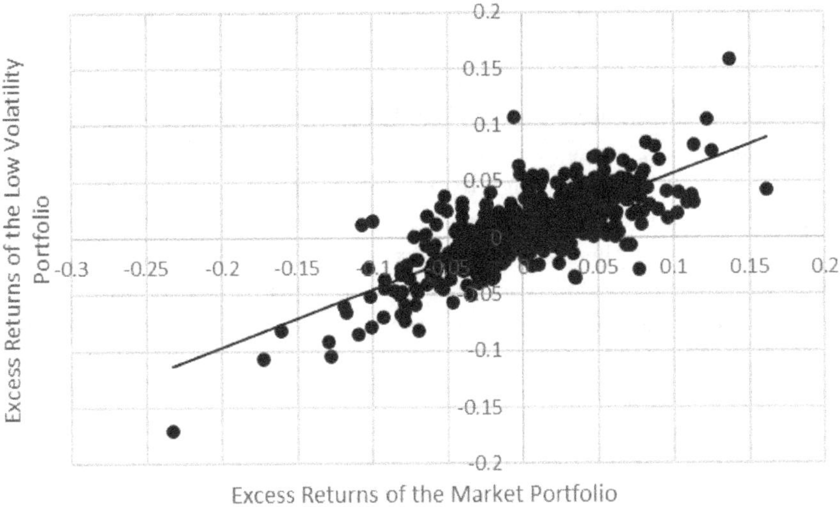

FIGURE 3: Estimated Regression for the Low-Volatility Portfolio of the Least-Volatile 10% of the US Stocks

TABLE 3: Output for the Single-Factor Low-Volatility Anomaly Regression Model

	Intercept	**Slope**
Estimate	0.004431	0.5194
Standard error	0.00073	0.0166
t-Statistic	6.032	31.24
p-Value	(0.0000)*	(0.0000)*
	$r^2 = 0.599$	$df = 653$

return of the low-volatility strategy is 0.00723 and that of the market portfolio is 0.00539. These numbers look small, but on an annual basis, they are 8.67% and 6.46%, respectively, which are very decent average performances on top of the risk-free rate over a very long period of time. Because the slope coefficient is 0.5194, the average return earned due to the exposure to market risk is $0.5194 \times 0.00539 = 0.0028$. The remaining part, which equals the intercept (and is more than 60% of the total), is unexplained. Notice that on an annual basis the intercept amounts to $0.004431 \times 12 = 5.32\%$, which is a very high, economically significant return that is not explained by the market factor. Because of the presence of such anomalous performance, this phenomenon is called the *low-volatility anomaly.*

We continue with hypothesis testing. We are interested in testing the null hypothesis that the intercept is equal to zero. The t -statistic under the null hypothesis is 6.032. The p-value of obtaining such t-statistic is negligible and, therefore, we reject the null hypothesis. In fact, both regression coefficients are highly significant.

More generally, even though testing the model on a single risky asset is insufficient to draw deep conclusions, the results imply that the CAPM may be incomplete and there can be important systematic factors in addition to the market factor which should be used to explain the average return of risky assets. While such extensions do exist, it turns out that the volatility anomaly persists.

Multiple Linear Regression

When we study relationships between variables, it is natural to think of more than one explanatory variable for a given dependent variable. A natural generalization of the linear regression model discussed in the previous section is the multiple linear regression, which in the case of two explanatory variables is expressed as

$$Y_t = \alpha + \beta_1 X_{1t} + \beta_2 X_{2t} + u_t,$$

where α is the intercept, β_1 and β_2 are the slope coefficients corresponding to the first and the second explanatory variables, respectively, and u is the error term. The two slope coefficients are also known as the partial slope or partial regression coefficients. It is straightforward to generalize the multiple linear regression model to any number of explanatory variables,

$$Y_t = \alpha + \beta_1 X_{1t} + \beta_2 X_{2t} + \cdots + \beta_k X_{kt} + u_t.$$

However, here we consider only two explanatory variables for simplicity.

Because the multiple linear regression involves more than one explanatory variable, it is common to make an additional assumption to the ones discussed in the single variable case. The additional assumption is that no exact collinearity exists between X_{1t} and X_{2t}. The meaning of this assumption is that none of the explanatory variables can be expressed as an exact linear function of the other. Otherwise, one of the variables can be replaced by the corresponding linear function and there will be only one explanatory variable instead of two. Also, if the two explanatory variables are linearly dependent, then the coefficients β_1 and β_2 cannot be estimated uniquely.

The parameters of the multiple linear regression model are also estimated by using the least-squares method. Denote the observed samples by

$Y_1, Y_2, \ldots, Y_n$, $X_{11}, X_{21}, \ldots, X_{n1}$, and $X_{12}, X_{22}, \ldots, X_{n2}$. The parameters are estimated by solving the following problem:

$$\min_{\alpha,\beta_1,\beta_2} \sum_{t=1}^{n} (Y_t - \alpha - \beta_1 X_{1t} - \beta_2 X_{2t})^2,$$

where $u_t = Y_t - \alpha - \beta_1 X_{1t} - \beta_2 X_{2t}$ represents the errors. Closed-form expressions for the estimators can be derived and are provided in all econometric textbooks. The properties of the OLS estimator are not affected by the number of explanatory variables. That is, the nice properties of the estimator discussed in the single variable case continue to hold.

In the multiple linear regression, there is a goodness-of-fit measure denoted by R^2 similar to the coefficient of determination in the case of the single explanatory variable. It is called the coefficient of multiple correlation and is computed in the same way. It can be interpreted as the degree of association between the dependent variable and all explanatory variables jointly.

In practice, however, R^2 is not so important because it tends to decline mechanically if we increase the number of explanatory variables. As a result, it cannot be used to compare the goodness of fit of two linear regression models with a different number of explanatory variables. This problem is resolved by a modification that includes an adjustment factor. The modification is called the adjusted R^2, denoted by $\bar{R}^2$, and is calculated according to

$$\bar{R}^2 = 1 - (1 - R^2)\frac{n-1}{n-k},$$

where n denotes the number of observations and k denotes the number of estimated parameters. For example, if there are two X variables, then $k = 3$ because we estimate one intercept term and two partial regression coefficients. It is standard practice to compute both the adjusted R^2 and the unadjusted R^2 and software packages usually provide both.

Even though the adjusted R^2 provides a measure of goodness of fit, it is not informative about the significance of the partial regression coefficients. For example, it may be a high number indicating an excellent goodness of fit and at the same time some partial regression coefficients may be insignificant indicating that some of the explanatory variables may be unrelated to the dependent variable. To test if the partial regression coefficients are significant, we have to test each of them on a stand-alone basis.

The statistical test follows the same t-statistic as in the case of a single explanatory variable. One key difference is that the distribution of the statistic is Student t with $n - k$, where k equals the number of estimated parameters. Software packages report both the value of the statistic for each partial regression coefficient and also the corresponding p-value.

Apart from testing the partial regression coefficients on a stand-alone basis, we may be interested in testing the overall significance of the estimated multiple linear regression. We note that this is a new question that arises in the case of many explanatory variables. If there is only one explanatory variable, then the test of overall significance coincides with the test of significance of the slope coefficient. For example, with two explanatory variables the overall test of significance consists of testing if $\beta_1 = 0$ and $\beta_2 = 0$ jointly. This is different from testing if they equal zero on a stand-alone basis.

To test the overall significance of a multiple linear regression, we use a statistic known as the F ratio. This statistic can be expressed in terms of R^2,

$$F = \frac{R^2/(k-1)}{(1-R^2)/(n-k)},$$

where, as previously, k denotes the number of estimated parameters. Essentially, we test if R^2 is equal to zero or, to put it differently, if the degree of association between the dependent and all explanatory variables is equal to zero. The F ratio follows an F-distribution which is used to compute p-values. The F-distribution has two parameters which are associated with the numerator and the denominator of the F ratio — we say that the F ratio has an F distribution with $k-1$ degrees of freedom in the numerator and $n-k$ degrees of freedom in the denominator. In practice, however, we look at the p-value and if it is small enough (for instance, below 0.05) then we reject the hypothesis that the partial regression coefficients are jointly insignificant.

In the following, we provide two examples. In the first one, we revisit the low-volatility anomaly using a multiple linear regression with three explanatory variables, which is known in finance as the Fama-French three-factor model. We illustrate the t-tests of the partial regression coefficients as well as the F-test for overall significance.

The second example shows that the multiple linear regression can be used even when the right-hand side contains terms that are nonlinear functions of some of the explanatory variables. The nonlinear terms can be re-labeled as new variables and the regression can be estimated as a regular multiple linear regression.

The Fama-French three-factor model and the low-volatility anomaly

The discussion of the low-volatility anomaly example hinted that the celebrated single factor CAPM may be incomplete. Actually, this is a well-known fact in the field of finance. An extension of the model suggested in the 1990s by Fama and French [1992] includes two new factors. One of them is known as the size factor which captures the following empirically observed fact: smaller companies tend to have systematically higher returns than larger companies, in which the measure of size is the market capitalization of the company. The other factor is known as the value factor: companies which tend to have price per share much lower than their book value per share[5] also tend to have systematically higher returns than the companies that tend to be overpriced based on the same criterion. This asset pricing model has become known as the Fama-French three-factor model and has become a standard in both the theory and the practice of finance.

The Fama-French three-factor model is consistent with the following regression for the excess returns of a single stock or a portfolio of stocks:

$$R_t - r_f = \beta_1(R_{m,t} - r_f) + \beta_2 R_{\mathrm{BMS},t} + \beta_3 R_{\mathrm{HML},t} + u_t,$$

where the first term on the right-hand side is the excess return of the market factor, β_2 is the slope coefficient of the size factor, $R_{\mathrm{BMS},t}$ denotes the time series of the returns of the size factor, β_3 is the slope coefficient of the value factor, $R_{\mathrm{HML},t}$ is the time series of the returns of the value factor, and u_t is the residual which captures non-systematic risks.

Let us verify what happens with the anomalous performance of the low-volatility portfolio discussed in a previous example if we use the three-factor model. The regression is estimated with the same time series data for the dependent variable, the market portfolio, and the risk-free rate. The data for the size and the value factors for the corresponding period

[5]The book value per share is computed from information that public companies report in their financial statements on a regular basis. See Chapter 2.

TABLE 4: Output for the Fama-French Three-Factor Low-Volatility Anomaly Regression Model

	α	β_1	β_2	β_3
Estimate	0.0028	0.5246	0.2364	0.3201
Standard error	0.00062	0.0148	0.0208	0.0225
t-statistic	4.53	35.46	11.34	14.2
p-value	(0.0000)*	(0.0000)*	(0.0000)*	(0.0000)*
	R^2=0.724	Adj R^2 = 0.723		
	$F_{3,651}$= 569.6	p-Value = (0.0000)*		

are downloaded from the data library of Kenneth French.[6] The estimated regression is given by the following equation:

$$\hat{Y}_t = 0.0028 + 0.5246\, X_{1t} + 0.2364\, X_{2t} + 0.3201\, X_{3t}.$$

in which X_{1t} denotes the excess return of the market factor, X_{2t} denotes the returns of the size factor, and X_{3t} denotes the returns of the value factor. Additional information is provided in Table 4.

How does this model compare to the single factor CAPM from the previous example? First, the slope coefficients corresponding to the new factors have very high t values and negligible p-values. We can reject the null hypothesis that individually they are equal to zero. From the high value of the F-statistic we conclude that the overall regression is also highly significant; the joint hypothesis that $\beta_2 = \beta_3 = \beta_4 = 0$ is strongly rejected. The adjusted R^2 is 0.723, which is better than the r^2 value in Table 3. Overall, the three-factor model appears to be a better model for this portfolio.

From the standpoint of asset pricing theory, only systematic, non-diversifiable risks are rewarded and, therefore, the intercept is expected to be insignificant. However, in this case the null hypothesis that the intercept is equal to zero is strongly rejected. The estimate in the three-factor model is 0.0028, which implies that about 40% of the average returns of the low-volatility portfolio is left unexplained compared to about 60% in the previous example. Even though there seems to be progress, still a substantial proportion of the average return continues to be unexplained and, therefore, the anomaly has not been resolved.

[6]See http://mba.tuck.dartmouth.edu/pages/faculty/ken.french/data_library.html.

Finally, notice that in this example we do not look for additional explanatory variables by simply trying to maximize the adjusted R^2, which may be dangerous. In fact, in any asset pricing model the explanatory variables must be common for a large set of dependent variables. After all, if a given factor captures systematic risks, then it should be a relevant explanatory variable for potentially all risky assets of a certain class (e.g., for all stocks and portfolios of stocks). Therefore, concluding that a given factor model is incomplete and finding additional systematic factors that make logical sense is a subtle econometric exercise which has little to do with improving the adjusted R^2.

Evaluation of the market timing skills of portfolio managers

Portfolio managers running certain types of equity strategies attempt to profit more than the market portfolio by concentrating the portfolio into stocks they believe will perform better than the market (also known as stock selection) or by timing the market. The latter involves increasing a portfolio manager's investment in the stock market if the manager believes the stock market will rally and decreasing the investment if the manager believes the stock market will decline. If portfolio managers have superior skills and can correctly predict both the direction and the magnitude of the market return, then the portfolio returns are expected to exhibit a convex shape relative to the returns of the market portfolio — market turmoils/rallies are correctly identified and the portfolio performs progressively better with respect to the magnitude of the market decline or rally.

One way to check that hypothesis is to include a nonlinear term, usually the excess return of the market portfolio squared. For example, in the following regression:

$$R_t - r_f = \alpha + \beta_1(R_{m,t} - r_f) + \beta_2(R_{m,t} - r_f)^2 + u_t.$$

we would expect to find a positive curvature, i.e., $\beta_2 > 0$. Even though such a model contains a nonlinear term, the right-hand side is linear in the coefficients. As a consequence, the squared term can be re-labeled as a new variable and the estimation and the testing of hypotheses can be carried out using the standard multiple linear regression.

We verify if there are statistically significant skills of this type in all hedge fund managers who follow the so-called equity long-short strategy. To do so, we regress the monthly returns of the equity long-short index on

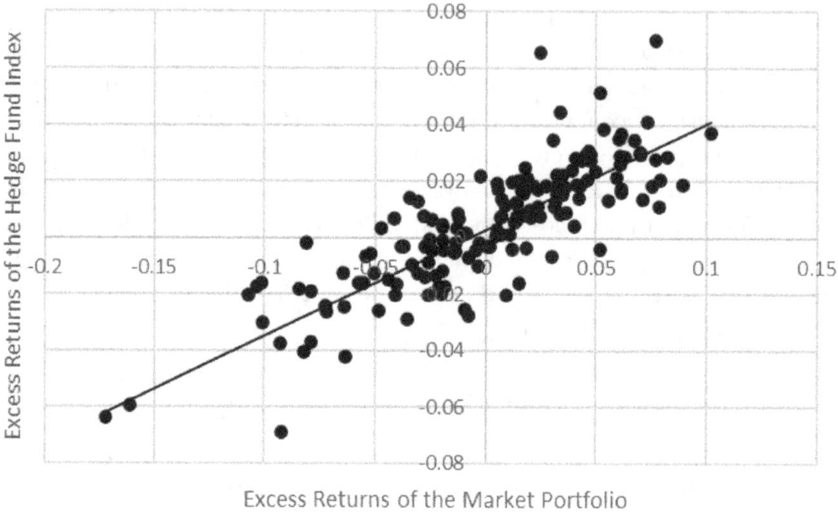

FIGURE 4: Estimated Regression for the Equity Long-Short Hedge Fund Index

TABLE 5: Output from the Nonlinear Market Timing Skills Model

	α	β_1	β_2
Estimate	0.0028	0.375	−0.042
Standard error	0.0009	0.016	0.2201
t-statistic	3.22	22.82	−0.191
p-value	0.0015	(0.0000)*	0.8487
	$R^2 = 0.7062$	$AdjR^2 = 0.7037$	
	$F_{2,233} = 280$	p-$Value = (0.0000)^*$	

the monthly excess returns of the market portfolio and the square of those returns.

The dataset consists of the 236 monthly returns of the equity long-short hedge fund index from January 1997 to August 2016.[7] The estimated regression is plotted in Figure 4 and a summary of the regression results is provided in Table 5.

The regression results show that we can reject the null hypothesis that the estimates of α and β_1 are equal to zero. However, the t-value of the

[7]This is the EDHEC Risk Equity Long-Short hedge fund index: http://www.edhec-risk.com/indexes/pure_style.

estimate of β_2 is rather low and the p-value under the null hypothesis that $\beta_2 = 0$ is very high; that is, the null hypothesis cannot be rejected. Nevertheless, the F statistic is very high and has a negligible p-value, which indicates that we cannot accept the hypothesis that $\beta_1 = \beta_2 = 0$. The adjusted R^2 is 0.706, which means that only about 30% of the variation in hedge fund index returns is unexplained by the market portfolio — an expected result. Another expected outcome is that the estimate of β_1 is positive.

The fact that we cannot reject that $\beta_2 = 0$ shows that if some hedge funds have skills to time the market and can correctly predict both the direction and the magnitude, on average such skills do not seem to be present in all hedge funds which specialize in this strategy.

Notice that our objective is not to disentangle stock selection skills from market timing skills. The estimate of the intercept indicates that the average return of the index unexplained by the market portfolio amounts to $0.0028 \times 12 = 3.36\%$, which in the context of this model can be interpreted as value added by an average hedge fund.

Principal Component Analysis

One problem with financial data is the so-called *curse of dimensionality* — there are many financial variables that we may need to analyze simultaneously because, for example, the portfolio we are analyzing contains many assets. The multiple linear regression offers a way to resolve that problem by considering only a few explanatory variables that capture the most significant aspects of the joint behavior of financial assets returns. If the objective is to model the expected risk premium, then it is common to consider factors such as the market, size, value, momentum, liquidity, etc. If the goal is to explain the risk of the portfolio return distribution, it is common to also include factors such as sector indices, exchange rates, interest rates, and so on. The factors are usually observable variables which are usually correlated and thus "overlap" when explaining the portfolio returns.[8]

Another approach in reducing dimensionality (the number of explanatory variables in the multiple linear regression) is to construct the factors

[8]For a more detailed discussion of PCA and its applications in asset management, see Rachev, Mittnik, Fabozzi, Focardi, and Jasic [2007, Chapter 13].

directly from the data. *Principal component analysis* (PCA) is a multivariate technique used to construct factors, called principal components, that explain as much of the variation in the original dataset of explanatory variables. By design, the principal components are not correlated and are ordered by importance so that the first few principal components account for most of the variability of all variables in the dataset. Because the factors are constructed from the data, they are regarded as non-observable, or latent.

Suppose that we have a set of correlated variables $Y_1, Y_2, \ldots, Y_d$. The goal of PCA is to describe the variation of that set of variables in terms of a new set of variables $X_1, X_2, \ldots, X_d$, which are not correlated. The new set of variables are constructed sequentially in the following way. The first one is represented as a linear combination of the original data

$$X_1 = a_{11}Y_1 + a_{12}Y_2 + \cdots + a_{1d}Y_d,$$

where $a_{11}, a_{12}, \ldots, a_{1d}$ are coefficients determined by the condition that the variance of X_1 should be maximal and the sum of the squares of the coefficients equals one,

$$a_{11}^2 + a_{12}^2 + \cdots + a_{1d}^2 = 1.$$

The reason behind the constraint is that the size of the coefficients, which can be positive or negative, needs to be bounded because otherwise the problem of finding the maximal variance makes no sense.

The second variable is constructed similarly. We represent X_2 also as a linear combination of the original data

$$X_2 = a_{21}Y_1 + a_{22}Y_2 + \cdots + a_{2d}Y_d,$$

in which the coefficients are such that the variance of X_2 is maximal subject to the constraints that the sum of the squares is equal to one and also that $a_{11}a_{21}+a_{12}a_{22}+\cdots+a_{1d}a_{2d} = 0$, which guarantees that X_1 and X_2 are not correlated. The remaining variables are constructed in a similar fashion.

By design, the new variables are ordered by significance. It remains to determine how many of them to use in a subsequent analysis. If we decide to use all of them, then we capture the entire variation in the original set of variables, but we end up with the same dimensionality. If the first few capture a significant proportion of the total variation, then using only the first few may be sufficient.

Because by construction the new variables are uncorrelated, the total variation of the data can be computed by adding up the variances of

$X_1, X_2, \ldots, X_d$. Denote that sum by S,

$$S = \sigma^2(X_1) + \sigma^2(X_2) + \cdots + \sigma^2(X_d).$$

The proportion of the total variation explained by the first K principal components is given by the following ratio:

$$\frac{\sigma^2(X_1) + \sigma^2(X_2) + \cdots + \sigma^2(X_K)}{S}.$$

One rule for deciding how many variables to select is to choose K such that this ratio is a number between 0.7 and 0.9.

Having fixed K, we can represent the variables $Y_1, Y_2, \ldots, Y_d$ in terms of $X_1, X_2, \ldots, X_K$ using the multiple linear regression. However, there is no need to estimate parameters because the partial regression coefficients coincide with the values of the coefficients that define the principal components. Mathematically, it is a consequence of the condition of no correlation that is imposed in the construction of the factors.

For instance, to keep things simple suppose that there are only four variables, $d = 4$, and we need only two principal components, $K = 2$. Then, mathematically the original variables can be represented in terms of the principal components in the following way:

$$\begin{aligned}
Y_1 &= a_{11}X_1 + a_{21}X_2 + \epsilon_1, \\
Y_2 &= a_{12}X_1 + a_{22}X_2 + \epsilon_2, \\
Y_3 &= a_{13}X_1 + a_{23}X_2 + \epsilon_3, \\
Y_4 &= a_{14}X_1 + a_{24}X_2 + \epsilon_4,
\end{aligned}$$

where the residuals absorb the remaining two principal components. Note that the partial regression coefficients of the principal components are also the coefficients that define the principal components as linear combinations of the original variables. If we decided to include all four PCs, there would be no residuals.

In practice, the principal components are computed by a method called eigenvalue decomposition, which is beyond the scope of the chapter. It is sufficient to know that given the initial set of variables $Y_1, Y_2, \ldots, Y_d$, the algorithm calculates all covariances between them, arranges the numbers in a matrix, and then calculates the eigenvalue decomposition of that matrix. The result consists of two items — the coefficients a_{ij} of all principal components and also their variances. Using that output, the researcher can determine the number K and also the data which correspond to the principal components.

The principal components are obtained as linear transformations of the original data and may not represent any observable quantities. However, in some cases, they have an interpretation. In the next example, we use PCA to analyze the Treasury yield curve, which is a standard application.

Analyzing the Treasury Yield Curve

The collection of all yield to maturities (YTM) of Treasury bonds, also known as the Treasury yield curve, represents a collection of correlated variables which are analyzed jointly. Because of their high correlation, PCA is a common technique to reduce dimensionality by isolating statistical factors that explain the behavior of the yield curve. We provide an illustration using daily data from August 1, 2019 to September 27, 2019 provided in Table 6.

As a first step, we calculate the coefficients a_{ij} and the variances of the principal components. The coefficients are provided in Table 7. The proportion of the total variation explained by PC1 is 87.7%, by PC1 and PC2 is 92.3%, and by the first three factors is 96.2%. Therefore, the first three PCs explain the vast majority of the total variation.

In most applications of PCA, the principal components have no particular interpretation. When applying PCA to the yield curve, however, the first three factors have a specific meaning — PC1 is called the *shift factor*, PC2 is known as the *slope factor*, and PC3 is known as the *curvature factor*. The reason is the values of the coefficients in Table 7.

Consider, for example, the first row of Table 7 which defines the coefficients of PC1 $a_{11}, a_{12}, \ldots, a_{1d}$. All the numbers are positive, which implies that if we consider the yields as dependent variables and the three PCs as independent variables, then the partial regression coefficients of PC1 will be the same positive numbers. As a result, if PC1 increases by a positive quantity, all yields increase by some positive amount as well and the yield curve "shifts" upwards. For this reason, PC1 is sometimes referred to as the shift factor.

As a next step, focus on the second row of Table 7. The first several coefficients are positive. They gradually decline and become negative for the longer maturities. Because the corresponding partial regression coefficients of PC2 are the same numbers, if PC2 increases by a positive quantity, then the front end of the yield curve shifts upwards while the other end shifts downwards implying that the impact is mostly on the slope.

TABLE 6: Daily Observations of the Yield to Maturity (in %) of Treasury Securities with Maturities from 2 Months (2 Mo) to 30 Years (30 Yr)

Date	2 Mo	3 Mo	6 Mo	1 Yr	2 Yr	3 Yr	5 Yr	7 Yr	10 Yr	20 Yr	30 Yr
8/1/2019	2.14	2.07	2.04	1.88	1.73	1.67	1.68	1.77	1.90	2.21	2.44
8/2/2019	2.12	2.06	2.02	1.85	1.72	1.67	1.66	1.75	1.86	2.16	2.39
8/5/2019	2.08	2.05	1.99	1.78	1.59	1.55	1.55	1.63	1.75	2.07	2.30
8/6/2019	2.08	2.05	2.00	1.8	1.60	1.54	1.53	1.62	1.73	2.03	2.25
8/7/2019	2.04	2.02	1.95	1.75	1.59	1.51	1.52	1.60	1.71	2.01	2.22
8/8/2019	2.07	2.02	1.96	1.79	1.62	1.54	1.54	1.62	1.72	2.02	2.25
8/9/2019	2.06	2.00	1.95	1.78	1.63	1.58	1.57	1.65	1.74	2.03	2.26
8/12/2019	2.06	2.00	1.94	1.75	1.58	1.51	1.49	1.56	1.65	1.92	2.14
8/13/2019	2.04	2.00	1.96	1.86	1.66	1.6	1.57	1.62	1.68	1.94	2.15
8/14/2019	1.98	1.96	1.92	1.79	1.58	1.53	1.51	1.55	1.59	1.84	2.03
8/15/2019	1.97	1.91	1.86	1.72	1.48	1.44	1.42	1.47	1.52	1.80	1.98
8/16/2019	1.95	1.87	1.85	1.71	1.48	1.44	1.42	1.49	1.55	1.82	2.01
8/19/2019	1.96	1.94	1.90	1.75	1.53	1.49	1.47	1.54	1.60	1.88	2.08
8/20/2019	1.96	1.94	1.89	1.72	1.50	1.44	1.42	1.49	1.55	1.84	2.04
8/21/2019	1.98	1.97	1.90	1.77	1.56	1.50	1.47	1.54	1.59	1.87	2.07
8/22/2019	2.02	2.00	1.91	1.79	1.61	1.53	1.50	1.56	1.62	1.90	2.11
8/23/2019	2.02	1.97	1.87	1.73	1.51	1.43	1.40	1.46	1.52	1.82	2.02
8/26/2019	2.03	2.01	1.90	1.75	1.54	1.47	1.43	1.49	1.54	1.84	2.04
8/27/2019	2.03	1.98	1.94	1.77	1.53	1.43	1.40	1.44	1.49	1.77	1.97
8/28/2019	2.04	1.99	1.89	1.74	1.50	1.42	1.37	1.42	1.47	1.76	1.94

(*Continued*)

TABLE 6: (*Continued*)

Date	2 Mo	3 Mo	6 Mo	1 Yr	2 Yr	3 Yr	5 Yr	7 Yr	10 Yr	20 Yr	30 Yr
8/29/2019	2.03	1.99	1.89	1.75	1.53	1.44	1.40	1.46	1.50	1.78	1.97
8/30/2019	2.04	1.99	1.89	1.76	1.50	1.42	1.39	1.45	1.50	1.78	1.96
9/3/2019	2.01	1.98	1.88	1.72	1.47	1.38	1.35	1.42	1.47	1.77	1.95
9/4/2019	2.02	1.97	1.87	1.69	1.43	1.36	1.32	1.40	1.47	1.77	1.97
9/5/2019	2.01	1.97	1.88	1.73	1.55	1.47	1.43	1.51	1.57	1.86	2.06
9/6/2019	2.00	1.96	1.88	1.73	1.53	1.46	1.42	1.50	1.55	1.83	2.02
9/9/2019	1.99	1.96	1.87	1.74	1.58	1.52	1.49	1.57	1.63	1.91	2.11
9/10/2019	1.99	1.95	1.89	1.81	1.67	1.61	1.58	1.66	1.72	2.00	2.19
9/11/2019	1.97	1.96	1.88	1.79	1.68	1.62	1.60	1.68	1.75	2.02	2.22
9/12/2019	1.97	1.95	1.90	1.82	1.72	1.67	1.65	1.72	1.79	2.06	2.22
9/13/2019	1.98	1.96	1.92	1.88	1.79	1.76	1.75	1.83	1.90	2.17	2.37
9/16/2019	2.02	1.99	1.93	1.86	1.74	1.71	1.69	1.77	1.84	2.11	2.31
9/17/2019	2.06	1.99	1.93	1.87	1.72	1.68	1.66	1.75	1.81	2.08	2.27
9/18/2019	1.93	1.95	1.91	1.87	1.77	1.72	1.68	1.76	1.80	2.06	2.25
9/19/2019	1.99	1.93	1.92	1.88	1.74	1.68	1.66	1.73	1.79	2.04	2.22
9/20/2019	1.94	1.91	1.91	1.84	1.69	1.63	1.61	1.68	1.74	1.99	2.17
9/23/2019	1.94	1.94	1.93	1.81	1.68	1.61	1.59	1.65	1.72	1.98	2.16
9/24/2019	1.90	1.92	1.91	1.78	1.60	1.53	1.52	1.58	1.64	1.91	2.09
9/25/2019	1.86	1.89	1.90	1.82	1.68	1.61	1.60	1.66	1.73	1.99	2.18
9/26/2019	1.90	1.83	1.88	1.79	1.66	1.61	1.59	1.65	1.70	1.96	2.15
9/27/2019	1.86	1.80	1.85	1.74	1.63	1.58	1.56	1.62	1.69	1.95	2.13

TABLE 7: The Coefficients that Define the Principal Components

	2 Mo	3 Mo	6 Mo	1 Yr	2 Yr	3 Yr	5 Yr	7 Yr	10 Yr	20 Yr	30 Yr
PC1	0.022	0.054	0.080	0.218	0.382	0.408	0.410	0.395	0.369	0.293	0.289
PC2	0.536	0.348	0.406	0.497	0.156	0.044	−0.012	−0.099	−0.184	−0.226	−0.243
PC3	0.550	0.236	0.028	−0.183	−0.345	−0.257	−0.171	−0.015	0.243	0.364	0.449
PC4	−0.542	0.741	0.280	−0.112	0.084	−0.077	−0.084	−0.111	−0.039	0.060	0.168
PC5	−0.323	−0.341	0.304	0.647	−0.251	−0.322	−0.075	−0.072	0.094	0.132	0.253
PC6	0.075	−0.313	0.464	−0.359	0.594	−0.350	−0.079	−0.163	0.182	−0.070	0.077
PC7	−0.034	−0.058	0.560	−0.300	−0.517	0.060	0.387	0.256	0.145	−0.147	−0.251
PC8	0.031	−0.205	0.271	−0.131	−0.082	0.537	−0.186	−0.093	−0.462	−0.148	0.541
PC9	−0.039	−0.090	0.180	−0.025	−0.050	0.428	−0.266	−0.441	0.210	0.552	−0.398
PC10	0.051	−0.024	−0.039	−0.042	0.023	−0.169	0.692	−0.431	−0.426	0.339	0.061
PC11	−0.003	−0.053	0.143	−0.049	0.103	−0.171	−0.222	0.579	−0.517	0.492	−0.201

Finally, similar arguments show that if PC3 increases by a positive quantity, the short and the long ends of the yield curve will shift upwards while the middle part shifts downwards implying a change of curvature.

Time Series Models for the Dynamics of Volatility

Recall that one of the assumptions in the classical linear regression model is that the error term is assumed to be homoscedastic; that is, its variance is not assumed to be time varying. In practice, however, financial time series such as stock prices, index levels, exchange rates, interest rates, etc. are characterized by a property known as *clustering of volatility,* which means that there are extended periods of wide price fluctuations followed by periods that are relatively calm. This behavior is not by accident, particular economic conditions that cause crises or expansions can persist for some time, which affects the behavior of all market participants and is, therefore, absorbed by market prices.

Modeling volatility is important for many areas in finance, such as risk management and asset pricing. In this section, we consider the most common time series models for volatility which include the autoregressive conditional heteroskedasticity (ARCH) model and the generalized ARCH (GARCH) model.[9]

The Autoregressive Conditional Heteroskedasticity Model

The *autoregressive conditional heteroskedasticity* (ARCH) model implements the following intuition. If empirically it appears that the levels of variance are relatively persistent, then the current level of variance can be expressed as the level of variance in the previous time instant multiplied by a constant term plus a constant term. That is, we can write down an expression similar to the linear equation behind the linear regression model in which the explanatory variable is simply the level of variance in the previous time instant. We need a way, however, to proxy variance in the first place and it is common to take the square of the residual.

Denote by R_t the return of a financial variable. The ARCH model can be expressed mathematically in the following way:

$$R_t = \mu + u_t,$$
$$\sigma_t^2 = \omega + \alpha u_{t-1}^2,$$

[9]For further explanations, see Engle, Focardi, and Fabozzi [2016].

where μ denotes the expectation of R_t, u_t denotes the error term, σ_t^2 denotes the variance of u_t at time t, ω is the intercept term and is related to a long-run variance level, and α is the slope coefficient that determines the level of persistence and is supposed to be non-negative. If at time $t-1$ there was an unexpected large return in absolute value, then at time t it increases the variance of u_t, which increases the probability of observing a large return at time t. The parameter α determines to what extent the past shock affects the current level of variance. As an extreme case, $\alpha = 0$ implies that the variance of the errors is not time varying.

The model described above is known as ARCH of order one, denoted by ARCH(1), because only the lag of order one is considered in the equation for variance. The model generalizes to any lag orders. For example, the general model of order q, ARCH(q) is given by

$$R_t = \mu + u_t,$$
$$\sigma_t^2 = \omega + \alpha_1 u_{t-1}^2 + \alpha_2 u_{t-2}^2 + \ldots + \alpha_p u_{t-q}^2.$$

When working with real financial returns data, very often going beyond ARCH(1) does not bring additional benefits.

The Generalized Autoregressive Conditional Heteroskedasticity Model

Historically, the ARCH model was developed first and was generalized later by the *generalized autoregressive conditional heteroskedasticity* (GARCH) model. The new component in the GARCH model is that the variance at time t depends not only on the size of the residual in the past but also on the past levels of the variance itself. More formally, considering only lags of order one, the GARCH model is defined in the following way:

$$R_t = \mu + u_t,$$
$$\sigma_t^2 = \omega + \alpha u_{t-1}^2 + \beta \sigma_{t-1}^2,$$

where the parameter β is assumed to be non-negative and determines the sensitivity of the current level of the variance to the level of variance in the previous time instant. If $\beta = 0$, then the GARCH model turns into an ARCH model. The two parameters should also satisfy the condition $\alpha + \beta < 1$ which guarantees that a spike in variance does not lead to an ever-increasing variance going forward.

The new term changes the way the model behaves because a big spike in variance at time $t-1$ necessarily leads to a relatively larger variance at time t if the parameter β has a value close to one. Then, over time variance gradually declines unless we observe new extreme values of the residual.

There is another useful way to interpret the equation for variance. It is possible to show that $V = \frac{\omega}{(1-\alpha-\beta)}$ equals the long-run variance. The equation for variance can then be equivalently re-stated in the following way:

$$\sigma_t^2 = V(1 - \alpha - \beta) + \alpha u_{t-1}^2 + \beta\sigma_{t-1}^2.$$

That is, the variance at time t can be represented as a weighted average of three terms — the long-run variance level V, the level of variance in the previous time instant σ_{t-1}^2, and a term which captures the impact of new information not available in σ_{t-1}^2.

Apart from explaining the dynamics of variance in the dataset, the so-called in-sample analysis, the GARCH model can be used to make forecasts about the future variance. Given a horizon h, using the estimated model we can build the forecast σ_{t+h}^2 conditional on the current estimated level of variance. Because as of time t, the future variance is treated as a random variable, the forecast equals the expected value of the future variance computed with the available information at the current time t, i.e., $\sigma_{t+h}^2 = E_t(\sigma_{t+h}^2)$, where the index t denotes that expectation is computed at time t. The expression for the forecast is given by

$$\hat{\sigma}_{t+h}^2 = \hat{V} + (\hat{\alpha} + \hat{\beta})^{h-1}(\hat{\sigma}_{t+1}^2 - \hat{V}),$$

in which $\hat{\sigma}_{t+1}^2 = \hat{\omega} + \hat{\alpha}\hat{u}_t^2 + \hat{\beta}\hat{\sigma}_t^2$ is a known quantity at time t. The interpretation of this equation is that the variance forecast h time steps ahead equals the long-run level of variance corrected with a term that captures the deviation of the $t+1$ forecast from the long-run level. Because $\hat{\alpha} + \hat{\beta} < 1$, the correction term disappears asymptotically if the horizon level is too far into the future and, therefore, the forecast converges to the long-run level. The rate of convergence depends on how close to one $\hat{\alpha} + \hat{\beta}$ is and in this sense, the sum of the two parameters is said to indicate the level of persistence. As an extreme case, if $\hat{\alpha} + \hat{\beta} = 1$, then the forecast h time steps ahead equals $\hat{\sigma}_{t+1}^2$, which does not depend on h.

The formulation of the GARCH model provided above is said to be of order "one-one", denoted by GARCH(1,1), meaning that lags of order one are used for both the error term and variance in the equation for variance. Lags of different orders, p and q, can be included for the two types of terms, respectively, and in this case we talk about GARCH(p,q),

$$R_t = \mu + u_t,$$
$$\sigma_t^2 = \omega + \sum_{i=1}^{q} \alpha_i u_{t-i}^2 + \sum_{j=1}^{p} \beta_j \sigma_{t-j}^2.$$

However, similar to the ARCH model, including more lags does not usually add more explanatory power and the most commonly used variation in the empirical literature is GARCH(1,1).

Unlike the multiple linear regression, the most common way to estimate parameters is not the OLS method but the method of maximum likelihood (ML). ML requires an assumption for the distribution of the residual term u_t and the standard assumption is that the distribution is Gaussian with a mean of zero and variance equal to σ_t^2, which is denoted by $u_t \in N(0, \sigma_t^2)$. Even though this assumption may not be true for a sample of real data, the estimator can be shown to have some nice properties.

In the following example, we provide an illustration with the daily returns of the S&P 500 index. For financial return time series, the clustering of the volatility effect is very strong for daily data and is known to become weaker for lower frequency returns, such as monthly and quarterly for example.

Estimating the volatility of the S&P 500 index

In this example, we estimate the parameters of the GARCH(1,1) model using the returns of the S&P 500 index provided in Table 8. The sample contains one year of daily returns data. Both the time period and the return frequency are standard. A plot of the time series is provided on the top plot of Figure 5.

The estimated parameters of the model and additional statistics are provided in Table 9. At the 95% confidence level, all the parameters that appear in the equation for variance are statistically significant. The sum of the estimated alpha and beta parameters is close to one, $\alpha + \beta = 0.954$, which implies a high level of persistence. That is, if volatility surges, then it will tend to remain high for a relatively extended period of time.

A plot of the estimated volatility, which has been annualized, is provided in Figure 5 (middle plot). The annualization is necessary because the original returns are daily and to present the volatility on an annual basis, the estimated numbers are multiplied by $\sqrt{250}$, which is a standard practice. We can clearly distinguish between periods of high volatility (at the beginning of the period) and periods of relatively lower volatility (in the

TABLE 8: Daily Returns of the S&P 500 Index from September 25, 2018 to September 20, 2019

Date	S&P 500	Date	S&P500	Date	S&P 500
9/25/2018	−0.131%	11/20/2018	−1.815%	1/22/2019	−1.416%
9/26/2018	−0.329%	11/21/2018	0.304%	1/23/2019	0.220%
9/27/2018	0.276%	11/23/2018	−0.655%	1/24/2019	0.138%
9/28/2018	−0.001%	11/26/2018	1.553%	1/25/2019	0.849%
10/1/2018	0.364%	11/27/2018	0.326%	1/28/2019	−0.785%
10/2/2018	−0.040%	11/28/2018	2.297%	1/29/2019	−0.146%
10/3/2018	0.071%	11/29/2018	−0.218%	1/30/2019	1.555%
10/4/2018	−0.817%	11/30/2018	0.817%	1/31/2019	0.860%
10/5/2018	−0.553%	12/3/2018	1.094%	2/1/2019	0.090%
10/8/2018	−0.040%	12/4/2018	−3.236%	2/4/2019	0.678%
10/9/2018	−0.142%	12/6/2018	−0.152%	2/5/2019	0.471%
10/10/2018	−3.286%	12/7/2018	−2.332%	2/6/2019	−0.222%
10/11/2018	−2.057%	12/10/2018	0.176%	2/7/2019	−0.936%
10/12/2018	1.421%	12/11/2018	−0.036%	2/8/2019	0.068%
10/15/2018	−0.590%	12/12/2018	0.542%	2/11/2019	0.071%
10/16/2018	2.150%	12/13/2018	−0.020%	2/12/2019	1.289%
10/17/2018	−0.025%	12/14/2018	−1.909%	2/13/2019	0.302%
10/18/2018	−1.439%	12/17/2018	−2.077%	2/14/2019	−0.265%
10/19/2018	−0.036%	12/18/2018	0.009%	2/15/2019	1.088%
10/22/2018	−0.430%	12/19/2018	−1.540%	2/19/2019	0.150%
10/23/2018	−0.551%	12/20/2018	−1.577%	2/20/2019	0.178%
10/24/2018	−3.086%	12/21/2018	−2.059%	2/21/2019	−0.353%
10/25/2018	1.863%	12/24/2018	−2.711%	2/22/2019	0.641%
10/26/2018	−1.733%	12/26/2018	4.959%	2/25/2019	0.123%
10/29/2018	−0.656%	12/27/2018	0.856%	2/26/2019	−0.079%
10/30/2018	1.567%	12/28/2018	−0.124%	2/27/2019	−0.054%
10/31/2018	1.085%	12/31/2018	0.849%	2/28/2019	−0.283%
11/1/2018	1.056%	1/2/2019	0.127%	3/1/2019	0.690%
11/2/2018	−0.632%	1/3/2019	−2.476%	3/4/2019	−0.388%
11/5/2018	0.560%	1/4/2019	3.434%	3/5/2019	−0.113%
11/6/2018	0.626%	1/7/2019	0.701%	3/6/2019	−0.652%
11/7/2018	2.121%	1/8/2019	0.970%	3/7/2019	−0.813%
11/8/2018	−0.251%	1/9/2019	0.410%	3/8/2019	−0.213%
11/9/2018	−0.920%	1/10/2019	0.452%	3/11/2019	1.467%
11/12/2018	−1.970%	1/11/2019	−0.015%	3/12/2019	0.295%
11/13/2018	−0.148%	1/14/2019	−0.526%	3/13/2019	0.695%
11/14/2018	−0.757%	1/15/2019	1.072%	3/14/2019	−0.087%
11/15/2018	1.059%	1/16/2019	0.222%	3/15/2019	0.498%
11/16/2018	0.222%	1/17/2019	0.759%	3/18/2019	0.371%
11/19/2018	−1.664%	1/18/2019	1.318%	3/19/2019	−0.013%

TABLE 8: (*Continued*)

Date	S&P 500	Date	S&P 500	Date	S&P 500
3/20/2019	−0.294%	5/23/2019	−1.191%	7/29/2019	−0.162%
3/21/2019	1.085%	5/24/2019	0.135%	7/30/2019	−0.258%
3/22/2019	−1.897%	5/28/2019	−0.838%	7/31/2019	−1.089%
3/25/2019	−0.084%	5/29/2019	−0.691%	8/1/2019	−0.900%
3/26/2019	0.718%	5/30/2019	0.210%	8/2/2019	−0.728%
3/27/2019	−0.464%	5/31/2019	−1.320%	8/5/2019	−2.978%
3/28/2019	0.359%	6/3/2019	−0.277%	8/6/2019	1.302%
3/29/2019	0.673%	6/4/2019	2.143%	8/7/2019	0.077%
4/1/2019	1.157%	6/5/2019	0.816%	8/8/2019	1.876%
4/2/2019	0.002%	6/6/2019	0.614%	8/9/2019	−0.662%
4/3/2019	0.215%	6/7/2019	1.050%	8/12/2019	−1.232%
4/4/2019	0.208%	6/10/2019	0.466%	8/13/2019	1.513%
4/5/2019	0.464%	6/11/2019	−0.035%	8/14/2019	−2.929%
4/8/2019	0.105%	6/12/2019	−0.204%	8/15/2019	0.246%
4/9/2019	−0.607%	6/13/2019	0.410%	8/16/2019	1.443%
4/10/2019	0.348%	6/14/2019	−0.161%	8/19/2019	1.211%
4/11/2019	0.004%	6/17/2019	0.093%	8/20/2019	−0.791%
4/12/2019	0.661%	6/18/2019	0.972%	8/21/2019	0.825%
4/15/2019	−0.063%	6/19/2019	0.299%	8/22/2019	−0.051%
4/16/2019	0.051%	6/20/2019	0.947%	8/23/2019	−2.595%
4/17/2019	−0.227%	6/21/2019	−0.126%	8/26/2019	1.098%
4/18/2019	0.158%	6/24/2019	−0.173%	8/27/2019	−0.320%
4/22/2019	0.101%	6/25/2019	−0.950%	8/28/2019	0.655%
4/23/2019	0.884%	6/26/2019	−0.123%	8/29/2019	1.269%
4/24/2019	−0.219%	6/27/2019	0.382%	8/30/2019	0.064%
4/25/2019	−0.037%	6/28/2019	0.576%	9/3/2019	−0.690%
4/26/2019	0.469%	7/1/2019	0.767%	9/4/2019	1.084%
4/29/2019	0.107%	7/2/2019	0.293%	9/5/2019	1.301%
4/30/2019	0.095%	7/3/2019	0.767%	9/6/2019	0.091%
5/1/2019	−0.750%	7/5/2019	−0.181%	9/9/2019	−0.009%
5/2/2019	−0.212%	7/8/2019	−0.484%	9/10/2019	0.032%
5/3/2019	0.964%	7/9/2019	0.124%	9/11/2019	0.723%
5/6/2019	−0.447%	7/10/2019	0.451%	9/12/2019	0.288%
5/7/2019	−1.651%	7/11/2019	0.229%	9/13/2019	−0.072%
5/8/2019	−0.161%	7/12/2019	0.462%	9/16/2019	−0.314%
5/9/2019	−0.302%	7/15/2019	0.018%	9/17/2019	0.258%
5/10/2019	0.372%	7/16/2019	−0.340%	9/18/2019	0.034%
5/13/2019	−2.413%	7/17/2019	−0.653%	9/19/2019	0.002%
5/14/2019	0.802%	7/18/2019	0.358%	9/20/2019	−0.490%
5/15/2019	0.584%	7/19/2019	−0.618%		
5/16/2019	0.890%	7/22/2019	0.283%		
5/17/2019	−0.584%	7/23/2019	0.685%		
5/20/2019	−0.675%	7/24/2019	0.469%		
5/21/2019	0.850%	7/25/2019	−0.526%		
5/22/2019	−0.282%	7/26/2019	0.739%		

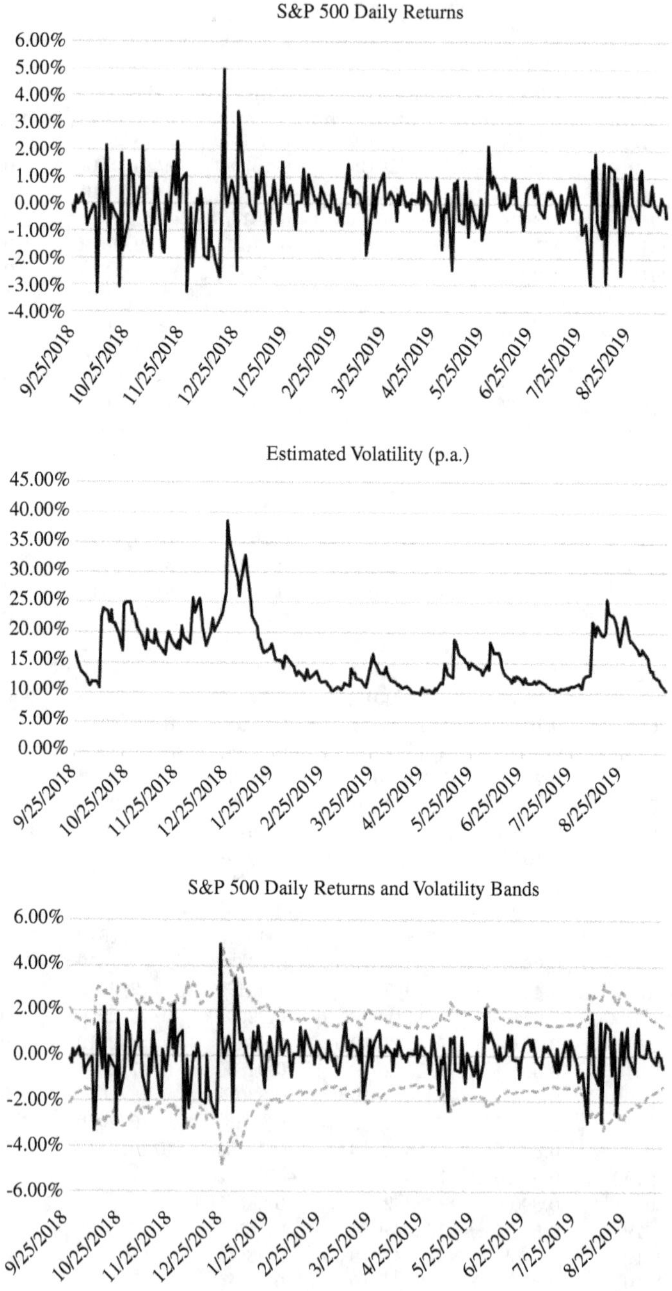

FIGURE 5: The S&P 500 Returns (top), the Estimated Annualized GARCH(1,1) Volatility $\hat{\sigma}_t$ (middle), and the Returns Together with Bands Equal to $\pm 2\hat{\sigma}_t$ (in gray)

TABLE 9: Estimates of the GARCH(1,1) Parameters, their Standard Errors, t Values, and the Corresponding p-Values Using the Daily Returns of the S&P 500 Index Provided in Table 8

	Estimate	**Std. Error**	***t*-Value**	**Pr(> |*t*|)**
mu	0.001	0.001	1.693	0.091
omega	6E-06	0.000	2.172	0.030
alpha	0.169	0.059	2.875	0.004
beta	0.786	0.056	13.947	0.000

middle of the period). By checking the economic news at these periods, one may be able to identify the likely sources of what looks like a high volatility regime in the first one-third of the time period.

Finally, the bottom plot in Figure 5 shows the historical data together with two curves which equal +/− two times the estimated daily volatility. These curves illustrate the approximate spread of the conditional return distribution at time t. Assuming that the conditional distribution is Gaussian, which would be consistent with the assumption behind the ML estimator, then the interval $[-2\sigma_t, 2\sigma_t]$ has a probability of 0.95 for any time t. Any observation that exceeds these bounds can be considered extreme for the corresponding time instant.

Other GARCH-Type Models

The GARCH model has become a standard econometric tool to analyze the volatility of time series. Its advantage is that it is capable of capturing the clustering of volatility effect, which is an important empirical characteristic of financial data, in a sufficiently simple way to allow for robust estimation and analytic transparency. However, one drawback of the model is that the variance at time t, σ_t^2, is affected in the same way by both positive and negative values of u_{t-1} because this term is squared in the equation for variance. Studies in the empirical literature suggest that negative values of u_{t-1} are expected to have a more significant effect than positive values and this is known as the *leverage effect*.

The family of asymmetric GARCH models accounts for the leverage effect. It includes models such as the exponential GARCH (EGARCH), threshold GARCH (TGARCH), and the more general asymmetric power GARCH (APARCH) models. Asymmetric GARCH models are beyond the scope of this chapter, an excellent reference is Francq and Zakoian [2010].

In this section, we discuss the exponentially weighted moving average model (EWMA), which is very common in the area of risk assessment and is closely related to the classical GARCH model.

The exponentially weighted moving average model

The *exponentially weighted moving average* (EWMA) model can be viewed as an extension of the sample estimator of variance which applies a higher weight to the relatively more recent observations in the sample. It was adopted by RiskMetrics in the 1990s in their first methodology for risk assessment and became a common approach.

Given a sample of returns $R_1, R_2, \ldots, R_n$, consider the following forecast for σ_t^2:

$$\sigma_t^2 = (1-\lambda)\sum_{i=1}^{n}\lambda^{i-1}R_{t-i},$$

where $0 < \lambda < 1$ determines the weights of the observations and is a parameter. The sum of all weights approximately equals $1/(1-\lambda)$ for large n and, therefore, the term $(1-\lambda)$ can be viewed as a normalizing factor making sure that the weights sum up to one. Because λ is raised to a higher power the further back in time the corresponding observation is, the corresponding weight $(1-\lambda)\lambda^{i-1}$ declines exponentially and for this reason the model is called exponentially weighted. Note that if all weights are equal to $1/n$, then this formula becomes similar to the sample estimator of variance.

It is possible to show that the formula above is consistent with the following recursive equation for variance which is reminiscent of the variance equation of the GARCH model when the parameter μ is negligible:

$$\sigma_t^2 = (1-\lambda)R_{t-1}^2 + \lambda\sigma_{t-1}^2.$$

The term $1-\lambda$ is similar to α, and λ corresponds to β. An important feature of the EWMA model, however, is that the sum of the two coefficients equals one, which makes it different from the classical GARCH model in which the corresponding sum is strictly less than one. As a consequence, the current volatility estimate is an unbiased forecast for any future period.

Even though the GARCH model is more flexible, the advantage of the EWMA model is that it captures the clustering of volatility effect in a very simple manner. There is only one parameter which can be either calibrated for each time series or set to a value on an *ad-hoc* basis depending on

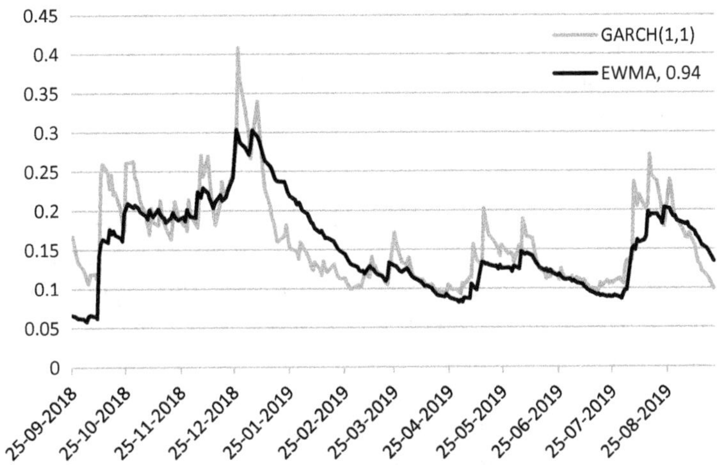

FIGURE 6: The Estimated Annualized Volatility Using GARCH(1,1) and the EWMA Model with $\lambda = 0.94$ and the S&P 500 Daily Data Provided in Table 8

the return frequency. For example, a common recommendation is to use $\lambda = 0.94$ with daily returns and $\lambda = 0.97$ with monthly returns.

An empirical illustration of the performance of the EWMA model compared to that of GARCH(1,1) is provided in Figure 6. We use the daily data for the S&P 500 index in Table 8 and the *ad-hoc* choice of $\lambda = 0.94$, which is consistent with current practices in risk assessment. The plot shows that the EWMA model indeed succeeds in capturing the clustering of volatility effect. The GARCH model is, however, more flexible and responds faster to the changes in the behavior of the underlying time series. If we assume that the underlying data generation process is consistent with the GARCH estimate, then the EWMA model tends to overestimate volatility when it increases and tends to underestimate it when it declines.

Key Points

- Regression analysis studies the relationship between a variable called the dependent variable and one or several other variables called explanatory, or independent, variables. When the relationship is linear, then the regression analysis is called linear.
- The regression coefficients are the parameters of the linear regression which are estimated from observations on the dependent and the explanatory variables. The free parameter is known as the intercept and the

parameters multiplying the explanatory variables are known as partial slope coefficients.

- The OLS method is the most common technique for parameter estimation. The parameters are estimated by finding the values that minimize the errors between what is predicted by the regression model and what is observed.
- The coefficient of multiple correlation R^2 is a goodness-of-fit measure which is interpreted as the degree of joint association between the dependent variable and all explanatory variables. R^2 increases mechanically as we add more explanatory variables.
- The adjusted R^2, denoted by $\bar{R}^2$, corrects for the number of explanatory variables and can be used to compare goodness-of-fit across models with a different number of explanatory variables.
- The t-test is used to test if the statistical relationship with a given explanatory variable is significant; that is, if the corresponding partial regression coefficient is significantly different from zero.
- The F ratio is used to test the overall significance of a multiple linear regression.
- Principal component analysis (PCA) is a multivariate method used to construct uncorrelated factors, called principal components, that explain as much of the variation in the original dataset of explanatory variables as possible.
- The principal components are constructed from the original data and are regarded as unobservable, or latent, variables.
- PCA is a common technique for modeling the yield curve. In this case, the first three principal components are interpreted as shift, slope, and curvature factors.
- Clustering of volatility is a property of financial asset returns which describes periods of wide price fluctuations followed by periods that are relatively calm. Autoregressive conditional heteroskedasticity (ARCH) model and the generalized ARCH (GARCH) model are used to model the dynamics of volatility.
- According to the GARCH model, the variance at time t can be represented as a weighted average of three terms — the long-run variance, the variance in the previous time instant, and a term which captures the impact of new information not available at the previous time instant.

References

Engle, R. F., S. M. Focardi, and F. J. Fabozzi, 2016. "Issues in applying financial econometrics to factor-based modeling in investment management," *Journal of Portfolio Management*, 42(5): 94–106.

Fabozzi, F. J., S. M. Focardi, S. T. Rachev, and B. Arshanapalli, 2014. *Basics of Financial Econometrics*. Hoboken, NJ: John Wiley & Sons.

Francq, C. and J-M. Zakoian, 2010. *GARCH Models: Structure, Statistical Inference, and Financial Applications*. UK: Wiley.

Rachev, S. T., S. Mittnik, F. J. Fabozzi, S. M. Focardi, and T. Jasic, 2007. *Financial Econometrics: From Basics to Advanced Modeling Techniques*. Hoboken, NJ: John Wiley & Sons.

Chapter 5

Monte Carlo Applications to Asset Management

Learning Objectives

After reading this chapter, you will understand:

- what the method of Monte Carlo simulations is;
- why Monte Carlo simulation is superior to other methods for assessing future outcomes;
- the steps involved in Monte Carlo simulation;
- the applications of Monte Carlo simulation in asset management;
- how to determine the number of trials;
- what a random number generator is for single variables;
- how a sample path is generated;
- methods that are used to choose parametric distributions; and
- generation of random numbers for dependent variables.

Introduction

In portfolio management, the performance of a portfolio or strategy will often depend on the outcome of many random variables. Moreover, changes in every random variable may proceed along a substantial number of possible paths. These eventualities make it impractical to evaluate all possible combinations of outcomes in order to assess the risks associated with a portfolio. For example, for a fixed income portfolio, the performance will be affected by the magnitude of the change in Treasury rates, the spread between non-Treasury and Treasury securities (or some other benchmark securities), changes in the shape of the yield curve, changes in the credit rating of individual corporate bond issues, changes in interest rate volatility, and, in the case of mortgage-backed securities, changes in prepayment speeds. It is common to consider a number of such variables jointly, which increases immensely the difficulty of evaluating their impact on the future performance of the portfolio.

Some measures of risk or performance, such as maximum drawdown, require the calculation of entire trajectories into the future regardless of the portfolio type. Yet in other applications, such as retirement planning, we are interested in increasing the stream of income the portfolio can generate which is also sample-path dependent. It is almost impossible to analyze such situations analytically.

The technique employed to deal with such problems faced by portfolio managers and analysts is *simulation*. There are many types of simulation techniques. When probability distributions are assigned to the random variables, the simulation technique is known as a Monte Carlo simulation — named after the famous gambling spot on the French Riviera. Monte Carlo simulation enables portfolio managers to determine the statistical properties of a problem that they face. More specifically, the product of a Monte Carlo simulation is a probability distribution and summary statistics (mean, standard deviation, skewness, and information in the tails) for the value of interest (e.g., strategy return or risk exposure). Armed with this information, an asset manager can evaluate a strategy in terms of the measure of interest. Monte Carlo simulation is also used in evaluating complex securities such as mortgage-backed securities (including collateralized mortgage obligations and interest-only/principal-only mortgage products) and plain vanilla and complex derivatives.[1]

In this chapter, we explain the basics of Monte Carlo simulation by describing the steps in a simulation and then provide several asset management applications. In Chapter 18, we explain how the Monte Carlo method is used in backtesting investment strategies.

[1]The use of Monte Carlo simulation to value derivatives was first suggested by Boyle [1977]. Schönbucher [2003] illustrates how to use Monte Carlo simulation to price credit derivatives.

Monte Carlo Simulations versus Other Methods for Financial Decision-Making

Suppose that an asset manager wants to assess the potential performance of a multi-asset portfolio over the next year and the manager has an absolute return target. The asset manager knows that the portfolio's performance will be determined by the actual outcome for each of nine random variables and that each of the nine random variables have seven possible outcomes. There are thus 4,782,969 (9^7) possible outcomes, representing all possible combinations of the nine random variables. Furthermore, each of the 4,782,969 outcomes has a different probability of occurrence. How can this asset manager assess the potential return from the multi-asset portfolio?

One approach for a portfolio manager is to take the "best guess" for each random variable and determine the impact on performance. The best-guess value for each random variable is usually the expected value of the random variable. However, there are serious problems with this short-cut approach. To understand its shortcomings, suppose the probability associated with the best guess for each random variable is 75%. If the probability distribution for each random variable is independently distributed, the probability of occurrence for the best-guess result would be only 7.5%. At this level of probability, no asset manager would have a great deal of confidence in this best-guess result.

Between the extremes of enumerating and evaluating all possible combinations and the best-guess approach is the Monte Carlo simulation technique. The returns generated from this technique do not represent an optimal solution to a problem. Rather, Monte Carlo simulation provides information about a problem so that an asset manager can assess the risks of a particular course of action. Because it offers a flexible approach to deal with investment decision-making, it is a commonly used tool for dealing with investment decisions when there are multiple random variables.

Steps for Monte Carlo Simulation

There are 12 steps in a Monte Carlo simulation. In practice, the first three steps are the responsibility of the asset manager. The last nine steps are performed by the Monte Carlo software and are described below so that a walk-through illustration can be demonstrated later in this chapter. The 12 steps are as follows:

Step 1: The performance measure must be specified. The performance measure may be, for example, the excess return over a specified benchmark, the absolute return from a strategy, or some risk exposure such as the maximum drawdown of a strategy.

Step 2: The problem that the asset manager seeks information about must be expressed mathematically. This means not only identifying the key variables but also the interactions among the variables which are quantified by using the correlation between variables. In a Monte Carlo simulation, there will be two types of variables: deterministic variables and random variables. A deterministic variable can take on only one value; a random variable can take on more than one value.

Step 3: For each random variable, a probability distribution must be specified.

Step 4: For each random variable, the probability distribution must be converted into a cumulative probability distribution.

Step 5: For each random variable, representative numbers must be assigned based on the cumulative probability distribution to each possible outcome specified. This is done via the Monte Carlo simulation software.

Step 6: A random number must be obtained for each random variable. This is done by the Monte Carlo software using a random number generator.

Step 7: For each random number, the corresponding value of the random variable must be determined.

Step 8: The corresponding value of each random variable found in the previous step must be used to determine the value of the performance measure.

Step 9: The value of the performance measure found in Step 8 must be recorded.

Step 10: Steps 6–9 must be repeated many times, say, 100-1,000 times. Each repetition of Steps 6–9 is known as a *trial.*

Step 11: The values for the performance measure for each trial recorded in Step 9 become the basis for the construction of a probability distribution and cumulative probability distribution.

Step 12: The cumulative probability distribution constructed in Step 11 is analyzed. This is done by calculating summary statistics for the performance measure such as the mean, standard deviation, skewness, and the range.

Determining the Number of Trials

How do we know how many trials to perform? In many applications, asset managers might want one estimate of the outcome of the simulation. For example, if an equity manager wants to assess the expected return for a potential strategy, the best estimate is the average value or mean from all the trials of the simulation. The estimated mean, however, may not be equal to the true mean. For example, if the exact same trial is repeated, the new average value will differ from the previous average value. The number of trials can be chosen to guarantee a certain level of accuracy.

A commonly used measure of accuracy is the mean standard error defined as

$$\text{Mean standard error} = \sqrt{\frac{\text{Variance of the trial performance measure}}{\text{Number of trials}}}.$$

A confidence interval for the estimate of the performance measure can be constructed using the mean standard error. The smaller the mean standard error, the greater the precision of performance measure's estimated value. One way to reduce the mean standard error is to increase the number of trials, which is evident from the formula above — increasing the number of trials increases the denominator while the numerator remains constant.

We illustrate this idea with the following simple example. Suppose that the goal is to estimate the expected return of a strategy whose annualized volatility is 10%. Also, suppose that the desired accuracy expressed in terms of a 95% confidence interval is 0.1% for the expected return. This means that the probability that the difference of the average return and the unknown mean in absolute value does not exceed 0.1% is 95%. How many trials do we need to guarantee this accuracy? We use the following formula:

$$\frac{\text{Desired accuracy}}{2} = 1.96\sqrt{\frac{\text{Variance of the trial performance measure}}{\text{Number of trials}}},$$

in which we use the squared annualized volatility as the variance of the trial performance measure. After solving for the number of trials, we obtain $(2 \times 0.1 \times 1.96/0.01)^2 = 1{,}536$ trials.

This formula can be interpreted also in the following way. Other things equal, to double the accuracy we need to quadruple the number of trials because of the square root on the right-hand side. Because of this, the Monte Carlo method may appear inefficient. However, we need to remember that it is a general method that can be applied to almost any problem. The relatively slow improvement of accuracy can then be viewed as the price that we pay for having a universal approach.

In Step 11, we recalculate the value of the performance measure for each trial. If higher accuracy is needed or if the calculation for each trial is computationally expensive, then it can be costly to increase the number of trials necessary to reduce the mean standard error to a satisfactory level. Alternatively, the mean standard error can be reduced by reducing the variance of the trial values. That is, we produce the Monte Carlo simulations in a way that reduces the numerator in the formula above. This approach to improving the precision of the estimated performance is called *variance reduction.*[2] Several variance reduction methods have been used in finance, and a discussion of these methods is beyond the scope of this chapter. They apply in special situations which, in the light of the discussion above, implies that for certain problems the Monte Carlo method can be adapted to have a faster improvement of accuracy with respect to the number of trials.

Walk-Through Illustration of the Steps of Monte Carlo Simulation

In our walk-through illustration, we consider a fixed income portfolio manager who has invested $60 million in three bonds. Table 1 shows the three hypothetical bonds and the relevant information about each issue. In our illustration, each bond is assumed to pay its next coupon interest six months from now. The portfolio manager wants to simulate the 6-month period total return if the only two random variables are (1) the change in the level and shape of the Treasury yield curve and (2) the change in the quality spread between Treasuries and BBB corporates.

The portfolio management team believes that there are six possible Treasury yield curves that may occur six months from now and that there are six possible Treasury/corporate spreads (i.e., quality spreads) assuming that spread is the same regardless of maturity. These six possible

[2]There are several variance reduction methods. These are described in Law and Kelton [2002, Chapter 11].

TABLE 1: Hypothetical Three-Bond Portfolio for Simulation Illustration

Bond	**Maturity (years)**	**Coupon (%)**	**Price ($)**	**Par ($)**	**Yield (%)**
Treasury	5.5	6.0%	$100	$20 million	6.0%
BBB corporate	15.5	9.0	100	16 million	9.0
BBB corporate	25.5	10.5	100	24 million	10.5

TABLE 2: Information for the Monte Carlo Simulation for the Bond Portfolio Illustration

Panel a: Six possible yield curves 6 months from now.

Treasury Yield Curve					
5-year	**15-year**	**25-year**	**Probability Distribution**	**Cumulative Probability Distribution**	**Representative Numbers Assigned**
4%	6%	7%	0.20	0.20	0–19
5	8	9	0.15	0.35	20–34
6	7	7	0.10	0.45	35–44
7	8	8	0.10	0.55	45–54
9	9	9	0.20	0.25	55–74
10	8	8	0.25	1.00	75–99

Panel b: Six possible BBB corporate/Treasury yield spreads 6 months from now.

BBB/Treasury Yield Spread (in basis points)	**Probability Distribution**	**Cumulative Probability Distribution**	**Representative Numbers Assigned**
75	0.10	0.10	0–9
100	0.20	0.30	10–29
125	0.25	0.55	30–54
150	0.25	0.80	55–79
175	0.15	0.95	80–94
200	0.05	1.00	95–99

Treasury yield curves are shown in panel a of Table 2 and the six possible Treasury/corporate spreads (i.e., quality spreads) are shown in panel b of Table 2. We use all this information to walk through each of the 12 steps of the Monte Carlo simulation technique and where we explain the last three columns in Table 2.

Step 1: The performance measure must be specified. The performance measure is the annualized 6-month total return for the three-bond portfolio.

Step 2: The problem under investigation must be expressed mathematically. To mathematically express the 6-month total return, the following notation will be used:

V_i = value of bond i at the end of 6 months ($i = 1$, 2, and 3, where 1 is the Treasury, 2 is the shorter BBB corporate bond, and 3 is the longer BBB corporate bond);

c_i = 6-month coupon payment for bond i.

Then the total future dollars from each bond at the end of the 6-month horizon is $p_i + c_i$. The 6-month total return for the three-bond portfolio whose initial portfolio value is \$60 million is then

$$\text{Total Return} = \frac{(V_1 + c_1) + (V_2 + c_2) + (V_3 + c_3)}{\$60,000,000} - 1.$$

Doubling the total return gives an annualized total return on a bond-equivalent yield basis.

Step 3: For those variables that are random variables, a probability distribution for each must be specified. In our illustration there are two random variables — the Treasury yield curve and the yield spread — and a probability distribution must be specified for both. Assume that the probability distributions for these two random variables are as shown in the two panels in Table 2. The coupon interest payments for each bond are a deterministic variable.

Step 4: For each random variable whose probability distribution must be specified, the probability distribution must be converted into a cumulative probability distribution. The cumulative probability of attaining a value less than or equal to a specified value is computed by summing the probabilities over the range of outcomes up to the specified value. The cumulative probability distribution for the two random variables in this illustration is shown in the next-to-the-last column in the two panels in Table 2.

Step 5: For each random variable, representative numbers must be assigned based on the cumulative probability distribution to each possible outcome specified by the probability distribution. The representative numbers assigned for the two random variables in this case are shown in the last column of the two panels in Tables 2. Note that there are 100 assigned two-digit numbers ranging from 0 to 99. Each possible outcome (value for the random variable) is assigned enough numbers so that the ratio of the total numbers assigned to 100 will equal the probability of the outcome. For example, for the Treasury yield curve (the first random variable), the first-yield curve outcome in panel a in Table 2 is assigned numbers from 0 to 19. There are 20 numbers in the range of 0 to 19, so 20 of the 100 numbers, or 20%, are assigned to the first possible Treasury yield curve shape to equal its probability of 20%. A similar choice applies for the fifth possible Treasury yield curve, which also has a probability of 20%. Here the 20 numbers assigned are 55–74; the numbers 0 to 19 are not assigned to this outcome because they were assigned at the outset to the first Treasury yield curve.

Step 6: *First Trial* Obtain a random number for each random variable. We can obtain a computer generated random number. For this illustration, we use the function RANDBETWEEN in Excel which generates an integer between two parameters called *bottom* and *top.* We set bottom to 0 and top to 99. In the next section, we cover random number generation in more detail. The first random number selected in Steps 6–9 will be for the random variable representing the Treasury yield curve. The second will be for the random variable representing the quality spread. Suppose that the first two random numbers generated by a computer are 91 and 12.

Step 7: *First Trial* For each random number, determine the corresponding value of the random variable. Given the random number of 91 for the Treasury yield curve and 12 for the quality spread, the corresponding outcome for the two random variables can be determined with the information in the two panels in Table 2. The Treasury yield curve 6 months from now in this trial would be

5-year Treasury = 10%, 15-year Treasury = 8%, 25-year Treasury = 8%.

The quality spread in this trial would be 100 basis points since that corresponds to random number 12. Therefore, the yield for the three bonds 6 months from now in this trial is

5-year Treasury = 10%, 15-year BBB corporate bond = 9%, 25-year BBB corporate bond = 9%.

Step 8: *First Trial* Using the corresponding value of each random variable found in the previous step to determine the value of the performance measure developed in Step 1, the total future dollars from each bond for the first trial are shown in the eighth, ninth, and 10th columns in Table 3. The next-to-last column shows the total future dollars for the portfolio, and the last column shows the total return percentage for the first trial.

TABLE 3: Results of 20 Trials for Total Return Simulation Illustration

		Treasury Yield Curve					Market Value of Each Bond ($)				
Trial No.	Random Variable	5-year	15-year	25-year	Random Variable	Quality Spread (bps)	5-year Treasury	15-yr BBB Corp	25-yr BBB Corp	Portfolio Value ($)	Total Return (%)
1	91	10%	8%	8%	12	100	17,511,308.00	16,720,000.00	28,817,160.00	63,048,468.00	10.16
2	64	9	9	9	18	100	18,226,184.00	15,490,204.00	26,355,356.00	60,071,744.00	0.24
3	48	7	8	8	54	125	19,768,340.00	16,398,960.00	28,165,020.00	64,332,316.00	14.44
4	44	6	7	7	20	100	20,600,000.00	18,103,364.00	31,704,656.00	70,408,020.00	34.69
5	85	10	8	8	84	175	17,511,308.00	15,784,364.00	26,935,284.00	60,230,952.00	0.77
6	10	4	6	7	76	150	22,396,516.00	18,859,508.00	30,202,336.00	71,458,360.00	38.19
7	66	9	9	9	53	125	18,226,184.00	15,204,420.00	25,797,268.00	59,227,872.00	−2.57
8	38	6	7	7	64	150	20,600,000.00	17,391,160.00	30,202,336.00	68,193,496.00	27.31
9	42	6	7	7	14	100	20,600,000.00	18,103,364.00	31,704,656.00	70,408,020.00	34.69
10	23	5	8	9	81	175	21,475,208.00	15,792,364.00	24,742,584.00	62,002,156.00	6.67
11	61	9	9	9	62	150	18,226,184.00	14,926,732.00	25,260,000.00	58,412,916.00	−5.29
12	90	10	8	8	5	75	17,511,308.00	17,050,624.00	29,495,820.00	64,057,752.00	13.53
13	57	9	9	9	51	125	18,226,184.00	15,204,420.00	25,797,268.00	59,227,872.00	−2.57
14	29	5	8	9	49	125	21,475,208.00	16,398,960.00	25,797,268.00	63,671,432.00	12.24
15	6	4	6	7	18	100	22,396,516.00	19,662,728.00	31,704,656.00	73,763,900.00	45.88
16	67	9	9	9	81	175	18,226,184.00	14,656,880.00	24,742,584.00	57,625,648.00	−7.91
17	38	6	7	7	40	125	20,600,000.00	17,741,956.00	30,938,116.00	69,280,072.00	30.93
18	42	6	7	7	8	75	20,600,000.00	18,475,752.00	32,503,532.00	71,579,288.00	38.6
19	68	9	9	9	86	175	18,226,184.00	14,656,880.00	24,742,584.00	57,625,648.00	−7.91
20	86	10	8	8	71	150	17,511,308.00	16,087,184.00	27,538,124.00	61,136,616.00	3.79

TABLE 4: Summary Statistics for Three-Bond Portfolio Illustration for 500, 1,000, 2,000, and 4,000 Trials

No. of Trials	Average Return (%)	Standard Deviation	Skewness	Minimum Return (%)	Maximum Return (%)
500	13.7	0.684	0.064	12.1	15.8
1,000	13.8	0.487	0.403	12.8	14.9
1,500	13.9	0.422	−0.106	12.7	14.8
2,000	13.9	0.322	−0.052	13.1	14.5
4,000	13.9	0.267	−0.050	13.3	14.6

Step 9: *First Trial* Record the value for the performance measure found in Step 8. The value of the performance measure for the first trial is 10.16%.

Step 10: Repeat Steps 6–9 (i.e., find the calculation of performance measure for new trials). Here we describe repeating Steps 6–9 for only one more trial. The results of the first 20 trials are shown in Table 3.

Step 11: The values for the performance measure for each trial recorded in Step 9 become the basis for construction of a probability distribution and cumulative probability distribution.

Step 12: The cumulative probability distribution constructed in Step 11 is analyzed. This is done by calculating summary statistics for the performance measure such as the mean, standard deviation, skewness, and the range. Table 4 provides summary statistics (average, standard deviation, skew, kurtosis, and range) for trials of 500, 1,000, 2,000, and 4,000 (using Excel). Based on the assumptions for the Treasury yield curve 6 months from now and the quality spread 6 months from now, the average total return is from 13.7% and 13.9% depending on the number of trials. The standard deviations can be used to create a confidence interval for the total return for each trial.

Generating Random Numbers

The algorithm in Steps 5 and 6 represents a very commonly used technique for generating random numbers from a prescribed distribution and is sometimes referred to as the *inverse cumulative distribution function method*, or more shortly, the *inverse transform method*. In this section, we discuss random number generation in simple terms.

A close inspection of Step 6 reveals that the integers generated are equally likely — on each trial Excel picks a new integer between 0 and 99 independently, without discriminating between the integers in that interval in any way. For this reason, these integers are said to be uniformly distributed. In fact, usually Steps 5 and 6 are merged into a single step in which at each trial we generate a random number between 0 and 1 in the same fashion — independently, without discriminating between the points in the interval [0, 1]. This probability distribution is known as the uniform distribution in the interval [0, 1]. In this case, Step 7 is completed by using the third column in Table 2 instead of the fourth one.

Every modeling environment has a random number generator which produces uniformly distributed numbers in the interval [0, 1]. In Excel, for example, this function is called RAND and is used without any arguments: "=RAND()". Even though we use the term random number generator, the numbers are produced by a deterministic algorithm and are, therefore, not truly random. They are also referred to as *pseudorandom numbers.*

A detailed discussion of an actual algorithm goes beyond the scope of this chapter. However, it is important to keep in mind that the pseudorandom numbers produced by the most common algorithm[3] behind the modern implementation of the RAND function in most modeling environments (including Excel) are of high quality as described by the following properties:

- The algorithm passes numerous tests for statistical randomness.[4]
- The pseudorandom sequence has a long period — it takes a very long sample before the sequence starts repeating itself. For a univariate sample, the period is about 4×10^{19937} observations.
- The pseudorandom sequence is produced quickly.

Discrete Distributions

The distribution function of the BBB corporate/Treasury yield spread provided in Panel b of Table 2 is plotted on the top plot of Figure 1 and the bar

[3]The most common algorithm is known as Marsenne Twister and is based on prime numbers known as Marsenne primes. The largest primes known to humankind are Marsenne primes.

[4]Examples include testing if the random numbers are uniformly distributed and also that in a sequence of pseudorandom numbers the next generated number does not depend statistically on the previous generated numbers (no autocorrelations).

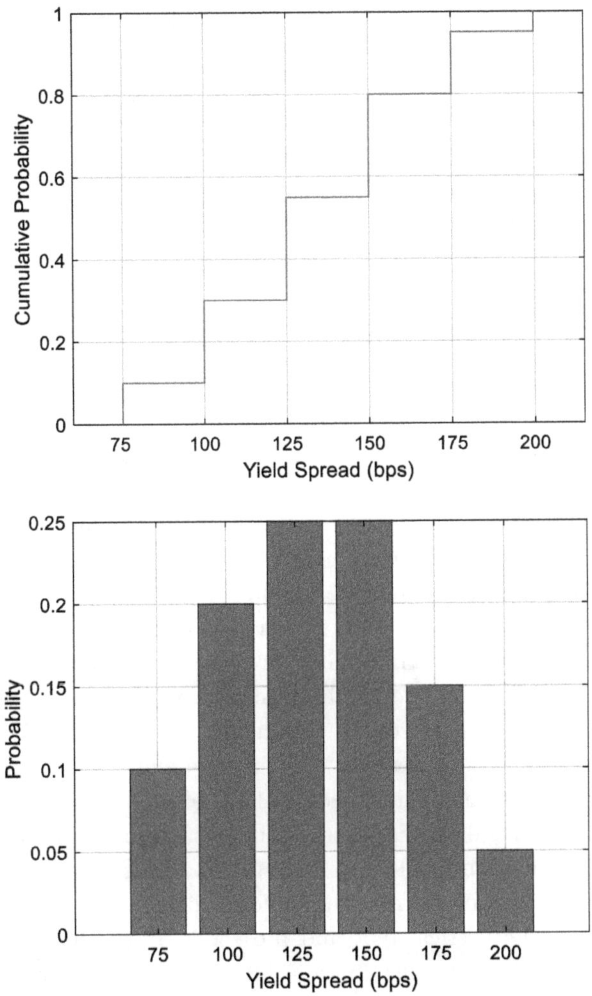

FIGURE 1: The Cumulative Probability Distribution Function (top) and the Individual Probabilities (bottom) of the BBB Corporate/Treasury Yield Spread Provided in Panel b of Table 2

plot below it shows the corresponding probabilities. This is an example of a discrete distribution because the number of possible outcomes is finite — only six possible values can occur.

To generate simulations from that distribution, first we generate a pseudorandom number using, for example, the RAND function in Excel. Then we locate the generated number on the vertical axis of the top plot of

Figure 1 and project the number using the graph of the function onto the horizontal axis. If, for instance, the generated number is 0.4, then the projection is 125 and it becomes a simulation for the yield spread. Because the pseudorandom numbers produced by the RAND function follow a uniform distribution, the probability of a specific outcome (such as 125) equals the size of the jump of the distribution at that value (0.25 for 125), which corresponds to the height of the corresponding bar of the box plot in Figure 1.

Continuous Distributions

Instead of assuming six possible values for the spread, we may decide to work with an infinite number of possible values. A discrete distribution may represent historical probabilities or our own forward-looking probabilities of what may occur and even though a popular method, it provides a limited number of possible outcomes. For instance, values higher than 200 basis points and lower than 75 basis points will not occur in a Monte Carlo simulation because such values are missing in the table.

One way to deal with this limitation is to assume a continuous distribution. Such a distribution is illustrated in Figure 2 — the top plot provides the distribution function and the bottom plot provides the density of that distribution. The plots are constructed in the following way. We have simply selected a Gaussian distribution with the same mean and standard deviation as the discrete distribution in Figure 1.

Even though this distribution is continuous, the same principle for generating random numbers holds. As a first step, we use the RAND function to draw a random number from the uniform distribution. Then, we locate the number on the vertical plot and project it on the horizontal plot by means of the graph of the distribution function. Clearly, if we draw a sufficiently large sample from the uniform distribution, its projection onto the horizontal axis will contain numbers higher than 200 and lower than 75 because those extreme spreads correspond to numbers close to 1 and 0 on the vertical axis.

This example shows that the inverse transform method is very general and applies to any distribution. However, it can be very inefficient computationally. For this reason, for specific distributions, such as the Gaussian, specialized algorithms exist which can generate random numbers from that specific distribution much faster. Even though highly specialized, these algorithms also depend on the RAND function.

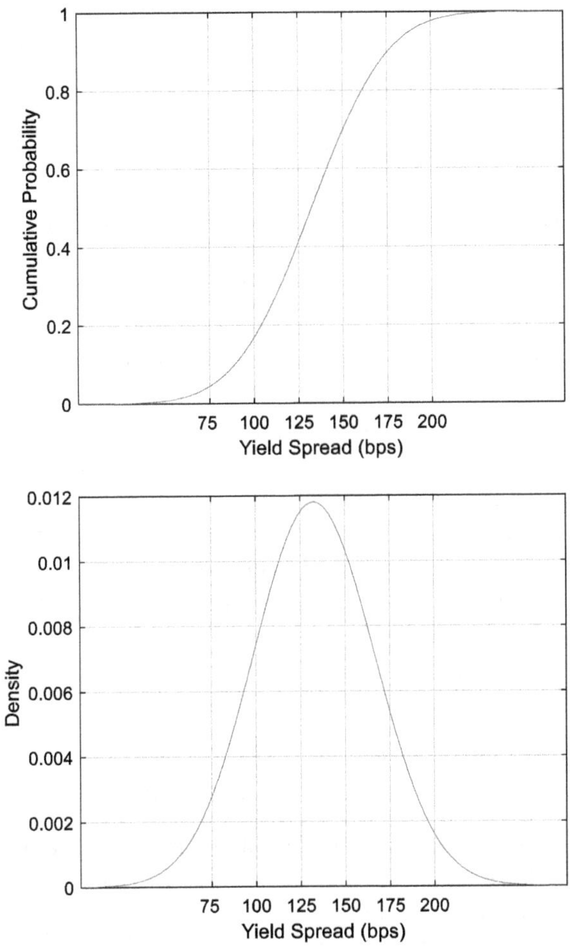

FIGURE 2: The Cumulative Probability Distribution Function (top) and the Individual Probabilities (bottom) of a Gaussian Random Variable used as a Model for the BBB Corporate/Treasury Yield Spread Data Provided in Panel b of Table 2

An Example with a Retirement Portfolio

We illustrate the power of the Monte Carlo simulation method with the following example. Consider an individual planning retirement in 10 years with retirement savings worth \$1 million today invested in a portfolio. The portfolio is 30% invested in a US Large Cap index and 70% in a Long-Term Treasury index. After retirement, the individual plans to withdraw \$150,000 at the beginning of every year over another 10 years, while the remaining funds are still invested in the same portfolio. The practical question facing the future retiree is what is the likelihood that the portfolio gets liquidated before the end of 10 years after retirement. If $150,000 is a target the individual is unwilling to change, then how does that probability change as the horizon after retirement is extended?

We illustrate how the problem can be solved by implementing the general algorithm in Steps 1–12. However, this problem is more involved because we need to simulate 20 years of future performance, which cannot be done in a single step. The reason is that after withdrawals start, the future portfolio performance needs to be simulated on a year-by-year basis. One trial in this context is a full simulation of the next 20 years, which is also known as a *sample path* or a *trajectory*.

Suppose that the individual has 10 years until retirement in January 2020. To simulate the next 20 years of history — 10 years before retirement and 10 years after retirement — we use data from the previous 20 years starting from January 2000. The monthly returns of a portfolio with 30% allocation to US Large Caps and 70% in Long-Term Treasuries in that period are provided in Table 5. Below is a sketch of the assumptions necessary to carry out the simulation:

Step 1: The performance measure is the probability that the investment portfolio is liquidated before year 10 after retirement.

Step 2: The mathematical expression of the performance measure is difficult to write down explicitly, but is easy to describe in terms of a short algorithm provided further below.

Step 3: The distribution of the monthly returns is assumed to be Gaussian with mean equal to the average monthly return in the past 20 years and standard deviation equal to the volatility of the monthly returns in the same time window. A simple calculation using the data in Table 5 shows that the annualized average monthly return is 7.5% and the annualized volatility equals 7.6%. To simulate, however, we do not use the annualized numbers but the monthly values, which are 0.624% average monthly return and 2.19% monthly volatility. We also assume that the monthly returns are independent; that is, to simulate the returns of two consecutive months, we draw two random numbers from the corresponding distribution independently.

TABLE 5: Monthly Returns of a 70–30 mix of a US Large Cap Index and a Long-Term Treasury Index from January 2000 to January 2020

Month	Return	Month	Return	Month	Return	Month	Return
Jan-2000	−0.63%	May-2003	5.55%	Sep-2006	1.87%	Jan-2010	0.78%
Feb-2000	1.50%	Jun-2003	−0.66%	Oct-2006	1.51%	Feb-2010	0.78%
Mar-2000	5.13%	Jul-2003	−5.48%	Nov-2006	1.90%	Mar-2010	0.75%
Apr-2000	−1.37%	Aug-2003	1.58%	Dec-2006	−1.08%	Apr-2010	2.41%
May-2000	−0.93%	Sep-2003	3.23%	Jan-2007	−0.15%	May-2010	0.56%
Jun-2000	2.36%	Oct-2003	−0.11%	Feb-2007	1.46%	Jun-2010	1.70%
Jul-2000	0.60%	Nov-2003	0.48%	Mar-2007	−0.46%	Jul-2010	1.98%
Aug-2000	3.31%	Dec-2003	2.43%	Apr-2007	1.93%	Aug-2010	3.60%
Sep-2000	−2.18%	Jan-2004	1.76%	May-2007	−0.31%	Sep-2010	1.40%
Oct-2000	0.97%	Feb-2004	1.79%	Jun-2007	−1.12%	Oct-2010	−1.17%
Nov-2000	−0.27%	Mar-2004	0.56%	Jul-2007	0.75%	Nov-2010	−1.12%
Dec-2000	1.87%	Apr-2004	−4.34%	Aug-2007	1.83%	Dec-2010	−0.51%
Jan-2001	1.26%	May-2004	0.02%	Sep-2007	1.26%	Jan-2011	−0.96%
Feb-2001	−1.48%	Jun-2004	1.19%	Oct-2007	1.45%	Feb-2011	1.89%
Mar-2001	−2.33%	Jul-2004	0.07%	Nov-2007	1.96%	Mar-2011	0.02%
Apr-2001	0.54%	Aug-2004	2.49%	Dec-2007	−0.55%	Apr-2011	2.31%
May-2001	0.34%	Sep-2004	0.98%	Jan-2008	0.04%	May-2011	1.96%
Jun-2001	−0.20%	Oct-2004	1.48%	Feb-2008	−0.73%	Jun-2011	−1.90%
Jul-2001	2.23%	Nov-2004	−0.36%	Mar-2008	0.58%	Jul-2011	2.31%
Aug-2001	−0.47%	Dec-2004	2.57%	Apr-2008	0.17%	Aug-2011	4.44%
Sep-2001	−1.81%	Jan-2005	1.08%	May-2008	−1.10%	Sep-2011	5.00%
Oct-2001	4.15%	Feb-2005	−0.24%	Jun-2008	−1.27%	Oct-2011	0.94%
Nov-2001	−1.25%	Mar-2005	−1.06%	Jul-2008	−0.04%	Nov-2011	1.21%
Dec-2001	−1.01%	Apr-2005	1.69%	Aug-2008	1.70%	Dec-2011	2.50%
Jan-2002	0.40%	May-2005	2.74%	Sep-2008	−2.48%	Jan-2012	1.39%
Feb-2002	0.29%	Jun-2005	1.19%	Oct-2008	−7.58%	Feb-2012	−0.18%
Mar-2002	−1.58%	Jul-2005	−0.69%	Nov-2008	6.30%	Mar-2012	−1.66%
Apr-2002	0.79%	Aug-2005	1.74%	Dec-2008	6.52%	Apr-2012	2.87%
May-2002	0.05%	Sep-2005	−1.71%	Jan-2009	−8.45%	May-2012	3.65%
Jun-2002	−0.91%	Oct-2005	−1.72%	Feb-2009	−3.91%	Jun-2012	0.23%
Jul-2002	−0.27%	Nov-2005	1.53%	Mar-2009	6.31%	Jul-2012	2.74%
Aug-2002	3.19%	Dec-2005	1.64%	Apr-2009	−0.63%	Aug-2012	−0.07%
Sep-2002	−0.45%	Jan-2006	0.17%	May-2009	−0.19%	Sep-2012	−0.70%
Oct-2002	0.65%	Feb-2006	0.65%	Jun-2009	0.56%	Oct-2012	−0.86%
Nov-2002	1.08%	Mar-2006	−2.01%	Jul-2009	2.83%	Nov-2012	1.11%
Dec-2002	1.07%	Apr-2006	−0.97%	Aug-2009	2.26%	Dec-2012	−1.12%
Jan-2003	−1.10%	May-2006	−0.89%	Sep-2009	2.50%	Jan-2013	−0.74%
Feb-2003	1.67%	Jun-2006	0.54%	Oct-2009	−1.58%	Feb-2013	1.28%
Mar-2003	−0.50%	Jul-2006	1.47%	Nov-2009	3.13%	Mar-2013	1.14%
Apr-2003	3.11%	Aug-2006	2.63%	Dec-2009	−3.38%	Apr-2013	3.28%

(*Continued*)

TABLE 5: (*Continued*)

Month	Return	Month	Return
May-2013	−3.66%	Oct-2016	−3.51%
Jun-2013	−2.69%	Nov-2016	−4.39%
Jul-2013	0.17%	Dec-2016	0.34%
Aug-2013	−1.77%	Jan-2017	1.02%
Sep-2013	1.55%	Feb-2017	2.29%
Oct-2013	2.30%	Mar-2017	−0.38%
Nov-2013	−0.83%	Apr-2017	1.42%
Dec-2013	−0.91%	May-2017	1.63%
Jan-2014	3.34%	Jun-2017	0.62%
Feb-2014	1.79%	Jul-2017	0.20%
Mar-2014	0.69%	Aug-2017	2.38%
Apr-2014	1.49%	Sep-2017	−0.97%
May-2014	2.61%	Oct-2017	0.68%
Jun-2014	0.50%	Nov-2017	1.36%
Jul-2014	0.00%	Dec-2017	1.58%
Aug-2014	4.16%	Jan-2018	−0.67%
Sep-2014	−1.82%	Feb-2018	−3.13%
Oct-2014	2.55%	Mar-2018	1.16%
Nov-2014	2.81%	Apr-2018	−1.32%
Dec-2014	1.90%	May-2018	1.97%
Jan-2015	5.37%	Jun-2018	0.65%
Feb-2015	−2.24%	Jul-2018	0.22%
Mar-2015	0.31%	Aug-2018	1.80%
Apr-2015	−1.86%	Sep-2018	−1.75%
May-2015	−1.13%	Oct-2018	−4.03%
Jun-2015	−3.19%	Nov-2018	1.86%
Jul-2015	3.57%	Dec-2018	1.14%
Aug-2015	−2.31%	Jan-2019	2.74%
Sep-2015	0.59%	Feb-2019	0.04%
Oct-2015	2.19%	Mar-2019	4.41%
Nov-2015	−0.48%	Apr-2019	−0.10%
Dec-2015	−0.72%	May-2019	2.75%
Jan-2016	2.17%	Jun-2019	2.82%
Feb-2016	1.96%	Jul-2019	0.58%
Mar-2016	2.07%	Aug-2019	7.00%
Apr-2016	−0.33%	Sep-2019	−1.28%
May-2016	1.02%	Oct-2019	−0.13%
Jun-2016	4.67%	Nov-2019	0.81%
Jul-2016	2.51%	Dec-2019	−1.20%
Aug-2016	−0.66%	Jan-2020	5.09%
Sep-2016	−0.92%		

Steps 4–9: The following steps describe how a single trial is carried out. Because one trial represents an entire sample path, the Monte Carlo simulation has a number of sub-steps which we summarize. The evaluation of the performance measure is also illustrated:

- Generate independently 120 monthly returns from the hypothesized Gaussian distribution. Compound the returns to find the value of $1 million 10 years from now, which is when the person retires.
- The person has just retired and withdraws $150,000. Check if the residual value, which equals the portfolio value computed in the previous step minus the withdrawn amount, is positive. If it is negative, stop here and mark that in this trial the portfolio has been liquidated before year 10. If it is positive, then draw 12 random monthly returns from the hypothesized Gaussian distribution and use them to compound the residual portfolio value to find the value one year further into the future.
- Repeat the previous step 10 times, one for each year after retirement. The sample path is regarded as completed if one of the following two conditions occurs: either the simulation is terminated before year 10 is reached or year 10 is reached. If early termination occurs, we record it.

Step 10: The steps above are repeated multiple times, each trial represents one possible version of the future.

Step 11: The results from the simulations are collected.

Step 12: To compute the probability, we divide the number of trials with early termination by the total number of trials.

Once this algorithm has been implemented in a modeling environment, it is very easy to run a large number of simulations (sample paths) and to calculate the probability that the retiree runs out of money before year 10 after retirement. It is also very easy to change some of the settings. For example, it may be of interest to repeat that simulation for periods of different lengths to see how the probability changes.

Results based on 5,000 simulated sample paths are provided in Table 6. The probability in the first cell is 0.0102, which corresponds to a period of 10 years after retirement. That is, the probability that the individual runs out of money appears to be relatively small. As we increase the number of

TABLE 6: The Probability that the Investment Portfolio is Liquidated Before the Year in the Column When the Monthly Returns are Assumed Gaussian Distribution Based on 5,000 Simulated Sample Paths

10 years	15 years	20 years	25 years	30 years
0.0102	0.1114	0.2306	0.349	0.417

years, however, we notice that the probability increases by a bit more than 0.1 every five years, and at 20 years, it is close to 0.23.

How to Choose a Distribution

When running a Monte Carlo simulation, it is important to think carefully about the assumptions made in order to evaluate their impact. One important assumption in the retirement portfolio example is the hypothesis that the portfolio returns in the future will follow a Gaussian distribution. How do we pick a distribution in the first place?

The guiding principle is that the hypothesized distribution should describe the historical data well and there are different ways to quantify what "well" means. A common first step is to inspect visually the histogram of the observed returns which typically has a bell-like shape. However, it may exhibit skewness and also there may be extreme returns far away from the body of the distribution, which is a sign of what is known as fat tails.

It is also common to visualize the histogram together with a fitted Gaussian distribution for two reasons. Firstly, it represents a classical distributional hypothesis in finance very often used by default and, secondly, it is symmetric and does not exhibit fat tails, which makes it a good benchmark.

On the top plot of Figure 3, we show the histogram of the portfolio returns data in Table 5 together with a fitted Gaussian distribution. The black curve is exactly the distribution used to generate monthly returns in the retirement portfolio example. Even though it generally fits the profile of the returns data, there are two issues that are very common when the Gaussian distribution is used to model financial asset returns. The first one is a slight skewness to the left of the empirical distribution which the Gaussian distribution does not seem to capture well. Although this is much more pronounced in daily returns time series, it can be a feature of monthly returns as well.

The second issue is the extreme negative returns whose empirical frequency of occurrence appears to be higher than that predicted by the fitted Gaussian distribution. This is also the reason why the fitted Gaussian distribution does not capture the central part of the histogram well. This phenomenon is also much more pronounced in higher frequency returns than that of monthly returns.

In Chapter 7, we discuss various distributional assumptions which represent more general families of distributions that include the Gaussian distribution as a special case. One of them is the location-scale Student's

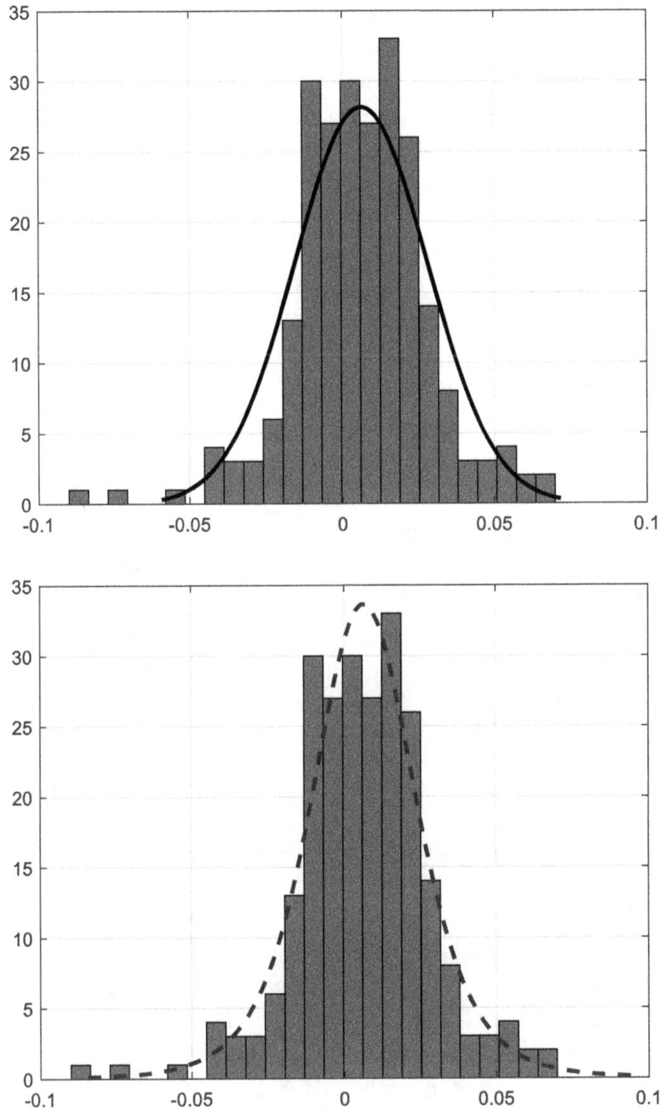

FIGURE 3: The Histogram of the Data in Table 5 with a Fitted Gaussian Distribution (top) and Fitted Location-Scale Student's t Distribution (bottom)

t distribution. The bottom plot in Figure 3 shows the same histogram, but this time with a fitted location-scale Student's t distribution. The differences with the top plot are visible — the central part of the empirical distribution and the negative returns in the left tail are captured better.

Apart from visually overlaying the histogram of the historical data on the density of a fitted distribution, there are other graphical comparisons that are commonly made. One example is the quantile–quantile plot, also known as the q–q plot, which compares the empirical quantiles to the quantiles of a fitted distribution.

In addition to the graphical approaches, there are also formal ways to calculate how close the fitted distribution is to the empirical data. Two widely used statistics include the Kolmogorov–Smirnov distance and the Anderson–Darling statistic. A standard way to analyze a given dataset is to calculate both statistics for several distributional assumptions and then check for which of them the statistics are minimal. Even though this is not a formal statistical test, such a comparison provides insight which complements the graphical approach.

Finally, it is possible to run formal statistical tests which often take the form of likelihood-ratio tests if one of the distributional assumptions is a special case of the other; for example, the Gaussian distribution is a special case of the Student's t distribution. This is, however, beyond the scope of this chapter.[5]

If it appears that a distribution different from the selected one fits the data better, then the Monte Carlo simulation can be repeated to evaluate the impact of a change in the distributional assumption on the final result. This is often viewed as a robustness check.

Generating Joint Scenarios

The portfolio returns provided in Table 5 are computed from the returns of two indices — a US Large Cap index and a Long-Term Treasury index. Financial assets return data are rarely independent. In this particular case, the US Large Cap index returns and the Long-Term Treasury index returns are negatively correlated in the period from January 2000 to January 2020; in fact, the correlation coefficient equals –0.29.

The example in the previous section assumes a fixed-mix portfolio (i.e., the allocation to the two indices is assumed constant across time). There are financial products, however, in which the allocation to the two funds evolves across time. For example, the so-called life-cycle or target-date funds

[5]For more information, see Rachev, Hochstotter, Fabozzi, and Focardi [2010].

increase the allocation to the fixed-income part of the portfolio deterministically as a function of the remaining time to retirement. In this situation, it is not possible to follow the same method and use the returns of the portfolio in the past in order to simulate the returns in the future because the portfolio in the future will become more conservative, and, therefore the past returns are not representative. To circumvent this problem, one would need to produce joint simulations for the future returns of the two portfolio constituents and then apply the correct portfolio weights depending on the time in the future we are simulating for. Because the returns of the two indices are not independent, the practical question is how to produce Monte Carlo simulations for variables that are correlated.

In this section, we provide an answer using the material on financial econometrics from Chapter 4. The main idea is first to generate a simulation for one of the variables and then, conditional on that realization, to generate a simulation for the other variable. Even though the same principle is used in the case of many variables, the discussion in this section is limited to two variables only for the sake of clarity.

Taking advantage of the notation behind the linear regression discussed in Chapter 4, we label the US Large Cap index a dependent variable and denote it by Y, and the Long-Term Treasury index an independent variable and denote it by X. The returns of the dependent variable can then be expressed in terms of the returns of the independent variable and an independent residual,

$$Y = \alpha + \beta X + \epsilon,$$

where α and β coefficients are estimated. This equation allows us to carry out a simulation in the way just described — the left-hand side is simulated conditionally on realizations of X which appears on the right-hand side.

The first step, however, is to estimate the regression. Using the monthly returns data from January 2000 to January 2020, the estimated equation is

$$Y = 0.0082 - 0.3896 \times X + \epsilon.$$

The estimated beta is negative which reflects the negative correlation between the returns of the two indices.

We follow the next steps to produce joint simulations of the US Large Cap index returns and the Long-Term Treasury index returns, which are essentially a modification of the steps between Steps 3 and 7 of the algorithm provided at the beginning of the chapter.

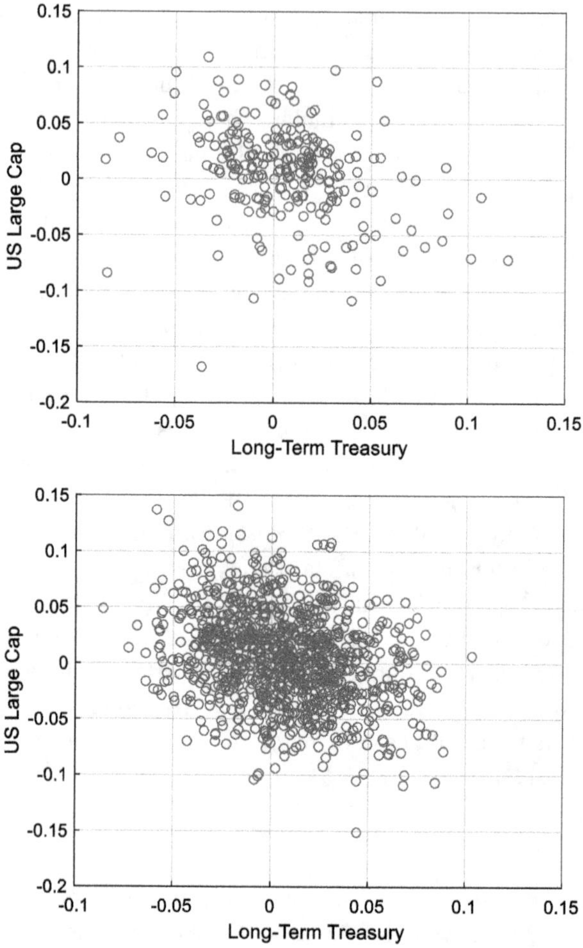

FIGURE 4: A Scatter-Plot of the Returns of the Long-Term Treasury Index and the Returns of the US Large Cap Index (top) and a Scatter Plot of 1,000 Joint Simulations of the Same Variables (bottom). Both Plots are Based on the Data Used to Construct the Portfolio Returns Provided in Table 5

Step 3′: The distribution of variable X is assumed to be Gaussian distributed with mean and standard deviation equal to the mean return and the volatility of the Long-Term Treasury index returns from January 2000 to January 2020. The estimated values are 0.65% and 3.13%, respectively. The distribution of the estimated residual ϵ is assumed to be Gaussian distributed with mean and standard deviation equal to the corresponding sample quantities. The estimated values are 0% and 4%, respectively. The residual and the variable X are assumed to be independent. Note that the assumptions made so far are sufficient to describe the variable Y by means of the right-hand side of the regression equation and, therefore, no distributional assumptions are made explicitly for Y.

Step 7′: Using Monte Carlo software, generate independently one random number from the distribution of X and one random number from the distribution of the estimated residual ϵ. Denote those numbers by X_1 and ϵ_1. Compute the random number for the dependent variable, denoted by Y_1, by plugging them into the estimated regression,

$$Y_1 = 0.0082 - 0.3896 \times X_1 + \epsilon_1.$$

By repeating Step 7′ many times, we obtain joint simulations for the variables X and Y. Note that, indeed, each simulation of Y is conditional on a given realization of X.

A scatter plot of the original data and 1,000 Monte Carlo simulations are provided in Figure 4. The top plot shows the observed returns of the two indices; the independent variable is plotted on the horizontal axis and the dependent variable is plotted on the vertical axis. The bottom plot shows the generated joint Monte Carlo simulations. A quick comparison of the two scatter plots reveals that the general shape of the cloud in the simulations is similar to the shape of the cloud of the real data and properly reflects the negative correlation of the observed data.

Key Points

- The Monte Carlo approach simulates possible future values of variables which influence the performance measure and, as a consequence, generates possible future values for that performance measure.
- The simulation method is very general and applies to a wide range of situations which makes it a useful component in the decision-making process of portfolio managers.
- Each simulation is known as a trial. The number of trials determines the accuracy of the calculated performance measure.
- The Monte Carlo method relies on making assumptions about the distribution of the random quantities being simulated.
- The actual simulation involves drawing random numbers from a uniform distribution and then transforming them so that they become draws from the desired distribution.

- A distribution is selected based on how well it describes the original data when fitted to the sample.
- Both graphical tools, such as comparing the estimated density to the empirical histogram, as well as quantitative methods which use certain statistics, are used in assessing the outcome of a Monte Carlo simulation.
- It is common to evaluate the significance of a given assumption, such as a distributional model, by modifying it and re-running the Monte Carlo simulation.
- The Monte Carlo method can be successfully applied in more complicated simulations when a full sample path of possible future portfolio return realizations is necessary to evaluate the selected performance measure.
- When the variables influencing the selected performance measure are dependent, a regression model can be used to incorporate the stochastic dependence into the Monte Carlo simulations.

References

Boyle, P., 1977. "Options: A Monte Carlo approach," *Journal of Financial Economics*, 4: 323–338.

Law, A. M. and W. D. Kelton, 2002. *Simulation Modeling and Analysis*, 3rd edn. New York: McGraw-Hill.

Rachev, S., M. Hochstotter, F. J. Fabozzi, and S. M. Focardi, 2010. *Probability and Statistics for Finance.* Hoboken, NJ: John Wiley & Sons.

Schönbucher, P. J., 2003. *Credit Derivatives Pricing Models*, Chichester, UK: John Wiley & Sons.

Chapter 6

Optimization Models for Asset Management

Learning Objectives

After reading this chapter, you will understand:

- what is mathematical programming;
- the steps needed to set up a mathematical programming model;
- the main types of mathematical programming models and the connections between them;
- the applications of optimization models in bond and equity portfolio construction and asset allocation.

Introduction

An *optimization model* prescribes the best course of action to be pursued in order to achieve an objective. The optimization models used in most asset management applications are *mathematical programming models*. We describe in this chapter the various types of mathematical programming models used for optimization in asset management and review some of the applications, without delving into the nuances of these models or the algorithms for solving a mathematical programming problem. Any real-world problem confronting an asset manager will be complex enough to require the use of commercially available software to solve.

Optimization models are used in making asset allocation decisions (i.e., decisions on allocation of funds among major asset classes). The most well-known such allocation model is the Markowitz portfolio selection model or mean–variance analysis. Conceptually, asset managers construct a portfolio that has minimal total risk subject to some expected return target and other constraints. In Chapters 15 and 16, where we demonstrate how multi-factor risk models are used in constructing and rebalancing equity and bond portfolio, respectively, the application of optimization models is described.

Apart from the problem of asset allocation, optimization problems are used in equity portfolio management. Similarly, the objective is to build a large portfolio of equities that has minimal risk subject to certain constraints. Because risk can be measured in different ways, there are a number of variations of the generic problem. In some applications, the portfolio manager is mandated to track an equity benchmark. Then, the risk of the equity portfolio is optimized relative to the corresponding benchmark.

Optimization models are commonly used in bond portfolio management with a considerable number of applications starting in the mid-1980s through the late 1990s. For example, structured portfolio strategies do not rely on expectations of interest-rate movements or changes in yield spreads. Instead the objective is to design of an optimal portfolio that will achieve the performance of a predetermined benchmark. The target could be (1) the return on a specific benchmark index, (2) sufficient dollars to satisfy a future single liability, or (3) sufficient dollars to satisfy each liability of a future liability stream. The structured bond portfolio strategy used when the target to be achieved is replication of a predetermined benchmark index is called a *bond indexing strategy*. When the objective is to generate sufficient funds to pay off predetermined future liabilities, the strategy is called a *liability funding strategy*.

Solving an optimization problem can be viewed as a problem of engineering. Generally, optimization problems are classified into groups which come with their own solution techniques. Therefore, to solve a problem in practice, we need to map the real-world problem to a particular type of optimization problem and then employ the corresponding toolbox to solve it. In this chapter, we explain the main classes of optimization problems and then discuss the most common asset allocation problems.

Mathematical Programming

Mathematical programming models are used to solve problems that involve the allocation of limited resources so as to optimize a quantitative goal. An allocation problem assumes there are many acceptable solutions that satisfy the decision maker's constraints or restrictions, but that there may be one best solution that optimizes the value of the specified goal. Depending on the types of constraints and objectives, we distinguish between different classes of optimization models. We begin by describing general steps that are followed when designing a mathematical programming model.

Setting Up a Mathematical Programming Model

There are four steps in setting up a mathematical programming or optimization problem.

Step 1: Define the variables on which a decision must be made. These variables are called *decision variables*. In an asset allocation problem, the decision variables are the amount to be allocated to each major asset class. In the construction of an equity portfolio to meet certain investment goals subject to constraints, the decision variables are the amount to be allocated to each stock. In a structured portfolio problem, the decision variables are typically the amount of a security that should be purchased or sold.
Step 2: Specify mathematically the objective the decision maker seeks to optimize. This mathematical expression is called the *objective function*. The linear or nonlinear nature of the objective function is what distinguishes the different types of mathematical programming models.
Step 3: Specify mathematically the constraints under which the objective function is to be optimized. One constraint, for example, might be that the portfolio's beta be equal to 1 or the duration of bond portfolio be equal to 4. To avoid concentration risk, a constraint may specify that the amount allocated to one sector of the market may not exceed a certain percentage of the portfolio, or that the maximum amount allocated to illiquid assets be a specified percentage. As with the objective function, the mathematical characterization of the constraints determines the type of mathematical programming problem.
Step 4: Solve for the optimal solution.

Optimization problems are solved in practice with the help of software. Even though it is true that under some conditions the optimal solution can be written down as a concrete mathematical expression, the practical problems one faces in real life are complicated and cannot be solved analytically. The software tools provide a way to define the objective function and the constraints and to solve the problem numerically.

Types of Mathematical Programming Models

There are different types of mathematical programming models depending on: (1) the nature of the objective function and the constraints, (2) whether the problem concerns a single decision (also known as *myopic problem*) or multiple decisions in time (*dynamic problem*), and (3) whether the inputs to the optimization problem are deterministic or stochastic. The most common mathematical programming models in each category are shown in Table 1. In the remainder of this section, we describe the main classes and provide simple examples.

Linear Optimization Models

The objective function and all the constraints in a linear programming problem are linear. An example of where this programming method can be used in bond portfolio management is a structured portfolio strategy.[1] Suppose that the acceptable universe of bonds is 950 issues made up of Treasuries, agencies, and all investment-grade corporate bonds. The decision variables are the percentage of the portfolio to be invested in an issue. There are then 950 decision variables, one representing each of the acceptable issues

TABLE 1: Most Common Mathematical Programming Models by Category

1. Classes of linear and nonlinear models
   - Linear optimization models
   - Quadratic optimization models
   - Convex optimization models
   - Mixed-integer optimization
2. Static and dynamic problems
   - Static or myopic problems
   - Dynamic optimization models
3. Type of parameters
   - Deterministic optimization models
   - Stochastic optimization models
   - Robust optimization models

[1]This strategy is explained in Chapter 8 in the companion book.

in the universe. Let

w_i = Par amount to purchase a particular issue ($i = 1, 2, \ldots, 950$);

p_i = Price of issue i (as a percent of par value P, e.g., $0.90, 1.00, 1.05$).

Then the total cost of the portfolio is

$$w_1 p_1 + w_2 p_2 + \cdots + w_{950} p_{950}.$$

This expression represents the objective function. The objective function is linear because each decision variable is multiplied by a constant equal to the price of the corresponding issues, and the portfolio manager would seek to minimize the objective function subject to the constraints imposed.

Two examples of a linear constraint would be that a minimum of \$25 million of the portfolio must be invested in Treasury issues and that no more than \$30 million may be invested in BBB-rated corporate bonds. Mathematically, if issues 1, 2, ..., 150 are the Treasury issues, the first constraint can be expressed as

$$w_1 p_1 + w_2 p_2 + \cdots + w_{150} p_{150} \geq \$20{,}000{,}000.$$

If issues 625 to 950 are triple-B-rated corporate bonds, the second constraint can be expressed mathematically as

$$w_{625} p_{625} + w_{626} p_{626} + \cdots + w_{950} p_{950} \leq \$30{,}000{,}000.$$

One common linear constraint in structured portfolio strategies is a restriction on portfolio duration. For example, an immunization strategy[2] would constrain portfolio duration to match the duration of the liability. Assuming no short selling, all the decision variables are then constrained to be greater than or equal to zero.

Linear programming models are solved in practice using linear programming solvers. Once the mathematical problem has been formulated, the objective function is defined in the solver by means of the coefficients multiplying the decision variables. The set of all constraints is described by means of a matrix of numbers which collects all coefficients multiplying the decision variables in the constraints and one vector of numbers which contains the right-hand side values of the constraints (e.g., \$20,000,000 and \$30,000,000 from the example).

[2]A bond immunization strategy sets the duration of a bond portfolio to match the investment horizon of the investor. The goal is to reduce the interest rate risk of the bond portfolio.

To solve the problem numerically, the solver employs specialized algorithms. Linear programming has been a topic of research since the 1940s and modern commercial solvers can handle millions of decision variables and millions of constraint equations. The mathematical theory behind linear models guarantees that when a solution exists, it can be discovered in a finite number of steps.

Quadratic Programming Models

Even though linear programming finds a lot of applications in economics, its application in the field of asset allocation is limited. The reason is that the notion of risk is critical to portfolio construction and is nonlinear. Therefore, the practical problems that arise do not qualify as linear programming models.

Quadratic programming models extend linear models by allowing the objective function to have a quadratic term. Because linear functions can be viewed as quadratic functions with no quadratic term, then by construction linear models represent a special case of quadratic programming models. The classical formulation of a quadratic model is an optimization problem in which the objective function is quadratic in the decision variables and the constraints are linear in the decision variables.

The classical example in portfolio construction is the mean–variance framework. The decision variables are the portfolio weights, which define what percentage of capital is allocated to a given stock. The objective function is portfolio risk proxied by the variance of the portfolio return distribution. The portfolio variance equals

$$\sigma^2 \left(R_p\right) = \sum_{k=1}^{K} \sum_{h=1}^{K} w_k w_h cov \left(R_k, R_h\right)$$

in which w_k denotes the weight of stock k, $cov\left(R_k, R_h\right)$ denotes the covariance of the returns of stocks k and h, and K denotes the number of stocks. The variance of the portfolio returns is essentially a sum of all possible products of two decision variables multiplied by a constant. Therefore, it is a quadratic function of the decision variables. The goal of risk-averse investors is to find a portfolio, or a set of weights, which minimizes portfolio risk. It is common to include several standard constraints as follows:

- *Budget Constraint*: The budget constraint states that the entire capital is allocated, or mathematically, that the weights should sum up to one,

$$w_1 + \cdots + w_K = 1$$

- *Expected Performance Constraint*: The optimal portfolio is required to have an expected return equal to a given target value,

$$w_1 E(R_1) + \cdots + w_K E(R_K) = E(R_p)$$

in which $E(R_1), \ldots, E(R_K)$ denote the expected stock returns and $E(R_p)$ is a number representing the targeted expected portfolio return.
- *Long-Only Constraint*: The portfolio can be required to be long-only, which means all weights are non-negative,

$$w_i \geq 0, \quad i = 1, \ldots, K$$

- *Single Holding Constraints*: To avoid concentration in a given asset, the weights can be required to be bounded below and above,

$$L_i \leq w_i \leq U_i, \quad i = 1, \ldots, K$$

where L_i and U_i are the lower and the upper bounds, respectively. The bounds can be positive and also negative numbers. Negative weights are interpreted as short positions. Also, notice that the long-only constraints can be formulated as single holding constraints.
- *Sector Constraints*: To avoid concentration in certain sectors, the weight allocated to a particular sector can be constrained in a similar fashion. Suppose that the first 10 stocks belong to a given sector. Then, the sum of the first 10 weights can be constrained similar to the single holding constraints

$$L \leq w_1 + w_2 + \cdots + w_{10} \leq U$$

If the objective function includes only portfolio risk, then it has only a quadratic part and no linear part. To give an example of a portfolio construction problem with an objective that has both parts, consider a risk-averse investor choosing a portfolio that maximizes the investor's utility function which consists of only two components — the expected portfolio return and portfolio variance. Because the investor is risk averse, a higher expected portfolio return increases utility (other things equal) and a higher portfolio variance decreases the utility of the investor. Mathematically, the objective of the investor is then to maximize

$$U(w) = w_1 E(R_1) + \cdots + w_K E(R_K) - \lambda \sum_{k=1}^{K} \sum_{h=1}^{K} w_k w_h \, cov(R_k, R_h)$$

in which the parameter λ is positive and describes the degree of risk aversion. The expected return part of the utility function is the linear component of the objective and the second component, which calculates portfolio variance, is the quadratic part. Notice that if we work with such an objective function, then we do not need the expected performance constraint.

Quadratic programming problems are solved numerically using quadratic solvers. The optimization problem is defined in the solver in the following way. The objective function, in this case portfolio risk, is defined by means of a matrix which includes all pairwise covariances, also known as the covariance matrix. Because all constraints are linear, the constraint set is defined in the same way as in the case of linear programming — by a matrix that contains the coefficients multiplying the decision variables in each constraint.

In contrast to linear programs, quadratic problems may not be possible to solve with a quadratic solver. A solution is guaranteed to exist and to be unique if the matrix defining the quadratic part of the objective function has certain properties — the matrix has to be such that for any values of the decision variables, the quadratic part should be a non-negative number. In portfolio construction, this property holds because for any values of the decision variables, the quadratic objective calculates the variance of the corresponding portfolio return distribution, which is a non-negative number. Thus, the covariance matrix has the necessary property and a quadratic solver can be used to solve the problem. Modern quadratic solvers can handle thousands of decision variables.

Convex Programming Models

As explained in Chapter 8, risk measures focused on the downside such as value-at-risk (VaR) and conditional value-at-risk (CVaR) have properties very different from variance. From a portfolio construction perspective, we can replace portfolio variance in the objective function with a different measure of risk. The corresponding optimization problem, however, is not in the class of the quadratic problems and, therefore, a quadratic solver cannot be used to solve it.

A more general class of models is that of *convex programming*. An important first step is to make sure that the risk measure has the important convexity property as described in Chapter 8. This property guarantees that the solution is unique, if it exists.[3] If the convexity property does not hold, then the portfolio construction problem cannot be solved with the help of

[3]The statement holds under additional mild regularity conditions which are not restrictive for practical problems.

convex programming. Some risk measures, such as CVaR, are known to be convex and others, such as VaR, do not have that property.

Finally, convex problems allow for more general types of constraints. Apart from linear constraints, we also can include convex constraints, such as the requirement that the portfolio risk as computed by CVaR does not exceed a specific number.

Solving convex problems is not as simple as solving linear or quadratic problems. The first reason is that the programming model is relatively more difficult to set up. The second reason is that convex programming is much more computationally intensive. Finally, even though there are standard algorithms which can be applied to any convex problem, there are also specialized algorithms which are more efficient if the objective function has certain additional properties. In contrast to linear and quadratic programming, modern convex solvers can handle only hundreds of decision variables.

Mixed Integer Programming

In the classical linear, quadratic, and convex programming models, the decision variables are assumed continuous. For example, the optimal portfolio solution from a mean–variance example may suggest purchasing 12.63 shares of stock A and selling 2.345 shares of stock B, while in practice an investor can purchase only an integer number of shares.

Even though assuming the decision variables are continuous can be a reasonable approximation, in some practical situations it is better to work with variables that can take only discrete values, such as integer-valued variables or binary variables. If all decision variables are integer-valued, then we have an *integer programming model.* If some variables are continuous and others are discrete, we have a case of *mixed-integer programming.* In general, we can have any combination of type of model and type of variables — we can distinguish between linear, quadratic, and convex mixed-integer programming models.

As a particular example, consider an investor who wants to invest in only 10 stocks using the mean–variance portfolio construction problem and the candidate list is the 500 stocks in the S&P index. We could simply take the optimal solution, sort by weight, take the top 10 stocks, and renormalize the weights so that they sum up to one. This, however, may result in a suboptimal solution. Such a problem can be solved by including the so-called *cardinality constraint* which leads to extending the set of continuous variables with binary variables, a given stock is either in or out of the portfolio. The resulting problem is a quadratic mixed-integer problem.

A mixed-integer model is much more difficult to solve than the corresponding continuous variable model. Depending on the structure of the particular optimization problem, the computational burden can increase by several orders of magnitude.

Myopic versus Dynamic Problems

The classical portfolio construction framework is also known as one-period, myopic, or static, because the optimal portfolio is supposed to be held until some unknown future time instant. From a practical perspective, it is clear that market conditions evolve and at some point the portfolio needs to be updated or rebalanced. The input to the optimization problem is re-estimated, the optimization problem is solved again, and the new portfolio is implemented.

Even though the practical implementation involves regular rebalancing, the framework is still myopic because the future dynamics of the input variables are not recognized in advance. Dynamic problems resolve this limitation. They are characterized by an explicit investment horizon and concrete assumptions about the dynamics of the stock prices.

Although dynamic programming appears to be a much more realistic framework, it is rarely used in practice because the computational complexity is enormous. Application in asset allocation remains mostly an academic exercise involving only a few variables.

Stochastic versus Deterministic Models

The inputs to the mean–variance problem consist of all pairwise covariances and the estimates of future expected return. From a practical standpoint, the inputs represent estimated quantities from real data. Because the real data are noisy and samples are generally small, the estimated quantities are also noisy. Presence of a certain level of noise, however, is not recognized in the optimization problem; the input variables are taken at face value assuming they are known with infinite precision. From this perspective, the classical framework uses a deterministic optimization model.

Note that the stochastic nature of the inputs has nothing to do with dynamics. In principle, a variable can be random with or without pronounced dynamics. We can have stochastic dynamic programming problems and also deterministic dynamic programming problems.

Robust optimization represents a relatively new technique which recognizes that the inputs to the optimization problem are noisy. To describe the main concept, we use a simple procedure based on Monte Carlo simulation.[4] Consider the mean–variance framework and an investor with a given risk-aversion parameter. The asset manager estimates the pairwise covariances and the expected returns from historical data and solves the problem. The asset manager, however, realizes that there is a lot of uncertainty related to the expected returns and pairwise covariances. Therefore, to simulate the uncertainty in that parameter, the asset manager adopts the following Monte Carlo algorithm:

Step 1: Choose a distribution that describes the uncertainty in the original data. A standard choice is the multivariate normal with a mean equal to the estimated expected returns and a covariance matrix equal to the estimated one.
Step 2: Draw a random sample from that distribution with the number of observations equal to the number of observations in the original data. Estimate a new vector of expected returns and a new covariance matrix from the simulated data.
Step 3: Calculate a new optimal portfolio and store it.
Step 4: Repeat Steps 2 and 3 many times.
Step 5: The average of the optimal portfolios represents the robust optimal solution.

The algorithm essentially generates multiple optimal solutions under different sets of realistic parameters. The simulated optimal portfolios can also be used to investigate the sensitivity of the optimal weights to the noise in the input. For example, we can look at histograms of each of the weights to see how they are affected by the noise in the input.[5]

This approach has two shortcomings. First, even though the Monte Carlo algorithm clearly illustrates the main concept of robustness in this context, it may be impractical because the optimization problem is solved multiple times. This is true especially for large portfolios. Second, due to

[4]See Chapter 5 for a description of Monte Carlo simulation.
[5]For additional details, Fabozzi, Kolm, Pachamanova, and Focardi [2007] and Kim, Kim, and Fabozzi [2016].

the process of averaging, the averaged portfolio may have many small positions, which may be undesirable. Although there are certain *ad-hoc* ways in which the two issues can be mitigated, robust portfolio optimization offers an alternative approach.

We illustrate the general idea with the expected returns parameters assuming that their noisiness is more significant than that of the pairwise correlations. This is a practical hypothesis given that it is well known that the optimal solution is most sensitive to the expected returns input.[6]

Robust optimization begins with a specification of the so-called *uncertainty set* — this is a set that describes the uncertainty in the expected returns parameters. To simplify notation, denote by the estimated expected return and by the unknown true value. One possible choice for this set is to assume that the true expected return belongs to some interval around the estimated value,

$$\hat{\mu}_i - \delta_i \leq \mu_i \leq \hat{\mu}_i + \delta_i$$

in which δ_i is a positive number selected for each stock. If the expected return of a stocks is characterized by higher uncertainty, then a larger parameter δ_i for that stock should be selected.

The objective in the optimization problem is then reformulated so that the stocks with more uncertain expected returns on a relative basis are penalized,

$$w_1\hat{\mu} + \cdots + w_K\hat{\mu} - |w_1|\,\delta_1 - \cdots - |w_K|\,\delta_K - \lambda\sum_{k=1}^{K}\sum_{h=1}^{K} w_k w_h cov(R_k, R_h)$$

Apart from the modification in the objective function, the constraints remain the same.

Even though this objective function looks much more complicated than the utility function discussed previously, it is possible to re-formulate it as a quadratic programming problem. That is, the computational complexity is not much different from that of the original problem.

Robust optimization is a comprehensive theory that offers an approach to formulate a portfolio construction problem consistent with a particular uncertainty set. It is possible to include uncertainty sets for the pairwise covariances as well.

[6]Best and Grauer [1991] investigate the effect of a small increase in a single asset on portfolio weights. Chopra and Ziemba [1993] find that errors in estimating expected returns are found to be at least 10 times more important than errors in estimating variances and covariances.

Applications

Mathematical programming has been used to provide solutions for many types of fixed income portfolio problems,[7] including immunization, dedicated portfolio strategies, indexing, optimized rebalancing, and asset allocation.

Immunization

Immunization is a structured portfolio strategy designed to protect against interest-rate changes. A single-period immunization addresses one future liability when the objective is to construct a portfolio to minimize the risk that changes in interest rates will result in not satisfying the objective. Life insurance companies use single-period immunization in managing portfolios to satisfy their obligations of guaranteed investment contracts. A requirement for single-period immunization is that the duration of the portfolio be equal to the maturity of the liability. However, duration is limited to a parallel shift in the yield curve. Other researchers have presented methodologies for immunizing under more general shifts in the yield curve.[8]

Multiperiod immunization is used in the case of more than one future liability. Examples of multiple liabilities are liabilities of a defined benefit pension fund, liabilities of annuity policies issued by life insurance companies, and liabilities resulting from a state-sponsored lottery. Once again, the objective is to construct a minimum-cost portfolio designed to satisfy all the liabilities, however interest rates change. Two requirements of multiperiod immunization are that (1) the duration of the portfolio be equal to the duration of the liabilities and (2) the convexity of the portfolio be greater than or equal to the convexity of the liabilities.

Zenios and Kang [1993] apply portfolio immunization strategy in a multiperiod stochastic optimization framework.

Dedicated Portfolio Strategies

A dedicated portfolio strategy involves construction of a portfolio to satisfy multiple liabilities but without duration or convexity requirements. Instead, a minimum-cost portfolio is constructed so that the portfolio's cash flow

[7] Beltratti, Consiglio, and Zenios [1998] and Zenios [1995].
[8] See Heuson, Gosnell, and Barrett [1995] and Barber and Cooper [1996].

matches as closely as possible the amount and the times when the liabilities must be paid. A dedicated portfolio strategy therefore is also referred to as a *cash flow matching strategy.*

A popular variation of the immunization and dedicated portfolio strategies is a *combination matching strategy,* also called a *horizon-matching strategy.* Here a portfolio is duration-matched, with the added constraint that it be cash-matched in the first few years, usually five years. The advantages of combination matching over immunization are that the liquidity needs are provided for in the initial cash-flow matched period. Because most of the positive slope or inversion of a yield curve tends to take place in the first few years, cash-flow matching the initial portion minimizes the risk associated with non-parallel shifts of a sloped yield curve.

Bond Indexing

Indexing involves constructing a portfolio to match the performance of a specified index. There are three popular methodologies for designing a bond portfolio to replicate an index: (1) the cell approach, (2) the optimization approach, and (3) the variance minimization approach.[9]

The cell approach divides the index into cells, each representing a different characteristic of the index. The most common characteristics used to distinguish a bond index are (1) duration; (2) coupon; (3) maturity; (4) market sector (Treasury, corporate, mortgage-backed); (5) credit rating; (6) call factors; and (7) sinking fund features. The objective is to select from all the issues in the index one or more issues in each cell that can be used to represent the entire cell. No optimization is involved with this methodology.

The optimization approach requires the portfolio manager to construct a portfolio that will not only match a cell breakdown and satisfy other constraints, but also optimize some objective. An objective could be to maximize the yield to maturity or some other yield measure, to maximize convexity, or to maximize total return.[10] Constraints other than matching the cell breakdown might include not investing more than a specified amount in one issuer or group of issuers and overweighting certain sectors

[9]For a model that uses both optimization and simulation to track an index, see Worzel, Vassiadou-Zeniou, and Zenios [1994].

[10]For a mathematical presentation of this methodology, as well as the variance minimization methodology, see Seix and Akoury [1985].

for enhanced indexing. Depending on the mathematical characterization of the objective function and constraints, either linear or quadratic programming is used to solve for the optimal portfolio.

The variance minimization methodology is by far the most complex. It requires the use of historical data to estimate the tracking error. This is accomplished by statistically estimating a price function for every issue in the index on the basis of two sets of factors: (1) the cash flows from the issue discounted at theoretical spot rates and (2) other characteristics such as those described earlier. Once the price function for each issue is estimated, the tracking error is computed. The objective then is to minimize the tracking error in constructing an indexed portfolio. Quadratic programming is used because the tracking error is a quadratic expression, and the objective is to minimize the tracking error.

Optimized Portfolio Rebalancing

Once the optimal solution or optimal portfolio is found in any application, the optimization process does not end. In most strategies, an initially optimal portfolio must be rebalanced periodically as the characteristics of the portfolio change. For example, in an immunized portfolio, the duration for the individual issues changes over time as the issues approach maturity and as yields in the market change. Therefore, the portfolio's duration will change or wander from its target.

Rebalancing requires the purchase of issues (either new issues not in the original optimal portfolio or additional amounts of issues included in the original portfolio) and the sale of some or all the issues in the original optimal portfolio. An optimization model can be used to minimize the transaction costs associated with rebalancing a portfolio.

Asset Allocation

The objective of an asset allocation model is to divide funds among major asset classes so as either (1) to maximize expected return subject to a certain level of risk or (2) to minimize risk subject to a certain level of expected return. The two are equivalent statements of the asset allocation problem. A third equivalent formulation is to maximize a utility function that subtracts the portfolio risk multiplied by a risk-aversion coefficient from the portfolio expected return. Because there are no clear guidelines as to how to choose the risk-aversion parameter, this formulation is less popular.

The main input in the classical asset allocation problem based on mean–variance is the expected returns of the asset classes, the pairwise covariances, and the constraints the asset manager chooses to impose or is required to impose by the client. The structure of the problem is the same as the equity portfolio selection problem discussed in this chapter. The only difference is in the nature of the variables involved.

If risk is not proxied by variance, then the problem is no longer quadratic. Popular alternative risk measures used in the practice of finance include VaR and CVaR. The mean–CVaR problem is a convex programming problem but is rarely solved by employing a convex solver unless the number of risky assets considered for the portfolio is limited. For large portfolios, the convex problem is computationally very expensive. The most popular method includes combining the mathematical programming problem with the Monte Carlo method. The use of scenarios allows casting the original convex problem as a linear programming problem at the cost of increasing the number of decision variables. Thus, we take advantage of the higher efficiency of linear solvers. In contrast, the mean–VaR problem is generally not convex and cannot be tackled in the same fashion.[11]

Even though robust portfolio construction problems offer a useful framework, they have not been widely adopted as of this writing. However, professionals recognize the importance of the noise in the parameter estimates. One possible way to deal with it is to ignore noisy input. For this reason, global minimum variance (GMV) portfolios have become popular. They are derived from the mean–variance framework by simply ignoring the constraint that involves the expected returns. GMV portfolios are generally characterized by a high concentration in low-volatility stocks, or asset classes in the asset allocation problem. This can be mitigated by imposing certain constraints.

Other variations from the main framework include risk-parity portfolios. The objective in that optimization problem is to find a portfolio such that each portfolio constituent has the same contribution to portfolio risk. Solving this problem efficiently requires specialized methods. Even though the objective appears *ad-hoc*, it is possible to connect risk-parity portfolios to the mean–variance framework.

Finally, and similar to bond indexing, the objective can be to construct an optimal asset allocation in the presence of a benchmark. In this situation,

[11]For additional details, see Rachev, Stoyanov, and Fabozzi [2008].

instead of total portfolio risk, the portfolio manager minimizes portfolio risk relative to the benchmark, which is also known as tracking error. Although the application is different, the structure of the problem is the same as the classical mean–variance problem.[12]

Key Points

- Mathematical programming models concern finding the best solution that optimizes the value of the specified goal provided that the solution satisfies the decision maker's constraints or restrictions.
- To set up a model, the decision variables, objective function which needs to be optimized, and the constraints must all be specified.
- Mathematical programming models are classified into groups depending on the properties of the objective function, the constraints, and the nature of the additional parameters.
- There are specialized algorithms developed for each group of problems.
- Depending on the properties of the objective function, a distinction is made between linear, quadratic, and convex programming problems with the decision variables assumed to be continuous.
- In most typical applications in portfolio construction, the constraints are linear.
- Common constraints in an optimization problem include the budget constraint, the expected performance constraint, single holding constraints, and sector constraints.
- If some of the decision variables can be integer-valued, then this is the case of mixed-integer programming.
- In general, the objective function can be linear, quadratic, or convex.
- If there is uncertainty associated with some of the parameters that enter the optimization problem, then robust optimization models that take the uncertainty into account when calculating the optimal solution can be used.
- Immunization is a structured portfolio strategy designed to protect against interest-rate changes.
- A requirement for single-period immunization is that the duration of the portfolio be equal to the maturity of the liability.

[12] For a discussion of risk budgeting, see Dopfel [2005].

- A dedicated portfolio strategy, or a cash-flow matching strategy, involves construction of a minimum-cost portfolio so that the portfolio's cash flow matches as closely as possible the amount and the times when the future liabilities must be paid.
- Indexing involves constructing a portfolio to match the performance of a specified index.
- The objective of an asset allocation model is to divide funds among major asset classes so as to minimize risk subject to a certain level of expected return and, possibly, other constraints imposed by the portfolio manager.

References

Barber, J. R. and M. L. Cooper, 1996. "Immunization using principal component analysis," *Journal of Portfolio Management,* 23(1): 99–105.

Beltratti, A., A. Consiglio, and S. Zenios, 1999. "Scenario modeling for the management of international bond portfolios," *Annals of Operations Research,* 85: 227–247.

Best, M. J. and R. R. Grauer, 1991. "On the sensitivity of mean-variance-efficient portfolios to changes in asset means: Some analytical and computational results," *Review of Financial Studies* 4(2): 315–342.

Chopra, V. K. and W. T. Ziemba, 1993. "The effect of errors in means, variances, and covariances on optimal portfolio choice," *Journal of Portfolio Management* 19(2): 6–11.

Dopfel, F. W., 2005. "Risk budgeting for fixed income portfolios." In *Advanced Bond Portfolio Management: Practices in Modeling and Strategies,* F. J. Fabozzi, L. Martellini, and P. Priaulet (eds.), Hoboken, NJ: John Wiley & Sons.

Fabozzi, F. J., P. Kolm, D. Pachamanova, and S. Focardi, 2007. *Robust Portfolio Optimization and Management.* Hoboken, NJ: John Wiley & Sons.

Heuson, A. J., T. F. Gosnell, and W. B. Barrett, 1995. "Yield curve shifts and the selection of immunization strategies," *Journal of Fixed Income,* 5(2): 53–64.

Kim, W. C., J. H. Kim, and F. J. Fabozzi, 2016. *Robust Equity Portfolio Management.* Hoboken, NJ: John Wiley & Sons.

Rachev, S., S. V. Stoyanov, and F. J. Fabozzi, 2008. *Advanced Stochastic Models, Risk Assessment and Portfolio Optimization.* Hoboken, NJ: John Wiley & Sons.

Seix, C. and R. Akoury, 1986. "Bond indexation: The optimal quantitative approach," *Journal of Portfolio Management,* 12(3): 50–53.

Worzel, K. J., C. Vassiadou-Zeniou, and S. A. Zenios, 1994. "Integrated simulation and optimization models for tracking fixed-income indices," *Operations Research,* 42: 223–233.

Zenios, S. A., 1995. "Asset/liability management under uncertainty for fixed-income securities," *Annals of Operations Research*, 59: 77–97.

Zenios, S. A. and P. Kang, 1993. "Mean-absolute deviation and portfolio optimization for mortgage-backed securities," *Annals of Operations Research*, 45: 433–450.

Chapter 7

Machine Learning and its Applications to Asset Management

Learning Objectives

After reading this chapter, you will understand:

- what machine learning (ML) is;
- why financial problems require very distinct ML solutions;
- terminology used in financial econometrics and ML;
- the advantages of ML compared to financial econometrics;
- the different types of data structures;
- the various applications of ML to asset management;
- how to develop ML strategies; and
- how to set up an ML investment team.

Introduction

In Chapter 4, we described financial econometric models that have been applied to various activities in the asset management process. For many decades, asset managers have relied on these statistical techniques to identify patterns in data. Machine learning (ML), the subject of this chapter, promises to change that by allowing researchers to use modern nonlinear and highly dimensional techniques, similar to those used in scientific fields like DNA analysis and astrophysics. At the same time, applying those ML algorithms to model financial problems and formulate ML strategies is non-trivial, and their misuse often leads to disappointing results. Financial problems require very distinct ML solutions. In this chapter we describe

ML, provide a brief overview of ML tools, and describe the various applications to asset management. We conclude the chapter by describing how to develop ML strategies.[1]

Asset managers seek to build predictive models regarding information that can be used in identifying attractive investment opportunities. This is done by being able to analyze data, both structured and unstructured, to discover complex patterns. The discipline of data science provides the analytical tools for extracting insights from a wide range of datasets. Data science is a combination of many disciplines, or probably better said a discipline that integrates the tools of many disciplines. These disciplines include applied statistics, probability modeling, artificial intelligence (AI), big data analytics, computer science, and signal processing.

The data used by asset managers are of two types: structured and unstructured. From these data types, asset managers seek to obtain insights for formulating investment strategies. Advanced analytical techniques have been developed in the fields of statistics and computer science that allow asset managers to leverage the use of the power of computers to aid them in obtaining investment insights from large distinct datasets. The discipline of AI provides the tools that allow computers to perform the tasks performed by human experts in a particular field. Within the discipline of AI is the field of *ML*.

ML is the discipline that studies how algorithms learn automatically from experience. ML can accomplish tasks that until recently only expert humans could perform. As it relates to finance, this is the most exciting time to adopt a disruptive technology that will transform how everyone invests for generations. In fact, some market observers believe that in terms of the quantitative revolution, ML is the second wave in that revolution, mean–variance optimization being the first wave. An approach that integrates the fundamental philosophy of asset management with quantitative techniques, ML will move asset management firms closer to the quantamental approach (i.e., combining quantitative and fundamental analysis). As noted by López de Prado [2018, p. 53], many former discretionary hedge funds are embracing this quantamental approach with the help of ML.

ML is a universal modeling framework that does not depend on any domain-specific theory. Therefore, when applied to the activities in the asset management process, the ML models do not use finance theory but

[1]For a further discussion of how machine learning can help asset managers discover economic and financial theories, see López de Prado [2020].

rely on purely statistical analysis of financial phenomena. ML methods place constraints on model complexity to ensure that they retain some forecasting capability out-of-sample.

In this chapter, we provide a non-technical description of ML methods as it applies to various activities in the investment management process. ML is far more complex than we describe in this chapter. Too often asset management firms fail to grasp the complexity of ML applications to various investing tasks. This seems to be particularly true for asset management firms moving into the quantamental space. In the 1990s, ML applications to financial modeling generated a lot of exaggerated claims and hype, receiving substantial attention by asset management firms, their clients, and the media. In most cases, those expectations were not met. However, this was not because ML failed, but because those firms used ML incorrectly for reasons described at the end of this chapter, where we outline how an ML group within an asset management firm that is seeking to generate strategies should be structured.

What is Machine Learning?

The objective of ML is to find patterns in data without providing a particular specification. This is accomplished by the development of a sequence of actions that optimizes automatically by means of experience.[2] That is, the sequence of actions makes it possible for the computer to improve performance with respect to solving the problem at hand as experience increases. The actions will involve either no human intervention during the learning process or limited human intervention.

The sequence of actions that is to be performed typically by the computer (i.e., machine) to solve the problem at hand is provided by a set of steps that the computer must follow. The steps or rules are referred to as *algorithms*. The ML algorithm searches for patterns in inputs, which are variables and datasets. Sometimes it also uses *outputs*, which are the results associated with the inputs. In that case, learning by the machine involves developing a *rule* that links the inputs and the output. That rule can be in the form of an equation that can be used in making predictions about some variable or it could be finding the structure of the data to identify

[2]A pioneer in AI research, Arthur Samuel, coined the term machine learning in 1959 and defined it as the "field of study that gives computers the ability to learn without being explicitly programmed ..." [Samuel, 1959].

patterns. In generating the rule, only a certain portion of the data from the dataset is used. The portion of the data used to generate the rule is called the *training data.* This rule is then tested using the portion of the data that was not used in developing the rule (i.e., the training data) which is referred to as the *testing data.* The purpose of testing the rule is to assess the performance of the rule on unseen data using various statistical measures for that purpose.

ML is particularly useful for analyzing large and complex data, where there is little chance that the researcher may be able to provide a specification. Because ML is able to learn the specification from the data, ML is particularly suitable for analyzing the phenomena involved in complex systems, such as modern economies and financial markets. In contrast, traditional statistical tools are not able to learn the specification from the data, leading to misspecified models and false discoveries.

A common criticism with regards to the use of ML for the development of investment strategies is that they are "black-box strategies". In fact, that is not the case. ML algorithms include tools that evaluate the importance of various inputs *regardless of the functional form that binds them.* It is hard to overestimate the importance of this property of ML: whereas traditional statistical models are easily misspecified, leading to the acceptance of useless inputs and/or the rejection of useful ones, ML can point the researcher in the direction of useful variables *before* a theory is formulated. This is the reason ML is used in all modern scientific fields.

How Financial ML Differs from Financial Econometrics

Financial econometrics, the subject of Chapter 4, is the application of classical statistical methods to financial datasets. The essential tool of econometrics is multivariate linear regression. The key mathematical operation in multivariate linear regression is inverting the covariance matrix to estimate the parameters for a forecasting model. In contrast to financial ML, standard financial econometric models do not learn. It is unrealistic to expect that something as complex as 21st-century finance could be grasped by something as simple as inverting a covariance matrix.

Theories in finance are based on observation and therefore employ empirical methods as the foundation for the theory. If the statistical toolbox used to model these observations is the multivariate linear regression, asset managers will fail to recognize the complexity of the data, resulting in theories that are awfully simplistic and thereby useless. Some market observers (for example, Calkin and López de Prado [2014a, 2014b]), believe that financial econometrics is the primary reason financial economics has not experienced meaningful progress over the past 70 years.

Financial ML methods do not replace theory but rather guide it. An ML algorithm finds complex learning patterns in a high-dimensional space without being specifically directed. Once members of an asset management team identify the features that are predictive of a phenomenon, they can build a theoretical explanation, which can then be tested on an independent dataset.

Factors Influencing the Use of AI and ML

The idea that there was a mathematical possibility that machines can be taught to learn how to solve problems and make decisions (i.e., that an intelligent machine can be built) was suggested by the British mathematician Alan Turing. His framework for building an intelligent machine is explained in his 1950 seminal paper entitled "Computing Machinery and Intelligence".[3] Although the philosophical framework was provided by Turing, the roots of the field of AI have been credited to the Dartmouth Summer Research Project on Artificial Intelligence held on the campus of Dartmouth College in 1956.

The potential use of AI and ML in asset management is by no means a recent revelation. For example, a book by Robert Trippi and Efraim Turban titled *Neural Networks in Finance and Investing* with the subtitle *Using Artificial Intelligence to Improve Real-World Performance* was published in 1992. The book contained numerous examples of how neural networks could be used in the analysis of financial conditions, business failure prediction, debt risk assessment, and financial forecasting. Moreover, the authors explained how neural networks could be used in forecasting stock prices. Four years later, the book was updated with a new coauthor, Jae Lee, with the new title *Artificial Intelligence in Finance & Investing: State-of-the-Art Technologies for Securities Selection and Portfolio Management* and included a chapter on ML.[4] That is 26 years from the publication of the

[3]Turing [1950]. The title of the second movie about Turing is the title of the opening section of his paper.

[4]There were two endorsements on the back cover of the 1996 book. The first was by one of the coauthors of this chapter, stating: "A landmark book. The first book to comprehensively and clearly address the role of AI in modern portfolio management."

first edition of the Trippi book to today. Yet, despite the advancements in AI and ML, it has only been recently that asset management firms have begun investing in this technology.

One reason why it took so long for asset managers to embrace ML is that until very recently the datasets were relatively small and the computing power scarce. As datasets have become larger and more complex, and computers have acquired the power to model them, asset managers have come to realize that traditional tools are inadequate. In particular, some of the most interesting datasets are unstructured and non-numeric, thus not amenable to econometric methods.

Machine Learning Terminology

All fields develop their own terminology, and ML is no exception. It is helpful to compare its terminology to that used in classical statistics. Here we will do so, explaining how the terms commonly used in classical statistics are often used interchangeably with those in ML.

In statistics, a "hypothesis" is a statement that can be supported or refuted by statistical testing using data or experimentation. Statistical testing requires the use of "observations" or "data points". In ML, the terms used are "examples" and "instances". The collection of the observations or data points is referred to in statistics as the "sample". In *hypothesis testing*, a sample is used in the statistical analysis. There are two types of samples used in statistical testing of predictive or classification models: *in-sample* and *out-of-sample*. The former is used to estimate the parameters of the model, while the latter is used to test the model on observations that were not used to estimate the model. In ML, the in-sample is the part of the sample that is used to train the algorithm and is called the *training sample*, *training data*, *training example*, and *training instance*. The out-of-sample portion of the sample in ML is called the *test sample* or *test set*.

The most common statistical tool is the multivariate linear regression or simply regression. In a later section, we discuss the different types of ML algorithms and explain what supervised ML is. There are two types of *supervised learning algorithms*: *regression* and *classification*.

The second was by the Nobel Laureate in Economics, Harry Markowitz, who wrote: "The book describes innovations which may become standard investment procedures of the twenty-first century."

In the field of statistics we refer to the following in using a regression: independent or explanatory variable or predictor, dependent variable, model, and fit or estimate a model. The independent variable or explanatory variable or predictor is a variable that it is hypothesized can explain the dependent variable (typically an independent variable is denoted by x and the dependent variable by y). There is only one dependent variable but there are one or more independent variables. In ML, an independent variable is referred to as the *attribute* or *input feature* or *feature*, while the dependent variable is referred to as the *response* or *output* or *target*. When estimating or fitting a model in ML, it is referred to as *learning a model*.

Another statistical tool commonly used in asset management is principal components analysis (PCA), which we describe in Chapter 4. Basically, PCA transforms a set of correlated variables into a set of uncorrelated variables, such that each uncorrelated variable is a linear combination of the correlated ones, and each uncorrelated variable maximizes the explained variance. It has been used in generating latent factors that can be used in factor-based investing strategies, both for equity and bond portfolio management. In ML, this is a type of algorithm called *unsupervised learning*, which we describe later.

Review of Data Types

Data are generated in a variety of ways: from market transactions, from businesses via the many reports that they are required to file with government entities, from individuals from their tweets and posted blogs, and from sensors which show satellite images, etc. Here we just recall two types of data: structured versus unstructured data, and labeled versus unlabeled data.

Structured versus Unstructured Data

In general, *structured data* refers to information that is characterized by a high degree of organization and is objectively represented (i.e., its representation is not subject to interpretation). The information generally consists of numerical values. Tabulated series of stock return data, fundamental company data, and bond attributes (coupon, maturity, price, and par value) are examples of structured data.

Because it is easily organized, structured data can be stored in a local database or spreadsheet, allowing for the user to easily conduct searches.

Structured Query Language (SQL), a programming language created for managing and searching data, is typically used for structured data.

Unstructured data has fundamentally opposite attributes to those of structured data. It does not have a structure that is recognizable and therefore this information is difficult to categorize. Although it includes textual and non-textual items, it is typically text heavy. Examples include computer satellite images of parking centers, news stories, sell-side analysts' reports, tweets, and social media posts.

There is a category that falls between structured and unstructured data: *semi-structured data*. The information fails to have a strict data model structure to be treated as structured data. Certain data within the semi-structured data will have a label but parts of the data will be unstructured. An example is emails. It is similar to structured data because it will have the name of the sender, the name of the recipient, and the time the email was sent. However, what makes it unstructured is the content of the email. Moreover, if there is an attachment, that is unstructured data, too.

Labeled versus Unlabeled Data

To understand the difference between *labeled data* and *unlabeled data*, let's first give examples of the latter. Examples of unlabeled data that relate to finance would be audio recordings of webcasts by security analysts or company representatives, printed articles about a company by the media or by sell-side security analysts, tweets, and SEC filings by a public company.

For a database with unlabeled data, some of that data can be enhanced by an expert assigning a meaningful or informative label to it. The task of labeling data that are unlabeled is sometimes referred to as *classifying* or *tagging the data*. For example, consider the use of tweets from social-media platforms such as StockTwits and Twitter for measuring tweets that are used for quantifying sentiment on a real-time basis. The objective is to provide a label representative of the overall sentiment of the tweet.

Labeling data is a critical task for supervised learning algorithms described in the next section. Labeling can be done manually by humans, or automatically by another ML algorithm that has been trained to perform that task. This is not a superfluous task, as any mistake or inaccuracy in labeling adversely impacts the informativeness of the data. As a result, this will adversely impact the performance of the output of an ML algorithm. The importance of the labeling task also shows why it is not possible to remove human judgment from the ML process. Experts are required to process unstructured data for the algorithm to work effectively.

Here are two examples involving sentiment analysis about a company. If there are predefined targets sought for the values in an ML algorithm, these values cannot be targeted if an expert has not mapped them. First, consider data in the form of recommendations of sell-side analysts who are following a specific stock and cast their views in a company report. The sell-side analyst might recommend to buy, sell, or hold the stock. The labeling of a specific analyst's report would then be one of the three recommendations. A labeler must be able to provide the label. Second, consider data obtained from social media about a stock. For such data, labels would indicate neutral, negative, or positive sentiment.

There are other approaches to labeling unstructured data. The task can be outsourced to a company with domain-specific knowledge. One advantage is the speed at which the labeling process can be completed. The cost may or may not be greater than if done internally. The outsourcing firm has an interest to do the best job possible in order to potentially be awarded further labeling engagements, as well as to protect/enhance its reputation in the industry. However, the major risk is that the labeler may perform its task without perfect knowledge of how these labels will be used. The compensation of the ML team will suffer if the performance of an ML strategy is poor as a result of the disconnect between the labeling task and the modeling task. Rather than risk that the labeling task provided by external consultants produced inaccurate labeling resulting in poor performance, the ML team may want to take on the labeling task.

In general, the cost of unlabeled data is low relative to labeled data. Labeled data can be costly, due to the use of experts.

Concepts of Learning and Learning Styles

When thinking about the term "learning" in ML, consider the process a child might go through in learning to ride a bike. The child may fall many times before learning how to properly ride a bike, but the child learns from failures until he is able to perform with higher proficiency. Likewise, a machine will go through many attempts before finding the optimal solution to a problem. The machine will continue to learn through trial-and-error with the goal of finding the best model for a certain problem.

Just as psychologists distinguish between different types of learning processes that occur in the human mind, data scientists also distinguish between different computer learning processes. There are three main categories of ML: unsupervised learning, supervised learning, and reinforcement learning.

Each learning style will differ based on the information provided to the machine during the training period. For example, a supervised learning algorithm will have correct "labels" associated with each training example. A *label* is the observed output from a given training example. Essentially, this means that the computer will have the correct answers based on past observations and use that information to make an inference based on a new (unseen) set of inputs. Conversely, *unlabeled* training sets will not have the correct output for a given set of training examples. When a training set is unlabeled, the goal of the computer will be to identify structures in the data, such as observations that share similar characteristics. Reinforcement learning occurs when an algorithm derives a rule of behavior that maximizes a notion of cumulative reward. For now, it is important to understand that the difference between learning styles depends on the feedback given to the computer during the training phase. As a result, each learning style will produce different answers to different types of questions and will be used for different applications in financial decision-making.

Supervised Learning Algorithms

In ML, supervised algorithms allow the computer to learn from training data that already contain the correct label for each input. In supervised learning, the computer will identify patterns that link the input variables to the response variable (i.e., explanatory variable). For example, an ML algorithm can be trained to identify whether a patient has a certain disease based on certain features or input variables that indicate the presence of a disease. This is considered to be supervised learning because the dataset will include the input variables as well as the correct labels, corresponding to whether the patient has the disease or not (as diagnosed by an expert). Because the computer has the correct answers to the question at hand (i.e., diseased or not diseased) the computer can search for patterns in the features space that discerns diseased patients from non-diseased patients.

There are two types of supervised learning: regression ML and classification ML algorithms. A regression algorithm is used to predict a numerical value as the output. This means that the response variable is continuous.

A simple example of a regression algorithm is an asset manager trying to predict the price of a stock in the following year. Because the asset manager is attempting to identify the price (i.e., a numerical value), the asset manager must use a regression algorithm.

The second type of supervised learning is a classification algorithm. The goal of a supervised classification algorithm is to produce discrete variable outputs. This means that the algorithm will take the input variables, identify the correct group or label associated with the training example, and develop a set of rules to determine which group a training example should belong to. This means that the "labels" for each training example will correspond to a category or group so that the algorithm can learn to identify patterns that allow the machine to categorize features that distinguish between groups or labels. An example of a supervised classification algorithm is an algorithm that will determine whether a corporate bond will be upgraded, downgraded, or remain the same. In this case, there are three responses that the algorithm will produce. It is not trying to determine a numerical value associated with the input values, but rather identify which of the three categories an example is most likely to fall into.

The approach that places the learning process in the context of generalization and forecasting is *statistical learning.* Given an efficient process of learning, statistical learning deals with how one can make sure that the learning process has good generalization and forecasting abilities. Statistical learning attempts to answer this question in a probabilistic framework. Classical learning theory places limits on the model complexity in order to improve the forecasting capabilities of learned models. It does so by adding a penalty function that constrains model complexity, as measured in terms of the number of variables included in the model. Vapnik [1995, 1998] introduced an important conceptual novelty by showing that not only does the complexity of the model matter but so also does the type of functions used. He was able to construct a mathematical framework to predict how well a given set of approximating functions would generalize.

Unsupervised Learning

Unsupervised learning is more difficult to define and understand than supervised learning. With unsupervised learning algorithms, there are no labels provided for the inputs. The objective of the algorithm is to determine the structure of the data based on statistical properties. Clustering is the typical discrete example of unsupervised learning, and PCA is a typical continuous example. One starts with a set of training data that is unlabeled and discovers groupings of data that have similar statistical characteristics.

For example, consider the problem of marking-to-market securities that are illiquid and difficult to price. An unsupervised ML algorithm can be developed to identify securities that have characteristics similar to that of illiquid security where a price is sought. If an unsupervised learning algorithm can identify an appropriate cluster for the illiquid security, the characteristics of the cluster can be used to mark-to-market the illiquid security and potentially other illiquid securities in the portfolio that are illiquid and difficult to price.

In principle, the method of unsupervised learning applies to all available data. One can apply unsupervised learning to a sample and then generalize to the entire population. For example, a financial application performs clustering of price time series on sample data and then applies the same clustering to new data. Unsupervised learning is often used for exploratory analysis to identify hidden patterns, particularly when there is a lack of labeled training data.

Semi-supervised Learning Algorithms

In semi-supervised learning algorithms, some of the training data include both labeled and unlabeled data. The goal of semi-supervised learning is to evaluate how combining unlabeled and labeled data may alter the learning behavior, and then create algorithms that benefit from using both data types. The appeal of semi-supervised learning is that it can utilize unlabeled data to improve supervised learning algorithms when there is limited labeled data or when it is too costly to obtain additional labeled data.

Another potential advantage of semi-supervised learning algorithms is that they can start with labeled and unlabeled data but eventually predict labels for new unlabeled data.

Deep Learning Algorithms

From the point of view of financial modeling, a deep learning algorithm is a universal function approximator. This means that it is a system that, given a set of inputs, provides an accurate estimate of the variable to be predicted. The primary way for implementing deep learning algorithms is via *artificial neural networks* (ANNs), where there is a large number of inner layers. This model architecture can be utilized for solving supervised, unsupervised, and semi-supervised problems.

Deep learning algorithms have been studied from the general point of view of connectionist structures able to imitate some of the functions of the brain. It is useful to separate the two areas. As we stated earlier, AI has been surrounded by a lot of hype. The hype created, in turn, a lot of disappointment, because results were inferior to expectations. Much of the hype resulted from the fact that it was often assumed that AI was about building artificial brains with human-like cognitive capabilities. In particular, although the properties of deep learning algorithms as nonlinear function approximators are well established, the possibilities that large neural networks exhibit cognitive ability similar to a human brain is far from being demonstrated.

Basically, deep learning algorithms can be used either in a supervised or an unsupervised mode. In a supervised mode, a deep learning algorithm is used to learn a function from samples — for example, the data generating process (DGP) of a series from its past realizations.

A deep learning algorithm is formed by *nodes* and *connections*. Nodes are placed in multiple layers. The number of layers and the number of nodes in each layer are defined by the user. Nodes in one layer are connected only to nodes in the layers immediately below or above. A node receives inputs from the nodes in previous layers. Inputs are weighted, in the sense that each connection has an associated weight. The output of each node depends on the sum of the weighted inputs. If the sum of the inputs is below a given threshold, the output is zero; if it is above the threshold, the output is a given fixed value. When the network is in operation, inputs are applied to the lowest layer and propagate to the highest layer. Typically, the inputs represent one or more binary numbers and the output represents one binary number. But many configurations are possible.

The parameters to be learned are the weights. During the training phase — that is, during the learning process — both the inputs and the outputs are known. The objective is to determine the weights. Therefore, designing a deep learning network is a question of intuition, trial and error, and testing.

Once the number of nodes and their connections have been fixed — referred to as the *network's topology* — the weights can be estimated by using either an optimizer or a specific learning procedure, such as backpropagation. An optimizer is a computer program that finds the maximum or minimum of a function. It considers all input–output sample data at the same time. First, one computes the errors as a function of the weights. The optimizer finds those weights that minimize errors. This process is similar to least-squares estimation in regression analysis. In backpropagation, input data are sequentially fed to the network and weights are updated as a function of output data. Backpropagation is an adaptive process: One starts with an initial guess of the weights, and the guess is progressively modified as a function of new data.

Deep learning algorithms can also be used in an unsupervised mode. A typical such application is *vector quantization* — a process that tries to find prototypes of a set of items. Suppose, for example, that one is given a set of companies defined by their financial ratios. The objective is to create a set of prototype companies so that each company is associated with a prototype.

Reinforcement Learning Algorithms

A fundamental principle of learning theory is that learning is interactive. The focus of reinforcement learning algorithms is more on learning that is goal directed from interaction with some entity such as a human than the other algorithms described above. The input to a reinforcement learning algorithm is an unlabeled dataset. From this dataset, the algorithm provides an action for each data point. At this point in the process, feedback is received from some entity such as a human and this feedback helps the computer to learn. The algorithm's objective is to maximize the cumulative reward.

Problem Solving, ML, and Optimization

In 1960, Herbert Simon forcefully argued that human decision-making processes can be automated through computational processes. At the time, it was difficult to believe the idea that a computer, which operates based on preprogrammed instructions, can exhibit creative power. The link between algorithmic processes — that is, the step-by-step processes of computers — and creative problem solving is the concept of *searching*.

Automatic problem solving is based on the concept that human decision-making and problem solving are ultimately the guided exploration of a set of predetermined possibilities. Automatic problem solving works by searching a "space", or "ensemble", of opportunities and choosing according to some criterion.

Problem solving entails (1) the ability to describe the set of various possibilities, (2) a quantitative way to rate various solutions, and (3) a search and optimization strategy. Ultimately, therefore, problem solving is an application of optimization.

The methodologies used in problem-solving have also been tackled from a different perspective. In exploring a vast set of opportunities, the temptation is to use probabilistic methods.

Role of Humans in ML

Does the adoption of ML by asset management firms mean that there is no space left for human investors? No human is better at chess than a computer. And no computer is better at chess than a human supported by a computer. When betting against an ML algorithm, discretionary portfolio managers are at a disadvantage. However, it is possible that the best results are achieved by arming discretionary portfolio managers with ML algorithms. This is what has come to be known as the "quantamental" way.

While we do not describe the wide-range of ML algorithms in this chapter, what is important to understand is that there are such algorithms that combine human guesses (inspired by fundamental variables) with mathematical forecasts that can be used by quantamental teams. For example, a technique called *meta-labeling* which allows a portfolio manager to add an ML layer on top of a discretionary one.

Although humans will not be cut-out of the investment process, there is likely to be certain tasks performed by humans that will be cut dramatically. For example, in the view of Kolanovic and Krishnamachari [2017], high-frequency trading is an area where the role of humans has declined dramatically because computers can quickly analyze and process earnings statements, tweets, and news feeds. Another example is in labeling. As explained earlier in this chapter, experts will be needed to label data.

The extreme view that the role of humans will be eliminated in investment decision-making is based on the biases humans have in making decisions. That suggests there are no biases in algorithms or basically that algorithms are neutral. That is not the case and, in fact, can be worse. The bias, referred to as *algorithmic bias*, is due to the way ML algorithms work, particularly deep learning algorithms. The performance of deep learning algorithms improves with more labeled data. However, if the additional data continue to underrepresent a category (i.e., is not sufficiently diversified) during the learning process, it can cause a serious bias.

An AI expert at ABN AMRO, Julia Krauwer, notes that

> Models can't look beyond the data they have been trained on, so whenever the training data is skewed or too narrow (and this is often the case), the model output will be biased too ... One should be aware that a model, however intelligent the output may seem, is a mere representation of reality. A model can help users grasp certain elements of reality (a prediction, a categorization) but doesn't necessarily show the complete picture. That is why a human in the loop is essential: we are, unlike machines, able to take into account context and use general knowledge to put AI-drawn conclusions into perspective. [Finextra, 2017, p. 23].

This view that the role of humans will not be eliminated has been expressed by Brian Cho, the head of quantitative research at Chiron Investment Management. This asset management firm has both quantitative and fundamental research teams using the investment approach that is referred to as quantamental. According to Cho, when discussing AI and data, what is often missing is the role of human judgment and in his view human intervention is needed. Gaurav Mallik, the chief portfolio strategist at State Street Global Advisors (the third largest asset management firm), agrees with this view. He argues that to obtain a "well-sounded" investment hypothesis, a combination of data tools and human talent is needed.

Applications

Financial ML offers asset managers the opportunity to gain the following insight from data:

- Modeling nonlinear relationships in a high-dimensional space;
- Analyzing unstructured data;
- Learning complex patterns;
- Focusing on predictability over variance adjudication;
- Controlling for overfitting.

At the same time, finance is not a plug-and-play subject as it relates to ML. Modeling financial data is more challenging than driving cars or recognizing faces. An ML algorithm will always find a pattern, even if there is none!

In this section, we review the following nine important financial ML applications:

- Price/rate/volatility prediction;
- Portfolio construction/risk analysis;
- Structural breaks/anomaly detection;
- Bet sizing;
- Feature importance;
- Controlling for effects;
- Credit ratings/analyst recommendations;
- Sentiment analysis/recommender systems;
- Detection of false investment strategies.

Price/Rate/Volatility Prediction

A common use of ML techniques is to predict values such as price, interest rates, or volatility. Financial econometric models have been the traditional techniques for doing so. Mullainathan and Spiess [2017] discuss some of the differences between ML and econometric approaches. The goal of supervised ML is to produce good predictions of y on out-of-sample data. In contrast, the goal of econometric models is to obtain the best linear unbiased estimate of the parameters for the purpose of variance adjudication in-sample.

Unfortunately, prediction and unbiasedness are not necessarily consistent goals. The best linear unbiased estimates for the parameters of a regression model used for prediction will not necessary minimize the squared errors on out-of-sample data. For example, although the ordinary least squares (OLS) method has minimum variance among all unbiased estimates, there are estimators that achieve lower mean-squared errors by accepting a small bias in exchange for lower variance. Linear examples of such estimators are Ridge, LASSO or elastics nets, and a non-linear example is the James-Stein estimator.

Financial econometric models adjudicate the variance of the explained variable to specific explanatory variables in-sample. The model is designed to decompose a combined effect as a sum of individual effects. Although this is helpful for analyses when assuming all other things remain equal, when the goal is prediction out-of-sample rather than adjudication in-sample, ML is a more appropriate tool. This is particularly true in the presence of multicollinear explanatory variables or missing explanatory variables.

Mullainathan and Spiess [2017] provide an illustration of why it is necessary to look beyond OLS and to ML for economic and financial analyses. Their illustration involves the prediction of house prices. These authors used 10,000 randomly selected owner-occupied units from the 2011 metropolitan sample of the American Housing Survey. The dependent variable was the value of each home. They used 150 explanatory variables. To compare different prediction techniques, using a test set (hold-out set) of 41,808 units, Mullainathan and Spiess evaluated how well each approach predicted home prices. The prediction methods tested were OLS and four ML methods.[5] The illustration produced two principal insights. The first insight highlights the need for a hold-out sample to assess performance. Specifically, they find that in-sample performance does not generalize well out-of-sample. They find this to be especially true for certain ML algorithms that are known to have a strong tendency to overfit, a problem that we discuss later in this chapter. The second insight is about out-of-sample performance. They find that ML algorithms can significantly outperform OLS. Moreover, this outperformance occurs even at moderate sample sizes and with a limited number of covariates.

Portfolio Construction/Risk Analysis

ML is particularly useful in portfolio optimization. The current landscape of portfolio construction and optimization is dominated by mean–variance optimization methods. This is a paradigm that dates back to the 1950s and 1960s based on the work of Harry Markowitz. Unfortunately, mean–variance portfolios are optimal in-sample, but tend to perform poorly out-of-sample.

The problem with implementing this type of optimization is that the asset management team must produce a complete picture of how each security relates to another. To do this, one must compute a covariance matrix that relates each security to all of the other securities in the portfolio. Thus if the portfolio manager seeks to construct a portfolio of size n, the asset management team must compute a covariance matrix of size $n \times n$. This requires computing $[n\times\ (n+1)]/2$ covariances independently, which will not be very robust in practice. For example, a portfolio manager who wants to create a 50 stock portfolio will require that members of the asset

[5]The four ML methods were (1) least absolute shrinkage and selection operator (LASSO), (2) regression tree tuned by depth, (3) random forest, and (4) ensemble.

management team produce a 50 by 50 covariance matrix based on daily observations. This covariance matrix will have 1,275 elements, of which 50 are variance estimates, and the balance are covariance estimates. Unless the portfolio manager has access to five years worth of daily returns, covering a period of stable covariances, the covariance matrix is guaranteed to be numerically ill-conditioned. When applying these covariances to solve convex optimization models as described in Chapter 6, the computation involved will typically magnify estimation errors.

A better way of solving the portfolio optimization problem is through the use of ML. To do so requires the calculation of a *minimum spanning tree* (MST), an ML technique. Without getting technical, MST is basically used to identify the securities that exhibit a relationship with all of the other securities without having to explicitly calculate the correlations between each of the variables. For example, once again assume that a portfolio manager wants to construct a portfolio with 50 securities. An MST will identify 49 relationships that implicitly capture the structure of the entire system. By using this ML technique, the MST will summarize the structure of the data and allow the portfolio manager to identify hierarchical relationships between the securities. This will result in a much more robust estimation of the relationships between variables. Furthermore, this technique only requires estimating $n-1$ relationships as opposed to calculating $[n\times\ (n{+}1)]/2$ independent covariances. This requires much less data for obtaining a more robust and reliable characterization of the market.

López de Prado [2016] introduced the technique just described for constructing portfolios. He referred to this technique for portfolio construction that uses ML and the mathematics in the field of graph theory as Hierarchical Risk Parity allocation. Based on Monte Carlo experiments, he finds that this technique outperformed the mean–variance approach out-of-sample. In particular, experiments show that the Sharpe ratio improved out-of-sample by 31% when using the new technique compared to mean–variance optimization.

Identification of Structural Breaks

The third beneficial application of financial ML is for identifying structural breaks in time series, or outliers in cross-sectional data. Some asset managers are skeptical about the benefits of using quantitative methods for investment decision-making because the models are "fit to fail". This is because quantitative models use historical observations to learn past market behavior in order to predict something in the future which is not likely to happen again. While there is some validity to this statement, this concern is often exaggerated in the context of ML. All models, even the models developed in our brains, are based on historical observations which allow us to make predictions about future events. ML is not necessarily at a disadvantage for this argument alone.

ML algorithms are particularly skillful at identifying structural breaks or bubble-like behavior. While these algorithms may not be better than humans at understanding future market behavior, they are capable of identifying when an observation is drawn from a distribution that is very different from the distributions that have been observed in the past. What this means is that ML algorithms can identify when an observation arises that is not relatable to the set of previous observations used to train the algorithm. This is an extremely useful application of ML because humans often fail to determine when there is a transition from one market behavior to another.

One technique that is used in ML to identify structural breaks is a test procedure called supremum augmented Dickey–Fuller test (SADF). Basically, SADF is a double-nested ADF test that determines whether a security or an asset is exhibiting an exponential growth or exponential decay in prices. This determines whether there is bubble-like behavior associated with the time-series of returns. SADF is particularly helpful at recognizing multiple bubble-burst actions within the same time series, even though the series as a whole may appear to be stationary. ML algorithms will use these sorts of statistics as features to identify the preconditions for the appearance of a bubble or whether a bubble is likely to burst. This is not to say that ML will determine when a bubble will burst, but rather, the algorithms seek to predict whether a bubble currently exists within the time-series. When these types of structural breaks are identified, portfolio managers would not want to implement mean–reverting pricing algorithms, or hold excessive risk in either direction.

Bet Sizing

A portfolio manager making a decision about a security must decide two things. First, the portfolio manager must decide the position or side to take. The position or side of the security means whether it should be long or short the security. This is referred to as the "side bet". Second, the portfolio manager must decide the amount or size to commit to the position. This is referred to as the "size bet". A bet size of zero means no bet at all. A portfolio manager can use an ML algorithm to recommend the size of a bet, where the side is determined by another algorithm. Splitting the size and side decisions can lead to better performance than modeling both together. To understand how, two concepts must be explained: *recall* and *precision*.

To understand precision and recall, picture an algorithm that is being used to determine securities that will appreciate (i.e., securities that the portfolio manager should buy). In this context, recall is the ratio of the number of securities that the model says are going to appreciate that actually did appreciate over the total number of securities that appreciated during the time period. For example, if there are 50 securities that appreciated and the model only identified 30 of them, the recall is then 30/50 or 0.6. Precision is the proportion of securities that appreciated relative to the number of securities that the model predicted would appreciate. Thus, it is the ratio of the number of correctly identified buy recommendations over the total number of predicted buy recommendations. If the model predicts that 40 securities will appreciate and only 20 of them actually do, then the precision of the model is 20/40 or 0.5. Therefore, recall can be thought of as the ability of the model to avoid false negatives, and precision as the model's ability to avoid false positives.

Let's return to the recommendation with respect to the side and the size of the bet. The ideal algorithm is one that has both high recall and high precision. Although a single ML algorithm can be used to make both a side recommendation and size recommendation, it will usually suffer from high recall and low precision or high precision and low recall.

Because it is difficult to develop a single ML algorithm with high recall and high precision, a portfolio manager should separate the decision-making process using two distinct ML algorithms: one that determines the side of the bet and the other that determines the size of the bet. Intuitively, the first ML algorithm should have high recall because the portfolio manager wants to be able to identify a large number of possible trade opportunities. Conversely, the second ML algorithm should have high precision because the manager will want to ensure that the recommendation of the first model is actually accurate. In practice, someone on the asset management team will develop the first ML algorithm with low precision and high recall and then supersede a second ML algorithm that is going to trade off some recall in exchange for higher precision. The overall objective is to maximize the harmonic average of precision and recall. The advantage of this is that the second ML algorithm is not making the decision of whether or not the portfolio manager should buy or sell a security, but it's making a decision about the size of the bet, not the side of the bet. The side of the bet is still determined by the primary ML algorithm.

In practice, however, the side decision does not need to involve an algorithm. It could come from a fundamental investor or a discretionary portfolio manager, where the second ML algorithm can determine the size of that discretionary investment. So the function of the second ML algorithm is to determine whether the portfolio manager should go or not for this bet. Here we see an example of using human intervention as part of an ML technique and, as we noted earlier in this chapter, how with the application of ML techniques, asset management teams can move closer to the quantamental approach.

Feature Importance

Supervised learning algorithms identify patterns in a high-dimensional space. These patterns associate features with outcomes. Although the nature of the relationship can be extremely complex, one can always study what features are more important regardless of the model's specification. Consequently, an application of ML that goes beyond forecasting is referred to as *feature importance*. The purpose of feature importance is to identify the relevant variables that appear to hold information needed to make accurate predictions.

Suppose that Sir Isaac Newton had had the ability to use computers during his investigation of the laws of gravity and the gravitational force equation (he certainly was well equipped to handle calculus!). With the help of feature importance analysis, Newton would have been able to distinguish the relevant variables to be used in the gravitational force equation from the variables that are not relevant for understanding gravitational force. With the knowledge that mass and distance are the two relevant variables, he could have then explored alternative model specifications. Instead, the lack of computational tools forced Newton to create a new field of mathematics (calculus) just to reach the same conclusion. In practice, we cannot expect researchers to create new fields of mathematics for every discovery. This is one reason ML has become a key tool in the scientific arsenal.

In finance, ML algorithms will rarely give us a closed-form solution because these are non-parametric methods in many cases. The way ML can assist asset managers is not by generating a closed-form solution. Rather, ML is used to assist in providing asset managers with the variables that are relevant in a particular phenomenon.

When using traditional statistical analysis, important variables are often missed by asset managers due to model misspecifications. This is why feature importance is particularly useful in financial analysis. Feature importance analysis provides asset managers with the best model inputs by identifying only the most useful variables. Once an asset manager has this information, he can either use that information to better understand what factors are at play and/or use that information to develop a theoretical model that explains why those variables are important.

Controlling for Effects

Econometric specifications usually involve two types of explanatory variables. The first type of explanatory variables involves hypothesized predictors of the dependent variable. The second type of explanatory variables involves control variables. Typically, control variables are not of particular interest to an asset manager. However, because they are related to the dependent variable, control variables must be included in a regression in order to remove their effects from the equation.

Mullainathan and Spiess [2017] argue that, since we are not interested in "understanding" the parameters associated with the control variable, they should not be estimated parametrically. Instead, the asset manager should replace the effect on the control variables with predictions from ML algorithms based on the features of the control variables. Doing so will give the asset manager a better estimate of the significance of the estimated parameters of the predictor variables.

Credit Ratings/Analyst Recommendations

Stock analysts apply a number of models and heuristics to produce credit and investment ratings. These decisions are not entirely arbitrary, and correspond to a complex logic that cannot be represented with a simple set of formulas or a well-defined procedure. ML algorithms have been successful at replicating a large percentage of recommendations produced by bank analysts and credit rating agencies.

An example by Bacham and Zhao [2017] of Moody's Analytics demonstrates the advantage of ML over traditional statistical analysis. Based on two explanatory variables to explain default rates, they show that the relationship is nonlinear and complex, as well as non-monotonic. When the logit or probit model is used to predict defaults, as expected the prediction performance was poor. Using an ML algorithm — specifically the random forest model — did a far superior job in predicting bond issues that would default.

The ML method performed better because it was not constrained to predicting linear or continuous relationships. Being unconstrained by the assumptions underlying statistical linear models offers asset managers much better insights, and the possibility of automating tasks performed by expert humans.

Sentiment Analysis

There have been several studies that have used ML to extract market sentiment using social media data.[6] Social media data have become a popular source for stock market prediction, and many have explored its relationship with financial markets. Kalampokis, Tambouris, and Tarabanis, [2013] summarize studies suggesting how social media data can be used for various types of predictions. For example, Amazon reviews have been used to predict product sales.

One of the earliest empirical studies was Antweiler and Frank [2004], who investigated the effect of social media on the stock market, focusing on the application of text on Yahoo!Finance message boards to predict stock market volatility. These studies suggest that predictive indicators can be derived from social media content.

Recently, researchers have explored Twitter as their source for social media content. Although each post or tweet is limited to 140 characters, in aggregate it is believed that the information may provide an accurate representation of public sentiment. Examining tweet analysis and initial public offering (IPO) performance, Liew and Wang [2016] find that there is a positive significant correlation between IPOs' average tweet sentiment and IPOs' first-day returns not only on the first trading day but also two or three days prior. Further, examining the relationship between tweets and earnings announcements, Liew, Guo, and Zhang, [2017] report that not only are the consensus earnings of crowdsourced information more accurate (by

---

[6]Part of the discussion in this section draws from Sun, Lachanski, and Fabozzi [2016].

more than 60%) but also tweet sentiment before the earnings announcement can predict post-announcement risk-adjusted excess returns.

Azar and Lo [2016] show that tweets during the Federal Open Market Committee (FOMC) meeting dates contain information that can be used to predict stock market returns and can be used to build benchmark-outperforming portfolios. In a subsequent study regarding FOMC meetings, Agrawal, Azar, Lo, and Singh [2018] found that coupling social media with new data offers greater insight about stock market panics and manias than just using traditional data. They find that investor sentiment influences the supply and demand for liquidity.

Liew and Budavri [2017] use StockTwits data to show that social media has significant power in explaining the time-series variation in returns. They subsequently propose that a sixth "Social Media Factor" for the Fama–French five-factor model that is both distinct from the previous five factors and significant in predicting returns.

Sun, Lachanski, and Fabozzi [2016] find that the ML method of support vector machine can be used to create market indicators from StockTwits streams to predict stock price direction. These findings support the claim of Wong, Liu and Chiang [2014] that support vector machine methods can be used in conjunction with text mining to predict the stock market.

Detection of False Investment Strategies

Another important application of ML that goes beyond forecasting is the detection of false investment strategies. Suppose that a researcher is given random data for the purpose of deriving an investment strategy. After many backtest iterations, the researcher finds a strategy with a backtested Sharpe ratio of 3. This is obviously a false positive because the data were random and there is no investment strategy to be discovered. The reason why the researcher found a false positive is that the probability of getting a false positive grows with the number of independent trials. (A false positive is also known as a Type I error and is discussed in Chapter 17 in the context of backtesting.) In order to derive the probability that a strategy is false, we must take into account the number of trials involved in the strategy's discovery.

Not each backtest counts as an independent trial, as sometimes the difference between two backtests is a small change in parameters. Here is where unsupervised ML algorithms help, namely clustering methods that determine blocks of low-correlated backtests. Once we have estimated the number of low-correlated clusters of backtests, we can use that information to deflate the Sharpe ratio for the effects of selection bias under multiple testing.

Setting up an ML Investment Team

How does one set up an ML investment team so that the likelihood of developing successful strategies is high? In this final section of the chapter, we will provide some guidelines for accomplishing that. There are three overall activities that are involved. The first is structuring of data in a manner that allows for ML algorithms to be applied. The second is to undertake the research so as to make an actual discovery through a scientific process rather than searching aimlessly until some unexpected result is discovered — a discovery that is likely to be false. Finally, backtesting of an investment strategy or investment opportunity must be performed while controlling for the probability of a false discovery.

Two Pitfalls to Avoid

In building an ML investment team, there are many pitfalls to avoid. Here we will discuss just two of them:[7] avoid research silos and avoid research through backtesting. After we describe these pitfalls, we will see how setting up an ML research team avoids these two pitfalls.

Avoid research silos

Security analysts analyze raw news and analyses, but mostly rely on their judgment or intuition in making decisions about individual securities. Similarly, discretionary portfolio managers do the same in formulating investment decisions. Both security analysts and discretionary portfolio managers may rationalize their decisions about a particular stock or bond or alternative asset based on some story. However, an analyst can always make a story up *ex post*, to justify any investment decision. Because no one fully understands the logic behind their bets, it is difficult for one analyst to build on the work of another in an objective manner. For this

[7]For a detailed explanation of the pitfalls faced by ML experts and the solutions for dealing with these pitfalls, see López de Prado [2018].

reason, investment firms typically ask their analysts to work independently from one another, in silos, believing that this will provide better views on securities being analyzed. Anyone who attends meetings of members of an asset management team and their clients, or in the case of registered investment companies, the board of trustees, would observe how long and aimless those meetings can be. Each participant seems obsessed about one particular piece of anecdotal information and giant argumentative leaps are made without fact-based, empirical evidence. This does not mean that security analysis and portfolio managers cannot be successful. On the contrary, a few of them are. The point is that they cannot naturally work as a team. Build a portfolio team of 40 analysts and they will influence one another until eventually the asset management firm is paying 40 salaries for the work of one. Thus, it would seem plausible for the analysts to work in silos so they interact as little as possible.

Unfortunately, when applied to quantitative or ML projects, that formula has been highly unsuccessful. The asset management firm's mentality is, let us do with quants what has worked with security analysts and portfolio managers. Let us hire 40 Ph.D's and demand that each of them produce an investment strategy within six months. This approach tends to backfire because each Ph.D will frantically search for investment opportunities and eventually settle for either (1) a false positive that looks great in an overfit backtest or (2) standard factor investing, which may be an overcrowded strategy with a low Sharpe ratio, but at least has academic support. Both outcomes will disappoint clients, and the effort will be discontinued. Even if three of those Ph.D's make a true discovery, the profits will not suffice to cover the expenses of 40, so those three will relocate somewhere else, searching for a proper reward.

If a researcher wants to develop ML strategies in isolation, the odds are stacked against doing so. It takes almost as much effort to produce one true investment strategy as to produce 100, and the complexities are overwhelming: data curation and processing, high-performance computing infrastructure, software development, feature analysis, execution simulators, backtesting, and the like. Even if management provides those charged with developing ML strategies with shared services in those areas, it is still difficult to achieve.

Successful quantitative firms set up their research teams following the *meta-strategy paradigm* as pointed out by López de Prado [2014]. Tasks are divided into subtasks, which are sequentially performed giving rise to an assembly line. Quality is independently measured and monitored for each subtask. The role of each quant is to specialize in a particular task, to become the best there is at it, while having a holistic view of the entire process. This set up allows teams to yield discoveries at a predictable rate, with no reliance on lucky strikes. This is fundamentally the same organization principle followed by National Laboratories.[8] No particular individual is responsible for these discoveries because they are the outcome of team efforts, in which everyone contributes. Of course, setting up these financial laboratories takes time and requires personnel who know what they are doing and have done it before.

Avoid research through backtesting

One of the most pervasive mistakes in financial research is to take some data, run it through an ML algorithm, backtest the predictions, and repeat the sequence until a nice-looking backtest shows up. Academic journals are filled with such pseudo-discoveries, and even large hedge funds constantly fall into this trap. A researcher who repeats a test over and over again using the same data will generate a discovery that is false.

As explained in Chapter 17 where we discuss backtesting, this methodological error is so notorious among statisticians that they consider it scientific fraud, and the American Statistical Association warns against it in its ethical guidelines.[9] Even at full recall, it typically takes about 20 such iterations to discover a (false) investment strategy subject to the standard significance level (false positive rate) of 5%.

How can we deal with this problem? Suppose we have a dataset that contains features and labels for a particular asset. The asset management team can use an ML technique to fit a classifier on the database and evaluate the generalization error through what is called *cross-validation*. Assuming that the model achieves good performance, the next step would be to try to understand what features contributed to that performance. Maybe the asset manager could add some features that strengthen the signal responsible for the classifier's predictive power. Maybe the asset manager could eliminate some of the features that are only adding noise to the system. Most critically, understanding feature importance opens up the proverbial black box, and can guide the researcher's quest for a theory that explains how those features are involved in a particular outcome.

---

[8]The 17 National Laboratories, part of the US Department of Energy, are among the world's leading institutions for scientific research.

[9]See Discussion #4 in American Statistical Association [2016].

Insights into the patterns identified by the classifier can be appreciated if the asset manager can understand what source of information is indispensable to it. This is one of the reasons why the black box mantra is somewhat overplayed by ML skeptics. While it is true that the algorithm has has identified a pattern without human intervention, directing the process (the whole point of ML) in a black box, that does not mean that an asset manager cannot (or should not) take a look at what the algorithm has found. Once an ML technique identifies what features are important, the asset manager can learn more by conducting a number of experiments. In doing so, ML tools provide greater and more insights into the connection between X and y than traditional methods. More specifically, the asset manager can assess

- whether the features identified are important all the time, or only in some specific environments;
- over time what triggers a change in importance of the features (i.e., regime changes);
- whether those regime changes can be predicted;
- whether those important features are also relevant to other, related financial instruments;
- what the most relevant features across all financial instruments are;
- whether there is a subset of features with the highest rank correlation across the entire investment universe.

This is a much better way of researching strategies than the foolish backtest cycle. Remember, feature importance is a research tool, and backtesting is not.

Setting up an ML Production Chain

There are different ways to think about how to set up an ML investment strategy team. One way suggested by López de Prado [2018] is in terms of the stations of a production chain. These stations include data curators, feature analysts, strategists, backtesters, deployment, and portfolio oversight.

The data curators' station

The members of the team at the data curators' station are responsible for collecting, cleaning (scrubbing), correcting for outliers and missing data, indexing, storing, adjusting, and delivering all data to the production chain.

They are experts in market microstructure and data protocols, and must understand the context in which that data arise. This is not a simple task. For example, was a quote canceled and replaced at a different level, or canceled without replacement? Are fills split arbitrarily by the matching engine, and if so can they be reconstructed? Each asset class, exchange, and product has its own nuances. For instance, in the case of bonds, they are routinely called or exchanged; stocks are subjected to splits, reverse-splits, voting rights, and the like; futures and options must be rolled; currencies are not traded in a centralized order book.

The feature analysts' station

It is at the feature analysts' station that the members of the team transform raw data provided by the data curator station into informative signals. These informative signals have some predictive power over financial variables. This station is populated by experts in information theory, signal extraction and processing, visualization, labeling, weighting, classifiers, and feature importance techniques. For example, feature analysts may discover that the probability of a stock market sell-off is particularly high when (1) quoted offers are canceled-replaced with market sell orders, and (2) quote buy orders are canceled-replaced with limit buy orders deeper in the book. Although such a finding is not an investment strategy on its own, it can be used in different ways: order execution, monitoring of liquidity risk, market making, position taking, etc. A common mistake is to believe that feature analysts formulate investment strategies. That is not the case. Feature analysts collect and catalog libraries of findings that can be useful to several of the other stations.

The strategists' station

It is at the strategists' station where informative features are transformed into actual investment algorithms. A strategist will analyze the libraries of features looking for ideas to develop an investment strategy. The library of features was discovered by different feature analysts studying a wide range of instruments and asset classes. The strategist's goal is to make sense of all these observations and to formulate a general theory that explains them. Consequently, the strategy developed is just an experiment designed to test the validity of this theory. Data scientists who possess a thorough knowledge of financial markets and the economy are members of this station.

The theory formulated by the strategist needs to explain a large collection of importance features. Specifically, a theory must identify the economic mechanism that causes another market participant to lose money systematically. It can be attributable to a behavioral bias, asymmetric information, regulatory constraints, and the like. Features may be viewed as being discovered by a black box, but the strategy is developed in a white box. Tossing together a number of features from a library does not constitute a theory. After finalizing the strategy, a member of the strategist station will prepare code that uses the full algorithm and submit that prototype to the backtesting station.

The backtesting station

At the backtesting station, the team members evaluate the profitability of an investment strategy under various scenarios. One of the scenarios of interest is how the strategy would perform if history repeated itself, recognizing full well that the historical path is merely one of the possible outcomes of a stochastic process, and not necessarily the most likely going forward. Alternative scenarios must be evaluated that are consistent with the knowledge of the weaknesses and strengths of a proposed strategy. Team members are data scientists with a thorough understanding of empirical and experimental techniques.

A good backtester incorporates into the analysis meta-information regarding how the strategy came about. In particular, the analysis performed must evaluate the probability of backtest overfitting by taking into account the number of trials it took to distill the strategy. The results of this evaluation will not be reused by other stations because of the dangers of backtesting that we discuss in Chapter 17. Instead, the results of the backtest are communicated to management and not shared with anyone else.

The deployment station

The members of the deployment station are charged with integrating the strategy code into the production line. Some components may be reused by multiple strategies, especially when the other strategies share common features. Algorithm specialists and hardcore mathematical programmers are members of this station. Part of their responsibility is to ensure that the deployed solution is logically identical to the prototype they received. It is also the responsibility of the deployment station to optimize the implementation sufficiently, such that production latency is minimized.

The portfolio oversight station

Once a strategy is deployed, the portfolio oversight station takes over. This station first runs the strategy on data observed after the end date of the backtest. This embargoed period may have been reserved by the backtesters intentionally, or it may be the result of implementation delays.

If performance is consistent with the backtest results, the strategy moves on to the next stage for which the portfolio oversight station is responsible. This is the paper trading stage which involves the strategy being run on a live, real-time feed. By doing so, performance will account for data parsing latencies, calculation latencies, execution delays, and other time lapses between observation and positioning. The length of time of the paper trading stage is not any fixed time period. Rather, paper trading will take place for as long as necessary to gather enough evidence that the strategy performs as expected.

Once the paper trading stage is completed and confirms the backtests, at this stage this station manages a real position, whether in isolation or as part of an ensemble. Performance is evaluated precisely, identifying the returns, attributed risks, and costs.

The role of this station does not stop there. Based on the production performance, the allocation to the strategy is frequently re-assessed within the context of a diversified portfolio. The initial allocation to the strategy is small. The allocation is increased if over time the strategy performs as expected. However, if over time the performance deteriorates, gradually a smaller allocation is made.

Strategies are not expected to perform well forever. Ultimately all strategies are discontinued when their performance drops below expectations for a sufficiently extended period of time so that management concludes that the supporting theory is no longer backed by the empirical evidence.

Key Points

- ML is a universal modeling technique that does not depend on any domain-specific theory.
- ML models do not use finance theory but they can assist researchers in the development of financial theories.
- ML methods place constraints on model complexity to ensure that they retain some forecasting capability out-of-sample.
- The objective of ML is to empower computers to find the sequence of actions that optimizes automatically by means of experience and will

involve either no human intervention during the learning process or limited human intervention.

- The training data is the portion of the data used to generate the rule.
- The algorithm is then tested using the portion of the data that was not used to train the model and is referred to as the test data.
- The purpose of testing the algorithm is to assess the performance of the rule using unseen data using various statistical measures.
- Because ML is able to learn the specification from the data, it is particularly suitable for analyzing the phenomena involved in complex systems such as financial markets.
- Financial econometric statistical tools are not able to learn the specification from the data, leading to misspecified models and false discoveries.
- If the financial econometric tool used to model observations is the multivariate linear regression, asset managers will fail to recognize the complexity of the data, resulting in theories that are of limited value.
- One reason why it took so long for asset managers to embrace ML is that until very recently the datasets were limited in size and variety, and the computing power scarce.
- Some of the most interesting datasets are unstructured and non-numeric and therefore not amenable to econometric methods.
- Statistical testing requires the use of "observations" or "data points", while in ML, the terms used are "examples" and "instances".
- The two types of samples used in statistical testing of predictive or classification models are in-sample and out-of-sample, while in ML they are referred to as training sample and test sample, respectively.
- In ML, multivariate regression is often used interchangeably with supervised learning.
- In statistics, in using a regression there are independent or explanatory variables or predictors, while in ML these are referred to as attributes or input features or features.
- In statistics, in using a regression there is a dependent variable which in ML is referred to as a response, output, or target.
- When estimating or fitting a model in ML, it is referred to as "learning a model".
- In general terms, we can think of two types of data classifications: structured versus unstructured data and labeled versus unlabeled data.
- Structured data refers to information that is characterized by a high degree of organization and is objectively represented (i.e., its representation is not subject to interpretation) and generally consists of numerical values.

- Unstructured data do not have a structure that is recognizable and therefore this information is difficult to categorize.
- Although unstructured data include textual and non-textual items, they are typically text heavy.
- Unlabeled data that relate to finance would be audio recordings of webcasts by security analysts or company representatives, printed articles about a company by the media or by sell-side security analysts, tweets, and SEC filings by a public company.
- The task of labeling data that are unlabeled is sometimes referred to as classifying or tagging the data.
- Data scientists distinguish between different computer learning processes, the three main categories of ML being supervised learning, unsupervised learning, and reinforcement learning.
- Each learning style will differ based on the information provided to the machine during the training period.
- In ML, supervised algorithms allow the computer to learn from training data that already contain the correct label for each input so that the computer will identify patterns that link the input variables to the response variable.
- There are two types of supervised learning: regression ML and classification ML algorithms.
- In unsupervised learning there are no labels provided for the inputs, the objective of the algorithm being to determine the structure of the data based on statistical properties.
- Clustering is the typical discrete example of unsupervised learning, and PCA is a typical continuous example.
- In semi-supervised learning algorithms, some of the training data include both labeled and unlabeled data and the objective is to appreciate how combining unlabeled and labeled data may alter the learning behavior, and then create algorithms to benefit from using both data types.
- From the point of view of financial modeling, a deep learning algorithm is a supervised learning algorithm that given a set of inputs provides an accurate estimate of the variable to be predicted.
- The primary way for implementing deep learning algorithms is via artificial neural networks (ANNs).
- The focus of reinforcement learning algorithms is learning with the objective of maximizing the cumulative reward.
- The quantamental approach to investing combines human guesses (inspired by fundamental variables) with mathematical forecasts.

- ML offers asset managers the opportunity to gain the following insight from data: (1) modeling nonlinear relationships in a high-dimensional space, (2) analyzing unstructured data, (3) learning complex patterns, (4) focusing on predictability over variance adjudication, and (5) controlling for overfitting.
- Following are applications of ML in asset management: (1) price/rate/volatility prediction, (2) portfolio construction/risk analysis, (3) structural breaks/anomaly detection, (4) bet sizing, (5) feature importance, (6) controlling for effects, (7) credit ratings/analyst recommendations, (8) sentiment analysis/recommender systems, and (9) detection of false investment strategies.
- In building an ML investment team, there are many pitfalls to avoid, two of them being avoiding research silos and avoiding research through backtesting.

References

Agrawal, S., P. Azar, A. Lo, and T. Singh, 2018. "Momentum, mean-reversion and social media: Evidence from StockTwits and Twitter." *Journal of Portfolio Management*, 44(7): 85–95.

Antweiler, W. and M. Z. Frank, 2004. "Is all that talk just noise? The information content of internet stock message board," *Journal of Finance*, 59(3): 1259–1294.

Azar, P. and A. W. Lo, 2016. "The wisdom of Twitter crowds: Predicting stock market reactions to FOMC meetings via Twitter feeds," *Journal of Portfolio Management*, 42(5): 123–134.

Bacham, D. and J. Zhao, 2017. "Machine learning: Challenges, lessons, and opportunities in credit risk modeling," *Moody's Analytics*. Available at https://www.moodysanalytics.com/risk-perspectives-magazine/managing-disruption/spotlight/machine-learning-challenges-lessons-and-opportunities-in-credit-risk-modeling.

Calkin, N. and M. López de Prado, 2014a. "Stochastic flow diagrams," *Algorithmic Finance*, 3(1): 21–42.

Calkin, N. and M. López de Prado, 2014b. "The topology of macro financial flows: An application of stochastic flow diagrams," *Algorithmic Finance*, 3(1): 43–85.

Finextra, 2017. "The next big wave: How financial institutions can stay head of the AI revolution." Available at https://www.finextra.com/newsarticle/30590/banks-must-get-on-ai-bandwagon-now--new-finextra-research/retail.

Kalampokis, E., E. Tambouris, and K. Tarabanis, 2013. "Understanding the predictive power of social media," *Internet Research*, 23(5): 544–559.

Kolanovic, M. and R. Krishnamachari, 2017. "Big data and AI strategies: Machine learning and alternative data approach to investing," JP Morgan.

Karpp, T. and K. Crawford, 2015. "Social Media, financial algorithms and the hack crash," *Theory Culture & Society*, 33(1): 73–92.

Liew, J. K.-S. and T. Budavri, 2017. "The sixth factor — Social media factor derived directly from tweet sentiments." *Journal of Portfolio Management*, 43(3): 102–111.

Liew, J. K.-S., S. Guo, and T. Zhang, 2017. "Tweet sentiments and crowd-sourced earnings estimates as valuable sources of information around earnings releases," *Journal of Alternative Investments*, 19(3): 7–26.

Liew, J. K.-S. and G. Z. Wang, 2016. "Twitter sentiment and IPO performance: A cross-sectional examination," *Journal of Portfolio Management*, 42(4): 129–135.

López de Prado, M., 2016. "Building diversified portfolios that outperform out-of-sample," *Journal of Portfolio Management*, 42(4): 59–69.

López de Prado, M., 2018. *Advances in Financial Machine Learning*. Hoboken, NJ: John Wiley & Sons.

López de Prado, M., 2020. *Machine Learning for Asset Managers*. Cambridge, UK: University Press.

Mullainathan, S. and J. Spiess, 2017. "Machine learning: An applied econometric approach," *Journal of Economic Perspectives*, 31(2): 87–106.

Samuel, A., 1959. "Some studies in machine learning using the game of checkers," *IBM Journal of Research and Development*, 44(1, 2): 221–229.

Sun, A., M. Lachanski, and F. J. Fabozzi, 2016. "Trade the tweet: Social media text mining and sparse matrix factorization for stock market prediction," *International Review of Financial Analysis*, 48: 272–281.

Trippi, R. and J. Lee, 1996. *Artificial Intelligence in Finance & Investing: State-of-the-Art Technologies for Securities Selection and Portfolio Management*. Chicago, IL: Probus Publishing.

Trippi, R. and E. Turban, 1992. *Neural Networks in Finance and Investing: Using Artificial Intelligence to Improve Real-World Performance*. Chicago, IL: Probus Publishing.

Turing, A. M., 1950. "Computing machinery and intelligence," *Mind*, 49: 433–460.

Vapnik, V. N., 1995. *The Nature of Statistical Learning Theory*. New York: Springer.

Vapnik, V. N., 1998. *Statistical Learning Theory*. New York: Springer.

Wong, F. M. F., Z. Liu and M. Chiang, 2014. "Stock market prediction from WSJ: Text mining via sparse matrix factorization," *IEEE International Conference on Data Mining*, arXiv:1406.7330v1.

Chapter 8

Risk Measures and Asset Allocation Problems

Learning Objectives

After reading this chapter, you will understand:

- the types of return distributions used in asset management;
- the difference between risk and uncertainty;
- asymmetric dispersion measures such as semi-standard deviation;
- the industry standard value-at-risk (VaR) and conditional value-at-risk (CVaR);
- how to interpret and calculate VaR and CVaR;
- how to solve the asset allocation problem beyond the classical mean–variance analysis; and
- extensions of the classical Sharpe ratio.

Introduction

In the classical asset allocation problem, variance is used as a proxy for risk even though it penalizes symmetrically both profit and loss. In this chapter, we describe extensions of mean–variance analysis capturing asymmetry of risk by means of a risk measure or an asymmetric measure of dispersion. We focus on the features which are most relevant for asset allocation decision-making. They include the capacity to capture the skewness and kurtosis present in the observed asset returns, the dependence which is most relevant for extreme losses, and most importantly, consistency with the principle of diversification.

Because it is common to use alternative risk measures in conjunction with a distributional assumption for the asset returns, we review the most popular distributional hypotheses with a focus on what makes the extended frameworks different from mean–variance analysis.

Finally, every extension of the mean–variance analysis is consistent with a risk-reward ratio which, just like the Sharpe ratio, can be used as a measure of risk-adjusted performance. We make connections with some of the alternative risk-reward ratios employed in the practice of finance and comment on their application in asset allocation problems.

Measures of Risk and Uncertainty

Conceptually, the asset allocation problem is about building a portfolio while balancing risks and rewards. In the classical mean–variance framework, portfolio risk is proxied by the standard deviation of the portfolio return distribution. The square of the standard deviation, also known as variance, equals the expected value of the squared differences between the return outcomes and the expected portfolio return. Because the differences are squared, the standard deviation is said to penalize symmetrically both profits and losses. Indeed, if we flip the signs of the portfolio return outcomes turning losses into gains and vice versa, the standard deviation would not be affected. As a consequence, two distinct portfolios may have equal variances and at the same time one of them may have more pronounced losses making it less attractive.

These properties illustrate that standard deviation is a measure of how dispersed the portfolio outcomes are around the expected portfolio return capturing uncertainty about the future realizations rather than portfolio risk. A standard deviation of zero indicates no uncertainty about the future outcomes.

In general, as argued by Holton [2004], risk involves both *uncertainty* and *exposure*. Managing portfolio risk is, therefore, about managing the exposure, or losses, caused by the uncertainty in the future realizations of certain risk factors. As a result, the measure of risk should be asymmetric, focused to a greater extent on the left side of the portfolio return distribution, which describes losses. Unlike variance, a measure of risk should be able to make a distinction between positively and negatively skewed return distributions.

In this chapter, we provide examples of alternative risk measures used to extend the mean–variance framework. Even though such extensions are more realistic and conceptually more appealing, the corresponding asset allocation problems are analytically less transparent and harder to solve, relying heavily on numerical algorithms. The lack of transparency can lead to difficulties when results need to be explained to senior-level management, board of trustees, and clients.

Alternative Measures of Dispersion

The *mean absolute deviation* (MAD) of the portfolio return distribution equals the expected value of the differences between the return outcomes and the expected portfolio return in absolute value. In contrast to variance, instead of squaring the differences, MAD uses their absolute value. Just like variance, MAD is a symmetric measure of dispersion. For some return distributions, there are simple formulae showing how MAD can be expressed through variance. For example, if the return distribution is normal, then

$$\text{MAD} = \sigma\sqrt{\frac{2}{\pi}},$$

where σ denotes standard deviation. As a result, in this case working with MAD is equivalent to working with standard deviation. The application of MAD in portfolio theory was suggested by Konno and Yamazaki [1991].

An example of an asymmetric measure of dispersion is *semi-variance.* The semi-variance of a portfolio return distribution is defined as the expected value of the squared deviations of the return outcomes from the portfolio mean provided that the outcomes are below the mean. Clearly, semi-variance is focused on the downside and disregards the return outcomes which are above the portfolio expected return. However, if there are no pronounced asymmetries in the return distribution, then semi-variance is close to one half of variance. For example, if the return distribution is symmetric around the mean, then semi-variance equals one half of variance. Application of semi-variance to portfolio theory was suggested by Markowitz [1952, 1959].

Certain extensions of the notion behind semi-variance include *lower partial moments.* Instead of squaring the distance of the return outcome to the expected return, in a lower partial moment of order n it is raised to the power of n, where the power is a positive integer and represents a parameter to be chosen by the investor. Lower partial moments are asymmetric and exhibit different sensitivities to extreme losses depending on the value of the parameter.

Measures of Risk

A systematic study of proper ways to measure risk started in the 1990s driven to a large extent by the development of banking regulations. From a regulatory perspective, a measure of portfolio risk would indicate an amount of capital to be kept in reserve in order to cover portfolio losses in case certain risks materialize. Regulations distinguish between market, credit, and operational risks and prescribe certain ways of measuring them as set forth in the Basel Committee on Banking Supervision accords issued as three standards in 1988, 2004, and 2010, which are also known as Basel I, II, and III.

Value-at-risk

A risk measure widely accepted since the early 1990s is *VaR*. It was popularized by JP Morgan and their service RiskMetrics, which was later spun off into a separate company. In the mid-1990s, VaR was approved by regulators as a valid approach to calculating capital reserves to cover market risks. According to regulations, the capital reserves equal VaR multiplied by a factor which takes into account the accuracy of the VaR forecast based on the historical accuracy of the adopted risk model.

VaR is defined as the minimum level of loss at a given, sufficiently high, confidence level for a predefined time horizon. Suppose, for example, that we are holding a portfolio with a 1-week VaR at 99% equal to $1 million. This means that over the horizon of one week, the portfolio may lose more than $1 million with a probability equal to 1%.

A similar example can be constructed for percentage returns. Suppose that the current portfolio value is $100 million. If the 1-week 99% VaR of the return distribution is 2%, then over the time horizon of one week, the portfolio can lose more than 2% ($2 million) of the portfolio current value with a probability of 1%.

Even though according to regulations VaR is stated in terms of its confidence level, it is more convenient to transform the confidence level into a probability which is called *tail probability*. The tail probability equals one minus the confidence level; if the confidence level is 99% as in the examples above, the tail probability equals 1%. With this small modification, VaR can be defined as the negative of the inverse distribution function of the portfolio return distribution evaluated at the tail probability.

Because VaR is just a quantile, it can be positive, negative, or zero, unlike variance or any other measure of dispersion. If, for example, the portfolio manager adds cash to the portfolio, the profit distribution shifts to the right (the loss distribution shifts to the left) because now all possible loss outcomes decline by the amount of cash added. This automatically reduces the portfolio VaR by the amount of cash added to the portfolio. For instance, if in the first example above the portfolio manager adds \$800,000 to the portfolio, then the VaR at 1% tail probability will decline from \$1 million to \$200,000. By the same argument, if \$1 million is added, then the VaR at 1% tail probability will decline to zero. However, this does not imply that the portfolio becomes riskless — with a smaller tail probability the portfolio may still lose a positive amount. This property, sometimes referred to as *translation invariance*, is crucial for the use of VaR as a basis for regulatory capital requirement.

In practice, the calculation of VaR from historical data is done in the following way. Suppose that the investor has a portfolio invested 30% in the US Large Cap asset class and 70% in Long-Term Treasury asset class. The historical returns of the two asset classes are provided in the second and the third column of Table 1.[1] The portfolio return is calculated by multiplying the US Large Cap by 0.3 and adding to the result 0.7 multiplied by the corresponding observation of the Long-Term Treasury. For instance, the portfolio return of −0.74% observed in January 2013 equals $0.3 \times 5.18 + 0.7 \times (-3.27)$.

To calculate VaR at 5% tail probability, we sort the portfolio return observations by size in increasing order and we look for the observation which is the row number equal to "number of observations" multiplied by "tail probability". In this case, the row number equals $78 \times 0.05 = 3.9$ (see Table 2). Because the result is not an integer, there are different methods to compute the quantile — they involve rounding the number up, down, to the nearest integer, or computing a weighted average of the VaRs corresponding to the two nearest integers (three and four in this case). The simplest approach is to round the number up to the nearest integer: the row number becomes four. The observation in row four is −3.51% and, therefore, the portfolio VaR at 5% tail probability becomes equal to 3.51% after flipping the sign.

In the general case, it is unclear how VaR is related to the expected return and standard deviation of the portfolio return distribution. It is

[1]All of the data for the illustrations in this chapter were obtained from Portfolio Visualizer and all of the calculations were performed using the Portfolio Visualizer software. https://www.portfoliovisualizer.com/.

TABLE 1: Monthly Returns of US Large Cap, Long-Term Treasury, and a Portfolio Invested 30% in US Large Cap and 70% in Long-Term Treasury

Month	US Large Cap	Long-Term Treasury	Portfolio	Month	US Large Cap	Long-Term Treasury	Portfolio
Jan-2013	5.18%	−3.27%	−0.74%	Apr-2016	0.37%	−0.63%	−0.33%
Feb-2013	1.34%	1.26%	1.28%	May-2016	1.78%	0.69%	1.02%
Mar-2013	3.74%	0.03%	1.14%	Jun-2016	0.25%	6.57%	4.67%
Apr-2013	1.91%	3.87%	3.28%	Jul-2016	3.68%	2.01%	2.51%
May-2013	2.33%	−6.23%	−3.66%	Aug-2016	0.13%	−1.00%	−0.66%
Jun-2013	−1.35%	−3.26%	−2.69%	Sep-2016	0.01%	−1.32%	−0.92%
Jul-2013	5.07%	−1.93%	0.17%	Oct-2016	−1.83%	−4.23%	−3.51%
Aug-2013	−2.91%	−1.28%	−1.77%	Nov-2016	3.70%	−7.86%	−4.39%
Sep-2013	3.12%	0.88%	1.55%	Dec-2016	1.96%	−0.35%	0.34%
Oct-2013	4.59%	1.32%	2.30%	Jan-2017	1.88%	0.65%	1.02%
Nov-2013	3.03%	−2.49%	−0.83%	Feb-2017	3.96%	1.57%	2.29%
Dec-2013	2.51%	−2.37%	−0.91%	Mar-2017	0.10%	−0.59%	−0.38%
Jan-2014	−3.47%	6.26%	3.34%	Apr-2017	1.02%	1.59%	1.42%
Feb-2014	4.56%	0.60%	1.79%	May-2017	1.39%	1.73%	1.63%
Mar-2014	0.82%	0.63%	0.69%	Jun-2017	0.61%	0.63%	0.62%
Apr-2014	0.72%	1.82%	1.49%	Jul-2017	2.04%	−0.59%	0.20%
May-2014	2.33%	2.73%	2.61%	Aug-2017	0.29%	3.27%	2.38%
Jun-2014	2.05%	−0.16%	0.50%	Sep-2017	2.06%	−2.27%	−0.97%
Jul-2014	−1.39%	0.59%	0.00%	Oct-2017	2.32%	−0.02%	0.68%
Aug-2014	3.98%	4.23%	4.16%	Nov-2017	3.06%	0.63%	1.36%
Sep-2014	−1.41%	−1.99%	−1.82%	Dec-2017	1.10%	1.78%	1.58%
Oct-2014	2.42%	2.61%	2.55%	Jan-2018	5.71%	−3.40%	−0.67%
Nov-2014	2.68%	2.86%	2.81%	Feb-2018	−3.70%	−2.89%	−3.13%
Dec-2014	−0.26%	2.82%	1.90%	Mar-2018	−2.56%	2.75%	1.16%
Jan-2015	−3.02%	8.97%	5.37%	Apr-2018	0.37%	−2.04%	−1.32%
Feb-2015	5.74%	−5.66%	−2.24%	May-2018	2.39%	1.79%	1.97%
Mar-2015	−1.59%	1.13%	0.31%	Jun-2018	0.61%	0.66%	0.65%
Apr-2015	0.95%	−3.07%	−1.86%	Jul-2018	3.71%	−1.28%	0.22%
May-2015	1.27%	−2.16%	−1.13%	Aug-2018	3.25%	1.18%	1.80%
Jun-2015	−1.93%	−3.73%	−3.19%	Sep-2018	0.55%	−2.74%	−1.75%
Jul-2015	2.08%	4.21%	3.57%	Oct-2018	−6.85%	−2.82%	−4.03%
Aug-2015	−6.04%	−0.71%	−2.31%	Nov-2018	2.03%	1.78%	1.86%
Sep-2015	−2.49%	1.91%	0.59%	Dec-2018	−9.04%	5.50%	1.14%
Oct-2015	8.42%	−0.48%	2.19%	Jan-2019	8.00%	0.49%	2.74%
Nov-2015	0.29%	−0.81%	−0.48%	Feb-2019	3.20%	−1.31%	0.04%
Dec-2015	−1.59%	−0.34%	−0.72%	Mar-2019	1.94%	5.47%	4.41%
Jan-2016	−4.98%	5.23%	2.17%	Apr-2019	4.04%	−1.88%	−0.10%
Feb-2016	−0.15%	2.86%	1.96%	May-2019	−6.36%	6.65%	2.75%
Mar-2016	6.78%	0.05%	2.07%	Jun-2019	7.03%	1.01%	2.82%

Source for monthly returns: Portfolio Visualizer (https://www.portfoliovisualizer.com/).

TABLE 2: The Monthly Returns of the Portfolio in Table 1 Sorted by Size in Increasing Order

Month	Sorted Returns	Month	Sorted Returns
Nov-2016	−4.39%	Mar-2014	0.69%
Oct-2018	−4.03%	May-2016	1.02%
May-2013	−3.66%	Jan-2017	1.02%
Oct-2016	**−3.51%**	Dec-2018	1.14%
Jun-2015	−3.19%	Mar-2013	1.14%
Feb-2018	−3.13%	Mar-2018	1.16%
Jun-2013	−2.69%	Feb-2013	1.28%
Aug-2015	−2.31%	Nov-2017	1.36%
Feb-2015	−2.24%	Apr-2017	1.42%
Apr-2015	−1.86%	Apr-2014	1.49%
Sep-2014	−1.82%	Sep-2013	1.55%
Aug-2013	−1.77%	Dec-2017	1.58%
Sep-2018	−1.75%	May-2017	1.63%
Apr-2018	−1.32%	Feb-2014	1.79%
May-2015	−1.13%	Aug-2018	1.80%
Sep-2017	−0.97%	Nov-2018	1.86%
Sep-2016	−0.92%	Dec-2014	1.90%
Dec-2013	−0.91%	Feb-2016	1.96%
Nov-2013	−0.83%	May-2018	1.97%
Jan-2013	−0.74%	Mar-2016	2.07%
Dec-2015	−0.72%	Jan-2016	2.17%
Jan-2018	−0.67%	Oct-2015	2.19%
Aug-2016	−0.66%	Feb-2017	2.29%
Nov-2015	−0.48%	Oct-2013	2.30%
Mar-2017	−0.38%	Aug-2017	2.38%
Apr-2016	−0.33%	Jul-2016	2.51%
Apr-2019	−0.10%	Oct-2014	2.55%
Jul-2014	0.00%	May-2014	2.61%
Feb-2019	0.04%	Jan-2019	2.74%
Jul-2013	0.17%	May-2019	2.75%
Jul-2017	0.20%	Nov-2014	2.81%
Jul-2018	0.22%	Jun-2019	2.82%
Mar-2015	0.31%	Apr-2013	3.28%
Dec-2016	0.34%	Jan-2014	3.34%
Jun-2014	0.50%	Jul-2015	3.57%
Sep-2015	0.59%	Aug-2014	4.16%
Jun-2017	0.62%	Mar-2019	4.41%
Jun-2018	0.65%	Jun-2016	4.67%
Oct-2017	0.68%	Jan-2015	5.37%

Note: The column Month indicates when the corresponding observation was made. The number in **bold** indicates the portfolio VaR at 5% tail probability.

intuitively clear, however, that if the dispersion of the distribution is small, then portfolio VaR is close to the expected return. For some concrete distributions, we can obtain a transparent connection. If the portfolio return distribution is normal with a mean equal to μ and standard deviation equal to σ, then

$$\begin{aligned}\text{VaR at 5\% tail probability} &= 1.645\,\sigma - \mu,\\ \text{VaR at 1\% tail probability} &= 2.326\,\sigma - \mu,\end{aligned}$$

in which the numbers multiplying the standard deviation are the negative of the 5% and the 1% quantiles, respectively, of the standard normal distribution. For any distribution symmetric around the mean, the VaR at $p\%$ tail probability takes the following general form:

$$\text{VaR at } p\% \text{ tail probability} = q(p)\,\sigma - \mu,$$

where $q(p)$ is the $p\%$ quantile of the corresponding standardized distribution (with standard deviation equal to one and mean equal to zero). Therefore, for any fixed tail probability, $q(p)$ is a number which can be precalculated and does not depend upon μ and σ. We come back to this observation further on when we discuss asset allocation with alternative risk measures.

Using the data in Table 1, we find that the standard deviation of the portfolio returns is 2.1% and the mean is 0.6%. Plugging in these values in the formula for the VaR at 5% tail probability, we obtain 2.86%. As a result, the normal VaR appears to be significantly lower than the historical VaR at 5%, which is an expected outcome given that the normal distribution underestimates the frequency of extreme losses.

Conditional value-at-risk

Any risk measure considered for application in portfolio construction should be consistent with the notion of diversification: the risk of a portfolio should not exceed the weighted average of the stand-alone risks of the single assets included in the portfolio. If this does not hold, then there are no incentives to build portfolios; it would be better to hold single assets. That is, we expect the following inequality to hold always regardless of the dataset or regardless of assumed model for the joint distribution of all asset returns,

$$\begin{aligned}\text{Risk}(w_1R_1 + w_2R_2 + \cdots + w_nR_n) \le\ & w_1\text{Risk}(R_1)\\ &+ w_2\text{Risk}(R_2) + \cdots + w_n\text{Risk}(R_n).\end{aligned}$$

Standard deviation, for instance, satisfies this inequality. A major deficiency of VaR is that it is not always consistent with diversification. One can construct examples in which the VaR of a portfolio exceeds the weighted average of the VaRs of the single assets. This property is also known as *convexity*; that is, a risk measure for which the above inequality holds for any portfolio is called a convex risk measure. VaR is not a convex risk measure in general.

To resolve this problem, Artzner, Delbaen, Eber, and Heath [1999] suggested *CVaR* as an alternative to VaR. CVaR is defined as the average of VaRs which are larger than the VaR at a given tail probability. By design, CVaR is more informative because it calculates the expected loss provided that the loss exceeds a VaR threshold. For example, suppose that the weekly CVaR of a portfolio at 1% tail probability equals \$2 million and the weekly VaR at 1% equals \$1 million. The VaR figure indicates that the portfolio may lose more than \$1 million over one week with a probability of 1%. It is, however, silent about the magnitude of losses beyond \$1 million if such an event occurs. The CVaR figure provides additional information — if the portfolio loses more than \$1 million, on average the extreme loss equals \$2 million.

Apart from the additional information that CVaR provides, Artzner, Delbaen, Eber, and Heath [1999] showed that it is always consistent with diversification; that is, if there are diversification opportunities in the data, CVaR will recognize them. As a result, CVaR is a good candidate for a risk measure in asset allocation and portfolio construction problems.

Because CVaR is an average of VaRs, it inherits the translation invariance property which makes it useful for financial regulation. Also, similar to VaR, in some special cases there is a direct connection between CVaR, the mean μ, and standard deviation σ of a return distribution. For instance, if the portfolio return distribution is normal, then a formula similar to that of VaR holds,

$$\text{CVaR at 5\% tail probability} = 2.063\,\sigma - \mu,$$
$$\text{CVaR at 1\% tail probability} = 2.665\,\sigma - \mu.$$

Likewise, for any return distribution symmetric around the mean, the following more general formula holds:

$$\text{CVaR at } p\% \text{ tail probability} = C(p)\,\sigma - \mu,$$

where $C(p)$ depends only on the tail probability.[2] We provide the corresponding expressions in the next section.

[2]For additional details, Rachev, Stoyanov, and Fabozzi [2008, 2011].

Given a sample of observations, CVaR can be calculated using a formula which follows directly from the definition. Denote by $R_{(1)} \leq R_{(2)} \leq \cdots \leq R_{(n)}$ the sorted sample of portfolio returns. Thus, $R_{(1)}$ equals the largest loss observed in the sample period and $R_{(n)}$ denotes the largest gain. The portfolio CVaR at $p\%$ tail probability equals,

$$\text{CVaR}_p(R) = -\frac{1}{pn}(R_{(1)} + R_{(2)} + \cdots + R_{(k)}) - \frac{1}{p}\left(p - \frac{k}{n}\right) R_{(k+1)},$$

in which k equals the largest integer smaller than pn. The first term equals the average loss provided that the loss exceeds the $p\%$ quantile (or the corresponding VaR) and the second term is a correction which appears because pn may not happen to be an integer. For example, suppose that a year of daily data amounts to 252 data points. Then, the 1% quantile for that sample happens to be between the second and the third observation in the sorted sample because $pn = 2.52$. In this situation, the second term in the formula will add a correction.

We illustrate how this formula is applied in practice using the data in Tables 1 and 2. Suppose that apart from VaR at 5% tail probability, the portfolio manager would like to see the CVaR at the same tail probability. The first step is to calculate $pn = 0.05 \times 79 = 3.9$. The largest integer smaller than 3.9 is $k = 3$. Plugging in the corresponding data points from Table 2, we obtain

$$\begin{aligned}\text{CVaR}_{5\%}(R) &= -\frac{1}{3.9}(-4.39 - 4.03 - 3.66) \\ &\quad - \frac{1}{0.05}\left(0.05 - \frac{3}{79}\right)(-3.51) = 3.94.\end{aligned}$$

Recall that the VaR at 5% tail probability equals 3.51%. The interpretation of the CVaR number is that if the portfolio loses more than 3.51%, which happens with a probability of 5%, then on average the portfolio loses 3.94%.

We can also calculate the CVaR from the formula assuming the normal distribution. We calculated previously that the standard deviation of the portfolio returns is 2.1% and the mean is 0.6%. With these values, the normal CVaR at 5% tail probability equals $2.063 \times 2.1\% - 0.6\% = 3.73\%$.

Using Risk Measures in Practice

An alternative risk measure can be employed for decision-making in two ways. The first approach is to estimate the risk measure directly from a historical sample. This approach is non-parametric because we do not make any assumptions about the data generating process. However, it has an important disadvantage. If we are interested in a risk measure focused on the left tail of the portfolio return distribution describing extreme losses, then the risk computed from the sample will rely on only several data points which may be unreliable. For example, if we use one year of daily data to estimate the daily CVaR at 1% tail probability, the risk figure will be based essentially on the first three numbers in the sorted sample. It is hard to believe that three data points can lead to a reliable risk statistic.

For this reason, risk measures, such as VaR and CVaR for low tail probabilities, are always used together with some parametric model for the portfolio return distribution. The parametric model is supposed to make the risk statistic more reliable. An important feature of the parametric model should be that it describes realistically the frequency of extreme gains and losses.

Common Parametric Models for Asset Return Distributions

In this section, we describe some of the most common parametric models for asset allocation and risk management. We provide closed-form expressions for VaR and CVaR if they are available. Because our focus is on asset allocation problems, we work with multivariate models which describe the joint probabilities for all assets. In this way, the risk measure becomes a function of the portfolio weights and the parameters of the distribution. This perspective is important in the discussion of optimal allocations.

Our objective is to make a connection with mean–variance analysis. We show that the criticism that mean–variance is consistent only with the multivariate normal distribution is incorrect. It is valid under much more general assumptions — it is possible to show that regardless of the choice of risk measure, the mean–variance analysis is still correct under those assumptions. It become unrealistic only if there is pronounced skewness or kurtosis in the returns across assets.

We assume that there are K assets and a portfolio invested in them is defined in terms of the portfolio weights $w_1, w_2, \ldots, w_K$. To keep the discussion simple, we provide comments only on the properties important for asset allocation decisions; we do not include probability density functions to keep the notation simple.

The multivariate normal distribution

Even though the normal distribution is known to be overly optimistic about the frequency of extreme events, it is a common distributional assumption. If the returns follow the multivariate normal distribution, then the return distribution of any portfolio is univariate normal with standard deviation $\sigma(R_p)$ and mean $E(R_p)$ where

$$\sigma^2(R_p) = \sum_{k=1}^{K}\sum_{h=1}^{K} w_k w_h \mathrm{cov}(R_k, R_h),$$

$$E(R_p) = w_1 E(R_1) + w_2 E(R_2) + \cdots + w_K E(R_K).$$

The portfolio VaR and CVaR at 1% tail probability are given by the following expressions:

$$\text{VaR at 1\% tail probability} = 2.326\,\sigma(R_p) - E(R_p),$$

$$\text{CVaR at 1\% tail probability} = 2.665\,\sigma(R_p) - E(R_p),$$

which differ from the ones provided previously only by the explicit dependence of the portfolio standard deviation and the portfolio expected return on the weights and the parameters of the multivariate normal distribution — all pairwise covariances of the asset returns and the expected asset returns.

More generally, for any tail probability the constant multiplying the portfolio standard deviation of the expression of VaR is the negative of the corresponding quantile of the standard normal distribution $q(p)$ and the corresponding constant $C(p)$ in the CVaR expression is given by the formula

$$C(p) = \frac{1}{p\sqrt{2\pi}} \exp\left(-\frac{q^2(p)}{2}\right).$$

As a consequence, the two basic quantities that change as we vary the allocation are the portfolio standard deviation and the portfolio expected return; the VaR and CVaR are characterized completely by means of these two quantities. This is not unique to VaR and CVaR. Under the assumption of normality, MAD and any other measure of dispersion can be represented as a scaled standard deviation.

The multivariate location-scale Student's t distribution

A more flexible family of distribution is the multivariate location-scale Student's t distribution, which can describe better the frequency of extreme events. This distribution has an additional parameter denoted by $\nu > 0$ and is called the degrees of freedom. This parameter describes the degree of tail thickness for all asset returns: the lower ν is, the thicker both tails of the distribution are.

This distribution has a property similar to that of the multivariate normal when $\nu > 2$; that is, if the joint return distribution is multivariate location-scale Student's t, then the return of any portfolio univariate location-scale Student's t and can be represented in the following way:

$$R_p = X\sigma(R_p)\frac{\sqrt{\upsilon - 2}}{\sqrt{\nu}} + E(R_p),$$

where X is a random variable which has the classical Student's t distribution with a degrees-of-freedom parameter equal to ν. The condition $\nu > 2$ ensures that the distribution has a finite variance. The normal distribution model is a special case due to the well-known property of Student's t distribution that as the degrees-of-freedom parameter increases indefinitely, then the Student's t distribution becomes a standard normal distribution.

The portfolio VaR and CVaR at $p\%$ tail probability are given by the following expressions:

$$\text{VaR at } p\% \text{ tail probability} = q\,(p, \nu)\frac{\sqrt{\upsilon - 2}}{\sqrt{\upsilon}}\sigma(R_p) - E\,(R_p),$$

$$\text{CVaR at } p\% \text{ tail probability} = C(p, \nu)\sigma(R_p) - E(R_p),$$

in which the constants $q(p, \nu)$ and $C(p, \nu)$ depend both on the tail probability and degrees-of-freedom parameter. The coefficient $q(p, \nu)$ is the negative of $p\%$ quantile of the Student's t distribution with ν degrees of freedom and $C(p, \nu)$ can be computed using the following formula:

$$C(p,\nu) = \frac{\Gamma\left(\frac{\nu+1}{2}\right)}{\Gamma\left(\frac{\nu}{2}\right)}\frac{\sqrt{\nu - 2}}{(\nu - 1)\,p\sqrt{\pi}}\left(1 + \frac{q^2\,(p,\nu)}{\nu}\right)^{\frac{1-\nu}{2}},$$

where $\Gamma(x)$ denotes the gamma function which is available in MS Excel and any other software for quantitative analysis.

It is important to keep in mind that neither $q(p,\nu)$ nor $C(p,\nu)$ depend on the portfolio weights. As a consequence, from an asset allocation perspective the basic quantities are the portfolio variance and the mean, like in the multivariate normal assumption.

In the following example, we illustrate how the portfolio VaR and CVaR are computed assuming multivariate normal and the multivariate location-scale Student t distributions. Suppose that the portfolio is equally invested in US Large Cap, Emerging Markets, and Long-Term Treasury. As in the example before, the portfolio return for a given month is calculated by summing up the observed returns of the three asset classes multiplied by 33%. Table 3 includes the returns of the equally weighted portfolio from January 2007 until June 2019.

For the multivariate normal VaR and CVaR at 1% tail probability, we need to calculate the standard deviation and the expected return of the portfolio. Using the data in Table 3, we obtain $\sigma(R_p) = 3.29\%$ and $E(R_p) = 0.6\%$. The monthly risk statistics are computed in the following way:

$$\text{Normal VaR at 1\% tail probability} = 2.326{}^{*}3.29\% - 0.6\% = 7.05\%,$$

$$\text{Normal CVaR at 1\% tail probability} = 2.665{}^{*}3.29\% - 0.6\% = 8.17\%.$$

To find the Student t VaR and CVaR at 1% tail probability, it remains to estimate the degrees of freedom parameter ν. Using the method of maximum likelihood, we find that for this sample the estimated value is $\nu = 4.03$. Plugging in that value in the formula for $C(p,\nu)$, we calculate first that $q(0.01,4.03) = 3.73$,

$$C(0.01, 4.03) = \frac{\Gamma\left(\frac{4.03+1}{2}\right)}{\Gamma\left(\frac{4.03}{2}\right)} \frac{\sqrt{4.03-2}}{(4.03-1)\,0.01\sqrt{\pi}} \left(1 + \frac{3.73^2}{4.03}\right)^{\frac{1-4.03}{2}} = 3.68.$$

The Student t monthly risk statistics equal

$$\begin{aligned}&\text{Student } t \text{ VaR at 1\% tail probability}\\ &= 3.73{}^{*}\frac{\sqrt{4.03-2}}{\sqrt{4.03}}{*}3.29\% - 0.6\% = 8.11\%,\\ &\text{Student } t \text{ CVaR at 1\% tail probability}\\ &= 3.68{}^{*}3.29\% - 0.6\% = 11.5\%.\end{aligned}$$

Both the Student t VaR and CVaR exceed the corresponding risk numbers of the normal distribution because the fitted value of the degrees of

TABLE 3: The Monthly Returns of an Equally Weighted Portfolio in US Large Cap, Emerging Markets, and Long-Term Treasury

Month	Return	Month	Return	Month	Return	Month	Return
Jan-2007	0.02%	Apr-2010	1.53%	Jul-2013	1.37%	Oct-2016	−1.81%
Feb-2007	−0.11%	May-2010	−4.37%	Aug-2013	−2.46%	Nov-2016	−2.84%
Mar-2007	1.36%	Jun-2010	−0.20%	Sep-2013	3.72%	Dec-2016	0.48%
Apr-2007	3.17%	Jul-2010	5.36%	Oct-2013	3.52%	Jan-2017	2.49%
May-2007	2.50%	Aug-2010	0.10%	Nov-2013	−0.49%	Feb-2017	2.94%
Jun-2007	0.64%	Sep-2010	6.09%	Dec-2013	−0.27%	Mar-2017	0.59%
Jul-2007	1.20%	Oct-2010	1.16%	Jan-2014	−1.49%	Apr-2017	1.33%
Aug-2007	0.84%	Nov-2010	−1.44%	Feb-2014	2.86%	May-2017	1.45%
Sep-2007	4.89%	Dec-2010	3.46%	Mar-2014	1.77%	Jun-2017	0.67%
Oct-2007	5.10%	Jan-2011	−0.93%	Apr-2014	1.02%	Jul-2017	2.27%
Nov-2007	−2.53%	Feb-2011	1.27%	May-2014	2.93%	Aug-2017	2.20%
Dec-2007	−0.52%	Mar-2011	1.87%	Jun-2014	1.63%	Sep-2017	−0.33%
Jan-2008	−4.82%	Apr-2011	2.82%	Jul-2014	0.22%	Oct-2017	1.58%
Feb-2008	0.58%	May-2011	−0.23%	Aug-2014	3.93%	Nov-2017	1.30%
Mar-2008	−1.07%	Jun-2011	−1.73%	Sep-2014	−3.52%	Dec-2017	2.12%
Apr-2008	3.70%	Jul-2011	0.44%	Oct-2014	2.45%	Jan-2018	3.57%
May-2008	0.33%	Aug-2011	−1.77%	Nov-2014	1.51%	Feb-2018	−3.77%
Jun-2008	−5.68%	Sep-2011	−4.36%	Dec-2014	−0.80%	Mar-2018	−0.34%
Jul-2008	−1.56%	Oct-2011	7.03%	Jan-2015	2.21%	Apr-2018	−1.23%
Aug-2008	−1.52%	Nov-2011	−0.61%	Feb-2015	1.20%	May-2018	0.44%
Sep-2008	−8.29%	Dec-2011	0.28%	Mar-2015	−0.85%	Jun-2018	−1.08%
Oct-2008	−16.03%	Jan-2012	5.22%	Apr-2015	1.89%	Jul-2018	1.87%
Nov-2008	−0.98%	Feb-2012	2.59%	May-2015	−1.42%	Aug-2018	0.29%
Dec-2008	6.08%	Mar-2012	−1.12%	Jun-2015	−2.68%	Sep-2018	−1.17%
Jan-2009	−8.36%	Apr-2012	0.66%	Jul-2015	−0.17%	Oct-2018	−5.75%
Feb-2009	−5.91%	May-2012	−3.10%	Aug-2015	−5.36%	Nov-2018	2.75%
Mar-2009	10.02%	Jun-2012	2.50%	Sep-2015	−1.28%	Dec-2018	−2.17%
Apr-2009	6.87%	Jul-2012	1.78%	Oct-2015	4.50%	Jan-2019	5.67%
May-2009	7.07%	Aug-2012	0.54%	Nov-2015	−1.26%	Feb-2019	0.85%
Jun-2009	−0.44%	Sep-2012	1.93%	Dec-2015	−1.46%	Mar-2019	3.10%
Jul-2009	6.64%	Oct-2012	−0.90%	Jan-2016	−1.93%	Apr-2019	1.41%
Aug-2009	1.55%	Nov-2012	1.08%	Feb-2016	0.61%	May-2019	−2.05%
Sep-2009	5.00%	Dec-2012	1.58%	Mar-2016	6.62%	Jun-2019	4.49%
Oct-2009	−1.56%	Jan-2013	0.84%	Apr-2016	0.17%		
Nov-2009	4.60%	Feb-2013	0.29%	May-2016	−0.31%		
Dec-2009	−0.04%	Mar-2013	0.74%	Jun-2016	3.95%		
Jan-2010	−2.40%	Apr-2013	2.37%	Jul-2016	3.45%		
Feb-2010	1.32%	May-2013	−2.54%	Aug-2016	0.27%		
Mar-2010	4.22%	Jun-2013	−3.58%	Sep-2016	−0.01%		

Source for monthly returns: Portfolio Visualizer (https://www.portfoliovisualizer.com/).

freedom parameter ν implies a much higher frequency of extreme losses than that implied by the normal distribution.

The multivariate elliptical distribution

The multivariate elliptical distribution is a larger family of distributions in which the multivariate location-scale Student's t distribution, and also the multivariate normal, is nested. Applications of this distribution in asset pricing were suggested by Owen and Rabinovitch [1983]. The name comes from the shape of the contour lines of the joint density — the contour lines are ellipses. The class contains both distributions with fat tails that can describe the frequency of extreme events and also light-tailed distributions, such as the normal distribution.

An illustration of the contour lines of an elliptical distribution is provided in Figure 1 in the bivariate case. The plot can be interpreted in the following way. If we have a sample of observations of the two variables and we create a scatterplot, then the shape of the observations would be approximately elliptical following the shape of the contour lines in Figure 1.

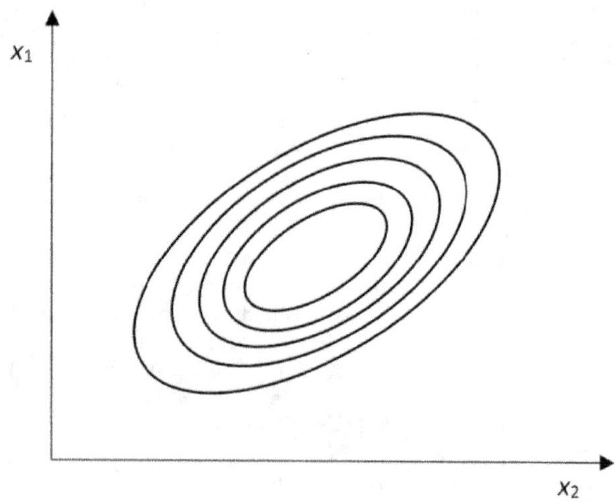

FIGURE 1: The Contour Lines of the Density of a Bivariate Elliptical Distribution Represent Concentric Ellipses

Note: A scatterplot of observations from such a distribution would have a similar elliptical shape.

If the multivariate elliptical distribution has finite variance, then the return of any portfolio can be represented in the following way:

$$R_p = X\sigma(R_p) + E(R_p),$$

where X is a random variable which has a univariate distribution symmetric around the mean with variance equal to one and a mean of zero; that is, the return distribution of any portfolio is a symmetric distribution around the mean. The degree of fat-tailedness of the multivariate elliptical distribution is captured by the term X and this representation shows that it is the same for all asset returns and all portfolios.

The portfolio VaR and CVaR at $p\%$ tail probability have the following representations:

$$\text{VaR at } p\% \text{ tail probability} = q_e(p)\sigma(R_p) - E(R_p),$$
$$\text{CVaR at } p\% \text{ tail probability} = C_e(p)\sigma(R_p) - E(R_p),$$

where $q_e(p)$ is the negative of the $p\%$ quantile of the random variable X in the representation above and $C_e(p)$ is the CVaR at $p\%$ tail probability of the same random variable. Unfortunately, it is impossible to write down a simple parametric expression as in the cases of the normal and Student's t distribution, but the important property is that these coefficients do not depend on the portfolio weights.

The multivariate skewed Student's t distribution

A common feature of all members of the *multivariate elliptical distribution* is that the return of any portfolio has a symmetric distribution around the mean. There are classes of distributions which can capture asymmetry. The multivariate skewed Student's t distribution is one such class.

There are, in fact, many different *skewed Student's t distributions*, the name is generic and does not identify a particular class. In this chapter, we refer to the multivariate hyperbolic Student's t distribution as multivariate skewed Student's t.[3] This class has a parameter for skewness for each asset, $b_1, b_2, \ldots, b_K$, and a parameter λ controlling the heavy tail which is common for all assets.

[3]See Banchi, Stoyanov, Tassinari, Fabozzi, and Focardi [2019].

If the joint distribution of the asset returns is *multivariate skewed Student's t with finite variance*, then the return distribution of any portfolio is univariate skewed Student's t, the following representation holds:

$$R_p = X_p\sigma(R_p) + E(R_p),$$

where X_p has a *univariate skewed Student's t distribution* with a skewness parameter b_p depending on the portfolio weights, variance equal to one, and a mean of zero.

The portfolio VaR and CVaR at $p\%$ tail probability have the following representations:

$$\text{VaR at } p\% \text{ tail probability} = q_h(p, b_p)\sigma(R_p) - E(R_p),$$
$$\text{CVaR at } p\% \text{ tail probability} = C_h(p, b_p)\sigma(R_p) - E(R_p),$$

where $q_h(p, b_p)$ is the negative of the $p\%$ quantile of the random variable X_p in the representation above and $C_h(p, b_p)$ is the CVaR at $p\%$ tail probability of the same random variable. In contrast to the multivariate elliptical distribution, it is no longer the case that the coefficients multiplying portfolio variance are invariant to the portfolio weights. As we vary the weights and rebalance the portfolio from more negatively to more positively skewed assets, the two coefficients decline, reflecting the fact that positively skewed portfolios are less risky than negatively skewed portfolios assuming all other parameters are held constant.

Other distributions

Other more general classes of distributions include the *multivariate hyperbolic distribution,* which contains the multivariate skewed Student's t as a special case along with the *multivariate hyperbolic*, the *normal inverse Gaussian*, and the *variance-gamma distributions* [see Bianchi *et al.*, 2019].

There are other classes, which allow the tail thickness to vary from asset to asset.[4] For those classes, the corresponding expressions for VaR and CVaR would be even more complicated because the coefficients multiplying portfolio variance would depend on both the skewness and the tail thickness of the portfolio return distribution.

The fact that there are so many distributions begs the question if there is a way to choose one that best describes the data. Comparing how different multivariate distributions perform is a challenging statistical problem. It is, however, possible to test the historical performance of a VaR or CVaR

[4]See Näf, Paolella, and Polak [2019].

model for a given portfolio, which is also known as risk backtesting. This is, however, not directly related to the problem of asset allocation.[5]

Risk Measures and Asset Allocation Problems

Replacing standard deviation with a more general downside risk measure changes the set of efficient portfolios because the optimization problem recognizes the skewness and excess kurtosis present in the data. Nevertheless, there are a lot of parallels with mean–variance, especially as far as the geometry of the efficient frontier is concerned. We discuss the parallels in this section.

Connections with Mean–Variance Analysis

In the absence of a risk-free asset, according to the mean–variance framework risk-averse investors build efficient portfolios by minimizing risk proxied by variance subject to an expected return target. As explained in Chapter 8 of the companion volume, under certain assumptions the problem investors are solving is

$$\text{Minimize } \sigma^2(R_p),$$
$$\text{Subject to: } E(R_p) = \mu,$$

where μ is a target expected return. The set of feasible portfolios and the set of efficient portfolios can be described graphically by plotting their standard deviation and expected returns, see Figure 8.2 in Chapter 8 of the companion volume. Under the assumptions of mean–variance analysis, investors are interested only in the expected return and variance and choose portfolios from the efficient set where the trade-off between these two parameters provides an optimal utility.[6]

Note that we can replace standard deviation for variance in the optimal allocation problem without modifying the optimal solution. An equivalent formulation of the mean–variance problem is

$$\text{Maximize } E(R_p) - \lambda\sigma(R_p),$$

where λ is a positive parameter interpreted as risk aversion. The set of efficient portfolios obtained by varying the expected return target μ coincides

[5] For additional information, see Rachev, Stoyanov, and Fabozzi [2008].

[6] See the corresponding analysis in Chapter 8 of the companion volume.

with the set of efficient portfolios obtained by varying the risk-aversion parameter. The value of this parameter for each investor determines the optimal trade-off between risk and return and identifies the particular optimal allocation on the efficient frontier.

If investors measure risk not in terms of standard deviation but using a risk measure focused on the downside, then the corresponding allocation problem takes the following form:

$$\text{Maximize } E(R_p) - \lambda_R \, \text{Risk}(R_p),$$

where λ_R is non-negative and has the same interpretation. The index R indicates that this parameter is different from the one associated with standard deviation. The risk measure can be, for example, CVaR or a lower partial moment, or any other measure which is consistent with the notion of diversification. Recall that VaR may not be a good choice.

Even if investors' attitude towards risk is asymmetric, under certain assumptions the mean–variance problem is still the right one. For example, suppose that we choose to measure risk by CVaR at 1% tail probability and we assume that the joint asset returns distribution is multivariate normal. Then, we plug in the corresponding expression for CVaR in the optimization problem above and we obtain

$$\text{Maximize } (1+\lambda_R)\left[E(R_p) - 2.665\frac{\lambda_R}{1+\lambda_R}\sigma(R_p)\right].$$

Because the coefficient $1+\lambda_R$ is positive, it does not change the optimal solution and can be ignored. As a result, we obtain an asset allocation problem which is identical to the mean–variance problem if we choose the risk-aversion parameter to be represented as $\lambda = 2.665\lambda_R/(1+\lambda_R)$. That is, for any choice of λ_R, under the assumption of normality the investor is actually solving a mean–variance problem.

This may be unsurprising, given that the portfolio return distribution under the normal assumption distribution is characterized in terms of its variance and expected return — the two parameters of the normal distribution. However, in a similar manner under the multivariate elliptical assumption, the CVaR optimal allocation at any tail probability level can be represented as

$$\text{Maximize } (1+\lambda_R)\left[E(R_p) - C_e(p)\frac{\lambda_R}{1+\lambda_R}\sigma(R_p)\right].$$

This problem is also equivalent to the mean–variance problem if we set $\lambda = C_e(p)\lambda_R/(1+\lambda_R)$. Recall that the multivariate normal and the multivariate location-scale Student's t are special cases.

It may appear that alternative risk measures are redundant. There are two arguments against that premature conclusion. First, for regulatory purposes the value of the risk measure is used as a guideline for building capital reserves. Because the financial asset returns are not normally distributed, the normal VaR and CVaR may significantly underestimate the capital reserves. In those applications, the factors that appear in front of variance in the VaR and CVaR expressions (for example, $q_e(p)$ and $C_e(p)$) are of critical importance because they capture the impact of tail thickness on portfolio risk. Clearly, for the purposes of regulation, alternative measures of risk play a significant role.

Second, in asset allocation applications under some assumptions these scaling factors do not depend on the portfolio weights and, therefore, have no effect on the optimal solution. This happens, for example, if there are no detectable asymmetries in the returns of the single assets, if there are no differences in the tail behavior across assets, and if there are no asymmetries in the correlations in downward versus upward markets. These conditions are satisfied by the multivariate elliptical distribution and, for this reason, the optimal allocation is determined by mean–variance analysis.

We mentioned one distributional assumption which may fail to meet one of these conditions. For example, if the skewness parameters of the single assets in the multivariate skewed Student's t distribution are different from zero, then the corresponding coefficients depend on portfolio skewness, which is a function of portfolio weights. In this case, using an alternative risk measure such as CVaR does not lead to a mean–variance optimal allocation problem.

Finally, if we work with historical data only without assuming a specific parametric hypothesis, then the solution of the mean–CVaR problem and the mean–variance problem coincide only by accident.

Shape of the Efficient Frontier

All *feasible portfolios* can be visualized as a set in a plane with expected portfolio return on the vertical axis and portfolio standard deviation on the horizontal axis. The optimal allocations which are solutions to the mean variance problem obtained by varying the expected return target (or, equivalently, by varying the risk-aversion parameter) form a subset known as the set of efficient portfolios. On the graphical representation, that set is known as the *efficient frontier*.

If investors worry about downside risk and replace standard deviation with an alternative risk measure, then how do these sets change? We can arrive at an alternative visualization by replacing standard deviation with the corresponding measure of risk. The efficient portfolios are obtained in a similar manner by solving the corresponding mean–risk problem for all possible risk-aversion levels. It is possible to show that the general shape of the efficient frontier remains the same.[7]

An illustration is provided in Figure 2. The set of feasible portfolios is denoted by gray and the set of efficient portfolios is the border of the set in black. The general shape of the efficient frontier follows the shape of the mean–variance efficient frontier even though the optimal portfolios are different.[8] The reason is that the concave shape of the black curve in Figure 2 is dictated by the convexity property; that is, the inequality that defines the consistency of a risk measure with diversification.

In general, it is difficult to illustrate the shape of the set of feasible portfolios because it is not possible to compute the risk and the return of all possible portfolios, there are just too many of them. We can, however, draw a random portfolio, compute its risk and return, and then plot the point that corresponds to it. If we repeat that process many times, the

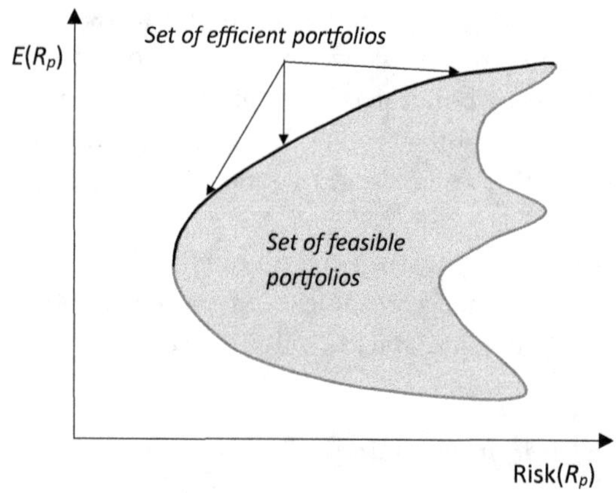

FIGURE 2: The Set of Feasible Portfolios (in gray) and the Set of Efficient Portfolios (in black) Obtained with an Alternative Measure of Risk Consistent with Diversification
Note: The general shape of the efficient frontier is very similar to that of the mean–variance problem.

[7]See Rachev, Stoyanov, and Fabozzi [2008].
[8]Compare this figure to Figure 8.2 in Chapter 8 in the companion volume.

TABLE 4: The Observed Monthly Returns of US Large Cap, Emerging Markets, and Long-Term Treasury for 2007 Together with a Portfolio Invested 30% in US Large Cap, 50% in Emerging Markets, and 20% in Long-Term Treasury

Month	US Large Cap	Emerging Markets	Long-Term Treasury	Random Portfolio
Jan-2007	5.18%	−3.27%	−0.74%	−0.01%
Feb-2007	1.34%	1.26%	1.28%	−0.65%
Mar-2007	3.74%	0.03%	1.14%	2.16%
Apr-2007	1.91%	3.87%	3.28%	3.61%
May-2007	2.33%	−6.23%	−3.66%	3.64%
Jun-2007	−1.35%	−3.26%	−2.69%	1.57%
Jul-2007	5.07%	−1.93%	0.17%	1.70%
Aug-2007	−2.91%	−1.28%	−1.77%	0.37%
Sep-2007	3.12%	0.88%	1.55%	6.53%
Oct-2007	4.59%	1.32%	2.30%	6.91%
Nov-2007	3.03%	−2.49%	−0.83%	−4.33%
Dec-2007	2.51%	−2.37%	−0.91%	−0.50%

Note: The allocation is chosen at random.
Source for monthly returns: Portfolio Visualizer (https://www.portfoliovisualizer.com/).

plotted points will start to approximate the shape of the set of feasible portfolios.

For this illustration, we select three asset classes — US Large Cap, Emerging Markets, and Long-Term Treasury — and we choose the time period from January 2007 until June 2019. We choose a random portfolio and we calculate the portfolio returns for each month in that period. For example, we choose at random that the allocation in the three asset classes is 30%, 50%, and 20%, respectively. Then, the portfolio returns for January 2007 are computed as the sum of the weights multiplied by the observed returns of the three asset classes in that month. Table 4 provides the observed returns for 2007 and the corresponding portfolio returns. The observation for January 2007 is computed in the following way: $0.3 \times 5.18\% + 0.5 \times (-3.27\%) + 0.3 \times (-0.74\%) = -0.01\%$.

Having computed the monthly returns of the selected portfolio, we compute the historical VaR and CVaR at 5% tail probability using the approach described in this chapter. Then, we plot a point in the mean–risk plane, which corresponds to the computed mean and risk numbers. As a next step, we select at random a new portfolio and repeat the process, which results in a second point, and so on.

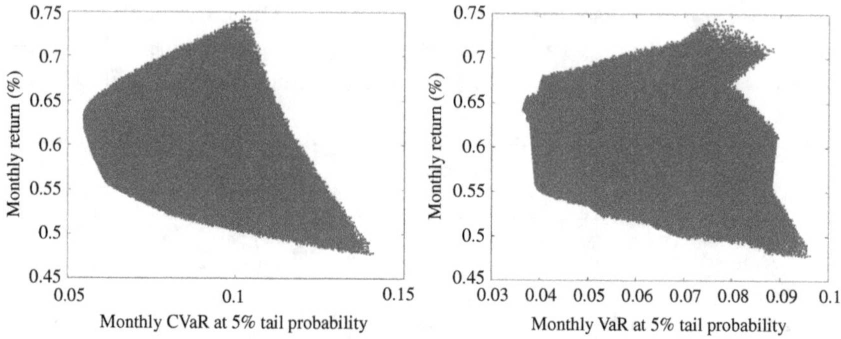

FIGURE 3: The Set of Feasible Portfolios with CVaR at 5% Tail Probability (left) and VaR at 5% Tail Probability (right) Produced from 1 Million Random Allocations in US Large Caps, Emerging Markets, and Long-Term Treasury

Note: Calculations were performed using the Portfolio Visualizer software (https://www.portfoliovisualizer.com/).

There are two plots shown in Figure 3. The left one shows the set of feasible portfolios invested in the three asset classes when CVaR at 5% is used as a risk measure and the right plot shows the set of feasible portfolios when VaR is used as a risk measure. To generate the plots, we use one million random portfolios. Because in general VaR is not consistent with the principle of diversification, the set has an irregular shape, while the set corresponding to CVaR is similar to the one in Figure 2. This has certain implications for portfolio optimization. For example, finding the global minimum VaR portfolio is much more difficult than finding the global minimum CVaR portfolio.

Solving the Mean–Risk Problem in Practice

It can be argued that the mean–variance framework has become so widely used because of its analytical transparency. Not only can we solve for the optimal allocation problem numerically, but we can understand which parameters drive the optimal solution. In some cases, it is possible to write down a formula for the optimal solution and analyze it further. For example, from the parameters that determine portfolio risk as proxied by variance, the most important ones for the optimal solution turn out to be the joint correlations which describe how asset returns covary with each other. It is also known that the optimal solution is very sensitive to the estimates of the expected returns as explained in Chapter 6.

Most of these advantages disappear when we use an alternative risk measure. For example, suppose that we use CVaR at 1% tail probability. It is not possible to write down a closed-form solution of the optimal allocation problem in the general case, which makes it hard to carry out a sensitivity analysis as in the case of mean–variance. Numerical studies indicate that the portfolio expected return and the portfolio standard deviation (the covariances and the asset expected returns) have a significant impact on the optimal allocation.[9] It is also intuitively clear that the dependence of the asset returns in times of market downturns, the skewness, and the tail thickness of the individual asset returns have an impact as well because the risk measure is focused on the downside. It has been, however, very difficult to compare the relative importance of these empirical characteristics.

Practitioners use numerical methods to solve the mean–risk problem. Without entering into unnecessary details, the most heavily exploited property is that of convexity. Recall that this property represents consistency with the principle of diversification. Convex risk measures can be optimized using the tools of convex programming and they have good optimality properties. In some cases, it is possible to formulate simpler and, thus, easier to solve problems. For example, the mean–variance problem is solved as a quadratic problem, which represents a special case. The mean–CVaR problem can be formulated as a linear programming problem.

As a particular example, suppose that an investor considers an asset allocation problem in four US equity asset classes (US Large Cap, US Mid Cap, US Small Cap, and US Micro Cap) and two fixed income asset classes (Long-Term Treasury and Long-Term Corporate Bond). The investor considers an upper bound of 25% on the allocation in each equity asset class and 30% in each fixed income asset class. Also, the investor sets a 0% lower limit on the allocation weight in the US Micro Cap and 5% for the remaining ones.

The optimal allocations when CVaR at 5% tail probability is minimized and when variance is minimized are included in Table 5, in the second and the third columns, respectively. The optimal solutions are obtained by using monthly returns in the period from January 2007 to May 2019. CVaR is computed without making any distributional assumptions using only the historical returns. The empirical properties of the return distributions include skewness and excess kurtosis and because of this, we would

[9]See Stoyanov, Rachev, and Fabozzi [2013a, 2013b].

TABLE 5: The Optimal Asset Class Allocation Using Variance and CVaR at 5% Tail Probability as Objectives in the Optimal Allocation Problem

Asset Class	Min CVaR at 5%	Min Variance
US Large Cap	25.00%	24.87%
US Mid Cap	10.00%	5.00%
US Small Cap	5.00%	5.00%
US Micro Cap	0.00%	5.13%
Long-Term Treasury	30.00%	30.00%
Long-Term Corporate Bonds	30.00%	30.00%

Note: The upper bounds on the asset weights are 25% for the group of equity and 30% for the group of fixed income. The lower bounds are 0% for US Micro Cap and 5% for the rest. To find the optimal solution, we use monthly data from January 2007 to May 2019. Calculations were performed using the Portfolio Visualizer software (https://www.portfoliovisualizer.com/).

expect the two optimal solutions to deviate from each other. Nevertheless, the fixed income asset classes are less risky and this should be recognized by both measures of risk. By comparing the optimal allocations, we find that the most significant difference is in the allocation to US Micro Cap and US Mid Cap.

Risk-Reward Ratios

In the presence of a risk-free asset, classical mean–variance analysis concludes that the optimal solution for any risk-averse investor can be characterized by a mix of two different portfolios, also known as "funds". This property of the optimal portfolio is known as two-fund separation. Depending on the level of risk-aversion, an investor should build a portfolio of the risk-free assets and a portfolio of risky assets known as the tangency portfolio, or the market portfolio. In equilibrium, when the market clears, the market portfolio turns into a cap-weighted portfolio. The tangency portfolio is the portfolio of risky assets with maximal Sharpe ratio. The Sharpe ratio is defined as the ratio of the expected excess return divided by the portfolio standard deviation.

A similar analysis can be performed with a general risk measure which has the convexity property. Figure 4 illustrates the tangency portfolio, which is the portfolio of risky assets with a maximal expected excess return

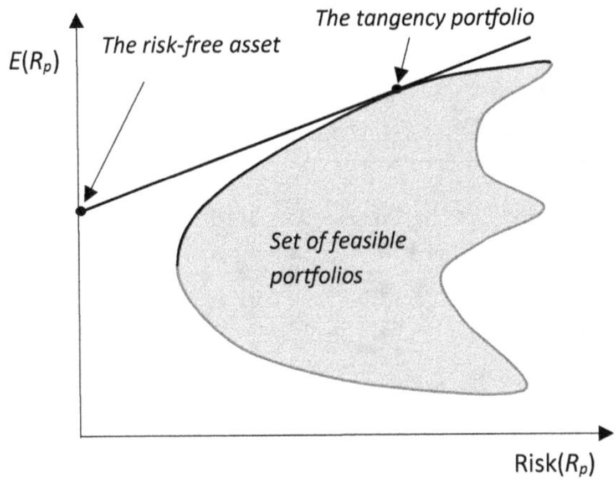

FIGURE 4: The Set of Feasible Portfolios (in gray), the Set of Efficient Portfolios of Risky Assets (in black), the Tangency Portfolio, and the Tangency Line Starting from the Risk-Free Asset and Passing through the Tangency Portfolio

to risk ratio, where risk is measured by the corresponding risk measure. If we choose to proxy risk by standard deviation, we obtain the Sharpe ratio. The tangency line represents all portfolios built as a mix of the risk-free asset and the tangency portfolio. The ratio of expected excess return to risk takes the general form

$$\frac{E(R_p) - R_f}{\text{Risk}(R_p)}.$$

Just like the Sharpe ratio, such ratios can be used to measure risk-adjusted performance. For instance, if CVaR at $p\%$ tail probability is used as a measure of risk, then the corresponding ratio is the expected excess return to CVaR,

$$\frac{E(R_p) - R_f}{\text{CVaR}_{p\%}(R_p)},$$

where R_f denotes the risk-free rate. In this ratio, the expected excess performance is adjusted for the risk in the left tail of the return distribution.

Some of the alternative performance ratios used in the practice of finance can be related to this more general framework. For instance, the Sortino ratio discussed in Chapter 7 in the companion book uses the standard deviation of the realized returns below a minimum acceptable level. If we choose that level to be the expected portfolio return, then the denominator becomes the square root of the semi-variance and the ratio can be viewed

TABLE 6: The Average Excess Return, Standard Deviation, VaR, CVaR, and the Corresponding Ratios of US Large Cap, US Mid Cap, US Small Cap, and Long-Term Corporate Bonds Using the Monthly Historical Data from January 2007 to June 2019

	US Large Cap	**US Mid Cap**	**US Small Cap**	**Long-Term Corporate Bonds**
Average Excess Return	0.17%	0.21%	0.24%	0.03%
Standard Deviation	4.28%	4.95%	5.51%	2.70%
VaR	7.17%	7.61%	9.41%	3.23%
CVaR	9.68%	11.17%	12.11%	5.24%
Sharpe Ratio	0.039	0.043	0.044	0.011
VaR Ratio	0.024	0.028	0.026	0.009
CVaR Ratio	0.017	0.019	0.020	0.006

Note: The VaR and CVaR are computed at 5% tail probability. Calculations were performed using the Portfolio Visualizer software (https://www.portfoliovisualizer.com/).

as the reward-to-risk ratio of a framework where the square root of semi-variance is used to measure risk.[10]

We provide a numerical example which illustrates how the VaR and CVaR ratios are calculated for several asset classes. We use monthly return data from January 2007 to June 2019. The average excess return for each asset class, which appears in the numerator of the ratios, is calculated as the difference between the average excess return of the asset class and that of the Long-Term Treasury.

Table 6 provides the average excess return, the standard deviation, VaR, CVaR, and the corresponding three ratios based on these risk measures. The VaR and CVaR are computed at 5% tail probability. We have not annualized any of the numbers and, therefore, all statistics are directly computed from the monthly data. For example, the VaR ratio is computed by dividing the average excess return of a given asset class by the VaR figure in the table: $0.17/7.17 = 0.024$.

Apart from asset classes, risk-adjusted returns are used to compare actively or passively managed funds or to evaluate and potentially justify adding a new fund or an asset class to an existing portfolio.

[10]A similar example can be constructed with the Sortino–Satchell ratio in which the numerator is the expected excess return and the denominator can be related to a general lower partial moment. See also the related discussion in Chapter 10 of Rachev, Stoyanov, and Fabozzi [2008].

The use of a ratio for risk-adjusted performance comparison does not need to be justified by an entire alternative framework for portfolio selection. However, if an investor wants to find a portfolio that has maximal risk-adjusted performance, then such a connection is highly desirable. Certainly, there is an implicit objective of maximization in ranking funds by any criterion because the investor's desire is to find the best among a given set of funds. This is, however, a simpler problem than an asset allocation decision because the set is discrete; that is, we typically work with a given number of funds and we can calculate the criterion for each fund (like the example in Table 6). When the goal is to make an allocation decision, it is impossible to compute the ratio (or the objective) for all possible portfolios and then rank and choose the best. We have to rely on certain geometric properties of the efficient frontier determined essentially by consistency with the principle of diversification (i.e., the convexity property) which makes sure that the computed optimal solution makes sense and is indeed globally optimal. In essence, the shape of the efficient frontier has to be like the one in Figure 4.

These arguments indicate that there is nothing wrong in ranking funds by a performance measure which uses, for example, VaR in the denominator. However, finding an asset allocation that maximizes that ratio is a much more involved problem, which makes practical sense only if we work with a set of assumptions which guarantee that VaR is convex. Even though there are numerical methods for global optimization, such as evolutionary algorithms, simulated annealing, etc., which do not rely on the objective being a convex function of portfolio weights, it is difficult to accept conceptually that working with risk measure inconsistent with the principle of diversification makes practical sense.[11]

Key Points

- Alternative symmetric measures of dispersion such as mean–absolute deviation (MAD) have been suggested for application to asset allocation problems. Conceptually, they are similar to variance because they penalize symmetrically both profits and losses.
- Asymmetric measures of dispersion, such as semi-variance, focus on the variability of the downside of the return distribution and reflect better the asymmetric nature of risk.

---

[11]For additional information, see Stoyanov, Rachev, and Fabozzi [2007].

- Financial regulation has been the main driver behind the development of alternative risk measures such as VaR and CVaR.
- For regulatory purposes, it is important that a risk measure can be employed to compute capital reserves, while for asset allocation applications the more important property is consistency with the principle of diversification. In contrast to CVaR, VaR does not always meet that condition.
- When risk measures are used to assess the risk of the very extreme losses, it is common to use a distributional hypothesis for the asset return distribution. If the asset return distribution is symmetric and does not reflect the skewness, kurtosis, and the tail dependence in the empirical data, then the mean–variance analysis is essentially an equivalent framework.
- Consistency of the risk measure with the principle of diversification is critical for the geometry of the efficient frontier. For such risk measures, the shape of the efficient frontier is similar to that of mean–variance. The efficient portfolios, however, can be different.
- Every mean–risk framework is consistent with a risk-reward ratio, defined as the expected excess return divided by the measure of risk, and can be used as a measure of performance. It is an alternative to the Sharpe ratio. The Sortino and the Sortino–Satchell ratios can be viewed as special cases.
- A risk-adjusted return ratio can be used for performance evaluation without requiring consistency with a mean–risk framework. However, for optimal allocation decisions such a consistency is desirable because the geometry of the efficient frontier guarantees good optimality properties of the ratio.

References

Artzner, P., F. Delbaen, J. M. Eber, and D. Heath, 1999. "Coherent measures of risk," *Mathematical Finance*, 9(3): 203–228.

Bianchi, M. L., S. V. Stoyanov, G. L. Tassinari, F. J. Fabozzi, and S. M. Focardi, 2019. *Handbook of Heavy-Tailed Distributions in Asset Management and Risk Management.* Singapore: World Scientific Press.

Holton, G. A., 2004. "Defining risk," *Financial Analyst Journal*, 60(6): 19–25.

Konno, H. and H. Yamazaki, 1991. "Mean-absolute deviation portfolio optimization model and its applications to Tokyo Stock Market," *Management Science*, 37(5): 519–531.

Markowitz, H. M., 1952. "Portfolio Selection," *Journal of Finance*, 7(1): 77–91.

Markowitz, H. M., 1959. *Portfolio Selection: Efficient Diversification of Investments*. New York: John Wiley & Sons.

Näf, J., M. S. Paolella, and P. Polak, 2019. "Heterogeneous tail generalized COMFORT modeling via Cholesky decomposition," *Journal of Multivariate Analysis*, 172: 84–106.

Owen, J. and R. Rabinovitch, 1983. "On the class of elliptical distributions and their applications to the theory of portfolio choice," *Journal of Finance*, 38(3): 745–752.

Rachev, S. T., S. V. Stoyanov, and F. J. Fabozzi, 2008. *Advanced Stochastic Models, Risk Assessment, and Portfolio Optimization*. Hoboken, NJ: John Wiley & Sons.

Rachev, S. T., S. V. Stoyanov, and F. J. Fabozzi, 2011. *A Probability Metrics Approach to Financial Risk Measures*. Hoboken, NJ: Wiley-Blackwell.

Stoyanov, S. V., S. T. Rachev, and F. J. Fabozzi, 2007. "Optimal financial portfolios," *Applied Mathematical Finance*, 14(5): 403–436.

Stoyanov, S. V., S. T. Rachev, and F. J. Fabozzi, 2013a. "Sensitivity of portfolio VaR and CVaR to portfolio return characteristics," *Annals of Operations Research*, 205(1): 169–187.

Stoyanov, S. V., R. T. Svetlozar, and F. J. Fabozzi, 2013b. "CVaR sensitivity with respect to tail thickness," *Journal of Banking & Finance*, 37(3): 977–988.

Chapter 9

Securities Lending and its Alternatives in the Equity Market*

Learning Objectives

After reading this chapter, you will understand:

- what securities finance is and the important role it plays in the market;
- what securities lending is and why it is used by beneficial owners;
- the mechanics of a securities lending program;
- the risks associated with securities lending;
- the role third-parties play in securities lending; and
- the alternatives to securities lending: contract for differences, single stock futures, equity swaps, and equity repos.

Introduction

In the secondary market for securities, there is a wide range of trading strategies employed by institutional investors. Some of the strategies will require that market participants borrow funds to purchase securities or to borrow securities. Because some investors need to borrow securities, other investors who own securities may be willing to lend them. For the market to accommodate these types of trades, a mechanism must be available in the marketplace whereby the financing of positions in securities can be done quickly and at a reasonable cost, and securities can be borrowed so that

*This chapter is coauthored with Steven Mann, Distinguished Professor Emeritus at the University of South Carolina.

short selling can take place. The financing of positions in securities and the borrowing of securities fall into a little-known but important area of finance called *securities finance*. Securities finance involves two activities: securities lending, the subject of this chapter, and repurchase agreements, the subject of the next chapter. Institutional investors can retain the services of a bank or a non-banking entity to operate a securities lending program to provide these services. Large asset management firms can use their own securities lending program rather than use a program offered by a third party. These entities generate fee income and interest income for their participation in these activities.

There are alternatives to a traditional securities lending program.[1] In the second part of this chapter, we review alternatives to securities lending: contract for differences, single stock futures, equity swaps, and equity repos.

Securities Lending

When an investor sells a security short, that investor benefits from a subsequent decline in the security's price. However, there needs to be a mechanism to accommodate short selling. When the short seller sells a security to a buyer, how does the short seller obtain the security to deliver to the broker, who then delivers the security to the buyer? Here is the short answer: the short seller borrows the security from the broker. That short answer, however, masks the role of a major activity in financial markets called securities lending and the motivation of the parties in a securities lending transaction. Although the need to borrow a security that has been sold short is the motivation for a securities lending transaction, securities lending can be used by beneficial owners to raise cash. The motivation for a repurchase agreement is typically driven by the need of the parties to borrow and lend cash. For an asset management firm, the lending of securities can produce revenue that can add to performance.

Mechanics of a Securities Lending Transaction

In a securities lending transaction, the owner of the security (i.e., the beneficial owner), for a limited time period gives legal title to a security or a

[1]For a discussion of the importance of securities lending and the development of the global securities lending market, see Dive, Hodge, Jones, and Purchase [2011].

basket of securities to another party. The securities lending agreement calls for the security borrower to return the borrowed security to the security lender either on demand or by a specified date. The party granting this right is referred to as the *security lender*. The party to whom the security is lent is called the *security borrower*. In exchange for the temporary transfer of ownership, the security lender receives some form of collateral which can be either cash or another security. The most common form of collateral is cash.[2]

When the collateral is cash for the right to the temporary ownership of the security, the security lender pays the security borrower an agreed upon amount called the *rebate rate*. This may seem odd that the security lender pays the security borrower for the right to borrow the security. The security lender, however, can invest the cash and earn a rate of return. The securities lender (or the entity managing the securities lending program) will invest the cash in a portfolio of short-term debt obligations. The expectation is that the security lender or the entity managing the securities lending program has the ability to earn a greater return on the cash collateral received from the security borrower than the rebate rate. If the security lender can earn a rate of return that exceeds the rebate rate, the difference accrues to the benefit of the security lender. Effectively, a security lending transaction is nothing more than a loan made by the security borrower to the security lender. The collateral for the loan is the security borrowed. The interest the security lender pays the security borrower is the rebate rate. The security lender seeks to earn a return that exceeds the rebate rate that must be paid by the security borrower. However, there is a risk, referred to as reinvestment risk, that the funds invested will earn a return lower than the rebate rate.

During the period when the security lender has loaned the security to the security borrower, the security lender faces the risk that the security borrower will not be able to return the lent security to the security lender. The concern is obviously that the market value of the lent security will increase, and the security lender will then realize a loss if the security borrower fails to return the security that has appreciated in value. To protect itself against this risk, the security lender will require that the security borrower post some type of collateral, which can be either cash or other securities.

[2]Baklanova, Caglio, Cipriani, and Copeland [2019] provide stylized facts about the securities lending market (as well as the repurchase agreement market).

If instead of cash collateral, securities are used by the securities borrower as collateral, then there is no cash to reinvest. In that case, the securities lender will negotiate a borrowing fee. This fee is based on the market value of the securities lent. The borrowing fee is split between the securities lender and the entity managing the securities lending program.

Securities Lending Programs

The various securities lending groups that can be used by institutional investors assist customers in negotiating the rebate rate, identifying acceptable counterparties in transactions, and investing the cash collateral to generate a spread over the rebate rate. Some institutional investors use the services of third-party managers of security lending programs.[3] These third-party entities then become the lending agent, lending on behalf of the beneficial owners. There are some asset management firms that have their own securities lending program rather than using the services of a third party. The purpose of a securities lending program is to optimize trading performance through its managed program. This involves determining who the counterparty in a transaction should be (i.e., counterparty credit analysis), monitor the counterparty and avoid concentration risk, avoid potential short squeezes in the market, and potentially assess long and short fund flow in the market that can be used by asset managers to support positions taken in their portfolio.[4]

A key in whether a client is willing to enter into a securities lending program is the performance of the investment program (i.e., the investment strategy for investing the cash collateral) used by the lending agent. The client can calculate, or retain an independent third-party to calculate, various performance measures to assess how effectively the cash collateral was invested. The client should thoroughly understand the investment strategy and its risks. Aggressive investment strategies can result in losses, in that the return earned is less than the rebate rate.

---

[3]Duffie, Gârleanu, and Pederson [2002] propose an asset valuation model when short-selling requires searching for security lenders and when bargaining the rebate rate.

[4]In addition to third-party vendors that provide services for managing programs mentioned above, there is a growing sector of financial technology (fintech) companies that offer services to assist companies in managing securities finance. The International Capital Market Association (ICMA) provides a directory of such services which include collateral management, corporate actions, exposure agreement, intraday liquidity (monitoring and reporting), matching, confirmation and allocation, and reconciliation.

When an asset manager uses its own securities lending program and there is a loss because the securities borrower fails to return the security, then the loss is absorbed by the portfolio managed by the asset manager. This occurred during the global financial crisis that began in 2008. When there is a lending agent, the treatment of losses varies. In some third-party lending programs, some lending agents may provide indemnification provisions to the securities lending program, while others do not provide such indemnification.

Equity Financing Alternatives to Securities Lending

Asset managers who want to establish a short position in common stock can borrow the stock via a security lending transaction. Those who want to implement a levered long position in common stock can simply buy stocks on margin. However, these positions can be replicated using derivative contracts such as contracts for differences (CFDs), single stock futures, and equity swaps, as well as equity repos. In this section, we describe these methods of equity financing.

Contracts for Differences

CFDs are derivative products that can be utilized to replicate both long and short positions in an underlying asset but do not carry any rights of ownership. The underlying asset for equity CFDs could be an individual common stock or an equity index.

A long position in an equity CFD creates a synthetic levered long position. Correspondingly, a short position in an equity CFD creates a synthetic short position. Asset managers create leverage, in that when an equity CFS position is opened, both the long and the short are required only to post a fraction (10–20%) of the position's value in the form of margin. A broker loans the balance of the contract's value and the asset manager in a long equity CFD pays interest on the contract's full value. Conversely, the asset manager in a short equity CFD receives interest on the contract's full value. The margin requirement varies across stocks and is a function of such factors as the stock's market capitalization and its price volatility. At the end of each trading day, CFDs are marked to market using the closing share prices. As long as the margin requirement is maintained, the position can remain open indefinitely.

Illustration

Let's illustrate how a long position in an equity CFD works with a hypothetical example. Suppose an asset manager buys 1,000 shares of XYZ Company stock as a CFD at a price of \$48.65 per share. The total market value of the position is \$48,650. Brokerage commission on the trade is assumed to be 0.25% or approximately \$122. The margin requirement is, say, 10% so the asset manager must deposit at least \$4,865 in an account with a broker to open the position. The asset manager is effectively borrowing money to establish a long equity position and must pay interest on the financing (i.e., the contract's full value). Suppose the interest rate is 3-month LIBOR + 200 basis points. Accordingly, interest is charged each trading day to the investor's margin account and is determined using the following expression:

$$1{,}000 \times \text{XYZ closing share price} \times (\text{3-month LIBOR} + 200\ \text{bp}) \times (1/360).$$

Now suppose that one month later the price of XYZ stock stands at \$51 a share and the asset manager desires to sell a CFD to close the position. The profit on this position is \$2,350 (= \$51,000 – \$48,650) plus any cash dividends paid while the position is open less the interest paid to finance the position as well as the commissions paid to open and close the CFD. Thus, a long position in this equity CFD creates a virtual leveraged long position in 1,000 XYZ shares.

A short position in an equity CFD profits when stock prices fall. The mechanics of a short equity CFD position are essentially the same as the long equity CFD with two important exceptions. First, an investor is required to post margin of say 10% of the total value of the position but instead of paying interest on the contract's full value. Second the short CFD investor receives interest each day the position is open. This feature is tantamount to the rebate an investor who borrows a security using a security lending agreement receives for providing cash collateral.

Advantages and disadvantages of CFDs

CFDs potentially offer the following advantages to asset managers:

- CFDs allow the asset manager to avoid certain trade-related costs (e.g., custody, clearing, and settlement), and there is no bid-ask spread because CFDs are valued at the prevailing market price at the time the position is opened.

- Greater leverage is possible with CFDs as compared to taking a physical position in the underlying common stock.
- After the short position is established, a CFD eliminates *recall risk*, the risk of the stock lender recalling the stock prior to the asset manager wanting to close out the short position.

To understand, the greater leverage advantage, suppose that an asset manager has a negative view on a stock and wants to establish a short position. To do so, the asset manager must borrow the stock and provide collateral based on the underlying value of the borrowed stock. Conversely, taking a short position using a CFD does not entail any physical ownership of the security so an amount of collateral needed in a security lending agreement is not required. A CFD requires only a margin of 10–20%. As a result, the CFD permits much greater leverage. In the United States, Regulation T requires that an asset manager who shorts a stock does not receive access to the proceeds of the short sale and in addition must put up at least 50% margin to secure the position.

There are some offsetting disadvantages of using CFDs as opposed to taking a long position in the underlying asset:

- Equity CFDs on individual common stocks do not carry any voting rights and thus for large institutional investors taking a long position in common stock using a CFD does not present any opportunities for shareholder activism.
- Equity CFDs positions will be closed out if a takeover of the corporation underlying the CFD is consummated. If this occurs, the final closing price will be the prevailing market price one day prior to the final day the shares are quoted in their existing form.
- Some institutional investors, especially mutual funds, are restricted as to the type of derivative products in which they are permitted to invest and CFDs may not be available to such fund managers.
- Equity CFDs on individual common stocks are non-deliverable.

CFD trading strategies

CFDs are utilized in a number of different trading strategies. For example, for an asset manager who has a view on the prospects of a particular common stock, CFDs are a low-cost vehicle to speculate on the expected change in price. Moreover, CFDs can be used to hedge short-term fluctuations in a portfolio's value. As an example, suppose an asset manager with a long position in a portfolio of common stocks believes that the risk of a substantial sell-off is uncomfortably high. There are several ways to hedge this risk. One obvious but relatively costly way is to liquidate the portfolio and then repurchase the shares when the risk has subsided. Taking a short position in CFDs offers a much more cost-effective method to hedge this risk exposure and avoids the possible tax liability incurred from liquidating the portfolio.

CFDs can also be employed to lock in a profit of a physical position in common stocks. To capture a profit due to a share price increase, one need only short a CFD in an equal amount at the prevailing market price. Accordingly, CFDs can be utilized for tax management. Finally, suppose an asset manager needs liquidity but desires to maintain an exposure. This is easily accomplished by converting a common stock position into a CFD at the prevailing market price. In the process, the investor releases the 90% of the cash in the position (assuming a 10% margin) while remaining fully exposed to the prospects of the common stock.

Single Stock Futures

Single stock futures are equity futures in which the underlying is the common stock of an individual corporation as opposed to an equity index. Not all stocks are the underlying for single stock futures, therefore an asset manager interested in taking a short position using these derivatives is limited to those stocks traded on either of these exchanges.

There are three advantages of using single stock futures rather than borrowing the shares in the cash market (via a stock lending transaction) if the asset manager seeking to short a stock has a choice. The first advantage is the transactional efficiency that the futures contract permits. In a stock lending program, the short seller may find it difficult if not impossible to borrow the stock in question for a variety of reasons. Moreover, an opportunity can be missed as the stock loan department seeks to locate the stock to borrow. A second advantage is that like CFDs, recall risk is eliminated. A third potential advantage is the cost savings by implementing a short sale via single stock futures rather than a stock lending transaction. The financing of the short sale position in a stock lending transaction is arranged by the broker through a bank. The interest rate that the bank will charge is called the *broker call loan rate* or the *call money rate*. The broker call loan rate with a markup is charged to the asset manager. However, if the short seller receives the proceeds to invest, this will reduce the cost of borrowing the stock.

There are several factors that determine whether or not there is a cost savings by taking a short position in a single stock futures contract. To understand these factors, we begin with the relationship between the price of the single stock futures contract and the price of the underlying stock. The following relationship must exist for there to be no arbitrage opportunity[5]:

$$\begin{aligned}\text{Futures price} = {} & \text{Stock price}[1 + r(d_1/360)] \\ & + \text{Expected dividend}[1 + r(d_2/360)],\end{aligned}$$

where r is the short-term interest rate, d_1 is the number of days until the settlement of the futures contract, d_2 is the number of days between receipt of the expected dividend payment and the settlement date.

As of this writing, the short-term rate in the pricing relationship above typically reflects the London Interbank Offered Rate (LIBOR).

The difference between the futures price and the stock price is called the *basis*. The basis is effectively the repo rate (for the period until the settlement date) adjusted by the expected dividend. The basis is also referred to as the *net interest cost or carry*. The buyer of the futures contract pays the net interest cost to maintain the long position; the seller of the futures contract earns the net interest cost for financing the buyer's long position. Note the similarity between single stock futures and equity CFDs. Recall that the long position in an equity contract for differences paid interest on the value of the contract while the short position receives interest.

Consequently, a comparison of the cost advantage to shorting single stock futures rather than using a stock lending transaction comes down to empirically determining which has the lower net interest cost.

Equity Swaps

Yet another way to replicate either a leveraged long equity position or a short sale is with an equity swap. *Equity swaps* are contractual agreements between two counterparties which provide for the periodic exchange of a schedule of cash flows over a specified time period where at least one of the two payments is linked to the performance of an equity index, a basket of stocks, or a single stock. Thus, asset managers can gain exposure to equities without entering the cash market directly.

---

[5]The derivation of this relationship is found in most books that cover futures contracts.

In its most basic form, in an equity swap one counterparty agrees to pay the other the total return to an equity index in exchange for receiving either the total return of another asset or a fixed or floating interest rate. All payments are based on a fixed notional amount and payments are made over a fixed time period. Equity swaps have a wide variety of applications including asset allocation, accessing international markets, return enhancement, hedging equity exposure, and synthetically shorting stocks.

The advantages of using equity swaps are no transaction costs, no sales or dividend withholding tax, and no tracking error/basis risk versus the index.

Equity swap structures are very flexible with maturities ranging from a few months to 10 years. The returns of virtually any asset can be swapped for another without incurring the costs associated with a transaction in the cash market. Payment schedules can be denominated in any currency regardless of the choice of the equity asset and payments can be exchanged monthly, quarterly, annually, or at maturity. The equity asset can be any equity index or portfolio of stocks denominated in any currency — hedged or unhedged.

Variations of the basic structure include: international equity swaps, where the equity return is linked to an international equity index; currency-hedged swaps, where the swap is structured to eliminate currency risk; and call swaps, where the equity payment is paid only if the equity index appreciates (depreciation will not result in a payment from the counterparty receiving the equity return to the other counterparty because of call protection).

The basic mechanics of equity swaps are the same regardless of the structure. However, the rules governing the exchange of payments may differ. If the investment objective is to reduce US equity exposure and increase Japanese equity exposure, for example, a swap could be structured to exchange the total returns to the S&P 500 for the total returns to the Nikkei 225 Index. If, however, the investment objective is to gain access to the Japanese equity market, a swap can be structured to exchange LIBOR plus a spread for the total returns to the Nikkei Index. This is an example of diversifying internationally and the cash flows can be denominated in either yen or dollars. The advantages of entering into an equity swap to obtain international diversification are that the investor exposure is devoid of tracking error and the investor incurs no sales tax, custodial fees, withholding fees, or market impact costs associated with entering and exiting a market. This swap is the economic equivalent of being long the Nikkei 225 Index financed at a spread to LIBOR at a fixed exchange rate.

There are numerous applications of equity swaps, but nearly everyone of them assumes the aforementioned basic structure. Asset managers can virtually swap any financial asset for the total returns to an equity index, a portfolio of stocks, or a single stock. Market makers are prepared to create structures that allow an investor to exchange the returns of any two assets. The schedule of cash flows exchanged is a function of the assets. For example, an active asset manager attempting to outperform an equity benchmark may be able to accomplish this by purchasing a particular bond and swapping the cash flows for the S&P total returns minus a spread.

Equity Repos

An *equity repo agreement* is the sale of a security with a commitment by the seller to buy the same equity security (or equivalent securities) back from the purchaser at a specified price at a designated future date or at call. As with repos in the bond market (as discussed in the next chapter), an equity repo agreement is a collateralized loan where the collateral is the equity security sold and subsequently repurchased. An equity repo is employed to finance long equity positions as well as to borrow securities to cover short positions.

Let's illustrate an equity repo transaction where a hypothetical common stock, ABC, serves as collateral for the loan. Suppose an asset manager desires to use an equity repo agreement to finance one million shares of ABC common stock which is currently trading at \$22 per share. The term of the agreement is assumed to be one month. Assume the relevant repo rate is 5%, which is the interest rate (i.e., borrowing rate) specified in the agreement. Then, as will be explained below, the asset manager would agree to deliver 1,000,000 shares of ABC common stock for \$20,000,000 and agree to repurchase the stock for \$20,083.333.33. The \$83,333.33 difference between the "sale" price of \$20,000,000 and the repurchase price of \$20,083,333.33 is the dollar interest on the financing.

In order to provide the lender of cash some cushion should the market value of ABC common stock decline during the 1-month agreement, the amount lent should be less than the current market value of ABC common stock. The amount by which the market value of the equity used as collateral exceeds the loan's value is called the initial margin or "haircut". While the initial margin is transaction specific, we will assume an initial margin of 10%. Accordingly, since the total market value of the common stock used as collateral is $22,000,000, the purchase price (i.e., amount borrowed) in our illustration is $20,000,000 ($22,000,000/1.10). The total repurchase price is the sale price plus repo interest. Using a repo rate of 5% and a repo term of 30 days, the dollar interest is $83,333.33 as follows:

$$\$20,000,000 \times 0.05 \times (30/360) = \$83,333.33.$$

The total repurchase price is $20,083,333.33.

One of the terms negotiated in an equity repo agreement is the procedure used for marking the equity collateral to market. Moreover, the conditions under which the initial margin needs to be reinstated via a margin call also needs to be determined. Usually in equity repo agreements, the party being called for additional margin has the right to deliver the required amount in either additional securities or in cash. In addition, if the term of an equity repo includes an ex-dividend date, the lender of cash (borrower of securities) is generally contractually required to make the payment equal to the amount of the dividend to the borrower of cash (lender of securities) on that date. Finally, the agreement may also include a right of substitution, which means the borrower of cash has the right to substitute equivalent collateral during the life of the equity repo agreement. This payment is termed the *manufactured payment.*

The illustration presented above is an example of a *cash-driven repo* transaction. The motivation for entering into a cash-driven repo is as a source of financing. By contrast, the motivation of a *stock-driven repo* transaction is to borrow common stock to cover a short position. There are also opportunities for arbitrage between an equity repo and other forms of equity financing. For example, an asset manager could borrow common stock using a securities lending agreement and then lend the shares via an equity repo.

Common stock that is in demand in the securities lending market (commonly called *specials* just as in the fixed-income repo market described in the Chapter 10) can be lent out and serve as a low-cost source of financing. Common stock that is not considered special will result in a higher repo rate. One of the differences between equity repo and the traditional repo market is that the term general collateral has little relevance in the equity repo market. Because common equity is more idiosyncratic than say US Treasuries, the repo rate negotiated between counterparties will be specific to a particular transaction. Thus, while there are certainly common stocks that are specials, the balance of common stock should not be viewed as close substitutes as collateral in equity repo transactions. As a result, these equity repo transactions will result in a wide range of repo rates.

One final element that requires mention is custody of the collateral. The three methods used in traditional repo agreements are also employed in equity repo agreements. The most straightforward approach is to physically *deliver-out* the securities to the cash lender, their clearing agent, or a designated third party. While this approach is logical and results in the least credit risk to the cash provider, this method is the most expensive in terms of time and administrative costs. The next method is termed *hold-in-custody*. With this method, the collateral remains in the possession of the borrower of cash. While this method is the least costly, it should be considered after a careful examination of the cash borrower's credit risk. The third method involves the use of a *collateral management facility* operated by a bank which performs the duties of holding the equity collateral, marking-to-market, margin calls, etc. for a fee. This arrangement is akin to a tri-party repo in the bond market described in Chapter 10.

Key Points

- Securities finance is an important part of the financial market landscape because it involves the financing of positions in securities and the borrowing of securities.
- Securities finance involves two activities: securities lending and repurchase agreements.
- Institutional investors can retain the services of a bank or a non-banking entity to operate a securities lending program to provide these services.
- In a securities lending transaction, the beneficial owner of a security temporarily transfers ownership for a limited time period to the security borrower.
- The securities lending agreement calls for the security borrower to return the borrowed security to the security lender either on demand or by a specified date.
- In exchange for the temporary transfer of ownership, the security lender receives some form of collateral, which can be either cash or another security, the former being the most common form of collateral.
- When the collateral is cash, the security lender pays the security borrower an agreed upon amount called the rebate rate, which the security lender invests.

- The expectation is that the security lender or the entity managing the securities lending program has the ability to earn a greater return on the cash collateral received from the security borrower than the rebate rate.
- One of the risks faced by the security lender is that the return realized when the cash is invested will be less than the rebate rate.
- A security lender should understand the strategy for investing the cash so that the investment risk can be evaluated.
- Another risk faced by the security lender is that the security borrower will not be able to return the lent security to the security lender; more specifically, the risk is that if the market value of the lent security increases, the security lender will then realize a loss if the security borrower fails to return the security that has appreciated in value.
- To protect itself against counterparty credit risk, the security lender will require that the security borrower post some type of collateral, which can be either cash or other securities.
- If securities are used as collateral, a borrowing fee based on the market value of the securities lent will be negotiated and that fee is split between the securities lender and the lending agent if one is used.
- A securities lending group can be used by institutional investors for negotiating the rebate rate, identifying acceptable counterparties in transactions, and investing the cash collateral to generate a spread over the rebate rate.
- The lending agent optimizes trading performance, which involves (1) determining who the counterparty in a transaction should be, (2) monitoring the securities borrowers and avoiding concentration risk, (3) avoiding potential short squeezes in the market, and (4) assessing long and short fund flow in the market that can be used by asset managers to support positions taken in their portfolios.
- A client in a securities lending program is exposed to the risk that the investment strategy will produce a return that is less than the rebate rate.
- The securities lender is exposed to counterparty risk (i.e., the securities borrower will fail to return the security if it has appreciated) when it manages its own securities lending program.
- In some third-party lending programs, the lending agents may provide indemnification provisions to the securities lending program, while others do not provide such indemnification.
- The alternative arrangements for securities lending and financing positions that can be used by asset managers include contracts for differences

(CFDs), single stock futures, and equity swaps, as well as equity repos.

- CFDs are derivative products that can be utilized to replicate both long and short positions in an underlying common stock or equity index but do not carry any rights of ownership.
- A long position in an equity CFD creates a synthetic leveraged long position, while a short position in an equity CFD creates a synthetic short position.
- Potential advantages of using CFDs are (1) avoids certain trade-related costs, (2) offers greater leverage compared to taking a physical position in the underlying security, and (3) avoids recall risk.
- Potential disadvantages of using CFDs are (1) equity CFDs on individual common stocks do not carry any voting rights should that be important for shareholder activism, (2) equity CFDs positions will be closed out if a takeover of the corporation underlying the CFD is consummated, (3) CFDs may not be permissible for some institutional investors, and (4) equity CFDs on individual common stocks are non-deliverable.
- When available, single stock futures are equity futures in which the underlying is the common stock of an individual corporation as opposed to an equity index.
- Advantages of using single stock futures to short a stock rather than borrowing the shares in a stock lending transaction are (1) the transactional efficiency that the futures contract permits, (2) recall risk is eliminated, and (3) the potential cost savings by implementing a short sale via single stock futures rather than a stock lending transaction.
- Equity swaps are contractual agreements between two counterparties which provide for the periodic exchange of a schedule of cash flows over a specified time period, where at least one of the two payments is linked to the performance of an equity index, a basket of stocks, or a single stock.
- Equity swaps allow asset managers exposure to equities without entering the cash market directly.
- In an equity swap, one counterparty agrees to pay the other the total return for an equity index in exchange for receiving either the total return of another asset or a fixed or floating interest rate.
- In addition to being used for synthetically shorting stocks, equity swaps can be used in asset allocation, accessing international markets, return enhancement, and hedging equity exposure.
- No transaction costs, no sales or dividend withholding tax, and no tracking error/basis risk versus the index are advantages of using equity swaps.

- An equity repo agreement is the sale of a security with a commitment by the seller to buy the same equity security (or equivalent securities) back from the purchaser at a specified price at a designated future date or at call.
- An equity repo is employed to finance long equity positions as well as to borrow securities to cover short positions.

References

Baklanova, V., C. Caglio, M. Cipriani, and A. Copeland, 2019. "The use of collateral in bilateral repurchase and securities lending agreements." *Review of Economic Dynamics*, 33: 228–249.

Dive, M., R. Hodge, C. Jones, and J. Purchase, 2011. "Developments in the global securities lending market." *Bank of England Quarterly Bulletin*, September.

Duffie, D., N. Gârleanu, and L. H. Pedersen, 2002. "Securities lending, shorting, and pricing." *Journal of Financial Economics*, 66(2–3): 307–339.

Chapter 10

Repurchase Agreements for Financing Positions and Shorting in the Bond Market*

Learning Objectives

After reading this chapter, you will understand:

- the mechanics of a repurchase agreement for bonds;
- credit risks associated with repurchase agreements and how they can be mitigated;
- the purpose of repo margin;
- the factors that impact the repo rate;
- what is meant by special collateral and general collateral;
- what are cross-currency repo, callable repo, and whole loan repo transactions; and
- non-repo instruments/arrangements for financing and/or leveraging bond positions: credit default swaps (CDSs), total return swaps (TRSs), and sell/buy-back arrangements.

Introduction

There are many bond strategies that require the asset manager to have access to short-term financing and the ability to borrow bonds to cover short positions. Consequently, the ability to finance bond positions and cover

*This chapter is coauthored with Steven Mann, Distinguished Professor Emeritus at the University of South Carolina.

short bond positions is an essential element of a liquid, well-functioning bond market. Although securities lending programs can be used by bond portfolio managers, repurchase and reverse repurchase agreements are the mechanisms most used by asset managers to accomplish these needs. Repurchase agreements occupy a central position in the money market and provide a relatively safe investment opportunity for short-term investors who are willing to lend to asset managers. The repo market is one of the largest sectors of the global money market. In this chapter, we discuss repurchase agreements and alternatives available to asset managers for financing positions and/or taking short positions.[1]

Repurchase Agreement

A *repurchase agreement* or simply *repo* is the sale of a bond with a commitment by the seller to buy the same bond back from the purchaser at a specified price at a designated future date. For example, an asset manager may need funding to implement an investment strategy. The asset manager can use holdings in the portfolio as collateral to obtain funding. For example, an asset manager who owns an investment-grade corporate bond might agree to sell this (the "seller") to another party (the "buyer") for cash today while simultaneously agreeing to buy the same corporate bond issue back at a certain date in the future (or in some cases on demand) for a predetermined price. The sale generates cash for the asset manager. The price at which the seller must subsequently repurchase the security is called the *repurchase price* and the date that the security must be repurchased is called the *repurchase date*.

Therefore, a repo is nothing more than a collateralized loan where the collateral is the security that is sold (the investment-grade corporate bond in our example) and subsequently repurchased. One party (the "seller") is borrowing funds and providing collateral for the loan; the other party (the "buyer") is lending money and accepting a security as collateral for the loan. As explained below, from the perspective of the borrower (i.e., the "seller"), the advantage of a repo is that the short-term borrowing rate is lower than the cost of bank financing, as we will see shortly. From the

[1]For a discussion of the role of repurchase transactions on th Global Financial Crisis of 2007-2009, see Gorton and Metrick [2012]. For an discussion of the European repo market and its role as an amplification channel for sovereign-debt crises, see Armakola, Douady, Laurent, and Molten [2020].

lender's perspective (i.e., the "buyer"), a repo offers an attractive yield on a short-term secured transaction that is highly liquid.

As for the type of collateral, any form of collateral acceptable to the lender of the funds can be used.

Repo Basics

To understand the basics of a repo, suppose that on March 16, an asset manager purchases a specific bond issued by Corporation ABC that matures in 10 years. The face amount of the position is $10 million, and the bond's full price (that is, flat price plus the accrued interest) is $10,200,000. Further, suppose the asset manager wants to hold the position until the next business day, March 17. Where does the asset manager obtain the funds to finance this position?

Of course, the asset manager can purchase the position in Corporation ABC bond with the cash from the portfolio being managed or by borrowing from a bank. Typically, though, the asset manager would use a repo to obtain financing. In the repo market, the asset manager can use Corporation ABC bond as collateral for a loan. The term of the loan and the interest rate the asset manager agrees to pay are specified. The interest rate is called the *repo rate*. When the length of a repo is one day, it is called an *overnight repo*. When the loan is for more than one day, it is referred to as a *term repo*. The transaction is referred to as a repurchase agreement because it calls for the security's sale and subsequent repurchase at a specified future date. Both the sale price and the purchase price are specified in the agreement. The difference between the purchase (repurchase) price and the sale price is the loan's dollar interest cost.

Let us return to the asset manager who seeks to finance a long position in Corporation ABC bond for one day. The settlement date is the day that the collateral must be delivered, and the money lent to initiate the transaction, which, in our example, is the next day. Likewise, the repo's termination date is the next day (i.e., an overnight repo). Suppose the amount of the loan that the asset manager needs to borrow to buy the bond is $10,200,000. Who might serve as the asset manager's counterparty (i.e., the lender of funds) in this transaction? Suppose that the treasurer of a municipality has excess funds in the amount of $10,200,000 to invest for one day. A repo offers the treasurer of the municipality a very low risk short-term investment opportunity. Accordingly, on the next day, the asset manager would agree to deliver ("sell") the \$10 million par value of Corporation ABC bond and buy the same corporate bond back for an amount determined by the repo rate the next business day, March 17. Note that in our illustration, we are assuming in this example that the borrower will provide collateral that is equal in value to the money that is loaned. In practice, lenders usually require borrowers to provide collateral in excess of the value of money that is loaned. We will illustrate how this is accomplished when we discuss repo margins.

Suppose the repo rate in this transaction is 2.9%. Then, as will be explained below, the asset manager would agree to deliver Corporation ABC bond for \$10,200,821.67 the next day. The \$821.67 between the "sale" price of \$10,200,000 and the repurchase price of \$10,200,821.67 is the dollar cost of the financing that the asset manager must pay.

Repo Rate and Dollar Interest

The following formula is used to calculate the dollar interest on a repo transaction:

$$\text{Dollar interest} = \text{Dollar principal} \times (\text{Repo rate}) \times (\text{Repo term}/360).$$

In our illustration, using a repo rate of 2.9% and a repo term of one day, the dollar interest is \$821.67 as follows:

$$\$10,200,000 \times 0.029 \times (1/360) = \$821.67.$$

Adding the dollar interest of \$821.67 to the amount borrowed of \$10,200,000 gives the repurchase price of \$10,200,821.67.

Reverse Repo

In our illustration, the asset manager is using the repo market to obtain financing for a long position. The repo market can correspondingly be used to borrow securities. Securities are routinely borrowed for a number of reasons, including opening a short position, the need to deliver securities against the exercise of a credit derivative contract, and the need to cover a failed transaction in the securities settlement system. Many arbitrage strategies involve the borrowing of securities (e.g., convertible bond arbitrage).

Suppose an asset manager established a short position in a 30-year Treasury bond one week ago and must now cover the position — namely, deliver the securities. The asset manager accomplishes this task by engaging in a *reverse repurchase agreement* or *reverse repo*. In a reverse repo, the asset manager agrees to buy securities at a specified price with a commitment to sell them back at a later date for another specified price. (Of course, the asset manager eventually would have to buy the 30-year Treasury bonds in the market in order to cover its short position.) In this case, the asset manager is making a collateralized loan to the agreement's counterparty. The counterparty is lending securities and borrowing funds obtained from the collateralized loan to create leverage.

Credit Risks

Just as in any borrowing/lending agreement, both parties in a repo transaction are exposed to credit risk. This is true even though there may be high-quality collateral underlying the repo transaction. Let us examine under what circumstances each counterparty is exposed to credit risk.

Suppose an asset manager is the borrower in a repo (i.e., sell the collateral and repurchase it) and suppose further the asset manager defaults; that is, the asset manager fails to repurchase the security from the counterparty. In such instances, the counterparty gains control over the collateral and retains any income generated by the security. The counterparty's risk is that bond yields increase subsequent to the repo transaction such that the collateral's market value is worth less than the unpaid repurchase price. Conversely, suppose the counterparty defaults (i.e., the counterparty fails to deliver the security to the asset manager) on the repurchase date. The risk is that bond yields have fallen over the agreement's life such that the asset manager is owed a security whose market value is worth more than the amount the asset manager used as collateral for the borrowed funds.

Repo Margin

While both parties are exposed to credit risk in a repo transaction, the lender of funds is usually in the more vulnerable position. Accordingly, the repo is structured to reduce the lender's credit risk. Specifically, the amount lent should be less than the market value of the security used as collateral, thereby providing the lender some cushion should the collateral's market value decline. The amount by which the market value of the security used as collateral exceeds the value of the loan is called *repo margin* or *haircut*.

Repo margins vary from transaction to transaction and are negotiated between the counterparties based on factors such as the following: term of the repo agreement, quality of the collateral, creditworthiness of the counterparties, and the availability of the collateral. Minimum repo margins are set differently across counterparty firms and are based on models and/or guidelines created by their credit departments. Repo margin is generally between 1% and 3%. For borrowers of lower creditworthiness and/or when less liquid securities are used as collateral, the repo margin can be 10% or more.

To illustrate the role of the haircut in a repurchase agreement, let us once again return to the asset manager who purchases a bond of Corporation ABC and needs financing overnight. The face amount of the position is $10 million and the bond's price including accrued interest is $10,200,000.

When a haircut is included, the amount the counterparty is willing to lend is reduced by a given percentage of the bond's market value. Suppose the collateral is set at 103% of the amount being lent. To determine the amount being lent, we divide the bond's full price of $10,200,000 by 1.03 to obtain $9,902,912.62, which is the amount the counterparty will lend. Suppose the repo rate is 2.9%. As a result, the transaction is structured as follows. The asset manager would agree to deliver the Corporation ABC bond for $9,902,912.62 and repurchase the same bond for $9,903,710.36 the next day. The $797.73 difference between the sale price of $9,902,912.62 and the repurchase price of $9,903,710.36 is the dollar interest on the financing. Using a repo rate of 2.9% and a repo term of one day, the dollar interest is calculated as follows:

$$\$9,902,912.62 \times 0.029 \times (1/360) = \$797.73.$$

Marking the Collateral to Market

Another practice to limit credit risk is to mark the collateral to market on a regular basis. Marking a position to market means simply recording the position's value at its market value. When the market value changes by a certain percentage, the repo position is adjusted accordingly. For complex securities that do not trade frequently, there is considerable difficulty in obtaining a price at which to mark a position to market.

Delivery of the Collateral and Credit Risk

One concern in structuring a repo is delivery of the collateral to the lender. The most obvious procedure is for the borrower to actually deliver the collateral to the lender or to the cash lender's clearing agent. If this procedure is followed, the collateral is said to be *delivered out*. At the end of a repo term, the lender returns collateral to the borrower in exchange for the repurchase price (i.e., the amount borrowed plus interest).

The drawback of this procedure is that it may be too expensive, particularly for short-term repos (e.g., overnight) owing to the costs associated with delivering the collateral. The cost of delivery is factored into the repo rate of the transaction, in that if delivery is required, this translates into a lower repo rate paid by the borrower. If delivery of collateral is not required, an otherwise higher repo rate is paid. The risk to the lender of not taking actual possession of the collateral is that the borrower may sell the security or use the same security as collateral for a repo with another counterparty.

As an alternative to delivering out the collateral, the lender may agree to allow the borrower to hold the security in a segregated customer account. The lender still must bear the risk that the borrower may use the collateral fraudulently by offering it as collateral for another repo transaction. If the borrower of the cash does not deliver out the collateral, but instead holds it, then the transaction is called a *hold-in-custody (HIC) repo*. Despite the credit risk associated with a HIC repo, it is used in some transactions when the collateral is difficult to deliver (e.g., mortgage loans) or the transaction amount is relatively small and the lender of funds is comfortable with the borrower's reputation.

Asset managers participating in an HIC repo must ensure that: (1) they transact only with counterparties of good credit quality since an HIC repo may be perceived as an unsecured transaction and (2) the investor (that is, the lender of cash) receives a higher rate in order to compensate for the higher credit risk involved. In the US market, there have been cases where dealer firms that went into bankruptcy and defaulted on loans were found to have pledged the same collateral for multiple HIC transactions.

Another method for handling the collateral is for the borrower to deliver the collateral to the lender's custodial account at the borrower's clearing bank. The custodian then has possession of the collateral that it holds on the lender's behalf. This method reduces the cost of delivery because it is merely a transfer within the borrower's clearing bank. If, for example, a dealer firm enters into an overnight repo with Customer A, the next day the collateral is transferred back to the dealer. The dealer can then enter into a repo with Customer B for, say, five days without having to redeliver the collateral. The clearing bank simply establishes a custodian account for Customer B and holds the collateral in that account. In this type of repo transaction, the clearing bank is an agent to both parties. This specialized type of repo arrangement is called a *triparty repo*. For some regulated financial institutions, this is the only type of repo arrangement permitted.

Determinants of the Repo Rate

Just as there is no single interest rate in the financial market, there is not one repo rate. The repo rate varies from transaction to transaction depending on the following factors:

- **Quality of the collateral:** The lower the credit quality of the collateral, all other factors equal, the higher the repo rate.
- **Term of the repo:** Typically, the longer the term of the repo, the higher the repo rate.
- **Delivery requirement:** When delivery of the collateral to the lender is required, the repo rate will be lower.
- **Availability of the collateral:** The more difficult it is to obtain the collateral, the lower the repo rate.
- **Prevailing federal funds rate:** While the above factors determine the repo rate on a particular transaction, the federal funds rate determines the general level of repo rates. The repo rate generally will trade lower than the federal funds rate because a repo involves collateralized borrowing, while a federal funds transaction is unsecured borrowing.

To understand why the availability of the collateral is important, remember that the borrower (or equivalently the seller of the collateral) has a security that lenders of cash want for whatever reason. (Perhaps the security is in great demand to satisfy borrowing needs.) Such collateral is said to be "on special". Collateral that does not share this characteristic is referred to as *general collateral*. The party that needs collateral that is "on special" will be willing to lend funds at a lower repo rate in order to obtain that collateral.

Special Collateral and Arbitrage

There are a number of investment strategies in which an asset manager borrows funds to purchase securities. The asset manager's expectation is that the return earned by investing in the securities purchased with the borrowed funds will exceed the borrowing cost. The use of borrowed funds to obtain greater exposure to a particular bond issue than is possible by using only cash results in leverage. In certain circumstances, a borrower of funds via a repo transaction can generate an arbitrage opportunity. This occurs when it is possible to borrow funds at a lower rate than the rate that can be earned by reinvesting those funds.

Such opportunities present themselves when an asset manager's portfolio includes securities that are "on special" and the manager can reinvest at a rate higher than the repo rate. For example, suppose that an asset manager has a bond in the portfolio that is "on special", say, Bond X. Lenders of funds are willing to take Bond X as collateral for two weeks charging a repo rate of say 2%. Suppose further that the asset manager can invest the funds in a 2-week Treasury bill (the maturity date being the same as the term of the repo) and earn 3%. Assuming that the repo is properly structured so that there is no credit risk, then the asset manager has locked in a spread of 100 basis points for two weeks. This is a pure arbitrage and the asset manager faces no risk. Of course, the asset manager is exposed to the risk that Bond X may decline in value, but the manager is exposed to this risk anyway as long as the asset manager intended to hold the bond anyway.

Structured Repos

Structured repos introduce variations on the basic agreement and are designed to accommodate specialized clienteles or users. They include cross-currency repo, callable repo, and whole loan repo.

A *cross-currency repo* is an agreement in which the cash lent and securities used as collateral are denominated in different currencies, say, borrow US dollars with UK gilts used as collateral. Of course, fluctuating foreign exchange rates mean that it is likely that the transaction will need to be marked to market frequently in order to ensure that cash or securities remain fully collateralized.

In a *callable repo*, the lender of cash in a term fixed-rate repo has the option to terminate the repo early. In other words, the repo transaction has an embedded interest rate option which benefits the lender of cash if rates rise during the repo's term. If rates rise, the lender may exercise the option to call back the cash and reinvest at a higher rate. For this reason, a callable repo will trade at a lower repo rate than an otherwise similar conventional repo.

A *whole loan repo* developed in the US market as a response to investor demand for higher yields in a falling interest rate environment. Whole loan repo trades at a higher rate than conventional repo because a lower quality collateral is used in the transaction. There are generally two types: mortgage whole loans and consumer whole loans. Both are unsecuritized loans or interest receivables. The loans can also be credit card payments and other types of consumer loans. Lenders in a whole loan repo are not only exposed to credit risk but prepayment risk as well. This is the risk that the loan package is paid off prior to the maturity date, which is often the case with consumer loans. For these reasons, the yield on a whole loan repo is higher than conventional repo collateralized by say US Treasuries.

Non-repo Instruments for Financing and/or Leveraging Bond Positions

There are other vehicles or instruments that can be used for financing and/or leveraging bond positions. These include credit default swaps, total return swaps, and buy/sell-back arrangements.

Credit Default Swaps

Credit derivatives can be used to effectively create a leveraged position or short an individual bond, bond sector, or bond index. Two examples are a credit default swap (CDS) that we discuss in this section and a total return swap (TRS) that we discuss in the next section. The type of credit derivative that is the most commonly used is a CDS.

A CDS that involves only one entity is called a *single-name CDS*. The entity that is the underlying for the contract is either referred to as the reference entity or reference obligation. The *reference entity* is the issuer of the bond and hence is also referred to as the *reference issuer*. The underlying for a single-name CDS could be a specific bond issue. In such cases, the underlying is referred to as the *reference obligation*. Typically, the underlying for a single-name CDS involving a corporate entity is a reference entity.

The mechanics of a single-name CDS are as follows. There are two parties to the contract: the buyer of the CDS and the seller of the CDS. The buyer of the CDS is the party that is seeking credit protection for the reference entity. The seller of the CDS is the party that is providing protection to the CDS buyer for the reference entity. The credit protection being sought is against the occurrence of a *credit event*. That is, if a credit event occurs with respect to the reference entity, the protection seller (i.e., seller of the CDS) must compensate the protection buyer (i.e., buyer of the CDS). To understand the mechanics of the contract, we need to understand: (1) what a credit event is and (2) what the potential cash flows are for the two parties to the contract.

What constitutes a credit event is defined in the legal documentation for a CDS trade. That documentation, which is the standard contract for a CDS trade developed by the International Swap and Derivatives Association (ISDA), defines eight credit events that attempt to capture every type of situation that could cause the credit quality of the reference entity to deteriorate, or cause the value of the bonds of the reference entity to decline in value.[2]

How CDS can be used to create a leveraged position and short corporate bonds

The credit protection buyer pays a premium periodically (typically every quarter) to the credit protection seller in return for the right to receive a payment conditional upon the occurrence of a credit event by the reference entity. The premium is called the *swap payment.* If no credit event occurs over the life of the contract, then the credit protection buyer makes the payments up to the contract's maturity date. At that time, the contract terminates. If a credit event occurs, the credit protection buyer is responsible for the accrued premium up to the date of the credit event and the credit protection seller must perform depending on the settlement procedure set forth in the legal documentation. The contract terminates after the credit event occurs.

The most obvious way for an asset manager to use a single-name CDS is to acquire credit protection for the holding of a corporate bond in its portfolio. For example, suppose an asset manager wants to purchase the obligation of a corporate entity (i.e., gain long exposure), then the most obvious way to do so is to purchase the bond in the cash market. The selling of credit protection on a corporate entity provides long credit exposure to that entity. To understand why, consider what happens when an asset

[2]These eight credit events include (1) bankruptcy, (2) failure to pay, (3) repudiation/moratorium, (4) downgrade, (5) restructuring, (6) credit event upon merger, (7) cross-acceleration, and (8) cross-default. The definition for each credit event is set forth in more detail in the *1999 ISDA Credit Derivatives Definitions* as modified in 2001 by the *Restructuring Supplement to the 1999 ISDA Credit Derivatives Definitions* and then in 2003 by the *2003 ISDA Credit Derivative Definitions.*

manager sells credit protection on a reference entity. The asset manager receives the swap premium and if there is no credit event, the swap premium is received over the life of the CDS contract. However, this is equivalent to buying the bond of the corporate entity. Instead of receiving coupon interest payments, the asset manager receives the swap premium payments. If there is a credit event, then the asset manager, under the terms of the CDS, must make a payment to the credit protection buyer. However, this is equivalent to a loss that would be realized if the bond was purchased. Hence, selling credit protection via a single-name CDS is economically equivalent to a long position in the reference entity.

Suppose that an asset manager wants to short a corporate bond because it is believed that the corporation is going to experience a credit event that will cause a decline in the value of the bond. In the absence of a CDS, the asset manager would have to short the bonds in the cash market. However, it is extremely difficult to short corporate bonds. With a liquid single-name CDS, it is easy to effectively short the bond of a corporate entity. Remember that shorting a bond involves making payments to another party and then if the asset manager is correct and the bond's price declines, the asset manager sells the bond at a higher price (i.e., realizes a gain). That is precisely what occurs when a single-name CDS is purchased: the asset manager makes payments (the swap premium payments) and realizes a gain if a credit event occurs. Hence, buying credit protection via a single-name CDS is equivalent to shorting.

For an asset manager seeking a leveraged position in a corporate bond, this can be achieved by selling credit protection. As just noted, selling credit protection is equivalent to a long position in the reference entity. Moreover, as with other derivatives, a CDS allows this to be done on a leveraged basis.

CDS index

An asset manager is not restricted to using the CDS to leverage or short a single reference name. There are CDSs in which the underlying is a corporate bond index (CDX) that includes a standardized basket of reference entities.

The mechanics of a CDX are different from that of a single-name CDS. For both types of CDS, there is a swap premium that is paid periodically. If a credit event occurs, the swap premium payment ceases in the case of a single-name CDS and the contract is terminated. In contrast, for a CDX, the swap payment continues to be made by the credit protection buyer.

However, the amount of the quarterly swap premium payment is reduced. This is because the notional amount is reduced as a result of a credit event for a reference entity.

What we said earlier about how an asset manager can use a single-name CDS applies equally to CDX. However, rather than managing exposure to a single reference entity, a CDX allows a portfolio manager to reduce exposure to a diversified portfolio of investment-grade corporate names.

Total Return Swaps

A derivative instrument that is economically identical to a repo is a TRS. In a TRS, one party makes periodic floating-rate payments to a counterparty in exchange for the total return realized on a reference asset (or underlying asset). For bond portfolio managers, the reference asset could be one of the following: credit-risky bond, a bank loan, a reference portfolio consisting of bonds or loans, or an index representing a sector of the bond market. While a repo is governed by the repo agreement, a TRS is governed by the ISDA agreement.

The total return of a reference asset includes all cash flows that flow from it as well as the capital appreciation or depreciation of the reference asset. The floating rate is a reference interest rate (historically Libor) plus or minus a spread. The party that agrees to make the floating-rate payments and receive the total return is referred to as the *total return receiver*; the party that agrees to receive the floating-rate payments and pay the total return is referred to as the *total return payer*.

A TRS is typically used by an asset manager to increase credit exposure. A TRS transfers all of the economic exposure of a reference asset to the total return receiver. In exchange for accepting this exposure, the total return receiver pays a floating interest rate to the total return payer. TRS applications fall into two categories: (1) asset managers using a TRS for leveraging purposes and (2) asset managers using a TRS as a more transactionally efficient means for implementing a portfolio management strategy.

Using a TRS to create a synthetic repo

There are reasons why asset managers may want to utilize a TRS. As noted above, one of these is to reduce or remove credit risk. Using a TRS as a credit derivative instrument, a party can remove exposure to an asset without having to sell it. In a basic TRS, the total return payer retains rights to the reference asset. This assumes that the reference asset is part of the asset manager's holding. The total return receiver gains an exposure to the reference asset without having to pay out the cash proceeds that would be required to purchase it. As the maturity of the swap rarely matches that of the reference asset, in a positive yield curve environment the swap receiver may gain from the positive funding or carry that derives from being able to roll over short-term funding of a longer-term asset. In contrast, the total return payer benefits from protection against interest rate and credit risk for a specified period of time, without having to liquidate the asset itself. At the maturity of the swap, the total return payer may reinvest the asset if it continues to own it, or it may sell the asset in the open market. In this respect, a TRS is in essence a *synthetic repo.*

Buy/Sell-Back

Another securities lending arrangement that is functionally equivalent to a repo is a *buy/sell-back agreement.* A buy/sell-back agreement separates a securities lending transaction into separate buy and sell trades that are entered into simultaneously. The security borrower buys the security in question and agrees to return the borrowed security (that is, sell back) at some future date for an agreed upon forward price. The forward price is usually derived using a repo rate. A buy/sell-back agreement differs from a repurchase agreement in that the security borrower receives legal title and beneficial ownership of the securities for the length of the agreement. Moreover, the security borrower retains any accrued interest and coupon payments until the security is returned to the lender. Nevertheless, the price on the termination date reflects the fact that the economic benefits of the coupon interest are being transferred back to the seller.

Key Points

- A repurchase agreement (repo) is the sale of a bond with a commitment by the seller to buy the same bond back from the purchaser at a specified price at a designated future date.
- The repurchase price is the price at which the seller must subsequently repurchase the security and the repurchase date is the date the security must be repurchased.

- A repo is nothing more than a collateralized loan where the collateral is the security that is sold and subsequently repurchased.
- The "seller" in a repo is borrowing funds and providing collateral for the loan; the buyer is lending money and accepting a security as collateral for the loan.
- The advantage for an asset manager using a repo is that the short-term borrowing rate is lower than the cost of bank financing; from the lender's (buyer's) perspective, a repo offers an attractive yield on a short-term secured transaction that is highly liquid.
- The repo rate is the interest rate paid by the seller.
- The difference between the purchase (repurchase) price and the sale price is the loan's dollar interest cost.
- An overnight repo is a repo where the length of the agreement is one day; a term repo has a length of more than one day.
- A repo can be used to borrow securities to create a short position by using a reverse repo.
- Both parties in a repo transaction are exposed to credit risk.
- A repo is structured to reduce the lender's credit risk should the collateral's market value decline and is achieved by specifying repo margin or haircut.
- Repo margin is the amount by which the collateral's market value exceeds the value of the loan.
- Repo margin varies from transaction to transaction and is negotiated between the counterparties based on the term of the repo agreement, quality of the collateral, creditworthiness of the counterparties, and the availability of the collateral.
- One concern in structuring a repo is delivery of the collateral to the lender.
- An alternative to delivering the collateral to the lender is that the lender may agree to allow the borrower to hold the security in a segregated customer account.
- If the borrower of the cash does not deliver out the collateral, but instead holds it, then the transaction is called a hold-in-custody (HIC) repo and lenders must ensure that they (1) transact only with counterparties of good credit quality since an HIC repo may be perceived as an unsecured transaction and (2) receive a higher rate in order to compensate them for the higher credit risk involved.

- Another method for handling the collateral is for the borrower to deliver the collateral to the lender's custodial account at the borrower's clearing bank using a triparty repo arrangement.
- The repo rate depends on the following factors: (1) quality of the collateral, (2) term of the repo, (3) delivery requirement, (4) availability of the collateral, and (5) prevailing federal funds rate.
- Other types of repos include cross-currency repo, callable repo, and whole loan repo.
- A credit default swap (CDS), total return swap (TRS), and buy/sell-back arrangement are other vehicles or instruments that can be used for financing and/or leveraging a bond position.
- Credit derivatives can be used to effectively create a leveraged position or short an individual bond, bond sector, or bond index, the most common one being CDSs.
- In a CDS, the credit protection buyer pays a premium (the swap payment) periodically to the credit protection seller in return for the right to receive a payment conditional upon the occurrence of a credit event by the reference entity. If no credit event occurs, then the credit protection buyer makes the payments up to the contract's maturity date.
- Selling credit protection via a single-name CDS is economically equivalent to a long position in the reference entity.
- Buying credit protection via a single-name CDS is equivalent to shorting.
- For an asset manager seeking a leveraged position in a corporate bond, this can be achieved by selling credit protection.
- A TRS is a derivative instrument that is economically identical to a repo.
- One party in a TRS makes periodic floating-rate payments to a counterparty in exchange for the total return realized on a reference asset (or underlying asset).
- The total return receiver agrees to make the floating-rate payments and receive the total return; the total return payer agrees to receive the floating rate payments and pay the total return.
- For bond portfolio managers, the reference asset could be a credit-risky bond, a bank loan, a reference portfolio consisting of bonds or loans, or an index representing a sector of the bond market.
- TRS applications fall into two categories: (1) asset managers using a TRS for leveraging purposes and (2) asset managers using a TRS as a more transactionally efficient means for implementing a portfolio management strategy.

- A securities lending arrangement that is functionally equivalent to a repo is a buy/sell-back agreement.
- A buy/sell-back agreement separates a securities lending transaction into separate buy and sell trades that are entered into simultaneously.

References

Armakola, A., R. Douady, J.-P. Laurent, and F. Molten, 2020. "Repurchase agreements and systemic risk in the European sovereign debt crises: The role of European clearing houses." Available at http://hal-paris1.archives-ouvertes.fr/hal-01479252/fr/.

Gorton, Gary B. and A. Metrick, 2012. "Securitized banking and the run on repo." *Journal of Financial Economics*, 104(3): 425–451.

Chapter 11

Implementable Quantitative Research*

Learning Objectives

After reading this chapter, you will understand:

- the process of performing quantitative research;
- how to convert research into implementable trading strategies;
- the differences in the discovery process in the physical sciences and in financial economics analysis that is used to implement trading strategies;
- the issues associated with the quantitative approach to asset management;
- what econophysics is;
- the two principles that are fundamental in financial analysis: (1) model simplicity and (2) out-of-sample validation;
- what is data snooping;
- the common objective of a quantitative research process;
- issues in selecting a sample that is free from survivorship bias;
- issues in selecting a methodology to estimate a model;
- the tradeoff between better estimations and prediction errors; and
- the issues in risk control.

*This chapter is coauthored with Sergio M. Focardi, professor and researcher at the Finance Group of the Pole Universitaire De Vinci in Paris, and a founding partner of The Intertek Group, and K.C. Ma, the Mary Ball Washington/Switzer Bros. Endowed Professor of Finance at The University of West Florida. This chapter is primarily drawn from the article published in *The Journal of Alternative Investments*, Fall 2005.

Introduction

The accessibility to increased computing power, large datasets, mathematical software, and the dominant role of institutional trading have resulted in the inevitable trend of implementing quantitative research and investment strategies. The gradual move of replacing traditional human judgments with machine calculations is based on the assumption that financial systems operate according to rules, which can be discovered and applied to make objective systematic decisions. Since a quantitative process is capable of systematically handling a large amount of information quickly and consistently, ambiguity and unpredictability, which are often associated with subjective choices during decision-making, can be kept to a minimum. Moreover, systematic decision-making can be improved over time, unlike their discretionary counterpart. For fact or fancy, most portfolio managers include some form of quantitative approach in their overall investment process.

However, the quantitative approach has its issues. First, the low signal-to-noise ratio in finance makes it easy to mistake a fluke for a real pattern. Fast computing power often increases the chances of making false discoveries. Second, using the conventional criterion of significance at some statistical level, researchers often quickly jump to the wrong conclusion. What they sometimes fail to realize is that statistical significance is neither a necessary nor sufficient condition for implementable abnormal returns. Third, humans have a tendency to only look at the unusual. Does an analyst notice an event because it is interesting or is it interesting because the analyst notices it? The resulting bias is that theories are established or tests are performed more easily on extraordinary events, and correlations are easily mistaken for causalities. This bias is further reinforced by high-speed computing, since quantitative tools are very efficient in locating outliers and finding correlations.

In this chapter, we explain the process of performing quantitative research and converting that research into implementable trading strategies. We begin by comparing the discovery process in the physical sciences and in financial economic analysis used by asset managers.

The Rise of Econophysics

Before outlining a general framework for quantitative research, let's briefly compare the discovery process in the physical sciences and in financial economics. The classical view of scientific discovery (albeit grossly oversimplified) is one of empirical observations plus human genius. Vast amounts of data are collected and then a theoretical synthesis is made. The end result is a mathematical model that explains the data and allows accurate predictions, which can be replicated in independent tests. In modern science, this process forces us to make model revisions when even very small discrepancies occur between prediction and observation.

There are a few points that have become pivotal to modern scientific methodology and that are important as well to financial economics:

1. "Observation" is far from being an obvious term. Any observation presupposes some theory.[1] Thus we see a stratification of science, where advanced theories live on the back of simpler theories. For example, the so-called "stylized facts" are an example of first level theories. They are empirical observations that presuppose a significant amount of theory.
2. There is an ongoing debate as to whether science actually "describes" an objective reality or simply provides recipes for predicting the outcome of observations without any descriptive pretension.[2]
3. In general, different (infinite) models can explain the same data. The criterion of choice between different theories is often "aesthetic" in the sense of mathematical simplicity and elegance. Theories can always be mended to accommodate new facts: eventually they are replaced by simpler and more elegant theories.
4. It is questionable whether the process of discovery is an inexplicable product of human genius or if there is some compelling logic that inevitably leads to discoveries.

We do not want to discuss these points here, but only to point out that in the physical sciences theories are constructed and validated on empirical data with a high level of accuracy. Scientists construct experiments and test different empirical settings. However, the level of statistical significance of theories in the physical sciences is extremely high.

[1] In the parlance of the modern philosophy of science, we say that observations are "theory laden".

[2] In economics, the latter point of view was forcefully made by Friedman [1953].

Methodologies used in financial economics[3] are different from those used in the physical sciences in five key ways:

1. The "laws" in financial economics are never validated with a high level of precision: There is ample room for ambiguity.
2. The financial market is a human artifact as well as an intelligent processor of information: Investors cannot think of the financial market as a permanent physical object. In today's parlance, financial markets are evolving, self-reflecting, complex systems.
3. Most models rely on historical data, which is easy to overfit.
4. Experimentation is limited or impossible in financial economics. Asset managers cannot repeat the events of the past, and control for the environmental variables, to determine the precise cause–effect involved in a phenomenon. Consequently, experiments cannot be independently replicated.
5. With the advent of computers, human creativity is complemented and even replaced by a learning approach based on statistics and data mining.

The relatively new field of "econophysics"[4] has tried to bridge the gap between the two worlds, drawing attention to the need for strict scientific validation of laws and results. Still it is important to realize that true differences exist. To avoid the forcing upon economics of an impossible scientific paradigm, we have to ask on what genuine knowledge implementable strategies are based.

The level of significance of economic theories is low: No financial economic model fits data with a very high level of significance. Many different models fit data and it is often impossible to separate true positives from false positives. The financial literature is full of bona fide defenses of contradictory facts. As a consequence, in financial economics it is very difficult to generalize and integrate theories. This happens because every theory or model is somehow misspecified and passes tests only within a given level of approximations and significance. When different models are integrated and generalized, approximations no longer hold.

For these reasons, two principles are fundamental in financial analysis: (1) model simplicity and (2) out-of-sample validation. Analysts can place a

[3]The same considerations apply to other scientific domains ranging from biology, medicine, ecological studies, and so on.

[4]See Mantegna and Stanley [2000].

higher level of confidence on a simple model validated on data different from those on which it has been built. These principles apply in particular when a "learning" approach is deployed. A learning approach is based on models of unbounded complexity able to perfectly fit any set of data. For example, an autoregressive model can have an arbitrary number of lags, a neural network can have an arbitrary number of nodes, and so on. Models of this type can describe any set of data with arbitrary precision. For instance, provided that a sufficient number of lags are allowed, an autoregressive model can describe *any* time series with zero error.

A General Framework

The common objective of a quantitative research process is to identify any persistent pattern in the data and, in finance, convert it into implementable and profitable investment strategies. To understand the general research process of a quantitative procedure, it is necessary to identify some of the commonly induced biases in this process. Specifically, Figure 1 provides a flowchart which demonstrates the process of how quantitative research is performed and converted into implementable trading strategies. Generally, it includes developing underlying economic and financial theories, explaining actual returns, estimating expected returns, and formulating corresponding portfolios. In what follows, we discuss each step.

Develop a Truly Ex Ante Economic Justification

A sound economic hypothesis is a necessary condition for the birth of an implementable and replicable investment strategy. True economics, however, can only be motivated with creative intuitions and scrutinized by strict logical reasoning, but it does not come from hindsight or prior experience. This requirement is critical since scientific conclusions can easily be contaminated by the process of data snooping, especially when a truly independent economic theory is not established first.

Data snooping (or data mining) is identifying seemingly significant but in fact spurious patterns in the data.[5] All empirical tests are at risk from this problem, especially if a large number of studies have been performed on the same datasets. Given enough time and trials, people who are convinced of the existence of a pattern will eventually manage to find that pattern,

[5] See Ross [1994] and Lo [1994].

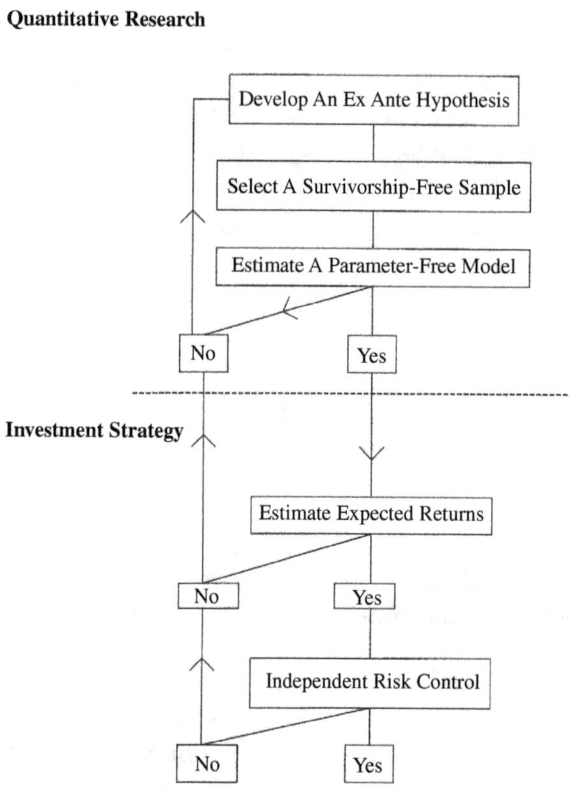

FIGURE 1: Process of Quantitative Research and Investment Strategy

real or imagined. Furthermore, there is an identical life cycle of experience in data snooping. Researchers are often confronted with the exact same issues and will have to make the same types of choices in the process.

The process of data snooping comes in several forms. At some basic but subtle level, an economic hypothesis is founded by the knowledge of past patterns in data. Researchers may establish their "prior" from their knowledge, learning, experience, or simply what others have said (as long as that knowledge or experience is not derived from the same or a similar dataset used to assess that hypothesis). A good example of a classic yet wrong way to model the excess return is "market capitalization should be included in the model because there is evidence of a size effect".

From then on, the problem can only get worse as long as there is more room for choices. A researcher may choose to design the same statistical tests because of what others have done using similar data. The choices in these tests include, but are not limited to, the selection of explanatory variables, how to measure them, the functional form of the model, the length of the time period, arbitrary preservation or removal of outliers, use of unrobust estimation methods, the underlying probability distribution, and test statistics. The difference in each of these artificial choices by itself may be small, but its resulting investment performance impact is often significant.

Ideally, there should be no need to make artificial selections since all of the tests should have been dictated by the underlying economic theories. However, even the best economic concept, being abstract and simplified, does not always fully specify its application in reality. There are ample opportunities where decision makers have to find proxies and instruments to complete the process.

Controlling for Data Snooping

A common fallacy, however, is that researchers tend to go back to the most immediate prior step in searching for solutions when the result is not what they expect to see. Of course, this attitude reflects the general human tendency to overweight the information in the most recent period in their decision-making. This could easily lead to the mindless trials of numerous alternatives, which are most likely not justified.

Therefore, a direct way to control for data snooping at all levels is that the entire process will have to be reconstructed right from the beginning whenever the output at any step cannot pass the quality test. If the estimated model cannot explain the variation of excess returns to some satisfactory degree, the process needs to be stopped and abandoned. We need to go back to Step 1 and develop a new theory. If the predicted model does not produce acceptable excess returns, go back to Step 1. Finally, if the level of the actual risk-adjusted excess return found from following the strategy "does not pass muster" — go back to Step 1. This "trial-and-error" process may correct for most, but not all, of the data snooping problem. As we throw away the obvious, "bad" models through testing, we learn from the experience of trial and error. This experience itself inevitably affects the seemingly "independent" creation of the economic intuition of the next generation.

Of course, most of us would agree that there is almost no way to completely eliminate some form of data snooping since even the most rigorous scientific process is no more than a sequence of choices, subjective or not. As suggested by Lo [1993], as in most forms of substance abuse, the first sign of recovery is the recognition of the problem. The next step is to facilitate a research environment which avoids the temptations of making choices. (This reluctance is probably the single most important reason for the recently developed machine learning techniques described in Chapter 7.) What this conclusion also means is that in formulating investment strategies, portfolio managers should be extremely disciplined at every step of the process in making choices, with the explicit understanding of the problem and bias induced from data snooping.

Select a Sample Free from Survivorship Bias

Since all backtest research, discussed in more detail in Chapters 17 and 18, is performed on a dataset which looks back in time, the entire history of an observation will not be available if it does not survive the present. The sample that researchers can work with is a set of observations which have been pre-selected through time by some common denominators. A sample of a sample should not pose a problem if the subset is selected randomly. But this is not the case for most samples which suffer from *survivorship bias*. This bias is a type of selection bias where the survivors of a particular outcome are disproportionately evaluated. Those who did not survive may even be ignored. A researcher's focusing on the survivors can result in a false, or incorrect, estimate of probability. Survivorship bias becomes relevant if the common bond to survive the observation is related to the pattern we are looking for. A finding of a statistically significant pattern merely reflects the underlying common bond which was used to construct the testing sample.

One typical point of interest, which is severely affected by the survivorship bias, is performance comparison. By only looking at the portfolios currently outstanding, it is obvious that portfolios which did not survive through time due to poor performance are excluded from the sample. By design, the sample only contains good portfolios. How can the true factors which have caused the bad performance ever be identified?

Commercial data vendors are not helping on this issue. Because of cost consideration, most datasets are only provided on a live basis. That is, for a currently non-existent sample observation, the common practice is to delete its entire history from the dataset. To simulate the true historical situation, it is the researchers' responsibility to bring these observations back to the sample. The sample collection procedure should be reversed in time. Cases which existed at the beginning of the sample period should be included and tracked through time.

Select a Methodology to Estimate the Model

The selection of a certain methodology should pass the same quality tests as developing financial economic theories and selecting samples. Without strong intuition, researchers should choose the methodology which needs the least amount of human inputs. A good example is the machine-learning method which uses computerized algorithms to discover the knowledge (pattern or rule) inherent in data. Advances in modeling technology such as artificial intelligence, neural network, and genetic algorithms fit in this category. The beauty of this approach is its vast degree of freedom. There are none of the restrictions which are often explicitly specified in traditional, linear, stationary models.

Of course, researchers should not rely excessively on the power of the method itself. Learning is impossible without knowledge. Even if you want to simply throw data into an algorithm and expect it to spit out the answer, you need to provide some background knowledge, such as the justification and types of input variables. There are still numerous occasions which require researchers to make justifiable decisions. For example, a typical way of modeling stock returns is using the following linear form:

$$E(R_{it}) = a + b_{1t}(F1_{it-1}) + b_{2t}(F2_{it-1}) + \cdots + b_{nt}(Fn_{it-1}), \qquad (11.1)$$

where $E(R_{it})$ is the excess return for the ith security in period t, Fj_{it-1} is the jth factor value for the ith security at the beginning of period t, and b_{kt} is the market wide payoff for factor k in period t.

How Many Explanatory Variables

Undoubtedly, in testing and estimating Equation (11.1), the first task is to decide which and how many explanatory variables should be included. This decision should not be a question if the test is justified by a truly *ex ante* financial economic hypothesis. Financial economic theories, however, are often developed with abstract concepts which need to be measured by alternative proxies. The choice of proper proxies, while getting dangerously close to data snooping, makes the determination of both the type and the number of explanatory variables an art rather than a science. The choice of a particular proxy based on the rationale "because it works!" is not sufficient unless it is first backed up by the theory.

Tradeoff between Better Estimations and Prediction Errors

One rule of thumb is to be parsimonious. A big model is not necessarily better, especially in the context of a predictable risk-adjusted excess return. While the total power of explanation increases with the number of variables (size) in the model, the marginal increase of explanatory power drops quickly after some threshold. Whenever a new variable is introduced, what comes with the benefit of the additional description is the increase of estimation error of an additional parameter. In Table 1, we demonstrate the explanatory power of a typical multifactor model for stock returns by including one additional variable at a time. The second and the third columns clearly show that although by design the R^2 increases with the number of the variables, the adjusted R^2, which also reflects the impact of the additional estimation error, levels off and starts decreasing after some point. This example suggests that in the process of estimation, there is an optimal number of explanatory variables in each model.

The cost of estimation error is even compounded when new prediction is further extended into the forecast period. In Table 1, we also perform out-of-sample prediction based on the estimated multifactor model in each

TABLE 1: Marginal Contribution of Additional Explanatory Variables

In-Sample			Out-of-Sample		
Additional Explanatory Variable	**Explanatory Power (R^2)**	**Explanatory Power (Adj. R^2)**	**Annualized Excess Return (%)**	**Annualized Standard Deviation (%)**	**Information Ratio**
1st	0.091	0.078	2.66	7.24	0.367
2nd	0.145	0.088	3.08	7.03	0.438
3rd	0.185	0.127	3.72	6.91	0.538
4th	0.206	0.176	3.94	6.67	0.591
5th	0.211	0.187	4.11	6.01	0.684
6th	0.274	0.221	4.03	6.10	0.661
7th	0.289	0.233	3.89	6.12	0.636
8th	0.295	0.227	3.81	6.17	0.618
9th	0.299	0.215	3.72	6.23	0.597
10th	0.303	0.189	3.61	6.47	0.558

Source: Ma [2005c].

stage. Columns 4 and 5 show a more striking pattern wherein the risk-adjusted excess return, in the form of the information ratio, deteriorates even more quickly when the model becomes large.

Animal Spirits

It is with the exact same objectivity that quantitative analysts are proud of regarding their procedures that often lead to the question, "If everyone has the algorithms, will they not get the same answers?" The "over-mining" on the same dataset using simple linear models almost eliminates the possibility of gaining economic profit.

Pessimism resulting from the competition of quantitative research also justifies the need to include some form of "animal spirit" in the decision process. Being able to do so is also probably the single most important advantage that traditional security analysis can claim over quantitative approach. Casual observations provide ample examples that investor behavior determining market pricing follow neither symmetric nor linear patterns: investors tend to react to bad news much differently than to good news;[6] information in more recent periods is overweighed in the decision process;[7] investors ignore the probability of the event but emphasize the magnitude of the event;[8] stocks are purchased for their glamour but not for intrinsic value;[9] and low price/earnings (PEs) stocks paying high returns do not imply that high PEs stocks pay low returns.[10] This does not mean that a quantitative model should include all these phenomenon, but the modeling methodology should be flexible enough to entertain such possibilities if they are warranted by the theory.

Statistical Significance Does Not Guarantee Excess Returns

As a result, staunch defenders of quantitative research argue that profitable strategies cannot be commercialized by quantitative analysis;[11] the production of excess returns will stay idiosyncratic and proprietary. Excess returns will originate in those proprietary algorithms that outperform commercially standardized packages for data analysis. In other words, researchers will

[6] See Brown, Harlow, and Tinic [1988].
[7] See DeBondt and Thaler [1985].
[8] See Ma [2005a].
[9] See Lakonishok, Shleifer, and Vishny [1994].
[10] See Ma [2005c].
[11] For an example, see Fogler [1995].

have to learn to gain confidence even if there is no statistical significance, while statistical significance does not guarantee economic profit.

Since quantitative investment strategists often begin with the identification of a pattern which is defined by statistical standards, it is easy to assume excess returns from conventional statistical significance. To show that there is not necessarily a link, we perform a typical momentum trading strategy which is solely based on the predictability of future returns from past returns. A simplified version of the return-generating process under this framework follows:

$$E_{t-1}(R_t) = a + b_{t-1}(R_{t-1}),$$

where $E_{t-1}(R_t)$ is the expected return for the period t, estimated at point $t-1$, a is time-invariant return, and b_{t-1} is the momentum coefficient observed at time $t-1$. When b_{t-1} is (statistically) significantly positive, the time-series returns are said to exhibit persistence and positive momentum. To implement the trading strategy using the information in correlations, stocks with at least a certain level of correlation are included in portfolios at the beginning of each month, and their returns are tracked. The performance of these portfolios apparently reflects the statistical significance (or lack of) in correlation between successive returns. In Table 2, we summarize the performance of some of the representative portfolios.

It is not surprising that higher excess returns are generally associated with higher correlation between successive returns. More importantly, higher risk seems to be related to lower statistical significance of the relationship (correlation). The bottom line is that an acceptable level of risk-adjusted excess return, in the form of information ratio (e.g., 1), cannot

TABLE 2: Statistical Significance and Economic Profits

Correlation Coefficient[a]	*t*-Value[b]	Annual Excess Return (%)	Annual Standard Deviation (%)	Information Ratio
0.10	2.21[b]	0.48	4.07	0.118
0.25	4.22[b]	1.88	3.10	0.606
0.50	6.75[b]	3.27	2.15	1.521
0.15	1.34	0.61	4.10	0.149
0.35	2.86[b]	2.07	3.80	0.545
0.60	1.12	4.50	4.05	1.111

Notes: [a]Significant at the 1% level.
[b]*t*-value is for the significance of correlation coefficient.
Source: Ma [2005a].

always be achieved by statistical significance alone. A more striking observation, however, is that, sometimes without conventional statistical significance, the portfolio was able to deliver superior risk-adjusted economic profit. While the driving force may yet be unknown, evidence is provided for the disconnection between statistical significance and economic profit.

A Model to Estimate Expected Returns

The estimation for the model to explain past returns from Step 3, by itself, is not enough, since the objective of the process is to predict future returns. A good model for expected returns is much harder to come by since we simply do not have enough data. As pointed out by Black [1993], people are often confused between a model to explain average returns and a model to predict expected returns. While the former can be tested on a large number of historical data points, the latter requires such a long time period (sometimes decades) to cover various conditions to predict the expected returns. Since in practice a researcher does not have that much time to wait, one common shortcut is to simply assume that the model to explain average returns will be the model to predict expected returns. Of course, such prediction is highly inaccurate, given the assumption of constant expected returns.

We can easily find evidence to show it is a bad assumption. For example, if a researcher can look at the actual model which explains the cross-sections of short-term stock returns, even the naivest researcher can easily conclude that there is little resemblance between the models from one period to the next. This would in turn suggest, at least in the short term, that the model to explain past returns cannot be used to predict expected returns.

This calls for brand new efforts to establish an *ex ante* expected returns model. The process has to pass the same strict tests for quality which are required for any good modeling, as discussed earlier. These tests would include the independent formulation of the hypothesis for expected return and a methodology and sample period free from data snooping and survivorship bias. While they are not necessarily related, the process of developing hypotheses for conditional expected return models can greatly benefit from the insights from numerous models of past returns estimated over a long time period.

Largest Value Added

Apparently, the final risk-adjusted returns from a strategy can be attributed to the proper execution of each step described in Figure 1. The entire process can be generally described in a three-step procedure — economic hypothesis, model estimation, and prediction. It is only natural for researchers to ask how to allocate their efforts among the three steps to maximize the return contribution.

To answer this question, let's examine the return contribution from model estimation and prediction. For this purpose, we use a typical multi-factor model to explain the returns for all stocks in the Standard and Poor's 500 Index. Assume that at the beginning of each period, the best model actually describing the return in the period is known to the portfolio manager. Using this information, a portfolio consisting of the predicted top quartile is formed. The excess return from this portfolio generated with perfect information would suggest the extent of the return contribution from model estimation. Accordingly, in Table 3, the annual mean excess return of the top predicted quartile is between 13% and 28%, depending on the length of the investment horizon.

In contrast, the annual mean excess return of the actual top quartile in the S&P 500 Index is between 50% and 132%. The difference in excess returns between the actual top quartile portfolio and the predicted top quartile portfolio, between 36% and 110%, would suggest the extent of the return contribution from model prediction. It is clear then that for all investment horizons, the return contribution from model prediction is on average two to five times the excess returns from model estimation.

TABLE 3: Potential Returns for Perfect Estimation and Prediction (S&P 500 Stocks: 1975–2004)

	Annualized Excess Returns if Perfect Foresight for			
	Best Model[a] for S&P 500		**Actual[b] S&P 500 Quartiles**	
	Top Quartile	**Bottom Quartile**	**Top Quartile**	**Bottom Quartile**
Monthly period[c]	21.7%	−18.4%	132.4%	−92.3%
Quarterly period	28.4	−24.1	100.7	−79.5
Annual period	13.7	−10.6	50.5	−23.4

Notes: [a]The parameters of the actual model to explain S&P 500 performance is known beforehand.
[b]The performance of each stock, in terms of the actual quartile, is known beforehand.
[c]The length of investment horizon for each portfolio is rebalanced based on the perfect information.
Source: Ma [2005b].

Estimation	Testing	Forecast	Estimation	Testing	Forecast	.....
Period I	Period I	Period I	Period II	Period II	Period II	Now

FIGURE 2: The Sample Period

Therefore, for all practical purposes, the step of identifying a predictable model is responsible for the largest potential value added in generating predictable excess returns. The implication is that resources allocated to research should be placed disproportionally toward the effort of out-of-sample prediction.

Retesting the Prediction

Another safeguard against data snooping is to scrutinize the model once more through time. That is, the conditional model to estimate expected returns needs to be tested again in a "fresh" data period. As it requires multiple time periods to observe the conditional model for expected returns, the prediction model derived under a single condition has to be confirmed again. In Figure 2, we specify the relationship in time periods among estimation, testing, and confirmation.

The sequential testing of the prediction model in the forecast period would affirm that the condition that converts the model of actual returns to the model of expected returns still produces an acceptable level of performance. As the conditioning factor varies from one period to anther, the consistent performance of the three-period process suggests that it is not driven by a constant set of artificial rules introduced by data snooping.

Risk Control

Even if the expected return is modeled properly at the individual stock level, the bottom line of implementable investment strategies is evaluated by an acceptable level of risk-adjusted portfolio excess returns. As most institutional portfolios are benchmarked, the goal is to minimize tracking error (standard deviation of excess returns), given some level of portfolio excess returns. Consequently, risk control becomes technically much more complex than the conventional efficient portfolio concept. As shown by Roll [1992], an optimal portfolio which minimizes tracking error subject to a level of excess return is not a mean–variance efficient portfolio. It should be noted that, due to the objective and competitive nature of the quantitative approach in its strong form, most models produce similar rankings in expected returns. The variation in performance among quantitative portfolios is mainly attributed to a superior risk control technology.

One commonly used, but less preferred, practice in risk management is often performed right at the stage of identifying the model for expected returns. It involves revising the estimates from the model to explain the actual return. The purpose is to control the risk by attempting to reduce the estimation error for the model of expected returns. This approach has several flaws. First, in most cases, the procedure of revising the parameter estimates (from the model of actual returns) so they can be used in the model of expected returns is often performed on an *ad hoc* basis, and is vulnerable to data snooping. Second, in revising the parameter estimates, the task of building a relevant expected model with low prediction errors is mistaken for risk control on portfolio returns. Finally, there is a lesser degree of freedom, in that estimates are made based on the estimates of previous steps. The "risk control" procedure becomes dependent on the process of estimating expected returns. Consequently, an independent risk control procedure, usually through an optimization process, should be performed as an overlay on the stock selections which are determined initially by the predicted expected returns.

For computing efficiency, the iterations can be significantly reduced if several other conditions are simultaneously imposed. For example, Ma [2005b] has shown that the largest source of tracking error is the deviation of portfolio sector weights from its benchmark sector weights. Consequently, most optimal benchmarked portfolios are "sector neutral", that is, portfolios do not make sector bets against the benchmark. This consideration would indicate the need to include a constraint which sets maximum acceptable deviations of portfolio sector weights from benchmark sector weights.

Along the same line, tracking error can be further controlled when the individual stock weight is constrained to conform to its corresponding weight in the benchmark. It is also accomplished by setting a maximum allowed deviation of stock weight in the portfolio from the weight in the benchmark.

Additional realistic portfolio constraints may be considered. Examples would include specifying (1) a minimum level of market liquidity for individual stocks, (2) a maximum absolute weight in which any stock is allowed to invest, (3) a minimum total number of stocks held, (4) a minimum number of stocks held in each sector, and (5) a maximum level of portfolio turnover allowed.

Key Points

- The inevitable trend of implementing quantitative research and investment strategies has been facilitated by asset managers' accessibility to increased computing power, large datasets, and mathematical software.
- There are several issues associated with the quantitative approach.
- Fast computing power often increases the chances of making false discoveries.
- Using the conventional criterion of significance at some statistical level results in researchers often quickly jumping to the wrong conclusion.
- In evaluating quantitative strategies, humans have a tendency to only look at the unusual.
- In the physical sciences, theories are constructed and validated on empirical data with a high level of accuracy.
- Methodologies used in financial economics that differ from those used in the physical sciences are (1) the "laws" in financial economics are never validated with a high level of precision, (2) financial markets are a human artifact as well as an intelligent processor of information, (3) most models rely on historical data, which is easy to overfit, (4) experimentation is limited or impossible in financial economics, and (5) with the advent of computers, human creativity is complemented and even replaced by a learning approach based on statistics and data mining.
- The field of econophysics has drawn attention to the need for strict scientific validation of laws and results of financial economic empirical testing.
- Many different models fit data and it is often impossible to separate true positives from false positives.
- Because the financial literature offers defenses for contradictory facts, it is difficult in financial economics to generalize and integrate theories.
- The two principles that are fundamental in financial analysis are model simplicity and out-of-sample validation.
- An asset manager can place a higher level of confidence on a simple model validated on data different from those on which the two principles in financial analysis are built.
- In the quantitative research process, the common objectives are identifying any persistent pattern in the data and converting it into implementable and profitable investment strategies.
- To understand the general research process of a quantitative procedure, some of the commonly induced biases in this process must be identified.
- The steps needed in the quantitative research process in order to convert research into implementable trading strategies generally include

developing underlying economic and financial theories, explaining actual returns, estimating expected returns, and formulating corresponding portfolios.

- All backtest research should be performed on a dataset which looks back in time and should be free of survivorship bias.
- The selection of a methodology for testing an investment strategy should pass the same quality tests as developing financial economic theories and selecting samples.
- The methodology chosen to backtest an investment strategy should be one which needs the least amount of human inputs.
- There is a tradeoff between better estimations and prediction errors, the rule of thumb being to be parsimonious.
- A big model is not necessarily better, especially in the context of predictable risk-adjusted excess returns.
- Statistical significance does not guarantee excess returns.
- A safeguard against data snooping is to scrutinize the model at several points in time; that is, the conditional model to estimate expected returns needs to be tested again in a "fresh" data period.

References

Black, F., 1993. "Estimating expected return," *Financial Analysts Journal*, 49(5): 36–38.

Brown, K. C., W. V. Harlow, and S. M. Tinic, 1988. "Risk aversion, uncertain information, and market efficiency," *Journal of Financial Economics*, 22(2): 355–386.

DeBondt, W. F. and R. Thaler, 1985. "Does the stock market overreact?" *Journal of Finance*, 40(3): 793–805.

Fogler, H. R., 1995. "Investment analysis and new quantitative tools," *Journal of Portfolio Management*, 21(4): 39–47.

Friedman, M., 1953. *Essays in Positive Economics*. Chicago, IL: University of Chicago Press.

Lakonishok, J., A. Shleifer, and R. W, Vishny, 1994. "Contrarian investment, extrapolation, and risk," *Journal of Finance*, 49(5): 1541–1578.

Lo, A., 1994. "Data-snooping biases in financial analysis," in *Proceedings of Blending Quantitative and Traditional Equity Analysis*. Charlottesville, VA: Association for Investment Management and Research.

Ma, K. C., 2005a. "Preference reversal in futures markets," Working paper, Stetson University.

Ma, K. C., 2005b. "Nonlinear factor payoffs?" Research Paper # 97-5, KCM Asset Management, Inc.

Ma, K. C., 2005c. "How many factors do you need?" Research Paper # 96-4, KCM Asset Management, Inc.

Mantegna, R. N. and H. E. Stanley, 2000. *An Introduction to Econophysics: Correlations and Complexity in Finance.* Cambridge, UK: Cambridge University Press.

Roll, R. R., 1992. "A mean-variance analysis of tracking error," *Journal of Portfolio Management*, 18: 13–22.

Ross, S. A., 1994. "Survivorship bias in performance studies," in *Proceedings of Blending Quantitative and Traditional Equity Analysis.* Charlottesville, VA: Association for Investment Management and Research.

Chapter 12

Quantitative Equity Strategies*

Learning Objectives

After reading this chapter, you will understand:

- what is meant by quantitative equity management/systematic asset management;
- the differences between systematic and discretionary asset management;
- the different types of quantitative equity strategies (multifactor strategies, factor strategies, event-based strategies, statistical arbitrage strategies, textual strategies, and alternative data strategies);
- the scientific approach to quantitative modeling;
- how to formulate quantitative strategies;
- what signals are and how they are developed and analyzed;
- computational methods used in empirical work;
- critical aspects of quantitative strategies;
- characteristics of good data;
- best practices for data that an asset manager must follow to increase the likelihood of producing a successful quantitative strategy; and
- the key properties of good quantitative investment models and strategies: parsimony, tractability, conceptual insight, predictability, and adaptability.

*This chapter is coauthored with Joseph Cerniglia, an adjunct professor at the Courant Institute of Mathematics at New York University and visiting scholar at the University of Pennsylvania, and Petter N. Kolm, Clinical Professor of Mathematics and Director of the Mathematics in Finance, M.S. Program at New York University's Courant Institute.

Introduction

In Chapter 11, implementable quantitative equity research was discussed. In this chapter, we describe the research process and principles that are needed to create successful models that can be used in quantitative equity strategies. To build successful strategies, asset managers need to combine judgment with the scientific approach to identify and validate new opportunities in ever-changing markets. Asset managers must understand the data and computational techniques that are needed to obtain empirical evidence to support their investment ideas. (We describe these techniques in other chapters in this book.) There is no doubt that the research and development of successful quantitative models are a blend of science and art. The endeavors that asset managers must pursue in model building require constant innovation and rigorous analytics to be successful.

Asset managers are described as quantitative when they apply a systematic, model-driven approach to investing. The investment management process followed by quantitative asset managers is systematic in how securities are chosen from among a universe of securities and how portfolios are constructed from those securities. This approach is also referred to as *systematic asset management.* Moreover, they can be applied to equity markets as well as to several asset classes.[1]

Fundamental equity investment style approaches to investing emphasize human judgment of the analyst and portfolio manager. The fundamental process begins by developing an understanding of the company and then using that understanding to develop forecasts to value a company. The process uses both qualitative and quantitative information. Typically, this approach uses the insights that come from qualitative information. This approach is also referred to as *discretionary asset management.*

Central to the formulation of successful quantitative strategies is the research process. The elements for their success are the availability of more and better data (e.g., Big Data and alternative data), and advanced computational methods, advanced analytical techniques (e.g., econometric, machine learning, and robust optimization methods), and a better understanding of how to enhance judgment in the research process. We do not provide a set of rules for an asset manager to follow but identify and examine

[1]See Tucker [2018] for a discussion of systematic fixed income investing.

the characteristics of quantitative strategies. We also highlight some best practices in quantitative modeling.[2] The characteristics that we describe may not be strictly statistical or mathematical in nature, but rather they emphasize the integration of market dynamics, data, research design, modeling techniques, and economic and financial judgment. The framework we describe for building quantitative forecasting models apply to all asset classes. Although we focus on quantitative research methodologies, we think that some of the ideas presented in this chapter are valuable for a fundamental research process.

Quantitative versus Fundamental Investment Strategies

Let's begin by describing the difference between quantitative equity investing and fundamental equity investing. Bukowski [2011] describes the difference by looking at how asset managers select stocks.

A fundamental asset manager begins the investment process by screening a list of candidate stocks for inclusion in the portfolio. For example, the asset manager may only want to include stocks comprising the S&P 500. The asset manager then selects characteristics for filtering the stock candidates to create a shorter list of acceptable stocks. For example, the asset manager may establish as its criteria that a company has to have earnings growth greater than or equal to 9% over the past five years and a profit margin that exceeds 18% over the same time period. The characteristics are based on what indicators the fundamental asset manager believes will help identify stocks that have superior company value and potential mispricing. The view is that these characteristics will create long-term value.

The list of companies that satisfy the criteria is what the asset management team will then focus on. Suppose that there are 100 companies from seven industries that are on the list. The asset manager will then assign to each industry analyst group the stocks from the list. The analyst will then perform traditional equity analysis to determine which stocks to recommend to the senior portfolio manager.

Traditional equity analysis provides qualitative insight into a company's operations, management, and competitive strengths. Analysts meet

[2]For an excellent review of the current state of quantitative equity investing, as well as a history of quantitative equity investing, see Becker and Reinganum [2018].

with company management to learn these characteristics of a company. These meetings make available management's knowledge of the financial operations of the company and discuss corporate strategy and the competitive environment. Analysts will further their understanding of the company by consulting others, such as sell-side analysts and industry experts, which provides an outside view on these characteristics of a company.

Equity analysis also involves using quantitative information. Analysts begin with exploring the numeric information in the financial statements. This understanding offers inputs into the financial position of the company that is useful for forecasting the sales, expenses, earnings and cash flow of the company that are later used to value the company. *Peer analysis* is useful in developing a broader view of how a company ranks relative to various quantitative measures such as financial ratios.

Based on the recommendations of the analysts about the prospects for each, a portfolio is constructed (i.e., amount assigned to each stock) based on further research regarding the future state of the economy as well as other macro factors. In the case of fundamental asset management, the majority of the team's time is devoted to traditional equity analysis.

A quantitative asset manager will also begin the investment process by screening the candidate list based on characteristics that are believed, based on the team's research or academic studies, will achieve the portfolio's investment objective. A quantitative asset manager believes that the characteristics provide sufficient information for selecting a company based on firm value and the biases that investors exhibit in the market. The bulk of the team's time is spent on deciding on the characteristics to be used in filtering candidates for the list of companies. Suppose that the screen produces 250 stocks. The asset manager then will purchase all 250 stocks.

Both approaches use characteristics in screening for candidates. In the quantitative management approach, the characteristics are used in a manner that is systematic and automated. In the fundamental management approach, the characteristic use a more qualitative criteria.

Differences between Fundamental and Quantitative Equity Approaches

In describing quantitative asset management, Clifford Asness, co-founder of the third largest hedge fund in the world, relates a conversation that he overheard that he believes exemplifies the difference between fundamental asset managers — who he refers to as "quals" — and quantitative asset managers or "quants":

> ...one day our qual manager came up to our quant manager and said, with obvious excitement in his voice: "We just added Philip Morris at maximum weight. We never hold anything at maximum weight, but we did all the analysis, and we're very enthusiastic. We think Philip Morris has taken a beating and will come roaring back. What do you guys think?" The quant looked at him and said: "You know, I'm not sure if we're long or short." Asness [2008, p. 47]

Why did the quant manager not know the position, if any, in the quant constructed portfolio? Why do fundamental asset managers know their holdings while quantitative asset managers might not be familiar with their holdings? Why are fundamental asset managers intimately familiar with the companies in their portfolio while quantitative asset managers do not necessarily have a detailed knowledge of the companies in their portfolio?

To understand why, it is necessary to understand the five differences between quantitative and fundamental investment management. Bukowski [2011] provides the following five differences between the two management approaches: (1) company versus characteristic focus, (2) narrow versus broad focus, (3) position concentration/size of bets, (4) risk perspective, and (5) past versus future focus. Basically, the difference in the two approaches is how the asset manager views information. We describe each as follows.

Company versus characteristic focus

The principal focus of a fundamental asset manager is on the companies that the filtering based on characteristics has identified as potentially acceptable investments. The analyst groups that are part of the asset management team will apply fundamental analysis to screen the companies allocated to the group to determine whether each company should be considered by the portfolio management team. In contrast, in quantitative asset management, the is no further screening of the companies on the filtered list since the characteristics used for the screening are believed to be sufficient to warrant the portfolio manager to allocate funds.

Narrow versus broad focus

The filtered list is used by a fundamental asset manager for further narrowing the potential stocks to be included in the portfolio. The equity analysts search not only the current filing by the company but other sources of information that will help them in differentiating companies in terms of potential returns. In quantitative asset management, the characteristics are believed to contain all of the information that will result in superior returns.

Position concentration/size of bets

In fundamental asset management, the position size in stocks tend to be larger. The detailed qualitative work done by the fundamental portfolio manager and analysts result in a higher level of confidence which influences the portfolio manager's judgment regarding the position size. Consequently, fundamental asset managers are basically making larger bets on stocks. For a quantitative asset manager, a portfolio optimization algorithm drives the position size. This process prioritizes diversification in the allocation process, which results in spreading the portfolio over a larger number of stocks. As a result, the bet is lower for each stock.

Risk perspective

Given the nature of the portfolios created by the two approaches, one can see the difference in risk perspective. The fundamental asset manager focuses on the risk of the individual companies in the portfolio. The risk of the portfolio is the perspective taken by a quantitative asset manager. As Asness notes:

> Good quants play a statistical game. They do something that works based on an average tendency. So, the advantage of quant management is that the manager does not have to make a big bet on any one position. Its disadvantage is that quant managers tend to know far less about any given situation than qualitative managers do. The flip side of this disadvantage, however, is that if qual managers expect to stay in business, they need to be right when they make a choice because they tend to take on a lot of risk in any given situation. [Asness, 2008, p. 47]

Past versus future focus

In selecting potential stocks and then performing additional analysis, analysts on a fundamental asset management team use not just past information in recommending the selection of stocks but also future prospects for the company. That is, this approach relies more heavily on qualitative, forward-looking research rather than just historical information.

Quantitative asset management looks at significant amounts of current and past information and gives less consideration to qualitative future prospects for the companies in the selection process. The argument for quantitative managers is that "history does not repeat itself but it often rhymes".

Quantitative Strategy Defined

A *quantitative strategy* is a systematic, data- and model-based approach for making decisions on the various activities in the asset management process. Quantitative strategies can be further understood by appraising the underlying core characteristics of the models at the heart of the investment process. By looking closely at these core characteristics, we evaluate how the model delivers returns and the type of risk they take to achieve those returns. We can also learn about the judgments and assumptions made in constructing the model as each one contributes to the outcome of the strategy.

The most important characteristic of the quantitative modeling approach is the scientific approach (1) formulating meaningful hypotheses or theses to be evaluated, (2) using empirical work to attempt to put precision around investment decisions and economic reasoning, (3) developing high standards of analytical rigor, (4) using sensitivity analysis to challenge assumptions and context in which the strategy was developed, (5) incorporating adjustments to the strategy based on judgment, (6) measuring results, and (7) incorporating revisions or updates to the model as new information becomes available.

Taxonomy of Quantitative Equity Strategies

Quantitative strategies exist across different markets. The characteristics underlying these strategies vary substantially. Strategies can be categorized along a number of dimensions, such as the asset class, type of securities, horizon, trading style, and investment philosophy. Each of these categories influences the quantitative modeling process, often starting with the research design, data, modeling techniques, and evaluation methods.

Commonality in these traits allows us to classify strategies into groups. The list of companies described earlier in this chapter attempts to create a simple taxonomy of quantitative strategies. There is some overlap in this categorization because quantitative strategies share common traits.

Quantitative investment strategies differ in their motivation to trade, the frequency of trading, information used to trade, and the markets traded. The strategies employ different holding periods and trading frequencies — the latter of which can occur in milliseconds, or extend to months or years. Separately, the holding period of each trade varies along similar horizons. Both trading frequencies and holding periods are functions of the investment theory underlying the strategy and the empirical results uncovered in research.

In equity asset management, there are numerous quantitative strategies. The six major ones are described as follows:

Multifactor Strategies

Multifactor strategies are the most common type of investment strategy among quantitative investors. As described earlier, quantitative researchers start by looking for common characteristics (factors) that forecast returns. Individual factors have different risk and return characteristics over assorted investment horizons and throughout market cycles. The next step is to assemble these factors in a way to optimize risk-adjusted performance by increasing predictive accuracy and delivering more consistent performance.

Key considerations in developing multifactor strategies include how to represent the underlying investment rationale and choosing the computational approach. The investment rationale provides us with the cause and effect on why these strategies will be successful. The computational approach provides the mathematical algorithm that implements this investment rationale.

Common explanations from investment rationale as to why multifactor strategies are successful include (1) the superior ability to earn excess returns from consistently applying a successful approach without behavior influences from humans, (2) algorithms integrate larger and more diverse types of information than human-based investing, and (3) algorithms can identify more complex patterns and relationships than humans are able to see.

Computational approaches to combine and weigh factors translate the empirical work on factors into a working model. We classify the approaches into four types: (1) data-driven approach, (2) factor model approach, (3) heuristics approach, and (4) optimization approach.

A *data-driven approach* uses statistical methods to select and weigh factors in a forecasting model. There are a variety of estimation procedures, such as neural networks, classification trees, and principal components, that can be used to estimate these models. The algorithm of the statistical method evaluates the data and compares the results against the criteria. *Factor models* are well-established statistical approaches such as multivariate regression. We can evaluate the fit, forecast ability, and economic significance of the model. *Heuristics* are based on common sense, intuition, and market insight and are not formal statistical or mathematical techniques designed to meet a given set of requirements. *Optimization* uses various computational approaches to fit an objective function and parameters to find an optimal solution to selecting and weighing individual factors.

Factor Strategies

Factor strategies are *rule-based strategies* to trade well-known equity risk premiums to earn returns. Factor strategies involve two major tasks (1) identification of the factors and (2) how to construct a portfolio from the identified factors. Identification of the factors results jointly from financial theory and empirical work to decide what characteristics of an investment will receive a return premium relative to a benchmark. Importantly, not all factors deliver a return premium; some explain the risk of securities. The second task is how to take that factor and build an investable factor mimicking portfolio (FMP). The FMP should track the performance and risk characteristics of the factors. Other considerations in the implementation challenges include liquidity and trading costs of the positions in the portfolio. Moreover, as constraints and other desired parameters are added to the portfolio construction process, other inherent risks often become present.

Event-Based Strategies

Strategies that attempt to take advantage of mispricing that can occur before or after some type of event takes place are called *event-based strategies*. Quantitative models look to identify price patterns that typically occur before or after events. Events include earnings releases, economics data announcements, corporate actions, spin-offs, takeovers, and regulatory changes.

Market Microstructure Strategies

Strategies that exploit profitable opportunities arising from the trading flows and dynamics of the equity market are called *market microstructure strategies*. During the late 1980s and early 1990s, markets abandoned the open-outcry trading venues system in favor of electronic trading. Since then, increased technological advances, deregulation, and changes in market structures have created the ideal conditions for the spread of high-frequency trading.

High-frequency trading firms deploy fully automated trading strategies to identify and profit from intra-day price patterns. These strategies rely on computer algorithms which decide the timing, price, and order quantity of various trades. These strategies try to earn small amounts of money on each trade which can be amplified by high trading volume. A key aspect of these strategies is the speed of execution with most strategies trading in the horizon of milliseconds.

Statistical Arbitrage Strategies

Statistical arbitrage strategies, commonly referred to as "stat arb strategies", focus on investing in securities, both long and short positions, centered on a mathematical or statistical algorithm that identifies a comoving relationship between the securities. These strategies work because they exploit systematic relationships among equity securities with similar characteristics. Typically, univariate statistical pairs trading strategies are structured as follows: In a formation period, two securities are identified whose prices have moved together historically. We say these securities have an equilibrium relationship, which is identified by a statistical model. Next, the spread of their price movements is monitored in a subsequent trading period. If the prices diverge and the spread widens between the pair, a trade is placed where the better performing stock is sold short and the worse performing stock is bought. Because of this equilibrium relationship between the securities, we expect the spread will revert to its historical mean, resulting in a profit.

The straightforward concept of univariate pairs trading is often extended into more sophisticated strategies. We could implement a strategy in a quasi-multivariate framework where one security is traded against a weighted portfolio of comoving securities. Another strategy would trade groups of stocks against other groups of stocks that comove together.

Stat arb strategies rely heavily on sophisticated statistical models. Econometric techniques such as cointegration are used to unveil stationary price series between securities to identify trading candidates. Techniques from statistical learning such as non-parametric distance metrics are used to identify pairs trading opportunities. Time series models are applied to find optimal trading rules for mean-reverting spreads.

Furthermore, stat arb arbitrage is closely related to other long-short anomalies, such as violations of the law of one price, lead-lag anomalies, and return reversal anomalies. In contrast to pure riskless arbitrage discussed in the academic finance literature, statistical arbitrage is a risky form of strategy.

Textual Strategies

Textual strategies involve trades based on qualitative textual signals such as news reports, company documents, or social media.

The field of computational linguistics has made considerable progress extracting meaning from different sources of text. Within finance, the most common content analysis methods focus on identifying market sentiment. Quantitative approaches to textual analysis range from simple dictionary approaches to more sophisticated algorithms that involve machine learning algorithms such as deep learning. Dictionary approaches score text according to a predetermined set of words that are believed to correlate with some theme that investors hypothesize will forecast returns. More sophisticated algorithms can identify topics or measure sentiment by identifying latent patterns using words and sentences from documents.

Textual analysis presents challenges as well as rich opportunities. Textual analysis is a high-dimensional problem because we need to interpret words in light of complex grammatical structures and the rich interactions among words. The vast quantities of data present quantitative opportunities to integrate and interpret tremendous amount of information that lead to more accurate forecasts. This is an area that will continue to see explosive growth in the future.

Alternative data strategies

The amount of data is growing exponentially as the processes and activities of companies, people, and governments become more data driven. As noted by Fortado, Wigglesworth, and Scannell [2017], examples of these data include website scraping, data from credit card tracking, geolocation data from smartphones, and satellite data. Some of these data are now being packaged and sold to investment firms, marketed as "alternative" data. Investment firms, particularly quantitative firms, are beginning to analyze these data to see if they can forecast the earnings or economic activity of companies that might not be available from more traditional data sources. Research involving alternative data uses various machine learning algorithms as well as traditional statistical techniques.

How to Develop Quantitative Strategies

As just noted, the most important characteristic of the quantitative modeling approach is the scientific approach. This approach provides an asset manager with a way to examine and understand phenomena, develop new theories, or modify or integrate existing theories based on the presentation of empirical and measurable evidence subject to specific principles of reasoning. Typically, research based on the scientific approach involves six steps: (1) define a question, (2) collect information and resources, (3) form an explanatory hypothesis, (4) test the hypothesis by performing experiments and collecting data in a reproducible manner, (5) analyze the data, and (6) interpret the data and draw conclusions. After drawing these conclusions, the asset manager may then go back to reformulate the explanatory hypothesis and repeat steps (3)–(6) as many times as necessary to strengthen the conclusions.

Within the context of asset management, empirical analysis utilizes data and tools to design, research, and evaluate hypotheses/models. The principal purpose of empirical research is to create (some) evidence to support or reject trading models. A major aspect of empirical analysis is research design. A well-thought-out research design provides support and credibility for validating the investment insights underlying trading models.

The following steps are commonly followed in developing quantitative strategies: (1) formulate trading ideas and strategies, (2) develop signals, (3) acquire and process data, (4) analyze the signals, (5) build the strategy, (6) evaluate the strategy, (7) backtest the strategy, and (8) implement the strategy. We discuss each, as follows.

Formulating Investment Ideas and Strategies

Typically, the formulation of a successful quantitative strategy begins as an idea based on economic intuition, a market insight, or an anomaly.

Background research can be helpful for understanding what others have tried or implemented in the past.

Differentiating between a trading idea and a quantitative strategy involves looking at the economic motivation for each. Often a *trading idea* has a shorter-term horizon that is associated with a specific event or mispricing. In contrast, a *quantitative strategy* has a longer time span and exploits opportunities to process information better, receive premiums associated with anomalies, or identify mispricings.

Developing Signals

Once the idea of the strategy is established, an asset manager proceeds from the economic concepts to the construction of signals that may be able to capture the intuition that led to the strategy. *Signals* are the building blocks for the model that the asset manager uses to create an investment strategy. Signals are quantitative measures constructed from the data. They represent an investment idea. The way in which signals are constructed varies depending on the investment thesis and the data representing the thesis. For example, a quantitative signal could be based on a stock's underlying characteristics such as its return on equity or valuation ratio. A *sentiment signal* could be developed from unstructured text from various company-issued reports or news about the company.

Acquiring and processing data

Data are critical to a strategy's success. For constructing signals, a strategy relies on accurate and clean data. Data need to be carefully stored in an infrastructure that is scalable and flexible. Upon acquiring new data sources, an asset manager expands the information set necessary to construct new insights.

Analyzing the signals

The asset management team must perform a variety of statistical tests on the data to assess the empirical properties of the signals constructed. This empirical research is used to understand the risk-and-return potential of a signal. For example, an asset manager might be interested in statistically testing whether a signal's Sharpe ratio exceeds one. This analysis may form the basis for constructing a more complete trading strategy.

Building the strategy

A model represents a mathematical or systematic specification of the trading strategy. The two key considerations in this specification are the selection of the specific signals and how these signals are combined. Both considerations may be motivated by the economic intuition driving the trading strategy.

Evaluating, testing, and implementing the strategy

The final steps involve assessing the estimation, specification, and forecast quality of the model. This analysis includes examining the goodness of fit (often done in-sample), forecasting ability (often done out-of-sample), and sensitivity and risk characteristics of the model.

Empirical validation and testing are key drivers in formulating quantitative trading strategies. They bridge the gap between stylized financial models and the real world represented by the markets. Financial models are nothing more than crude approximations of reality — with regimes in which they work acceptably, and regimes in which they do not work at all or work very poorly at best. Careful systematic empirical research can help the asset manager in identifying these regimes. The asset management team's judgment and experience become a critical factor in this step.

Models and Judgment

In explaining what quantitative asset management is, Clifford Asness notes the following about the role of judgment in this approach to managing money:

> Many people believe that quantitative asset management is all about numbers, and it is true that judgment and intuition do not play a big role in a quant portfolio, particularly on a daily basis. But in model construction and in process and risk control construction, sound judgment and intuition based on years of experience play a surprisingly important role in quant management. Asness [2008, p. 47]

Deciding how to cleanse the data, how to select a specific model, how to aggregate signals, and which risk measures to rely on are all examples of judgment calls. Of course, the asset management team makes these judgment calls based on its experience and preferences. Besides the research process itself, judgment is also prevalent in the feedback mechanism of backtesting and running the strategy.

Most quantitative models are based on two ways of thinking — hypothesis based (deductive) and pattern based (inductive). Each way of thinking requires a different model-building research process. The starting point for the hypothesis-based approach is some insight about why a trading opportunity exists. It is dependent on an economic thesis or hypothesis on how the market works or why the opportunity exists. Frequently, there is a "story" that precedes the empirical work.

The second approach — inductive or pattern based — is exploratory in nature, and the discovery of insights emerges from the empirical work. Learning occurs throughout the process.

In this approach, it is critical to be able to differentiate between correlation and causation. It must be determined whether the measured statistical correlations are spurious or causal. Understanding the underlying economic mechanisms and theory may offer insights in making this determination. Best practices involve understanding how to make better decisions in the research design process. It is useful to draw on sciences from other disciplines that study decision-making, often in experimental settings; these include psychology, philosophy, and organizational behavior.

There are benefits of using quantitative models that extend beyond pure quantitative trading. These models provide valuable analytical tools in a traditional, fundamental investment decision-making process. It is important to distinguish between how purely quantitative asset managers utilize model forecasts and how fundamental asset managers use them. For quantitative managers, model forecasts produce an expected return forecast on a security or a set of securities. For fundamental asset managers, model forecasts create new insights to synthesize with other qualitative information (e.g., management meetings and industry strategy) being acquired to make investment decisions. Fundamental asset managers must apply quantitative models to understand complex relationships, to verify investment theses, and to discover new opportunities.

Within an asset management firm that has both a quantitative management team and a fundamental management team is a social experience that can create an "investment edge". The process of building a quantitative model jointly produces unique investment insights. Numerous studies and anecdotes provide evidence that combining computer-based forecasting and human judgment results in better outcomes.

Techniques for Empirical Work

In addition to insights about the market, quantitative computational methods are critical for success. Many of the traditional financial econometric techniques that are described in Chapter 4 continue to be widely used in asset management. Their success results from their tractability — being well understood and fairly straightforward to implement.

Asset managers continue to extend and innovate upon traditional computational approaches. New computational methods continue to emerge and flourish. An increasingly popular computational field among quantitative researchers is statistical learning/machine learning that is described in Chapter 7. These tools — which can be classified into supervised and unsupervised methods — are valuable for building models because they reveal the structure of data, incorporate nonlinearities into the model, and provide robust predictions. These approaches should not be viewed or used as "black boxes" but rather as analytical tools.

Researchers in finance are applying these newer methodologies to create insights into the dynamics of equity markets. Moritz and Zimmermann [2016], for example, address the research question of which variables provide independent information about the cross-section of stock returns. Their computational approach, called *deep conditional portfolio sorts*, is designed to deal with a large number of variables and potential nonlinearities and interactions. When estimating the model, Moritz and Zimmermann incorporate concepts from the statistical learning literature, mirroring methods used to estimate a decision tree and ensemble methods.

Unstructured data have become more valuable in developing quantitative signals for equities. Textual analysis of corporate disclosures such as financial statements, earnings releases, and conference call transcripts are sources of unstructured, qualitative data. Li [2010] provides a survey of various techniques to extract signals from textual data, showing that the communication patterns of management could reveal certain management characteristics that have an impact on understanding corporate decisions and forecasting stock returns. Here are some recent examples:

- Heston and Sinha [2017] compare different methods of textual analysis using news reports from Dow Jones to predict cross-sectional stock returns. They analyze the horizons over which returns are realized for sentiment signals created using different computational methods. Some signals provide a forecasting horizon of up to a quarter, whereas others forecast returns over shorter horizons, such as a day.

- Klevak, Livnat, and Suslava [2019] document the most commonly used clichés in earnings conference calls and construct a dictionary of these expressions. They use natural language processing (NLP) — a fast-growing field within financial data science concerned with the interactions between human language and computers — to detect clichés and use the findings to signal potential negative tone. Controlling for other characteristics and signals conveyed in earnings calls that are most correlated with excessive use of clichés, these authors find using NLP that corporate management's excessive use of clichés is negatively correlated with excess stock returns. The excessive use of clichés, the authors find, are associated with negative earnings growth and prior stock returns. Corporate management appears to use clichés to "soften the blow" associated with bad news. Their evidence provide guidance for asset management in making decisions because it suggests that (1) market returns around earnings calls are incrementally and significantly more negative after controlling for the surprise in earnings and the tone of the conference call itself and (2) economic and statistically significant returns in a hedge portfolio holding long positions in all the companies that used no clichés in their earnings conference calls and short positions in companies that used at least four clichés.
- Rapach, Strauss, Tu, and Zhou [2019] used least absolute shrinkage and selection operator (lasso), a powerful and popular technique in machine learning, to analyze return predictability for 30 US industries based on the information in lagged industry returns. They report significant in-sample evidence of industry return predictability. Lagged returns for the financial sector and commodity and material-producing industries exhibit widespread predictive ability. This finding is consistent with the gradual diffusion of information across economically linked industries. Out-of-sample industry return forecasts that incorporate the information in lagged industry returns are economically valuable: controlling for systematic risk using leading multi-factor models, an industry-rotation portfolio that goes long (short) industries with the highest (lowest) forecasted returns delivers an annualized alpha of over 8%. The industry-rotation portfolio also generates substantial gains during economic downturns. Their findings offer machine-learning-based evidence against the weak form of market efficiency.

- Das, Seoyoung, and Kothari [2019] demonstrate how NLP can be applied to develop an early warning system for identifying corporate failure. Potential indicators within employees' sent email content and sender/recipient networks are explored to determine whether they can effectively predict changes in a firm's risk and subsequent financial performance. Sentiment-based indicators in the message bodies and non-textual structural characteristics (e.g., the number of emails sent, the average email length, and the shifting sender/recipient networks within the company over time) are explored and found to be useful indicators.

A growing amount of information comes from Twitter, Internet searches, and other sources of text-based social media. These data sources can also be useful for building quantitative measures of investor sentiment and how investor sentiment may impact various types of investment decisions. Dredze, Kambadur, Kazantsev, Mann, and Osborne [2016] provide a survey of the impact of social media and news on asset prices. Here are a few examples:

- Curtis, Richardson, and Schmardebeck [2016] found higher return sensitivity is associated with a high volume of social-media messages.
- Karagozoglu and Fabozzi [2017] used social-media sentiment to develop a strategy that trades VIX futures and showed that this strategy outperforms a benchmark, even after taking into account transaction costs.
- Agrawal, Pablo, Lo, and Taranjit [2018] analyze the relation between intra-day liquidity in the stock market and measures of sentiment that they estimate from social-media platforms StockTwits and Twitter. Extreme sentiment they find is associated with higher demand for and lower supply of liquidity. Negative sentiment tends to have a much larger effect on demand and supply than positive sentiment.

An understanding of the intuition, assumptions, and strengths and weaknesses of computational approaches is critical for the asset manager to understand. The choice of an analytical method involves trade-offs. The computational approach should be consistent with the data structure, research design approach, and underlying investment strategy being assessed. For example, research that uses a hypothesis-based (deductive) approach to modeling typically relies on more traditional computational approaches, such as regression and information coefficients. Pattern-based approaches are applied to unstructured data sources and/or data that contain nonlinearities or other unusual features.

Some Critical Aspects of Quantitative Strategies

There are many advantages to using a quantitative model in asset management. The scientific approach to developing models brings advantages such as rigor, creativity, avoidance of biases, and process.

A rigorous approach, the underlying principle of the scientific approach, allows the asset management team to validate ideas through a framework incorporating statistical rigor by employing backtests, in-sample/out-of-sample comparisons, and Monte Carlo analysis to study the robustness and sensitivity of a strategy to a given choice of parameters. This verification should also incorporate new market and theoretical developments. New assumptions paradigms/theories require the reconstruction of prior assumptions and the reevaluation of prior facts.

The numerous computational tools — from statistical learning to traditional statistical approaches — and the expanding set of data sources provide tools and raw materials to explore new trading ideas. The asset management team benefits from creativity — which results from hard work, introspection, and inspiration. This creativity is the driver for new investment ideas. With the right tools, researchers have the ability to develop ideas about investing strategies and create models.

All decisions are subject to biases. In investing, the behavioral biases are well documented and described in Chapter 17, where backtesting is described. Quantitative models can provide clients with more objective benchmarks by which to measure the decisions of the asset managers that they engage, as well as offering asset managers ways to (partially) eliminate investment biases.

The decisions asset managers make to build quantitative strategies are also affected by biases. Based on the data that they see, asset management teams sometimes construct a story to explain what happened by looking backward and creating a story to fit events. Asset managers' recognizing the potential biases and understanding how assumptions drive the choices in the modeling process are key to building successful strategies.

Quantitative strategies are systematic; that is, the underlying strategy is consistently applied to identify and implement trading opportunities in a structured framework. A framework brings structure and logic to a disorderly and complex activity of identifying opportunities in the market. This framework provides a process — a common plan of direction and action to use in developing, evaluating, and implementing investment ideas through quantitative models. In markets filled with near-constant information flow, not all information influences asset prices. The benefit of having a systematic model is having a consistent process to focus efforts on information that influences prices — and to avoid reacting to noise (useless information).

Empirical research is often based on historical data, and there is a limit to how much information about the future an asset manager can infer from the past. Sometimes, quantitative asset managers are at risk of being too systematic in their approach. There is always the risk of low-probability events that will challenge the underlying assumptions. Because markets change and the current environment looks different from the past, asset managers need to evaluate whether those changes are structural or transitory. Asset managers must understand how both types of changes will impact the performance of quantitative models. They need to continually evaluate their models and the markets in which they operate, revising a model when their judgment and experience indicate it is no longer effective or a different opportunity set for alpha arises.

Data are at the Core of a Quantitative Model

At the core of any quantitative model are the data used in building and testing the model. Quantitative analysis relies on non-experimental inference. The source and how the data are used is of critical importance. That is, the quantitative process is only as good as the data used.

In any dataset used in the quantitative process, there are some data features we understand, and some that we do not. For researchers, it is critical to explore data features and expose unexpected features of the data. Data can be classified in a number of different ways. One common way is as structured data or unstructured data. *Structured data* are organized into tables with clearly identified and organized information. *Unstructured data*, such as text containing natural language, do not have a formal structure. Specialized processes to extract the important attributes that can be used in various computational techniques are required for unstructured data. Consequently, unstructured data introduce new opportunities and challenges in formulating and testing quantitative strategies. The infrastructure to store and access this information is still evolving, requiring substantial effort to utilize this information in modeling.

Data containing errors, missing values, and other flaws impact the validity of the analysis. For example, Kothari, Sabino, and Zach [2005] find that non-surviving firms tend to be either extremely bad or extremely good performers. Survivorship bias implies truncation of such extreme observations. They show that even a small degree of such non-random truncation can have a strong impact on sample moments of stock returns.

Typically, data are often available from multiple sources, and the number of available data sources has been increasing. Different data sources maintain a different level of detail. These differences can have a significant impact on strategy development. It is important that an asset manager recognize the comparative characteristics of databases. In particular, in analyzing an investment strategy, an asset manager must be able to explain how discrepancies between databases affect the results and determine whether the use of a particular data source might have influenced the results.

Characteristics of good data include the following:

- clear and consistent definitions of what the data represent;
- reasonable detail underlying the data;
- appropriate data availability: length, frequency, timeliness;
- consistent view of history;
- free from survivorship bias; and
- free from look-ahead bias.

The following are just seven best practices for data that an asset manager must follow to increase the likelihood that working with data will produce a successful quantitative strategy:

1. ***Best Practice 1*:** The asset manager must understand the nuances of data sources.
2. ***Best Practice 2*:** The asset manager must understand how the database evolves over time.
3. ***Best Practice 3*:** The asset manager must understand how the database's standard procedures work and how they differ among different data sources.
4. ***Best Practice 4*:** The asset manager must recognize potential biases in the data.
5. ***Best Practice 5*:** If possible, the asset manager should select one data source to build the model and a second data source to confirm the model.
6. ***Best Practice 6*:** The asset manager must include statistics that describe and compare the usability of data items with regard to standard empirical applications in finance.

7. ***Best Practice 7*:** The asset manager must look for economic explanations of any outliers.

The above list of best practices is by no means exhaustive but does cover the major aspects that asset managers should follow.

Best Practice 2 should be followed by asset managers because most databases change over time, and those changes include what data were collected, how the data were collected, and their coverage. Because most databases have standardized procedures for reporting certain items in their system in order to ensure comparability, Best Practice 3 should be followed. Brown, Lajbcygier, and Li [2008] provide a good example for why Best Practice 7 should be followed by asset managers. Examining the economic significance of outliers in their dataset, they demonstrate that the outliers result from firms with materially different financial situations. In contrast to outliers caused by bad data, this set of outliers had material implications for the conclusions of their results.

An asset manager may have an opportunity to use less clean data sources or data with shorter history. This type of data might provide a source of alpha that other data sources overlook because of the work and patience required to make the data usable for a research process.

To appreciate how high-quality data are critical to success because the validity and power of the results rely on well-prepared datasets, consider the study by Ljungqvist, Malloy, and Marston [2009]. They document changes in the collection and recording of historical I/B/E/S analyst stock recommendations. They then show that these changes are non-random, and the consequences of these changes affect returns generated on trading signals using these data.

Five Key Properties of "Good" Quantitative Investment Models and Strategies

There are five key properties of "good" quantitative investment models. Gabaix and Laibson [2008] describe critical properties for building economic models. These properties are intended to be broad guidelines and we will apply them to quantitative investment models and to investment strategies. They are parsimony, tractability, conceptual insight, predictability, and adaptability.

Parsimony Property

Parsimony means models with few assumptions. All models are only approximations of the real world, and some features will always be omitted in developing a quantitative model. The assumptions made by an asset manager are based on the results of empirical research (parameter estimates), economic intuition, and judgment and theory (e.g., priors, structural assumptions). Overfitting tends to be the result of using too many assumptions. When overfitting does occur, the models are unable to provide accurate out-of-sample predictions.

Tractability property

Models that are tractable are easy to analyze, providing transparency to the user. Asset managers should have explicit descriptions that have been made with respect to the data, research design, and computational choices. *Tractability* allows the asset manager to question the model's assumptions and make changes when it is appropriate to do so.

Conceptual insightfulness property

The model should be consistent with market dynamics, investor behavior, and investment theory. The empirical analysis and the asset manager's hypothesis about why the strategy works should be mutually reinforcing.

Predictability property

The *predictability property* relates to the asset manager's desire for models that provide robust forecasts. Asset managers are primarily concerned with the profitability and risk of a strategy and how well the model's motivation fits economic theory and market behavior.

Adaptability property

Financial markets are constantly evolving, subject to sudden, unpredictable changes. Market changes challenge the assumptions made in constructing a quantitative model. It is critical that an asset manager understand and forecast the potential impact of market changes. For example, change may be the result of innovation of financial products, change in the preferences of market participants, and/or responses to exogenous financial and economic shocks. Flexibility in an asset management team's thinking and models is necessary to adapt to changing market conditions and is what we mean by a model's *adaptability property.*

Key Points

- In seeking to formulate quantitative investment strategies, asset managers need to combine judgment with the scientific approach to identify and validate new opportunities in ever-changing markets.
- Asset managers must understand the data and computational techniques that are needed to obtain empirical evidence to support their investment ideas.
- The endeavors that asset managers must pursue in model building require constant innovation and rigorous analytics to be successful.
- The differences between the systematic and fundamental approaches of asset managers can be seen by how they differ in selecting stocks and constructing portfolios.
- A fundamental asset manager begins the investment process by screening a list of candidate stocks for inclusion in the portfolio and from the list of companies that satisfy the criteria that the asset management team will then focus on.
- A fundamental asset manager will the select companies based on traditional equity analysis (i.e., an analysis of the company and industry in which it operates).
- The portfolio manager will use the recommendations of the analysts about a company's prospects to construct a portfolio after considering the future state of the economy as well as other macro factors.
- In fundamental asset management, the majority of the portfolio management team's time is devoted to traditional equity analysis.
- A quantitative asset manager starts the investment process by screening the candidate list based on characteristics that are believed will achieve the portfolio's investment objective.
- A quantitative asset manager believes that the characteristics identified provide sufficient information for selecting a company.
- The bulk of the portfolio management team's time in the case of systematic investing is spent on deciding on the characteristics to be used in filtering the candidate list of companies.

- When systematic investing is pursued, all companies selected are included in the portfolio with no further analysis.
- The differences in the approaches used by fundamental and quantitative asset management are (1) company versus characteristic focus, (2) narrow versus broad focus, (3) position concentration/size of bets, (4) risk perspective, and (5) past versus future focus.
- A quantitative strategy is a systematic, data- and model-based approach for making decisions on the various activities in the asset management process.
- The most important characteristic of the quantitative modeling approach is the scientific approach.
- The scientific approach involves (1) formulating meaningful hypotheses, (2) using empirical work to evaluate the investment strategy, (3) developing high standards of analytical rigor, (4) challenging assumptions of the strategy, (5) incorporating adjustments to the strategy based on judgment, (6) measuring results, and (7) incorporating revisions or updates to the model as new information becomes available.
- The major quantitative equity strategies are multifactor strategies, factor strategies, event-based strategies, statistical arbitrage strategies, textual strategies, and alternative data strategies.
- Multifactor strategies start by looking for common characteristics (factors) that forecast returns and construct a portfolio based on these factors in a way so as to optimize risk-adjusted performance.
- Key considerations in developing multifactor strategies include how to represent the underlying investment rationale and choosing the computational approach.
- The four computational approaches to combine and weigh factors are (1) data-driven approach, (2) factor model approach, (3) heuristics approach, and (4) optimization approach.
- Factor strategies are rule-based strategies involving well-known equity risk premiums to earn returns and involve two major tasks (1) identification of the factors and (2) how to construct a portfolio from the identified factors.
- Event-based strategies seek to take advantage of mispricing that can occur before or after some type of event takes place by identifying price patterns that typically occur before or after events.
- Market microstructure strategies attempt to exploit profitable opportunities arising from the trading flows and dynamics of the equity market.

- Using sophisticated statistical models, statistical arbitrage strategies focus on investing in securities, both long and short positions, based on a mathematical or statistical algorithm that identifies a comoving relationship between the securities.
- Textual strategies involve trades based on qualitative textual signals such as news reports, company documents, or social media.
- Alternative data strategies use "alternative data" (website scraping, data from credit card tracking, geolocation data from smartphones, and satellite data) and various machine learning algorithms as well as traditional statistical techniques to make investment decisions.
- Typically, research based on the scientific approach involves six steps: (1) define a question, (2) collect information and resources, (3) form an explanatory hypothesis, (4) test the hypothesis by performing experiments and collecting data in a reproducible manner, (5) analyze the data, and (6) interpret the data and draw conclusions.
- Within the context of asset management, empirical analysis utilizes data and tools to design, research, and evaluate hypotheses/models.
- The steps commonly followed in developing quantitative strategies are (1) formulate trading ideas and strategies, (2) develop signals, (3) acquire and process data, (4) analyze the signals, (5) build the strategy, (6) evaluate the strategy, (7) backtest the strategy, and (8) implement the strategy.
- Differentiating between a trading idea and a quantitative strategy involves looking at the economic motivation for each.
- A trading idea has a shorter-term horizon that is associated with a specific event or mispricing, while a quantitative strategy has a longer time span and exploits opportunities to process information better, receive premiums associated with anomalies, or identify mispricings.
- Signals are the building blocks for a quantitative model that the asset manager uses to create an investment strategy where the signals are quantitative measures constructed from the data.
- The asset management team must perform a variety of statistical tests on the data to assess the empirical properties of the signals constructed.
- A model represents a mathematical or systematic specification of the trading strategy and involves two key considerations: the selection of the specific signals and how these signals are combined.
- The final steps in developing a quantitative strategy involves assessing the estimation, specification, and forecast quality of the model.

- Judgment calls by the asset manager in formulating quantitative strategies include how to cleanse the data, how to select a specific model, how to aggregate signals, and deciding on the risk measures.
- Most quantitative models are based on two ways of thinking — hypothesis based (deductive) and pattern based (inductive).
- In addition to insights about the market, quantitative computational methods are critical for success.
- An understanding of the intuition, assumptions, and strengths and weaknesses of computational approaches is critical for the asset manager.
- The numerous computational tools — from statistical learning to traditional statistical approaches — and the expanding set of data sources provide tools to explore new trading ideas.
- At the core of any quantitative model are the data used in building and testing the model.
- The quantitative process is only as good as the data used.
- One common way of classifying data is as structured data or unstructured data.
- Structured data are organized into tables with clearly identified and organized information, while unstructured data (e.g., text containing natural language) do not have a formal structure.
- Specialized processes to extract important attributes that can be used in various computational techniques are required for unstructured data and therefore introduce new opportunities and challenges in formulating and testing quantitative strategies.
- Characteristics of good data are (1) clear and consistent definitions of what the data represent, (2) reasonable detail underlying the data, (3) appropriate data availability (i.e., length, frequency, timeliness), (4) consistent view of history, (5) free from survivorship bias, and (6) free from look-ahead bias.
- There are best practices for data that an asset manager must follow to increase the likelihood that working with data will produce a successful quantitative strategy.
- The five key properties of "good" quantitative investment models are (1) parsimony, (2) tractability, (3) conceptual insight, (4) predictability, and (5) adaptability.
- Parsimony means models with few assumptions.
- Tractability allows the asset manager to question the model's assumptions and make changes when it is appropriate to do so.

- Predictability relates to the asset manager's desire for models that provide robust forecasts.
- A model's adaptability property involves the flexibility afforded by an asset management team's thinking and ability to adapt to changing market conditions.

References

Agrawal, S., P. D. Azar, A. W. Lo, and T. Singh, 2018. "Momentum, mean-reversion, and social media: Evidence from StockTwits and Twitter," *Journal of Portfolio Management*, 44(7): 85–95.

Asness, C. S., 2008. "The past and future of quantitative asset management," *CFA Institute Conference Proceedings Quarterly*, December: 47–53.

Brinson, G. P., R. Hood, and G. L. Beebower, 1986. "Determinants of portfolio performance," *Financial Analysts Journal*, 42(4): 39–48.

Becker, Y. L. and M. R. Reinganum, 2018. *The Current State of Quantitative Equity Investing*. Charlottesville, VA: CFA Institute Research Foundation.

Brown, S., P. Lajbcygier, and B. Li, 2008. "Going negative: What to do with negative book equity stocks," *Journal of Portfolio Management*, 35(1): 95–102.

Bukowski, P., 2011. "An introduction to quantitative equity investing," in *Equity Valuation and Portfolio Management*, edited by F. J. Fabozzi and H. M. Markowitz (pp. 1–24). Hoboken, NJ: John Wiley & Sons.

Curtis, A., V. J. Richardson, and R. Schmardebeck, 2016. "Investor attention and pricing of earnings news," Chapter in *Handbook of Sentiment Analysis in Finance*, G. Mitra and X. Yu (eds), Amazon.com Services.

Da, Z., J. Engelberg, and P. Gao, 2011. "In search of attention," *Journal of Finance*, 66(5): 1461–1499.

Da, Z., J. Engelberg, and P. Gao, 2015. "The sum of all FEARS investor sentiment and asset prices," *Review of Financial Studies*, 28(1): 1–32.

Das, S. R., K. Seoyoung, and B. Kothari, 2019. "Zero-revelation RegTech: Detecting risk through linguistic analysis of corporate emails and news," *Journal of Financial Data Science*, 1(2): 8–34.

Fortado, L., R. Wigglesworth, and K. Scannell, 2017. "Hedge funds see a gold rush in data mining," *Financial Times*, August 28.

Dredze, M., P. Kambadur, G. Kazantsev, G. Mann, and M. Osborne, 2016. "How Twitter is changing the nature of financial news discovery," in *Proceedings of the Second International Workshop on Data Science for Macro-Modeling*. New York: ACM.

Gabaix, X. and D. Laibson, 2008. "The seven properties of good models," in *The Foundations of Positive and Normative Economics: A Handbook*, edited by A. Caplin and A. Schotter (pp. 292–299). New York, NY: Oxford University Press.

Heston, S. and N. Sinha, 2017. "News versus sentiment: Predicting stock returns from news stories," *Financial Analysts Journal*, 73(3): 67–83.

Klevak, J., J. Livnat, and K. Suslava, 2019. "When more or less is less: Managers' clichés," *Journal of Financial Data Science*, 1(3): 57–67.

Kothari, S., J. Sabino, and T. Zach, 2005. "Implications of survival and data trimming for tests of market efficiency," *Journal of Accounting and Economics*, 39(1): 129–161.

Li, F., 2010. "Textual analysis of corporate disclosures: A survey of the literature," *Journal of Accounting Literature*, 29: 143–165.

Ljungqvist, A., C. Malloy, and F. Marston, 2009. "Rewriting history," *Journal of Finance*, 64(1): 1935–1960.

Moritz, B. and T. Zimmermann, 2016. "Tree-based conditional portfolio sorts: The relation between past and future stock returns." Available at http://dx.doi.org/10.2139/ssrn.2740751.

Rapach, D. E., J. K. Strauss, J. Tu, and G. Zhou, 2019. "Industry return predictability: A machine learning approach," *Journal of Financial Data Science*, 1(3): 9–28.

Tucker, M., 2008. "The time for systematic fixed income investing is now," *BlackRock Research from Systematic Fixed Income*. July. Available at https://www.blackrock.com/institutions/en-us/literature/whitepaper/by-the-numbers-july-2018.pdf.

Chapter 13

Challenges in Implementing Equity Factor Investing Strategies*

Learning Objectives

After reading this chapter, you will understand:

- how factor strategies bring innovative investment options to asset owners;
- the ways in which asset owners such as institutional investors and retail investors can obtain access to factor strategies;
- the current state of factor research;
- the critical questions in factor research;
- the critical issues and practical implementation considerations associated with moving from research on factors to the formulation of factor strategies;
- the impact of the following on asset managers in implementing factor strategies: (1) increased impact of flows into factor portfolios, (2) timing of factors, (3) distinguishing value added of active managers from factors investment strategies, and (4) the benefits of innovation; and
- the investment risks faced by asset owners when they allocate funds to equity factor strategies.

---

*This chapter is coauthored with Joseph Cerniglia, an adjunct professor at the Courant Institute of Mathematics at New York University and visiting scholar at the University of Pennsylvania, and Petter N. Kolm, Clinical Professor of Mathematics and Director of the Mathematics in Finance M.S. Program at New York University's Courant Institute.

Introduction

As explained in the previous chapter, the most common quantitative equity strategy is one that focuses on factors. Factor investing is a quantitative investment strategy that employs a set of rules to select stocks that should be included in an equity portfolio. Factors are groupings of stocks into buckets which share similar attributes. Asset management firms offer asset owners either a dedicated team that focuses on factor investing from among several investment strategies or they will offer only factor investing strategies.

Factor strategies bring innovative investment options to asset owners. They give asset owners the ability to access the return and risk characteristics of a particular investment style in a cost-effective and efficient standardized investment product. Asset owners can acquire exposure to a range of styles with intra-day trading on exchanges. Previously, asset owners had to pay much higher fees to obtain that exposure if it was possible to obtain access at all.

There are several ways in which asset owners such as institutional investors and retail investors can obtain access to factor strategies. Typically, institutional investors such as pension funds can engage an asset management firm to do so. Some institutional investors and retail investors can gain exposure to factors by investing in exchange-traded funds (ETFs). ETFs are becoming increasingly popular as evidenced by the number of factor ETFs available to trade, the number of firms marketing ETFs, and the amount of assets under management in these factor ETFs. *The Economist* (2018) estimates there are $658 billion in factor ETFs. Retail investors can obtain exposure to factors via registered investment companies (i.e., mutual funds (open-end funds) and closed-end funds). Factor investment products blend the characteristics of active and passive investment products to varying degrees depending on their methodology. They can be considered passive because the construction of a factor portfolio is created from static and hopefully transparent rules, applied in an algorithmic process. For example, these products share features of actively managed portfolios most notably by their tracking error (sometimes large tracking error) relative to a market capitalization-weighted stock market index.

In this chapter, we provide a summary of the current state of factor research. We then discuss the challenges associated with how to move from research about factors to implementation of a factor investment strategy and the risks faced by asset owners.

Current State of Factor Research

Factor investing strategies in the equity space are based on the findings of numerous research studies by academics and practitioners. Factors are constructed from cross-sectional characteristics of stocks such as size, value, momentum, and quality. In equities, the number of factors is large with published research on over 400 characteristics. Factors can be derived from broad economic measures such as interest rates, inflation, and economic growth.

Research on factors dates back to the 1930s when Graham and Dodd (1934) wrote about the "value premium". Two economic models formulated the relationship between asset returns and factors: the capital asset pricing model (CAPM) and the arbitrage pricing theory (APT). The CAPM, introduced in 1964, provided an important fundamental principle of modern finance, stating that a stock's return is solely a function of the market factor. Ross [1976] developed APT, demonstrating that stock returns can be modeled as a function of many factors in addition to the market factor. His theory provides a framework that was empirically based, beginning with the tradition of using multiple factors as research tools and providing a way to understand risk and return characteristics of different stocks. In the late 1970s, academics began to identify groups of stocks that outperformed the market portfolio as measured by stock market indexes. Since the 1980s, work on factors has accelerated among academics. There are several papers that summarize the vast literature on equity factors.

The current state of factor research focuses on several research questions prompted by Cochrane [2011] based on his 2011 American Finance Association presidential address. He refers to the current state of research as a "factor zoo", highlighting that there have been many research papers over the last three decades identifying different factors as providing returns above risk-adjusted models such as the CAPM or the Fama–French three-factor model. Economic theories are used to explain why a specific factor should deliver superior performance and a large body of empirical work reports that these returns are statistically significant and persistent. However, the large number of these factors raises concerns.

Specifically, John Cochrane identifies the following three critical questions:

1. Which factors are independent?
2. Which factors are important?
3. Why do factors move prices?

Academic researchers have begun to examine these questions. Since 2010, there have been numerous papers addressing these critical issues.

One approach is to set a higher statistical bar to determine if factors predict returns reliably. Harvey, Liu, and Zhu [2014] review 300 variables published papers in various journals over 30 years. To address concerns that Cochrane identified, they propose a framework for the multiple testing problems associated with examining the expected return and recommend much higher levels of statistical significance as a benchmark.[1] They also emphasized that a factor that is derived from theory should have a lower statistical benchmark than one derived from pure empirical work.

Green, Hand, and Zhang [2016] attempt to find independent and significant cross-sectional factors in equities from a universe of 94 factors from 1980 to 2014. Their research indicates that there are 12 factors that are significant after adjusting for the influence of microcap stocks and concerns regarding data-snooping. They conclude that the number of independent determinants of asset returns is small and the magnitude of these returns have been diminishing since 2003.

Another concern is whether returns to factors disappear as more investors learned about them. McLean and Pontiff [2016] examine the performance of 97 factors from samples used both before and after the factor is published. They show that returns to factors are 50% lower post-publication. Examining the performance of 38 factors in these two out-of-sample periods — the pre-publication period and the post-publication period — Linnainmaa and Roberts [2016] report that only 12 of these factors earn significantly positive returns in both out-of-sample periods. They conclude that data-snooping bias could be distorting the research on other factors in their study.

Machine learning techniques are being used by financial researchers to make sense of the high dimensionality of factors. Feng, Giglio, and Xiu [2017] test the marginal importance of a factor for pricing assets using the statistical technique of least absolute shrinkage and selection operator (LASSO). Their methodology selects the best parsimonious model out of the large set of existing factors. Similar to research of others, they identify a small set of factors that seem to be significant and stable in explaining returns.

[1]For a discussion of this issue and a recommended solution, see Fabozzi and López de Prado [2018].

Combining factors or signals is another vital area of research which has received increased attention. How you combine factors is as important as what factors are used in a model. Finding the optimal approach of combining factors is as much an art as it is a science. Techniques range from bootstrapping human judgment to linear regressions to machine learning approaches. Well-known models in academia include Piotroski's F-Score as developed in Piotroski [2000] and Mohanram's G-score that combine traditional fundamental factors into a composite score to rank stocks. Asness, Frazzini, and Pedersen [2019] create a quality score using 21 different factors.

Novy-Marx [2015] raises several important issues related to these factor strategies. He argues that because the performance of these strategies often suffers from bias caused by overfitting as well as selection bias, backtesting needs to be carefully designed. While acknowledging that combining signals can lead to better performance, he recommends that the marginal contribution of each factor should be evaluated individually. Variable selection for models and combining variables is an area where there are many open research questions.

Transaction and trading costs, which we discuss in Chapter 14, are also important aspects that impact our understanding of factors. Many studies on anomalies ignore the costs associated with trading, thereby overstating the returns these strategies achieve. Some studies provide a better understanding of transaction costs. Novy-Marx and Velikov [2015] evaluate the transaction costs associated with a large number of well-known factors within a mean–variance efficient portfolio framework. In addition, they propose three strategies (limiting trading to low transaction costs stocks, lowering the frequencies of rebalancing, and a more stringent spread criteria for trading) to lower the trading costs for implementing strategies.

Over the past 30 years, we have seen market events that have moved asset prices spectacularly — dot-com crash (2000–2001), Asian Financial Crisis (1997), Global Financial Crisis (2007–2008), the Great Moderation (1990–2000), the European Debt Crisis (2010), and the Corona Virus Pandemic. In these periods, we have observed a complex link between factor returns and macroeconomic outcomes. Claessens and Kose [2017] survey the literature on asset prices and macroeconomic environments, providing insights on some of the theoretical mechanisms driving these relationships. More work needs to be done to better understand the link between factor returns and the macroeconomic environment.

Table 1 is a list of some well-known factors and their underlying economic rationale.

TABLE 1: Some Well-Known Factors and Their Underlying Economic Rationale

Factor	Economic Rationale
Market	Higher market sensitivity as measured by beta results in high returns.
Size (market capitalization)	Smaller companies tend to outperform larger companies.
Value	Investors prefer stocks with low valuations.
Momentum	Investors prefer stocks that have had good past performance.
Profitability	A company's current profitability as measured by gross profits-to-assets is a good predictor of future profitability.
Investment	There is an inverse relationship between corporate investments and expected returns.
Dividend yield	Investors prefer to immediately receive receipt of their investment returns.
Idiosyncratic risk	Stocks with high idiosyncratic risk in the current month tend to have lower returns the following month.
Volatility risk	Investors prefer stocks with lower volatility.
Asset turnover	This measure evaluates the productivity of assets employed by a firm. Investors believe higher turnover correlates with higher future returns.
Earnings revisions	Positive analysts' revisions indicate stronger business prospects and earnings for a firm.
Return reversal	Stocks overreact to information, that is, stocks with the highest returns in the current month tend to earn lower returns the following month.
Earnings surprises	Investors like positive earnings surprises and dislike negative earnings surprises.
Growth of Fiscal Year 1 and Fiscal Year 2 Earnings Estimates	Investors are attracted to companies with growing earnings.
Accounting accruals	Companies with earnings that have a large cash component tend to have higher future returns.
Accounting risk factors	Companies with lower accounting risk tend to have higher future returns.
Executive compensation factors	Firms that align compensation with shareholders interest tend to outperform.

Practical Considerations in Implementing Research Findings

There are critical issues and practical implementation considerations associated with moving from research on factors to the formulation of factor strategies.

Practitioners aligned their investment strategies with groups of stocks such as value stocks as suggested by Graham and Dodd [1932], growth as suggested by Fisher [1958] or other stock characteristics such as income. Historically, these factors were viewed as investment styles which are grounded in an underlying investment philosophy and economic rationale.

For active managers, factors have been part of the active management investment tool kit for four decades. As a research tool, factors became vital to designing investment strategies, managing risk, and constructing portfolios.

Both fundamental and quantitative equity portfolio managers use factors in designing investment strategies. Fundamental managers often describe their investment styles based on stocks that share common characteristics. For quantitative managers, factors are the instruments they often use in multifactor models to identify stocks that are expected to outperform.

Factor models provide insight as to how to identify, measure, and manage risk in a portfolio. The factors in risk models measure how the risk of the portfolio is attributed to the individual securities' exposure to these factors.

Factor exposure is a key consideration in constructing portfolios. Portfolio construction reflects the tradeoff between risk and return. Any additional risk taken on by a portfolio manager should be compensated with additional returns. Factors are used to measure and position how risks are manifested in a portfolio. Risk models become an important input to portfolio construction decisions. Other tools such as portfolio optimization are utilized in constructing a portfolio.

One of the key challenges to practitioners is how to reflect the empirical research findings regarding the return potential of factors into actually investable portfolios. There are a number of critical considerations such as implementation costs, rebalancing methodology, transaction costs, liquidity, and risk management. All of these considerations will impact how much of the returns presented in research papers on factors are realized. Moreover, although most studies emphasize the return potential, these studies do not necessarily explore the risks involved in these strategies in detail.

As factors move from a research tool in academia to investment products gathering assets, the impact on markets is potentially significant. Although factor investing impacts practitioners in many ways, we focus on the following four in our discussion: (1) increased impact of flows into factor portfolios, (2) timing of factors, (3) distinguishing value added of active managers from factor strategies, and (4) the benefits of innovation.

Increased Impact of Flows into Factor Portfolios

Crowding occurs when asset managers hold positions with similar investment theses. A contagion effect can be induced when asset managers are holding overlapping positions and investors react simultaneously to information related to the investment thesis. The rules-based approach of factor strategies is likely to contribute further to the negative impact of crowding.

Decaying returns to factor strategies can result from crowding flows into exchange-traded fund (ETF) factor strategies, and active managers compete away the excess return opportunity in the equity market. Crowding can contribute to overvaluation, which can push valuations beyond reasonable levels, and reduce potential future returns.

Crowding impacts the liquidity of individual stocks held in the portfolio of asset managers following factor strategies. Large withdrawals after substantial inflows create an environment prone to the rapid unwinding of positions. These trades are not driven by the changing underlying fundamentals of stocks. Khandani and Lo [2011] documented this effect in August 2007 when several highly successful quantitative long/short hedge funds realized large losses. A number of quant managers liquidated similar positions causing significant selling pressure that induced larger price movements. Trading by asset managers pursuing a factor strategy could contribute to indiscriminate buying of stocks that add to the potential for crowding. Liquidity events are relatively infrequent events making crowding a difficult concept to model.

Timing of Factors

Factor timing is an active topic of research in the industry. There is a debate among practitioners on whether it is possible to increase the allocation to factors when their expected returns are high and reduce the allocation when the expected returns are low. The potential returns to a successful strategy could be very large and beneficial to clients. It also provides an opportunity for active investors to distinguish their returns from factor returns.

Factor timing is a challenging endeavor. Asness [2016, p. 2] argues that "good factors and diversification . . . trump the potential of factor timing." He makes several strong points regarding the risk of timing strategies. However, as factors move increasingly from a research tool to an investment tool with increasing amount of assets, the opportunity set to allocate to various factors could increase.

Innovation in investing provides an opportunity to challenge conventional thinking. There is a strong economic rationale as to why varying the allocation to factors is a viable strategy. If we know that the underlying fundamentals of stocks are influenced by the economic environment, then the aggregate cross-sectional characteristics are likely to be sensitive to macroeconomic risks or other types of market risks. Researchers and asset managers view advancements in financial econometric techniques and machine learning algorithms as analytical tools to aid in discovering ways to manage the factor exposure of portfolios more actively.[2] Cerniglia, Fabozzi, and Kolm [2020] show how machine learning can contribute to forecasting factor returns in different economic environments.

Distinguishing Value Added of Active Managers from Factor Strategies

In the active management industry, a mounting challenge is how to distinguish manager performance from factor performance. This is an issue many managers will have to address with clients and consultants. Bender, Hammond, and Mok [2014] show that up to 80% of active excess returns garnered by equity managers can be explained by the factor exposures of their portfolios.

Factors might be highly correlated with active managers but not identical. Although 80% is a large number, the 20% difference could be a significant determinant of performance difference worth the additional costs. Active managers have the opportunity to innovate relative to the more rule-based factor strategies. As the investing environment changes, active managers have the flexibility to adjust quickly relative to the more rules-based approach.

Benefits of Innovation

Innovation is critical for success in active management. Developing new factors is one way that is useful for improving the performance of active managers. Tetlock and Gardner [2015] show how research in the field of decision science can assist in developing more accurate predictions.

---

[2] A review of financial econometrics and machine learning used in asset management is described in Chapters 4 and 7, respectively.

New factors will continue to be developed. Some of these factors will be created from "Big Data" sources as investment professionals continue to embrace new data sources as a competitive advantage. How useful new data will be is an open debate. Most of the data used by asset managers in factor research were created for investment research. In contrast, "Big Data" is often created by businesses, governments, and electronic devices when providing services or resulting from their business activities. As these new data are repurposed to develop new factors, new challenges will arise that require the necessary experience, domain knowledge, and technical expertise.

Risks Faced by Asset Owners

Asset owners are exposed to several investment risks when they allocate funds to equity factor strategies either in a separately managed fund or a collective investment vehicle. These risks extend beyond the risks associated with the factors used in the rules applied to securities in creating the factor portfolio. For example, the MSCI Value index is constructed from three factors (book value to price, 12-month forward earnings to price, and dividend yield) with limited portfolio turnover. In general, value strategies have time-varying risk exposures to other factors such as interest rates, economic growth, price momentum, and beta, among other characteristics. Without carefully controlling for these other risks, many asset owners might be exposing themselves to risks that they are not aware of. Most importantly, these uncontrolled risks vary through time.

There are two other investment risks asset owners face. First, there is the risk that a factor strategy will underperform the return on the market. Second, strategies based on specific factors that have performed well in the past may not perform well in the future.

Much of the empirical evidence on factor returns reflects the long-run average of backtest results. The stock market has evolved significantly over that time. Many asset owners are aware of these return "anomalies". There is a significant possibility that the premium will be traded away before it can be realized by an investment portfolio.

Most factor returns are time varying. Factors experience periods of underperformance and at times this underperformance can be dramatic. There is a question as to whether asset owners will have patience to invest in factor strategies over an entire market cycle. Cerniglia, Fabozzi, and Kolm [2021] discuss how factor performance, risk, and correlations are vulnerable to the economic and liquidity conditions of the financial markets.

Daniel and Moskowitz [2016] examine these questions for the momentum factor. From 1929 to 2015, they find that momentum has exhibited very strong performance in terms of average returns and Sharpe ratios. However, they note that "there are relatively long periods over which momentum experiences severe losses or crashes". Along with these points, Daniel and Moskowitz highlight several other interesting characteristics such as the asymmetry in returns between long and short sides of a momentum portfolio and the frequent option-like characteristics of the return series. Investors should be aware that other factors such as value, income, and quality also have their own unique risk and return properties.

Arnott, Harvey, Kalesnik, and Linnainmaa [2019] provide an in-depth discussion of the several challenges to factor investing for asset owners. Overall, they conclude that factor investing has not lived up to the hype promised by marketers of these investment products. In particular, they highlight the exaggerated expectations regarding the future performance of factors. Potential drags on future performance could result from data mining in the empirical work on factors as well as trading costs to implement these strategies. Also, they discuss how the benefits of diversification disappear in certain market and economic conditions.

Key Points

- The most common quantitative equity strategy is one that focuses on factors which employ a set of rules to select stocks that should be included in an equity portfolio.
- Factor strategies bring innovative investment options to asset owners because they give them the ability to access the return and risk characteristics of a particular investment style in a cost-effective and efficient standardized investment product.
- Asset owners such as institutional investors and retail investors can obtain access to factor strategies in several ways.
- Typically, institutional investors can hire an asset management firm to do so while some institutional investors and retail investors can gain exposure to factors by investing in exchange-traded funds.
- Factor investment products blend the characteristics of active and passive investment products to varying degrees depending on their methodology.
- Equity factor investing strategies are based on the findings of numerous research studies that identify from cross-sectional data the characteristics that have historically impacted equity returns.

- The current state of research on factors is referred to as a "factor zoo", highlighting that there have been many research papers identifying different factors as providing returns above risk-adjusted models.
- Economic theories are used to explain why a specific factor should deliver superior performance.
- There are three critical questions that academics and practitioners have begun to examine in factor research: (1) Which factors are independent? (2) Which factors are important? and (3) Why do factors move prices?
- One approach suggested in identifying factors when conducting factor research is to set a higher statistical bar to determine if factors predict returns reliably.
- Machine learning techniques are being used by financial researchers to make sense of the high dimensionality of factors.
- Transaction and trading costs are important in understanding factor strategies.
- There are four critical issues and practical implementation considerations associated with moving from research on factors to the formulation of factor strategies: (1) increased impact of flows into factor portfolios, (2) timing of factors, (3) distinguishing value added of active managers from factor strategies, and (4) the benefits of innovation.
- Crowding occurs when asset managers hold positions with similar investment theses.
- The rules-based approach of factor strategies is likely to contribute to the negative impact of crowding.
- Decaying returns to factor strategies can result from crowding.
- Crowding impacts the liquidity of individual stocks held in the portfolio of asset managers following factor strategies.
- Factor timing is a challenging endeavor with practitioners debating as to whether it is possible to increase the allocation to factors when their expected returns are high and reduce the allocation when the expected returns are low.
- In the active management industry, how to distinguish manager performance from factor performance is challenging and an issue that asset managers must address with clients and consultants.
- Developing new factors via innovation is one way that is useful for improving the performance of active managers.

- Asset owners are exposed to investment risks beyond the risks associated with the factors used in creating the factor portfolio when they allocate funds to equity factor strategies.
- Asset owners face risk that a factor strategy will underperform the return on the market and that strategies based on specific factors that have performed well in the past may not perform well in the future.

References

Arnott, R. D., C. R. Harvey, V. Kalesnik, and J. T. Linnainmaa, 2019. "Alice's adventures in factorland: Three blunders that plague factor investing," *Journal of Portfolio Management*, 45(4): 180–36.

Asness, C. S., 2016. "The siren song of factor timing," *Journal of Portfolio Management*, 42(5): 1–6.

Asness, C. S., A. Frazzini, and L. H. Pedersen, 2019. "Quality minus junk," *Review of Accounting Studies*, 24: 34–112.

Bender, J., P. B. Hammond, and W. Mok, 2014. "Can alpha be captured by risk premia?" *Journal of Portfolio Management*, 40(2): 18–29.

Bernard, V. L. and J. K. Thomas, 1989. "Post-earnings-announcement drift: Delayed price response or risk premium?" *Journal of Accounting Research*, 27: 1–36.

Cerniglia, J. A., F. J. Fabozzi, and P. N. Kolm, 2021. "Factor vulnerability," *Journal of Portfolio Management*, 47(2).

Cerniglia, J. A., F. J. Fabozzi, and P. N. Kolm, 2020. "Statistical vs. machine learning approaches in buy-side research," *Journal of Portfolio Management*, 47(1).

Claessens, S. and M. A. Kose, 2018. "Frontiers of macrofinancial linkages," Bank for International Settlement, Paper No. 95. Available at https://www.bis.org/publ/bppdf/bispap95.htm.

Cochrane, J. H., 2011. "Presidential address: Discount rates," *Journal of Finance*, 66(4): 1047–1108.

Daniel, K. and T. J. Moskowitz, 2016. "Momentum crashes," *Journal of Financial Economics*, 122(2): 221–247.

Fabozzi, F. J. and M. López de Prado, 2018. "Being honest in backtest reporting: A Template for disclosing multiple tests," *Journal of Portfolio Management*, 45(1): 141–147.

Feng, G., S. Giglio, and D. Xiu, 2017. "Taming the factor zoo," Chicago Booth Research Paper No. 17-04. Available at SSRN: https://ssrn.com/abstract=2934020.

Fisher, P. A., 1958. *Common Stocks and Uncommon Profits and Other Writings*. New York: John Wiley & Sons.

Graham, B. and D. Dodd, 1934. *Security Analysis.* New York: McGraw-Hill.

Green, J., J. R. M. Hand, and X. F. Zhang, 2013. "The supraview of return predictive signals," *Review of Accounting Studies*, 18(3): 692–730.

Harvey, C. R., Y. Liu, and H. Zhu, 2016. "... and the Cross-Section of Expected Returns," *Review of Financial Studies*, 29(1): 5–68.

Linnainmaa, J. T. and M. R. Roberts, 2016. "The history of the cross section of stock returns," National Bureau of Economic Research, Working Paper No. 22894.

Khandani, A. E. and A. W. Lo, 2011. "What happened to the quants in August 2007? Evidence from factors and transactions data," *Journal of Financial Markets*, 14(1): 1–46.

McLean, R. D. and J. Pontiff, 2016. "Does academic research destroy stock return predictability?" *Journal of Finance*, 71(1): 5–32.

Mohanram, P. S., 2005. "Separating winners from losers among low-book-to-market stocks using financial statement analysis," *Review of Accounting Studies*, 10(2–3): 133–170.

Novy-Marx, R. and M. Velikov, 2015. "A taxonomy of anomalies and their trading costs," *Review of Financial Studies*, 29(1): 104–147.

Novy-Marx, R., 2016. "Testing strategies based on multiple signals," Simon Graduate School of Business, Working Paper. Available at http://rnm.simon.rochester.edu/research/MSES.pdf.

Piotroski, J. D., 2000. "Value investing: The use of historical financial statement information to separate winners from losers," *Journal of Accounting Research*, 38(Supplement): 1–41.

Ross, S., 1976. "The arbitrage theory of capital asset pricing," *Journal of Economic Theory*, 13: 341–360.

Tetlock, P. E. and D. Gardner, 2015. *Superforecasting: The Art and Science of Prediction.* New York: Crown Publishers.

The Economist, 2018. "Maxing the Factors." February 1.

Chapter 14

Transaction and Trading Costs*

Learning Objectives

After you read this chapter, you will understand:

- how to categorize transaction costs;
- the difference between fixed and variable transaction costs;
- the difference between explicit and implicit transaction costs;
- what a bid–ask spread is and what it represents;
- the relationship between bid–ask spread and liquidity;
- the different types of implicit transaction costs: investment delay, market impact cost, price movement risk, market timing, and opportunity cost;
- the two types of market impact costs: temporary and permanent;
- why liquidity and transaction costs are interrelated;
- measures used to quantify market impact costs;
- the difficulties of measuring market impact costs;
- what empirical studies have found about market impact costs;
- how transaction costs can be measured: pre-trade measures, post-trade measures, and same-day measures;
- what the implementation shortfall approach is;
- the factors that are considered in forecasting market impact costs;

---

*This chapter is coauthored with Joseph Cerniglia, an adjunct professor at the Courant Institute of Mathematics at New York University and visiting scholar at the University of Pennsylvania, Petter N. Kolm, Clinical Professor of Mathematics and Director of the Mathematics in Finance M.S. Program at New York University's Courant Institute, and Sergio Focardi, professor and researcher at the Finance Group, ESILV EMLV, of the Pole Universitaire De Vinci, Paris.

- how transaction costs can be included in asset allocation models;
- what is meant by optimal trading and factors to be considered in optimal trading; and
- how to integrate transaction costs into portfolio management.

Introduction

Transaction and trading costs are an integral component of the asset management process. A poorly executed trade can significantly reduce portfolio returns and therefore investment performance. This is because financial markets are not frictionless, and transactions have a cost associated to them. In this chapter, we will first present a simple taxonomy of transaction costs and the linkage between transaction costs and liquidity, as well as the measurement of these quantities. Asset managers and traders need to be able to effectively model the impact of trading costs on their portfolios and trades. If possible, they would like to minimize total transaction costs. To address these issues, several approaches for the modeling of transaction costs have been proposed and we will identify them. We then provide a brief introduction to optimal execution strategies.[1]

A Taxonomy of Transaction Costs

Probably the easiest way to describe transaction costs is to categorize them in terms of fixed versus variable transaction costs, and explicit versus implicit transaction costs. *Fixed transaction costs* are independent of factors such as trade size and market conditions. In contrast, *variable transaction costs* depend on some or all of these factors. In other words, although fixed transaction costs are "what they are", asset managers and traders can seek to reduce, optimize, and efficiently manage variable transaction costs. *Explicit transaction costs* are those costs that are observable and known upfront, such as commissions, fees, and taxes. *Implicit transaction costs*, in contrast, are non-observable and not known in advance. Examples of transaction costs that fall into this category are market impact and opportunity costs. In general, the implicit costs make up the dominant part of the total transaction costs.

[1] In Chapter 3 of the companion book, descriptions of trading mechanics and trading arrangements used by institutional investors are provided.

Explicit Transaction Costs

Trading commissions and fees, taxes, and bid–ask spreads are explicit transaction costs. Explicit transaction costs are also referred to as observable transaction costs.

Commissions and fees

Commissions are paid to brokers to execute trades. Normally, commissions on trades are negotiable. Fees charged by an institution that holds the securities in safekeeping for an investor are referred to as *custodial fees.* When the ownership over a stock is transferred, the investor is charged a *transfer fee.*

Taxes

The most common taxes are *capital gains tax* and *taxes on dividends.* The tax law distinguishes between two types of capital gains taxes: *short term* and *long term.* In the United States, the tax law as of this writing requires that an asset must be held for more than one year to qualify for the lower long-term capital gains rate. Although tax planning is an important component of many investment strategies, this topic is outside the scope of this book.

Bid–ask spreads

The difference between the quoted sell and buy order is called the *bid–ask spread.* The bid–ask spread is the immediate transaction cost that the market charges anyone for the privilege of trading. High immediate liquidity is synonymous with small spreads. We can think about the bid–ask spread as the price charged by dealers for supplying immediacy and short-term price stability in the presence of short-term order imbalances. Dealers act as a buffer between the investors that want to buy and sell, and thereby provide stability in the market by making sure a certain order is maintained. In negotiated markets such as the New York Stock Exchange, market makers and dealers maintain a certain minimum inventory on their books. If the dealer is unable to match a buyer with a seller (or vice versa), he or she has the capability to take on the exposure on his book.

However, the bid–ask spread does not necessarily represent the best prices available, and the "half spread" is therefore not always the minimal cost for immediate buy or sell executions. Certain price improvements are possible and occur, for example, because:

- NYSE specialists fill the incoming market orders at improved prices (for example, see [Harris and Panchapagesan, 2005]).
- The market may have moved in the investor's favor during the time it took to route the order to the trading venue (a so-called "lucky saving").
- The presence of hidden liquidity.[2]
- Buy and sell orders can be "crossed".[3]

The bid–ask spread is misleading as a true liquidity measure because it only conveys the price for small trades. For large trades, due to price impact, the linkage between liquidity, trading costs, and market impact costs is discussed later in this chapter.

Implicit Transaction Costs

Investment delay cost, market impact cost, price movement risk, market timing, and opportunity cost are implicit transaction costs. Implicit transaction costs are also referred to as non-observable transaction costs.

Investment delay cost

Normally, there is a delay between the time when the asset manager makes a buy/sell decision of a security and when the actual trade is brought to the market by a trader. If the price of the security changes during this time, the price change (possibly adjusted for general market moves) represents the *investment delay cost*, or the cost of not being able to execute immediately. This cost depends on the investment strategy. For example, modern quantitative trading systems that automatically submit an electronic order after generating a trading decision are exposed to smaller delay costs. More traditional approaches where investment decisions first have to be approved by, for example, an investment committee, exhibit higher delay costs.

---

[2]For example, on electronic communication networks and on the Nasdaq, although it is possible to view the limit order book, a significant portion of the book cannot be seen. This is referred to as a *hidden order* or *discretionary order*.

[3]A *cross-order* is an offsetting or non-competitive matching of the buy order of one investor against the sell order of another investor. This practice is permissible only when executed in accordance with the Commodity Exchange Act, US Commodity Futures Trading Commission (CFTC) regulations, and the rules of the particular market.

Some practitioners view the investment delay cost as part of the opportunity cost discussed shortly.

Market impact costs

The *market impact cost* of a transaction, also referred to as *price impact cost*, is the deviation of the transaction price from the market (mid) price[4] that would have prevailed had the trade not occurred. The price movement is the cost, the market impact cost, of liquidity. The price impact of a trade can be negative if, for example, a trader buys at a price below the no-trade price (i.e., the price that would have prevailed had the trade not taken place).

We distinguish between two kinds of market impact costs, temporary and permanent. Total market impact cost is computed as the sum of the two. Figure 1 illustrates the different components of the market impact costs of a sell order. The *temporary market impact cost* is of transitory nature and can be seen as the additional *liquidity concession* necessary for the liquidity provider (for example, the market maker) to take the order, *inventory effects* (price effects due to broker-dealer inventory imbalances),

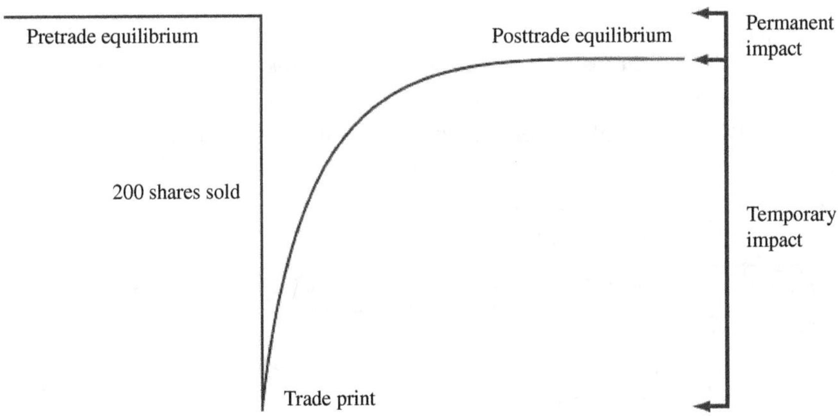

FIGURE 1: Market Impact Costs: Sell Order
Source: Kolm and Machlin [2008].

[4]Since the buyer buys at the "ask" and the seller sells at the "bid", this definition of market impact cost ignores the bid/ask spread, which is an explicit cost.

or *imperfect substitution* (for example, price incentives to induce market participants to absorb the additional shares).

The *permanent market impact cost*, however, reflects the persistent price change that results as the market adjusts to the information content of the trade. Intuitively, a sell transaction reveals to the market that the security may be overvalued, whereas a buy transaction signals that the security may be undervalued. Security prices change when market participants adjust their views and perceptions as they observe news and the information contained in new trades during the trading day.

Traders can decrease the temporary market impact by extending the trading horizon of an order. For example, a trader executing a less urgent order can buy/sell a position in smaller portions over a period and make sure that each portion only constitutes a small percentage of the average volume. However, this comes at the price of increased opportunity costs, investment delay costs, and price movement risk. We discuss this issue in more detail later in this chapter when we cover optimal execution models.

Several studies have found that market impact costs are often asymmetric; that is, market impact costs are different for buy and sell orders.[5] More specifically, empirical studies suggest that market impact costs are generally higher for buy orders.[6]

Despite the enormous global size of equity markets, the impact of trading is important even for relatively small funds. In fact, a sizable fraction of the stocks that compose an index might have to be excluded or their trading severely limited. For example, as reported in Kolm and Fabozzi [2011, p. 427], RAS Asset Management, which is the asset manager arm of the large Italian insurance company RAS, has determined that single trades exceeding 10% of the daily trading volume of a stock cause an excessive

[5]For instance, Bikker, Spierdijk, and van der Sluis [2007] estimated the market impact costs from a data sample consisting of 3,728 worldwide equity trades executed during the first quarter of 2002 at the Dutch pension fund Algemeen Burgerlijk Pensioenfonds (ABP). The trades, of which 1,963 were buys and 1,765 sales, had a total transaction value of €5.7 billion. They concluded that the temporary and persistent price effects of buy orders were 7.2 basis points and 12.4 basis points, respectively. For sell orders, on the other hand, these price effects were −14.5 basis points and −16.5 basis points.

[6]For example, a study by Hu [2003] shows that the difference in market impact costs between buys and sells is an artifact of the trade benchmark. (We discuss trade benchmarks later in this chapter.) When a pre-trade measure is used, buys (sells) have higher implicit trading costs during rising (falling) markets. Conversely, if a post-trade measure is used, sells (buys) have higher implicit trading costs during rising (falling) markets. In fact, both pre-trade and post-trade measures are highly influenced by market movement, whereas during- or average-trade measures are neutral to market movement.

price impact and have to be excluded, while trades between 5% and 10% need execution strategies distributed over several days.

There are two other types of market impact costs, crowding cost and cross-market impact cost. The basic view of capacity is that as the amount of assets under management increases for a given investment strategy, it becomes more costly to implement that strategy.[7] This adversely impacts performance due to several factors, including an increase in transaction costs. This not only applies to one asset management firm, but even other asset management firms when they use the same investment strategy. Because many asset managers may employ the same active management strategy and use the same model for stock selection, all may enter the market simultaneously to execute trades on the same stock. This results in an adverse impact on the prices of those stocks that are traded and is referred to as *impact cost due to crowding* or *crowding cost.*

The other type of market impact cost is the result of the price impact that the trading of one stock has on other stocks of companies in the same sector or industry. This cost is referred to as *cross-market impact cost.* For example, if an asset manager trades in some bank stock, for example, Bank of America, the trade may not just impact the price of that bank's stock but also other bank stocks. This is because investors in the bank sector are likely to base other bank stocks on the value of Bank of America stock.

Price movement risk

In general, the stock market exhibits a positive drift that gives rise to *price movement risk* or *trend risk.* Similarly, individual stocks, at least temporarily, trend up or down. A trade that goes in the same direction as the general market or an individual security is exposed to price risk. For example, when an asset manager is buying in a rising market, he might pay more than he initially anticipated to fully satisfy the order. In practice, it can be difficult to separate price movement risk from market impact costs. Typically, the price movement risk for a buy order is defined as the price increase during the time of the trade that is attributed to the general trend of a security, whereas the remaining part is market impact costs.

[7]Vangelisti [2006] explains what capacity means and provides how asset managers pursuing an active strategy can deal with it.

Market timing costs

Market timing costs are due to the movement in the price of a security at the time of the transaction that can be attributed to other market participants or general market volatility. Market timing costs are higher for larger trades, in particular when they are divided into smaller blocks and traded over a period of time. Practitioners often define market timing costs to be proportional to the standard deviation of the security returns times the square root of the time anticipated in order to complete the transaction.

Opportunity costs

The cost of not transacting represents an *opportunity cost.* For example, when a certain trade fails to execute, the asset manager misses an opportunity. Commonly, this cost is defined as the difference in performance between an asset manager's desired investment and the actual investment after transaction costs. Opportunity costs are in general driven by price risk or market volatility. As a result, the longer the trading horizon, the greater the exposure to opportunity costs.

Identifying Transaction Costs: An Example

We will use an example to highlight the key cost components of an equity trade.[8] Following the completion of an institutional trade, suppose that the ticker tape for XYZ stock reveals that 6,000 shares of XYZ stock were purchased at \$82.00. Although 6,000 XYZ shares were bought, the following indicates what may have happened behind the scenes — beginning with the initial security selection decision by the asset manager (the investment idea), to the release of the buy order by the equity trader, to the subsequent trade execution by the broker (the essential elements of trading implementation):

- Equity manager wants to buy 10,000 shares of XYZ at the current price of \$80.
- Trade desk releases 8,000 shares to broker when price is \$81.
- Broker purchases 6,000 shares of XYZ stock at \$82 plus \$0.045 (per share) commission.

[8]This illustration is similar to the example provided in Wagner and Edwards [1998]. The example used here is taken from Fabozzi and Grant [1999].

- XYZ stock jumps to \$85, and remainder of order is canceled.
- 15 days later the price of XYZ stock is \$88.

We can assess the cost of trading XYZ stock as follows. The commission charge is the easiest to identify — namely, \$0.045 per share, or \$270 on the purchase of 6,000 shares of XYZ stock.

Since the trade desk did not release the order to buy XYZ stock until it was selling for \$81, the assessed trader timing cost is \$1 per share. Also, the market impact cost is \$1 per XYZ share traded, as the stock was selling for \$81 when the order was received by the broker — just prior to execution of the 6,000 XYZ shares at \$82.

The opportunity cost — resulting from unexecuted shares — of the equity trade is more difficult to estimate. Assuming that the movement of XYZ stock's price from \$80 to \$88 can be largely attributed to information used by the equity manager in her security selection decision, it appears that the value of the asset investment idea to purchase XYZ stock was 10% (\$88/\$80 − 1) over a 15-day trading interval. Since 40% of the initial buy order on XYZ stock was "left on the table", the opportunity cost of not purchasing 4,000 shares of XYZ stock is 4% (10% × 40%).

The basic trading cost illustration suggests that without efficient management of the equity trading process, it is possible that the value of the manager's investment idea is impacted negatively by sizable trading costs in addition to commission charges, including trader timing, market impact cost, and opportunity cost. Moreover, trading cost management is especially important in a world where active equity managers are hard-pressed to outperform a simple buy-and-hold approach, such as that employed in a market index fund.

Liquidity and Transaction Costs

Liquidity is created by agents transacting in the financial markets when they buy and sell securities. Market makers, brokers, and dealers do not create liquidity. They are intermediaries who facilitate trade execution and maintain an orderly market.

Liquidity and transaction costs are interrelated. A highly liquid market is one were large transactions can be immediately executed without incurring high transaction costs. In an indefinitely liquid market, traders would be able to perform very large transactions directly at the quoted bid–ask prices. In reality, particularly for larger orders, the market requires traders to pay more than the ask when buying, and to pay less than the bid when selling. As we discussed above, this percentage degradation of the bid–ask prices experienced when executing trades is the market impact cost.

The market impact cost varies with transaction size: the larger the trade size, the larger the impact cost. Impact costs are not constant in time but vary throughout the day as traders change the limit orders that they have in the limit order book. A limit order is a conditional order; it is executed only if the limit price or a better price can be obtained. Therefore, a limit order is very different from a market order, which is an unconditional order to execute at the current best price available in the market (guarantees execution, not price). With a limit order a trader can improve the execution price relative to the market order price, but the execution is neither certain nor immediate (guarantees price, not execution).

At any given instant, the list of orders sitting in the limit order book embodies the liquidity that exists at a particular point in time. By observing the entire limit order book, impact costs can be calculated for different transaction sizes. The limit order book reveals the prevailing supply and demand in the market.[9] Therefore, in a pure limit order market, we can obtain a measure of liquidity by aggregating limit buy orders (representing the demand) and limit sell orders (representing the supply).[10]

However, few order books are publicly available and not all markets are pure limit-order markets. In 2004, the NYSE started selling information on its limit-order book through its new system called the *NYSE OpenBook*®. The system provides an aggregated real-time view of the exchange's limit-order book for all NYSE-traded securities.

In the absence of a fully transparent limit-order book, expected market impact cost is the most practical and realistic measure of market liquidity. It is closer to the true cost of transacting faced by market participants as compared to other measures such as those based upon the bid–ask spread.

[9]Even if it is possible to view the entire limit-order book, it does not give a *complete* picture of the liquidity in the market. This is because hidden and discretionary orders are not included. For a discussion of this topic, see Tuttle [2002].

[10]See Domowitz and Wang [2002] and Foucault, Kadan, and Kandel [2005].

Market Impact Measurements and Empirical Findings

The problem with measuring implicit transaction costs is that the true measure, which is the difference between the price of the stock in the absence of an asset manager's trade and the execution price, is not observable. Furthermore, the execution price is dependent on supply and demand conditions at the margin. Thus, the execution price may be influenced by competitive traders who demand immediate execution or by other investors with similar motives for trading. This means that the execution price realized by an investor is the consequence of the structure of the market mechanism, the demand for liquidity by the marginal investor, and the competitive forces of investors with similar motivations for trading.

There are many ways to measure transaction costs. However, in general this cost is the difference between the execution price and some appropriate benchmark, a so-called *fair market benchmark*. The fair market benchmark of a security is the price that would have prevailed had the trade not taken place, referred to as the *no-trade price*. Since the no-trade price is not observable, it has to be estimated. Practitioners have identified three different basic approaches to measure the market impact:[11]

- **Pre-trade measures** use prices occurring before or at the decision to trade as the benchmark, such as the opening price on the same day or the closing price on the previous day.
- **Post-trade measures** use prices occurring after the decision to trade as the benchmark, such as the closing price of the trading day or the opening price on the next day.
- **Same-day measures** or **average measures** use average prices of a large number of trades during the day of the decision to trade, such as the *volume-weighted average price* (VWAP) calculated over all transactions in the security on the trade day.[12]

The volume-weighted average price is calculated as follows. Suppose that it was a trader's objective to purchase 10,000 shares of XYZ stock. After completion of the trade, the trade sheet showed that 4,000 shares were purchased at \$80, another 4,000 at \$81, and finally 2,000 at \$82. In this

[11]See Collins and Fabozzi [1991] and Chan and Lakonishok [1993a, 1993b].
[12]Strictly speaking, VWAP is not the benchmark here but rather the transaction type.

case, the resulting VWAP is $(4{,}000 \times 80 + 4{,}000 \times 81 + 2{,}000 \times 82)/10{,}000 =$ \$80.80.

We denote by χ the indicator function that takes on the value 1 or -1 if an order is a buy or sell order, respectively. Formally, we now express the three types of measures of *market impact* (MI) as follows:

$$\mathrm{MI}_{\mathrm{pre}} = [(p^{\mathrm{ex}}/p^{\mathrm{pre}}) - 1]\chi,$$

$$\mathrm{MI}_{\mathrm{post}} = [(p^{\mathrm{ex}}/p^{\mathrm{post}}) - 1]\chi,$$

$$\mathrm{MI}_{\mathrm{VWAP}} = \left[\frac{\sum_{i=1}^{k} V_i p^{\mathrm{ex}}}{\sum_{i=1}^{k} V_i} \Big/ p^{\mathrm{pre}} - 1\right]\chi,$$

where p^{ex}, p^{pre}, and p^{post} denote the execution price, pre-trade price, and post-trade price of the stock, and k denotes the number of transactions in a particular security on the trade date. Using this definition, for a stock with market impact *MI* the resulting *market impact cost* for a trade of size V, *MIC*, is given by $\mathrm{MIC} = \mathrm{MI} \times V$.

It is also common to adjust market impact for general market movements. For example, the pre-trade market impact with market adjustment would take the form

$$\mathrm{MI}_{\mathrm{pre}} = [(p^{\mathrm{ex}}/p^{\mathrm{pre}}) - [(p_M^{\mathrm{ex}}/p_M^{\mathrm{pre}})]\chi,$$

where p_M^{ex} represents the value of the index at the time of the execution, and p_M^{pre} the price of the index at the time before the trade. Market-adjusted market impact for the post-trade and same-day trade benchmarks are calculated in an analogous fashion.

The previous three approaches to measure market impact are based upon measuring the fair market benchmark of a stock at a point in time. Clearly, different definitions of market impact lead to different results. Which one should be used is a matter of preference and is dependent on the application at hand. For example, Elkins/McSherry, a financial consulting firm that provides customized trading costs and execution analysis, calculates a same-day benchmark price for each stock by taking the mean of the day's open, close, high, and low prices. The market impact is then computed as the percentage difference between the transaction price and this benchmark. However, in most cases VWAP and the Elkins/McSherry approach lead to similar measurements.[13]

[13]See Willoughby [1998] and McSherry [1998].

As we analyze a portfolio's return over time, an important question to ask is whether we can attribute good/bad performance to investment profits/losses or to trading profits/losses. In other words, in order to better understand a portfolio's performance, it can be useful to decompose investment decisions from order execution. This is the basic idea behind the *implementation shortfall approach* suggested by Perold [1988].

In the implementation shortfall approach, we assume that there is a separation between investment and trading decisions. The asset manager makes decisions with respect to the investment strategy (i.e., what should be bought, sold, and held). Subsequently, these decisions are implemented by the traders.

By comparing the actual portfolio profit/loss (P/L) with the performance of a hypothetical "paper" portfolio in which all trades are made at hypothetical market prices, we can get an estimate of the implementation shortfall. For example, with a paper portfolio return of 6% and an actual portfolio return of 5%, the implementation shortfall is 1%.

Forecasting and Modeling Market Impact

As discussed in the previous section, the explicit transaction costs are relatively straightforward to estimate and forecast. With respect to market impact cost, several models are used in practice for forecasting and modeling this cost. These models are very useful in predicting the resulting trading costs of specific trading strategies and in devising optimal trading approaches.

We emphasize that in the modeling of transaction costs, it is important to factor in the objective of the trader or asset manager. For example, one market participant might trade just to take advantage of price movement and hence will only trade during favorable periods. Here the trading cost is different from that of an asset manager who has to rebalance a portfolio within a fixed time period and can therefore only partially use an opportunistic or liquidity searching strategy. In particular, this asset manager has to consider the risk of not completing the transaction within a specified time period. Consequently, even if the market is not favorable, the asset manager may decide to transact a portion of the trade. The market impact models described above assume that orders will be fully completed and ignore this point.

Although a complete description of these statistical models is beyond the scope of this chapter, we discuss the variables that are considered in these models.[14] The variables or forecasting factors used in modeling market impact costs are grouped in terms of trade-based and asset-based variables. We discuss each as follows.

Trade-Based Factors

Some examples of trade-based factors are:

- Trade size;
- Relative trade size;
- Price of market liquidity;
- Type of trade (information or non-information trade);
- Efficiency and trading style of the trader;
- Specific characteristics of the market or the exchange;
- Time of trade submission and trade timing;
- Order type.

Probably the most important market impact forecasting variables are based on absolute or relative trade size. Absolute trade size is often measured in terms of the number of shares traded, or the dollar value of the trade. Relative trade size, on the other hand, can be calculated as the number of shares traded divided by average daily volume, or number of shares traded divided by the total number of shares outstanding. The former can be seen as an explanatory variable for the temporary market impact and the latter for the permanent market impact. In particular, we expect the temporary market impact to increase as the trade size to the average daily volume increases because a larger trade demands more liquidity.

As discussed by Keim and Madhavan [1997], each type of investment style requires a different level of immediacy. Technical trades often have to be traded at a faster pace in order to capitalize on some short-term signal and therefore exhibit higher market impact costs. In contrast, more traditional long-term value strategies can be traded more slowly. These types of strategies can in many cases even be liquidity providing, which might result in negative market impact costs.

[14] For a general methodology for constructing forecasting models for market impact, see Kolm and Fabozzi [2011].

Several studies show that there is a wide variation in equity transaction costs across different countries.[15] Markets and exchanges in each country are different, and so are the resulting market microstructures. Forecasting variables can be used to capture specific market characteristics such as liquidity, efficiency, and institutional features.

The particular timing of a trade can affect market impact costs. For example, it appears that market impact costs are generally higher at the beginning of the month as compared to the end of it.[16] One of the reasons for this phenomenon is that many institutional investors tend to rebalance their portfolios at the beginning of the month. Because it is likely that many of these trades will be executed in the same stocks, this rebalancing pattern will induce an increase in market impact costs. The particular time of the day a trade takes place also has an effect. Many informed institutional traders tend to trade at the market open as they want to capitalize on new information that appeared after the market closed the day before.

As we discussed earlier in this chapter, market impact costs are asymmetric. In other words, buy and sell orders have significantly different market impact costs. Separate models for buy and sell orders can therefore be estimated.

Asset-Based Factors

Some examples of asset-based factors are:

- Price momentum;
- Price volatility;
- Market capitalization;
- Growth versus value;
- Specific industry or sector characteristics.

For a stock that is exhibiting positive price momentum, a buy order is liquidity demanding and it is therefore likely that it will have higher price impact cost than a sell order.

Generally, trades in high volatility stocks result in higher permanent price effects. It has been suggested by Chan and Lakonishok [1993a] and Smith, Alasdair, Turnbull, and White [2001] that this is because trades have

[15] For example, see Domowitz, Glen, and Madhavan [1999] and Chiyachantana, Jain, Jian, and Wood [2004].

[16] See Foster and Viswanathan [1990].

a tendency to contain more information when volatility is high. Another possibility is that higher volatility increases the probability of hitting and being able to execute at the liquidity providers' price. Consequently, liquidity suppliers display fewer shares at the best prices to mitigate adverse selection costs.

Large-cap stocks are more actively traded and therefore more liquid in comparison to small-cap stocks. As a result, market impact cost is normally lower for large-cap stocks.[17] However, if we measure market impact costs with respect to relative trade size (normalized by average daily volume, for instance), they are generally higher. Similarly, growth and value stocks have different market impact cost. One reason for that is related to the trading style. Growth stocks commonly exhibit momentum and high volatility. This attracts technical traders that are interested in capitalizing on short-term price swings. Value stocks are traded at a slower pace and holding periods tend to be slightly longer.

Different market sectors show different trading behaviors. For instance, Bikker, Spierdijk and van der Sluis [2007] show that equity trades in the energy sector exhibit higher market impact costs than other comparable equities in non-energy sectors.

Incorporating Transaction Costs in Asset Allocation Models

Standard asset-allocation models generally ignore transaction costs and other costs related to portfolio and allocation revisions. However, the effect of transaction costs is far from insignificant. On the contrary, if transaction costs are not taken into consideration, they can eat into a significant part of the returns. Whether transaction costs are handled efficiently or not by the asset manager can therefore make all the difference in attempting to outperform the peer group or a particular benchmark.

The typical asset-allocation model consists of one or several forecasting models for expected returns and risk. Small changes in these forecasts can result in reallocations which would not occur if transaction costs had been taken into account. Therefore, it is to be expected that the inclusion of transaction costs in asset-allocation models will result in a reduced amount of trading and rebalancing.

---

[17]See Keim and Madhavan [1997] and Spierdijk, Nijman, and van Soest [2003].

Given the complexity of the mathematical models that have been proposed for incorporating transaction costs into asset-allocation models such as the Markowitz mean–variance model, we cannot present them here. Instead, we provide some general remarks about these models.

Pogue [1970] gave one of the first descriptions of an extension of the mean–variance framework that included transaction costs. The formulation of more sophisticated modeling of portfolio rebalancing with transaction costs within the mean–variance framework was first proposed by Chen, Jen, and Zionts [1971]. Their model assumes that transaction costs are a constant proportion of the transaction's dollar value. Several other models were subsequently proposed. For example:

- Adcock and Meade [1994] add a linear term for the transaction costs to the mean–variance risk term and minimize this quantity.
- Yoshimoto [1996] proposes a nonlinear programming algorithm to solve the problem of portfolio revision with transaction costs.
- Best and Hlouskova [2005] give an efficient solution procedure for the case of proportional transfer costs where the transfer costs are paid at the end of the period, impacting both the risk and the return.
- Lobo, Fazel, and Boyd [2007] provide a model for the case of linear and fixed transaction costs that maximizes the expected return subject to the variance constraint.
- Chen, Fabozzi, and Huang [2009] demonstrate how the impact of transaction costs can be integrated into the mean–variance framework and show that even some analytical solutions under mild assumptions can be obtained via optimization techniques.

Transaction costs models can involve complicated nonlinear functions. Although there exists software for general nonlinear optimization problems, the computational time required for solving such problems is often too long for realistic investment management applications, and the quality of the solution is frequently not guaranteed. Very efficient and reliable software is available, however, for linear and quadratic optimization problems.[18] It is therefore common in practice to approximate a complicated nonlinear optimization problem by simpler problems that can be solved quickly. In particular, asset managers frequently employ approximations of some function

[18]See Chapter 6 for optimization models.

that represents the penalty due to transaction costs in the mean–variance framework.

Optimal Trading

The decisions of the asset manager and the trader are based upon different objectives. The asset manager constructs the optimal portfolio to reflect the best trade-off between expected returns and risk, given an assessment of the prevailing trading costs. The trader decides on the timing of the execution of the trades based upon the trade-off between opportunity costs and market impact costs.

One way of reducing market impact cost is to delay the trade until the price is right. However, this process will also lead to missed investment opportunities. This trade-off between market impact and opportunity costs is illustrated in Figure 2. The vertical axis represents unit cost, where the units could be cents per share, basis points, or dollars. The horizontal axis represents the time periods, which could be ticks, minutes, hours, days, and so on. First, we observe that market impact cost declines over time as it is positively related to the immediacy of execution. In other words, if a trader can "work an order" over time, the resulting transaction costs are expected to be lower. Second, opportunity cost increases over time as it is positively related to the delay in execution. This means that if a trader waits too long, a part of the extra return of the investment opportunity might disappear. Taken together, these two basic mechanisms give a total cost that is shaped like a parabola. As Figure 2 suggests, the total cost can be minimized by appropriately trading off market impact and opportunity costs.

Schematically, we can formulate this idea as an optimization problem where we attempt to minimize the expected total transaction costs. In general, this problem is a complicated stochastic and dynamic optimization problem. For example, Bertsimas, Hummel, and Lo [1999], Almgren and Chriss [2000/2001], and Almgren [2003] develop continuous-time models for optimal execution that minimizes average transaction costs over a specific time horizon. In particular, Almgren and Chriss [2000/2001] assume that securities prices evolve according to a random-walk process. Their model is an important contribution as it is one of the first of its kind that considers a dynamic model with market impact costs in which transactions occur over time.

As these techniques are rather involved mathematically, we describe only the basic ideas behind them. Realized transaction costs can deviate substantially from expected or average transaction costs. Therefore, it is

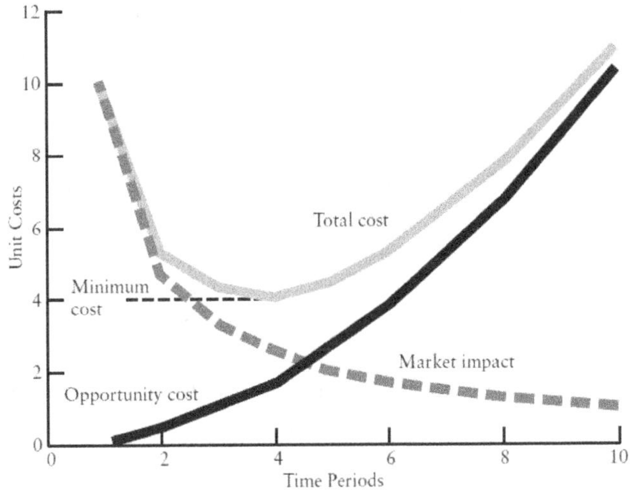

FIGURE 2: Cost Trade-Offs: Market Impact Cost versus Opportunity Cost

Source: Exhibit 2 in Fabozzi and Grant [1999].

convenient to use an objective function that takes this risk into account. Price volatility creates uncertainty in the realized trading costs in the same way it creates uncertainty in the realized return for an investment strategy. Therefore, we can think about opportunity costs as represented by the variance of the total transaction costs.

The models of optimal execution that have been proposed are designed to get the best execution of a single trade, or sometimes a sequence of trades. They achieve this objective by optimizing the trade-off between the risk and the mean cost of execution. Note that the risk considered here is the variance of execution costs. Intuitively, we can think of this as the risk of not getting a trade executed at a certain cost.

Depending on the size of the trade, it may take anything from a few minutes, a few hours, or even a few days to fully execute an order. The cost of trading is a random variable as some portions of the trade will be executed after prices have moved. Importantly, the delay in trading introduces price risk due to price movements beyond that which can be anticipated as a natural response to the trade itself. Now, if we think about the trade as part of a larger portfolio, then this price risk due to trading clearly affects the overall portfolio risk. However, often the models discussed in the literature ignore the effect of other stocks in the portfolio, including those whose positions are not changing during a trade.

In contrast, Engle and Ferstenberg [2007] developed a model that combines portfolio risk with execution risk in a single framework. Moreover, they studied characteristics of the joint optimization of positions and trades under different assumptions on the stock price processes and market impact of trades. While their results are rather technical to be presented here in detail, they provide several important insights. First, Engle and Ferstenberg show conditions under which the optimal execution of trades does not depend upon the holdings of the portfolio. That means that the generalized problem under these conditions reduces to two separate problems that are more familiar: the optimal allocation problem and the optimal execution problem. Second, they show that in order to hedge trading risks, sometimes it may be optimal to execute trades in stocks that may not have been in the trading order. Finally, they point out that taking trade execution risk into account leads to a natural measure of liquidity risk. Namely, typically the value of a portfolio is marked to market. Instead, they suggest looking at the portfolio liquidation value because it correctly represents the fact that the stocks in the portfolio cannot necessarily be liquidated at their current market prices. The portfolio liquidity risk can be estimated by computing a percentile of the possible distribution of portfolio liquidation values. There is, in fact, a range of possible distributions for future portfolio liquidation substantially from expected or average transaction costs. Therefore, it is convenient to use an objective function that takes this risk into account. Price volatility creates uncertainty in the realized trading costs in the same way it creates uncertainty in the realized return for an investment strategy. Therefore, we can think about opportunity costs as represented by the variance of the total transaction costs.

The models of optimal execution that have been proposed are designed to get the best execution of a single trade, or sometimes a sequence of trades. They achieve this objective by optimizing the trade-off between the risk and the mean cost of execution. Note that the risk considered here is the variance of execution costs. Intuitively, we can think of this as the risk of not getting a trade executed at a certain cost.

Integrated Asset Management: Beyond Expected Return and Portfolio Risk

As mentioned at the outset of this chapter, equity trading should not be viewed separately from equity asset management. On the contrary, the management of equity trading costs is an integral part of any successful investment management strategy. In this context, the firm of MSCI Barra points out that superior investment performance is based on careful consideration of four key elements[19]:

- Forming realistic return expectations;
- Controlling portfolio risk;
- Efficient control of trading costs;
- Monitoring total investment performance.

Unfortunately, most discussions of equity asset management focus solely on the relationship between expected return and portfolio risk — with little if any emphasis on whether the selected stocks in the "optimal" or target portfolio can be acquired in a cost-efficient manner.

To illustrate the seriousness of the problem that can arise with suboptimal portfolio decisions, Figure 3 highlights the "typical" versus "ideal" approach to (equity) asset management. In the typical approach (top portion of Figure 3), asset managers engage in fundamental and/or quantitative research to identify investment opportunities — albeit with a measure of investment prudence (risk control) in mind. Upon completion, the asset

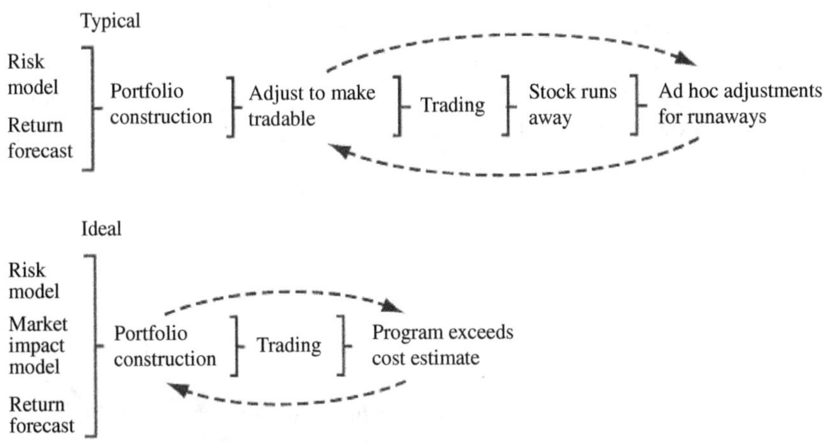

FIGURE 3: Typical versus Ideal Portfolio Management

Source: Torre [1998, Figure 4].

[19]The trading cost factor model described in this section is based on MSCI Barra's Market Impact Model™. A basic description of the model is covered in a three-part newsletter series. See Torre [1998].

manager reveals the list of stocks that form the basis of the target portfolio to the senior trader. At this point, the senior trader informs the asset manager of certain non-tradable positions — which causes the asset manager to adjust the list of stocks either by hand or some other *ad hoc* procedure. This, in turn, causes the portfolio to be suboptimal.

Figure 3 also shows that as the trader begins to fill the portfolio with the now suboptimal set of stocks, an additional portfolio imbalance may occur as market impact costs cause the prices of some stocks to "runaway" during trade implementation. It should be clear that any *ad hoc* adjustments by the trader at this point will in turn build a systematic imbalance in the portfolio — such that the asset manager's actual portfolio will depart permanently from that which would be efficient from a return–risk and trading cost perspective.

A better approach to equity asset management (lower portion of Figure 3) requires a systematic integration of asset management and trading processes. In this context, the returns forecast, risk estimates, and trading cost program are jointly combined in determining the optimal investment portfolio. In this way, the asset manager knows up front if (complete) portfolio implementation is either not feasible or is too expensive when accounting for trading costs.

Accordingly, the asset manager can incorporate the appropriate trading cost information into the portfolio construction and risk control process — before the trading program begins. The asset manager can then build a portfolio of securities whereby actual security positions are consistent with those deemed to be optimal from an integrated portfolio context.

Key Points

- Equity trading should not be viewed separately from equity portfolio management.
- Transaction costs are categorized in terms of fixed versus variable transaction costs, and explicit versus implicit transaction costs.
- Fixed transaction costs are independent of factors such as trade size and market conditions.
- Variable transaction costs depend on trade size, market conditions, and other factors.
- Asset managers and the portfolio team's traders seek to reduce, optimize, and efficiently manage variable transaction costs.

- Explicit transaction costs are those costs that are observable and known upfront, such as commissions, custodial fees, transfer fees, taxes (on capital gains and taxes on dividends), and bid–ask spreads.
- The bid–ask spread is the immediate transaction cost that the market charges anyone for the privilege of trading, with high immediate liquidity being synonymous with small spreads.
- From an economic perspective, the bid–ask spread is the price charged by dealers for supplying immediacy and short-term price stability in the presence of short-term order imbalances.
- As a true liquidity measure, the bid–ask spread is misleading because it only conveys the price for small trades.
- Implicit transaction costs are non-observable and not known in advance and include market impact and opportunity costs.
- In general, implicit costs make up the dominant part of the total transaction costs.
- Implicit transaction costs include investment delay cost, market impact cost, price movement risk, market timing cost, and opportunity cost.
- When a security's price may change adversely between the time when the asset manager makes a buy/sell decision and when the actual trade is brought to the market by a trader, this form of implicit transaction cost is referred to as investment delay cost.
- Investment delay cost depends on the investment strategy.
- Market impact cost (price impact cost) of a transaction is the deviation of the transaction price from the market (mid) price that would have prevailed had the trade not occurred.
- Market impact cost is the cost of liquidity.
- Market impact cost is the sum of temporary and permanent market impact costs.
- Temporary market impact cost is of transitory nature and can represent the additional liquidity concession necessary for the liquidity provider to take the order, inventory effects, or imperfect substitution.
- Permanent price impact cost is the persistent price change that results as the market adjusts to the information content of the trade.
- Several studies report that market impact costs are often asymmetric (i.e., market impact costs are different for buy and sell orders).
- In the stock market, typically price movement risk for a buy order is defined as the price increase during the time of the trade that is attributed to the general trend of a security, whereas the remaining part is market impact costs.

- Market timing costs are the result of the movement in a security's price at the time of the transaction that can be attributed to other market participants or general market volatility.
- Opportunity cost is the cost of not transacting and is defined as the difference in performance between an asset manager's desired investment and the actual investment after transaction costs.
- Liquidity is created by agents when they transact in the market and not by market makers, brokers, and dealers.
- Market makers, brokers, and dealers are intermediaries who facilitate trade execution and maintain an orderly market.
- Liquidity and transaction costs are interrelated.
- In a highly liquid market, large transactions can be immediately executed without incurring high transaction costs.
- In practice, for larger orders traders pay more than the ask when buying and pay less than the bid when selling.
- In general, transaction cost is measured by the difference between the execution price and some fair market benchmark.
- Measures of transaction cost include pre-trade measures, post-trade measures, and same-day (or average) measures.
- Pre-trade measures use prices occurring before or at the decision to trade as the benchmark.
- Post-trade measures use prices occurring after the decision to trade as the benchmark, such as the closing price of the trading day or the opening price on the next day.
- Volume-weighted average price (VWAP) is an example of a same-day measure.
- To better understand a portfolio's performance, it can be useful to decompose investment decisions from order execution and this is the basic idea behind the implementation shortfall approach.
- An estimate of implementation shortfall is obtained comparing the actual portfolio profit/loss with the performance of a hypothetical "paper" portfolio in which all trades are made at hypothetical market prices.
- Market impact cost models are useful in predicting the resulting trading costs associated with specific trading strategies and in devising optimal trading approaches.
- Examples of trade-based factors used in forecasting market impact costs are trade size, relative trade size, price of market liquidity, type of trade (information or non-information trade), efficiency and trading style of

the investor, specific characteristics of the market or the exchange, time of trade submission and trade timing, and order type.

- Probably the most important market impact forecasting variables are based on absolute or relative trade size.
- Examples of asset-based factors used in forecasting market impact cost are price momentum, price volatility, market capitalization, growth versus value, and specific industry or sector characteristics.
- Transaction costs can be included into asset allocation models and software is available to deal with the complexity associated with including these costs.
- An asset manager constructs the optimal portfolio to reflect the best trade-off between expected returns and risk, given his assessment of the prevailing trading costs.
- The trader decides on the timing of the execution of the trades based upon the trade-off between opportunity costs and market impact costs.
- Models of optimal execution have been proposed that are designed to obtain the best execution of a single trade, or sometimes a sequence of trades.
- Superior investment performance is based on careful consideration of four key elements: forming realistic return expectations, controlling portfolio risk, efficient control of trading costs, and monitoring total investment performance.

References

Adcock, C. J. and N. Meade, 1994. "A simple algorithm to incorporate transaction costs in quadratic optimization," *European Journal of Operational Research*, 79: 85–94.

Almgren, R., 2003, "Optimal execution with nonlinear impact functions and trading-enhanced risk," *Applied Mathematical Finance*, 10(3): 1–18.

Almgren, R. and N. Chriss, 2000/2001. "Optimal execution of portfolio transactions," *Journal of Risk*, 3: 5–39.

Bertsimas, D., P. Hummel, and A. W. Lo, 1999. "Optimal control of execution costs for portfolios," Working Paper, MIT Sloan School of Management.

Best, M. J. and R. R. Grauer, 1991. "On the sensitivity of mean–variance efficient portfolios to changes in asset means: Some analytical and computational results," *Review of Financial Studies*, 4(2): 315–342.

Best, M. J. and J. Hlouskova, 2005. "An algorithm for portfolio optimization with transaction costs," *Management Science*, 51(11): 1676–1688.

Bikker, J. A., L. Spierdijk, and P. J. van der Sluis, 2007. "Market impact costs of institutional equity trades," *Journal of International Money and Finance*, 26(6): 974–1000.

Chan, L. and J. Lakonishok, 1993a. "Institutional trades and intraday stock price behavior," *Journal of Financial Economics*, 33: 173–199.

Chan, L. and J. Lakonishok, 1993b. "Institutional equity trading costs: NYSE versus Nasdaq," *Journal of Finance*, 52(1): 71–75.

Chen, A. H., F. J. Fabozzi, and D. Huang, 2009. "Models for portfolio revision with transaction costs in the mean–variance framework," in *The Handbook of Portfolio Construction: Contemporary Applications of Markowitz Techniques*, edited by J. Geurard. New York: Springer.

Chen, A. H., F. C. Jen, and S. Zionts, 1971. "The optimal portfolio revision policy," *Journal of Business*, 44: 51–61.

Chiyachantana, C. N., P. K. Jain, C. Jian, and R. A. Wood, 2004. "International evidence on institutional trading behavior and price impact," *Journal of Finance*, 59: 869–895.

Collins, B. C. and F. J. Fabozzi, 1991. "A methodology for measuring transaction costs," *Financial Analysts Journal*, 47: 27–36.

Domowitz, I., J. Glen, and A. Madhavan, 1999. "International equity trading costs: A cross-sectional and time-series analysis," Technical Report, Pennsylvania State University, International Finance Corp., University of Southern California.

Domowitz, I. and X. Wang, 2002. "Liquidity, liquidity commonality and its impact on portfolio theory," Working Paper, Smeal College of Business Administration, Pennsylvania State University.

Engle, R. F. and R. Ferstenberg, 2007. "Execution risk," *Journal of Portfolio Management*, 33(12): 34–44.

Fabozzi, F. J. and J. L. Grant, 1999. *Equity Portfolio Management.* Hoboken, NJ: John Wiley & Sons.

Foster, F. D. and S. Viswanathan, 1990. "A theory of the interday variations in volume, variance, and trading costs in securities markets," *Review of Financial Studies*, 4: 593–624.

Foucault, T., O. Kadan, and E. Kandel, 2005. "Limit order book as a market for liquidity," *Review of Financial Studies*, 18(2): 1171–1271.

Harris, L. E. and V. Panchapagesan, 2005. "The information content of the limit order book: Evidence from NYSE specialist trading decisions," *Journal of Financial Markets*, 8: 25–67.

Hu, G., 2005. "Measures of implicit trading costs and buy-sell asymmetry," Working Paper, Babson College.

Keim, D. B. and A. Madhavan, 1997. "Transaction costs and investment style: An inter-exchange analysis of institutional equity trades," *Journal of Financial Economics*, 46: 265–292.

Kolm, P. N. and F. J. Fabozzi, 2011. "Modelling market impact costs," in *Equity Valuation and Portfolio Management*, edited by F. J. Fabozzi and H. M. Markowitz (Chapter 17). Hoboken, NJ: John Wiley & Sons.

Kolm, P. N. and L. Machlin, 2008. "Algorithmic trading: Where are we headed?" Working Paper, Courant Institute, New York University.

Lobo, M. S., M. Fazel, and S. Boyd, 2007. "Portfolio optimization with linear and fixed transaction costs," *Annals of Operations Research*, 152(1): 341–365.

Perold, A. F., 1988. "The implementation shortfall: Paper versus reality," *Journal of Portfolio Management*, 14(3): 4–9.

Pogue, G. A., 1970. "An extension of the Markowitz portfolio selection model to include variable transactions costs, short sales, leverage policies and taxes," *Journal of Finance*, 25(5): 1005–1027.

McSherry, R., 1998. *Global Trading Cost Analysis*. Elkins/McSherry Co., Inc.

Smith, B. F., D. Alasdair, S. Turnbull, and R. W. White, 2001. "Upstairs market for principal and agency trades: Analysis of adverse information and price effects," *Journal of Finance*, 56: 1723–1746.

Spierdijk, L., T. Nijman, and A. van Soest, 2003. "Temporary and persistent price effects of trades in infrequently traded stocks," Working Paper, Tilburg University and Center.

Torre, N., 1998. "The Market Impact Model™." Three-part series in *Barra Newsletters*, NL165–NL167.

Tuttle, L. A., 2002. "Hidden orders, trading costs and information," Working Paper, Ohio State University.

Vangelisti, M., 2006. "The capacity of an equity strategy," *Journal of Portfolio Management*, 32(2): 44–50.

Wagner, W. H. and M. Edwards, 1998. "Implementing investment strategies: The art and science of investing," in *Active Equity Portfolio Management*, edited by F. J. Fabozzi (pp. 179–194), Hoboken, NJ: John Wiley & Sons.

Willoughby, J., 1998. "Executions song," *Institutional Investor*, 32(11): 51–56.

Yoshimoto, A., 1996. "The mean–variance approach to portfolio optimization subject to transaction costs," *Journal of Operations Research Society of Japan*, 39(1): 99–117.

Chapter 15

Managing a Common Stock Portfolio with a Multifactor Risk Model Using Fundamental Factor*

Learning Objectives

After reading this chapter, you will understand:

- the way multifactor risk models based on fundamentals can be used to construct a portfolio;
- what tracking error is;
- the difference between backward-looking tracking error and forward-looking tracking error;
- the determinants of tracking error;
- what a return generating function is;
- the different ways that portfolio risk can be decomposed;
- how a fundamental multifactor risk model can be used to (1) assess whether the current portfolio is consistent with a manager's strengths, (2) control risk against a stock market index, and (3) construct a portfolio to make intentional bets.

*This chapter is coauthored with Frank J. Jones, Professor Finance and Accounting at San Jose State University and Raman Vardharaj, CFA, is the Head of Quantitative Analysis at OFI Global Asset Management, Inc. and a Vice President and Portfolio Manager at OppenheimerFunds, Inc.

Introduction

Equity portfolio managers who pursue a quantitative-oriented common stock strategy typically employ a multifactor model to construct a portfolio. There are two types of multifactor models. The first are models that are used to forecast expected returns. In equity portfolio management, the Fama–French three-factor and five-factor models are examples of such models. The second type of multifactor model forecasts risk when building and rebalancing a portfolio. Typically, the second type of model is provided by a third-party vendor.

In this chapter, we use a previously available commercial model to illustrate the general features of a multifactor model for forecasting risk using fundamental factors and how they are used to construct portfolios. We begin with a review of the concept of tracking error, which is a key concept in understanding the potential performance of a portfolio relative to a benchmark index and the actual performance of a portfolio relative to a benchmark index. In Chapter 16, the use of a multifactor risk model in managing a bond portfolio is explained and illustrated.

Tracking Error

The risk of a portfolio can be measured by the standard deviation of portfolio returns. This statistical measure provides a range around the average return of a portfolio within which the actual return over a period is likely to fall with some specified probability. The mean return and standard deviation (or volatility) of a portfolio can be calculated over a period of time.

The standard deviation or volatility of a portfolio or a market index is an absolute number. A portfolio manager or client can also ask what the variation of the return of a portfolio is relative to a specified benchmark. Such variation is called the portfolio's *tracking error*. Specifically, tracking error measures the dispersion of a portfolio's returns relative to the returns of its benchmark. That is, tracking error is the standard deviation of the portfolio's *active return* where active return is defined as

$$\text{Active return} = \text{Portfolio actual return} - \text{Benchmark actual return}.$$

A portfolio created to match the benchmark index (that is, an index fund) that regularly has zero active returns (that is, always matches its benchmark's actual return) would have a tracking error of zero. But a portfolio that is actively managed that takes positions substantially different from the benchmark would likely have large active returns, both positive and negative, and thus would have an annual tracking error of, say, 5–10%.

Tracking error calculated from these trailing active returns is referred to as *backward-looking tracking error* or *ex post tracking error*. A problem with a backward-looking tracking error is that it does not reflect the effect of current decisions by the asset manager on the future active returns and hence the future tracking error that may be realized. If, for example, the manager significantly changes the portfolio beta or sector allocations today, then the backward-looking tracking error that is calculated using data from prior periods would not accurately reflect the current portfolio risks going forward. That is, the backward-looking tracking error will have little predictive value and can be misleading regarding portfolio risks going forward.

An asset manager needs a forward-looking estimate of tracking error to accurately reflect the portfolio risk going forward. This is done in practice by using the services of a commercial vendor that has a model, called a *multifactor risk model*, that has defined the risks associated with a benchmark index. Statistical analysis of the historical return data of the stocks in the benchmark index are used to obtain the factors and quantify their risks. (This involves the use of variances and correlations.) Using the portfolio manager's current portfolio holdings, the portfolio's current exposure to the various factors can be calculated and compared to the benchmark's exposures to the factors. Using the differential factor exposures and the risks of the factors, a *forward-looking tracking error* for the portfolio can be computed. This tracking error is also referred to as the *predicted tracking error* or *ex ante tracking error*.

There is no guarantee that the forward-looking tracking error at the start of, say, a year would exactly match the backward-looking tracking error calculated at the end of the year. There are two reasons for this. The first is that as the year progresses and changes are made to the portfolio, the forward-looking tracking error estimate would change to reflect the new exposures. The second is that the accuracy of the forward-looking tracking error depends on the extent of the stability of the variances and correlations that were used in the analysis. These problems notwithstanding, the average of forward-looking tracking error estimates obtained at different times during the year will be reasonably close to the backward-looking tracking error estimate obtained at the end of the year.

Each of these estimates has its use. The forward-looking tracking error is useful in risk control and portfolio construction. The asset manager can immediately see the likely effect on tracking error of any intended change in the portfolio. Thus, an asset manager can do a what-if analysis of various portfolio strategies and eliminate those that would result in tracking errors beyond the asset manager's tolerance for risk. The backward-looking tracking error can be useful for assessing actual performance analysis, such as the information ratio.

Determinants of Tracking Error

Several factors affect the level of tracking error. According to Vardharaj, Fabozzi, and Jones [2004] the major factors are as follows:

- Number of stocks in the portfolio;
- Portfolio market capitalization and style difference relative to the benchmark;
- Sector deviation from the benchmark;
- Market volatility;
- Portfolio beta.

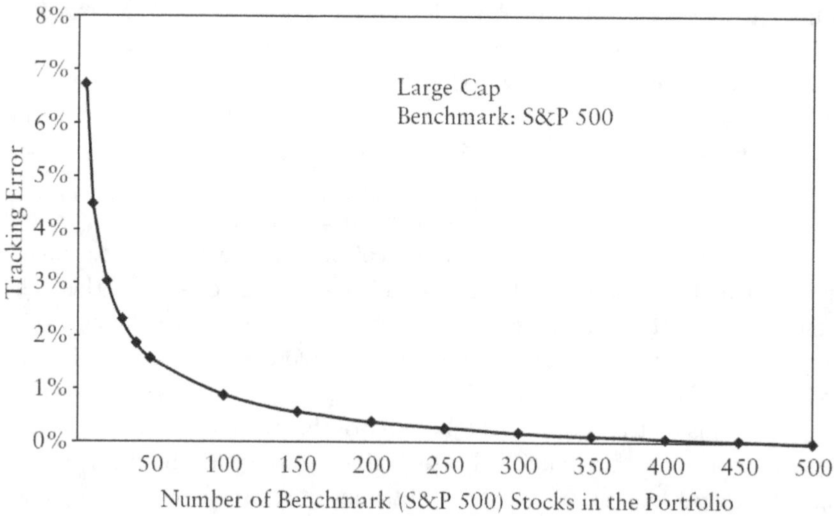

FIGURE 1: Typical Tracking Error versus Number of Benchmark Stocks in Portfolio for S&P 500

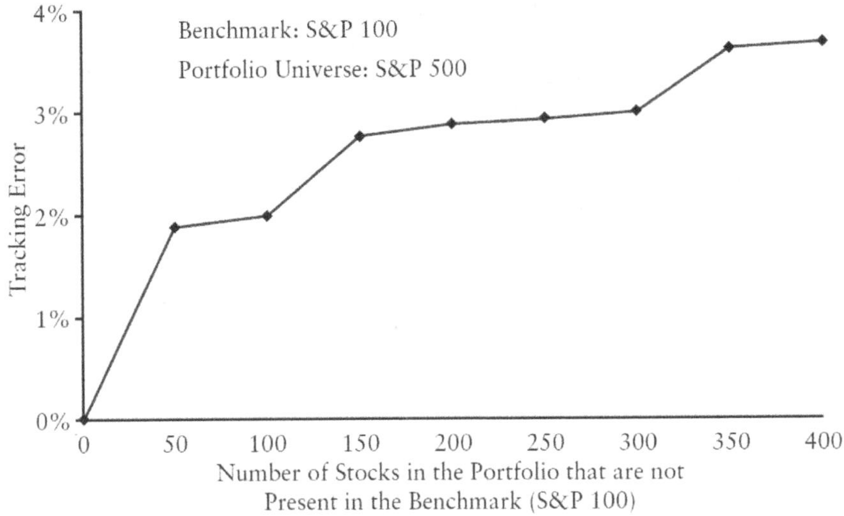

FIGURE 2: Tracking Error versus Number of Non-benchmark Stocks in Portfolio

Number of stocks in portfolio

Tracking error decreases as the portfolio progressively includes more of the stocks that are in the benchmark index. This general effect is illustrated in Figure 1, which shows the effect of portfolio size for a large-cap portfolio benchmarked to the S&P 500. Note that an optimally chosen portfolio of just 50 stocks can track the S&P 500 within 2.3%. For mid-cap and small-cap stocks, Vardharaj, Jones, and Fabozzi [2004] found that the tracking errors are 3.5% and 4.3%, respectively. In contrast, tracking error increases as the portfolio progressively includes more stocks that are not in the benchmark.

This effect is illustrated in Figure 2. In this case, the benchmark index is the S&P 100 and the portfolio progressively includes more and more stocks from the S&P 500 that are not in the S&P 100. The result is that the tracking error with respect to the S&P 100 rises.

Portfolio market cap and style difference relative to benchmark

Vardharaj, Jones, and Fabozzi [2004] found tracking error increases as the average market cap of the portfolio deviates from that of the benchmark index. Tracking error also increases as the overall style (growth/value) of the portfolio deviates from that of the benchmark index. First, holding style constant, they find that tracking error rises when the cap size difference increases. For example, a mid-cap blend portfolio has a tracking error of 7.07%, while a small-cap blend portfolio has a tracking error of 8.55% with respect to the S&P 500, which is a large-cap blend portfolio. Second, for a given cap size, tracking error is greater when the style is either growth or value than when it is the blend.

Sector deviation from benchmark

When a portfolio's allocations to various economic sectors differ from those of its benchmark, it results in tracking error. In general, when the differences in sector allocation increase, the tracking error increases. Vardharaj, Jones, and Fabozzi [2004] found that in general, the tracking error increased as the level of sector bets increased.

Market volatility

Managed portfolios generally hold only a fraction of the assets in their benchmark. Given this, a highly volatile benchmark index (as measured in terms of standard deviation) would be harder to track closely than a generally less volatile benchmark index. As market volatility rises, the portfolio tracking error increases. This correspondingly increases the probability of "dramatic underperformance", by which we mean an underperformance of 10% or more. This can be seen in Figure 3. On the horizontal axis of the figure is the tracking error and on the vertical axis is the probability of a shortfall of 10% or more from the benchmark index. (In this calculation, we assumed normal distribution of active returns and an alpha of −0.26%, which is the average alpha for domestic stock mutual funds.)

As the tracking error rises, the probability of dramatic outperformance increases just as much as the probability of dramatic underperformance. But, the portfolio management consequences of these two types of extreme relative performances are not symmetric — dramatic underperformance can cause a manager to be terminated. Another implication is that since an increase in market volatility increases tracking error and thereby the chances of dramatic underperformance, there is an increased need for managers to monitor the portfolio tracking error more frequently and closely during periods of high market volatility.

Portfolio beta

The beta for the market portfolio is 1 and beta for the risk-free portfolio (cash) is zero. Suppose an investor holds a combination of cash and the

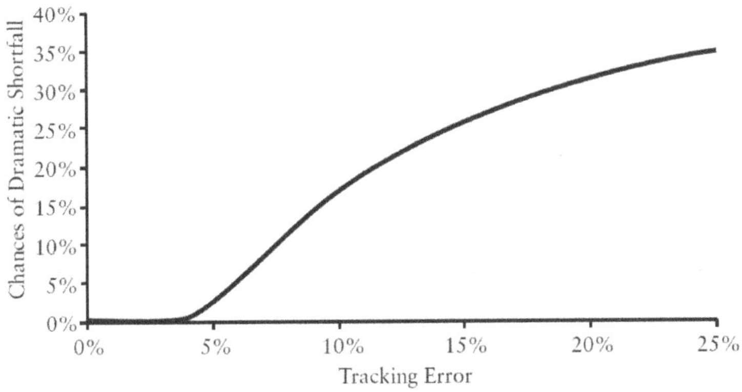

FIGURE 3: Tracking Error and Dramatic Shortfall

market portfolio. Then, the portfolio beta falls below 1. The managed portfolio is less sensitive to systematic risk than the market, and is therefore less risky than the market. Conversely, when the investor holds a leveraged market portfolio by borrowing at the risk-free rate and investing in the market portfolio, the beta is above 1 and the portfolio is riskier than the market.

It can be demonstrated that the portfolio tracking error, with respect to the market portfolio, increases both when the beta falls below 1 and when the beta rises above 1. So, as the portfolio increases the proportion of cash held, even though its absolute risk falls, its tracking error risk rises. As shown in Figure 4, tracking error rises linearly as the beta deviates from 1.

In the above example, we make the simplistic assumption that the manager only chooses between holding the market portfolio and cash when making changes to its beta. In the more general case where the fund can hold any number of stocks in any proportion, its beta can differ from 1 due to other reasons. But, even in this general case, the tracking error increases when the portfolio beta deviates from the market beta.

Marginal contribution to tracking error

Since tracking error arises from various bets (some intentional and some unintentional) placed by the manager through overweighting and underweighting relative to the benchmark index, it would be useful to understand how sensitive the tracking error is to small changes in each of these bets.

Suppose, for example, a portfolio initially has an overweight of 3% in the semiconductor industry relative to its benchmark index, and that the tracking error is 6%. Suppose that the tracking error subsequently increases

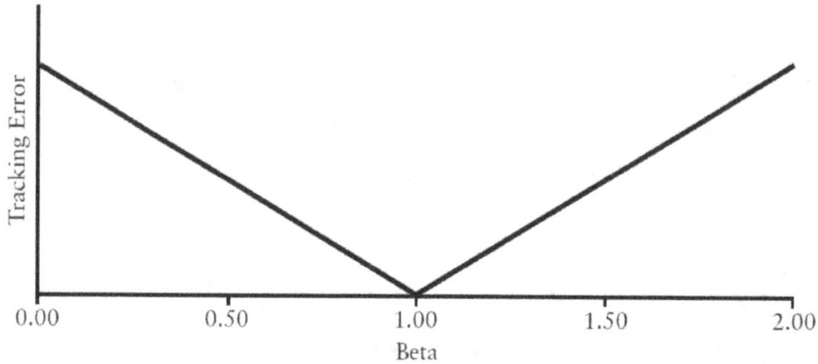

FIGURE 4: Tracking Error and Beta

to 6.1% due to the semiconductor industry weight in the portfolio increasing by 1% (and hence the overweight goes to 4%). Then, it can be said that this industry adds 0.1% to tracking error for every 1% increase in its weight. That is, its marginal contribution to tracking error is 0.1%. This would hold only at the margin, that is, for a small change, and not for large changes.

Marginal contributions can also be calculated for individual stocks. If the risk analysis employs a multifactor risk model, then similar marginal contribution estimates can be obtained for the risk factors also.

Generally, marginal contributions would be positive for overweighted industries (or stocks) and negative for underweighted ones. The reason is as follows. If a portfolio already holds an excess weight in an industry, then increasing this weight would cause the portfolio to diverge further from the benchmark index. This increased divergence adds to tracking error, leading to a positive marginal contribution for this industry. Suppose, however, the portfolio has an underweight in an industry. Then, increasing the portfolio weight in this industry would make the portfolio converge towards the benchmark, thus reducing tracking error. This leads to a negative marginal contribution for this industry.

An analysis of the marginal contributions can be useful for an asset manager who seeks to alter the portfolio tracking error. Suppose an asset manager wishes to reduce the tracking error, then she should reduce portfolio overweights in industries (or stocks) with the highest positive marginal contributions. Alternatively, the asset manager can reduce the underweights (that is, increase the overall weights) in industries (or stocks) with the most negative marginal contributions. Such changes would be most effective in reducing the tracking error while minimizing the necessary turnover and the associated expenses.

Fundamental Factor Model Description and Estimation

The basic relationship to be estimated in a fundamental factor model is

$$R_i - R_f = \beta_{i,F1} R_{F1} + \beta_{i,F2} R_{F2} + \cdots + \beta_{i,FH} R_{FH} + e_i,$$

where R_i is the rate of return on stock i, R_f is the risk-free rate of return, $\beta_{i,Fj}$ is the sensitivity of stock i to risk factor j, R_{Fj} is the rate of return on risk factor j, and e_i is the non-factor (specific) return on security i.

The above function is referred to as a *return generating function.*

In our illustration to demonstrate how a multifactor model is used to construct and rebalance a portfolio, we will use an old version of a model developed by Barra,[1] the E3 model. While that model has been updated, the discussion and illustrations provide the essential points for appreciating the value of using fundamental factor models.

The Barra fundamental factor model uses company and industry attributes and market data as "descriptors". Examples of descriptors are earnings/price ratios, book/price ratios, estimated earnings growth, and trading activity. The estimation of a fundamental factor model begins with an analysis of historical stock returns and descriptors about a company. In the Barra model, for example, the process of identifying the risk factors begins with monthly returns for hundreds of stocks that the descriptors must explain. Descriptors are not the "risk factors". They are the candidates for risk factors. The descriptors are selected in terms of their ability to explain stock returns. That is, all of the descriptors are potential risk factors but only those that appear to be important in explaining stock returns are used in constructing risk factors.

[1]Here is some history about this model. The genesis of this fundamental factor model is the work of Barr Rosenberg, at the time an associate professor of finance at the University of California, Berkeley, who in a series of research papers in the 1970s developed the theory that microeconomic or fundamental characteristics of a company can be used to explain stock returns (see, for example, Rosenberg and Marathe [1976] and Rosenberg and Guy [1976]). Rosenberg went on to found Barr Rosenberg & Associates (BARRA, Inc.), a quantitative consulting firm. The firm developed several fundamental factor models, one of which is used in the illustration in this chapter, the E3 model. In 2004, BARRA, Inc. was acquired by Morgan Stanley Capital International (MSCI) and referred to as MSCI BARRA.

Once the descriptors that are statistically significant in explaining stock returns are identified, they are grouped into "risk indexes" or "factors" to capture related company attributes. For example, descriptors such as market leverage, book leverage, debt-to-equity ratio, and company's debt rating are combined to obtain a risk index or factor referred to as "leverage". Thus, a risk index is a combination of descriptors that captures a particular attribute of a company.

For example, the Barra fundamental factor model, the E3 model used for illustration purposes only in this chapter, has 13 risk indexes and 55 industry groups. Table 1 lists the 13 risk indexes in the Barra model. Also shown in the table are the descriptors used to construct each risk index. The 55 industry classifications are further classified into sectors. For example, the following three industries comprise the energy sector: energy reserves and production, oil refining, and oil services. The consumer non-cyclicals sector consists of the following five industries: food and beverages, alcohol, tobacco, home products, and grocery stores. The 13 sectors in the Barra model are basic materials, energy, consumer non-cylicals, consumer cyclicals, consumer services, industrials, utility, transport, health care, technology, telecommunications, commercial services, and financial.

Given the risk factors, information about the exposure of every stock to each risk factor ($\beta_{i,Fj}$) is estimated using statistical analysis. For a given time period, the rate of return for each risk factor (R_{Fj}) also can be estimated using statistical analysis. The prediction for the expected return can be obtained from equation (1) for any stock. The non-factor return (e_i) is found by subtracting the actual return for the period for a stock from the return as predicted by the risk factors.

Moving from individual stocks to portfolios, the predicted return for a portfolio can be computed. The exposure to a given risk factor of a portfolio is simply the weighted average of the exposure of each stock in the portfolio to that risk factor. For example, suppose a portfolio has 42 stocks. Suppose further that stocks 1–40 are equally weighted in the portfolio at 2.2%, stock 41 is 5% of the portfolio, and stock 42 is 7% of the portfolio. Then the exposure of the portfolio to risk factor j is

$$0.022\beta_{1,Fj} + 0.022\beta_{2,Fj} + \cdots + 0.022\beta_{40,Fj} + 0.050\beta_{41,Fj} + 0.007\beta_{42,Fj}.$$

The non-factor error term is measured in the same way as in the case of an individual stock. However, in a well-diversified portfolio, the non-factor error term will be considerably less for the portfolio than for the individual stocks in the portfolio.

TABLE 1: Barra E3 Model Risk Definitions

Descriptors in Risk Index	Risk Index
Beta times sigma Daily standard deviation High-low price Log of stock price Cumulative range Volume beta Serial dependence Option-implied standard deviation	Volatility
Relative strength Historical alpha	Momentum
Log of market capitalization	Size
Cube of log of market capitalization	Size Nonlinearity
Share turnover rate (annual) Share turnover rate (quarterly) Share turnover rate (monthly) Share turnover rate (five years) Indicator for forward split Volume to variance	Trading Activity
Payout ratio over five years Variability in capital structure Growth rate in total assets Earnings growth rate over the last five years Analyst-predicted earnings growth Recent earnings change	Growth
Analyst-predicted earnings-to-price Trailing annual earnings-to-price Historical earnings-to-price	Earnings Yield
Book-to-price ratio	Value
Variability in earnings Variability in cash flows Extraordinary items in earnings Standard deviation of analyst-predicted earnings-to-price	Earnings Variability
Market leverage Book leverage Debt to total assets Senior debt rating	Leverage
Exposure to foreign currencies	Currency Sensitivity
Predicted dividend yield	Dividend Yield
Indicator for firms outside US-E3 estimation universe	Non-estimation Universe Indicator

The same analysis can be applied to a stock market index because an index is nothing more than a portfolio of stocks.

Risk Decomposition

The real usefulness of a fundamental factor model lies in the ease with which the risk of a portfolio with several assets can be estimated. Consider a portfolio with 100 assets. Risk is commonly defined as the variance of the portfolio's returns. So, in this case, we need to find the variance-covariance matrix of the 100 assets. That would require us to estimate 100 variances (one for each of the 100 assets) and 4,950 covariances among the 100 assets. That is, in all, we need to estimate 5,050 values, a very difficult undertaking. Suppose, instead, that we use a three-factor model to estimate risk. Then, we need to estimate (1) the three factor loadings for each of the 100 assets (that is, 300 values), (2) the six values of the factor variance-covariance matrix, and (3) the 100 residual variances (one for each asset). That is, in all, we need to estimate only 406 values. This represents a nearly 90% reduction from having to estimate 5,050 values, a huge improvement. Thus, with well-chosen factors, we can substantially reduce the work involved in estimating a portfolio's risk.

A fundamental factor model allows a portfolio manager and a client to decompose risk in order to assess the potential performance of a portfolio to the factors and to assess the potential performance of a portfolio relative to a benchmark. This is the portfolio construction and risk control application of the model. Also, the actual performance of a portfolio relative to a benchmark can be assessed.

Barra [1998] suggests that there are various ways that a portfolio's total risk can be decomposed when employing a fundamental factor model.[2] Each decomposition approach can be useful to managers depending on the equity portfolio management that they pursue. The four approaches are (1) total risk decomposition, (2) systematic-residual risk decomposition, (3) active risk decomposition, and (4) active systematic-active residual risk decomposition. We describe each in what follows and explain how managers pursuing different strategies will find the decomposition helpful in portfolio construction and evaluation.

[2]The discussion to follow in this section follows that in the 1998 handbook of Barra [1998] in describing the firm's model.

In all of these approaches to risk decomposition, the total return is first divided into the risk-free return and the total excess return. The *total excess return* is the difference between the actual return realized by the portfolio and the risk-free return. The risk associated with the total excess return, called *total excess risk*, is what is further partitioned in the four approaches.

Total Risk Decomposition

There are managers who seek to minimize total risk. For example, an asset manager pursuing a long-short or market neutral strategy, seeks to construct a portfolio that minimizes total risk. For such managers, total risk decomposition which breaks down the total excess risk into two components — common factor risks (e.g., capitalization and industry exposures) and specific risk — is useful. This decomposition is shown in Figure 5.[3] There is no provision for market risk, only risk attributed to the common

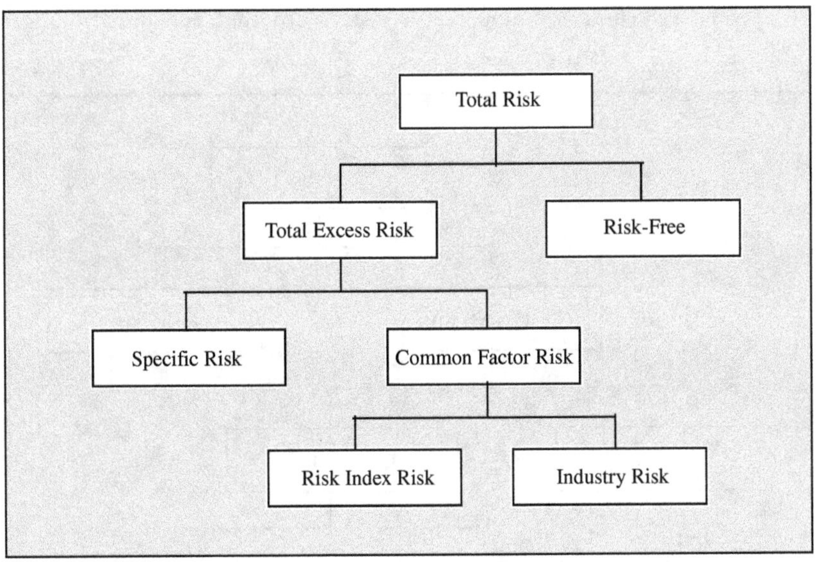

FIGURE 5: Total Risk Decomposition
Source: Barra [1998, p. 34, Figure 4.2]. Reprinted with permission.

[3]The discussion to follow in this section follows that in the 1998 handbook of Barra [1998] in describing the firm's model.

factor risks and company-specific influences (that is, risk unique to a particular company and therefore uncorrelated with the specific risk of other companies). Thus, the market portfolio is not a risk factor considered in this decomposition.

Systematic-Residual Risk Decomposition

There are managers who seek to time the market or who intentionally make bets to create a different exposure than that of a market portfolio. Such managers would find it useful to decompose total excess risk into systematic risk and residual risk as shown in Figure 6. Unlike in the total risk decomposition approach just described, this view brings market risk into the analysis.

Residual risk in the systematic-residual risk decomposition is defined in a different way than residual risk is in the total risk decomposition. In the systematic-residual risk decomposition, residual risk is risk that is uncorrelated with the market portfolio. In turn, residual risk is partitioned into specific risk and common factor risk. Note that the partitioning of

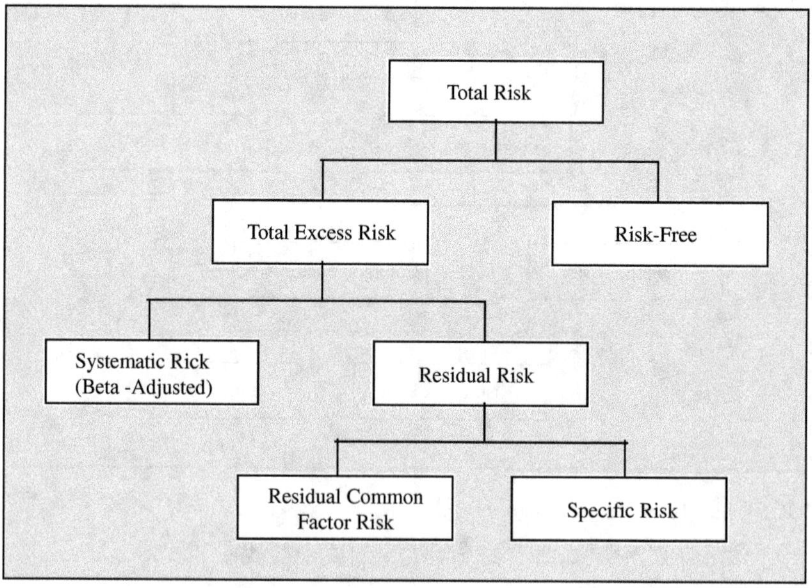

FIGURE 6: Systematic-Residual Risk Decomposition
Source: Barra [1998, p. 34, Figure 4.3]. Reprinted with permission.

risk described here is different from that in the Arbitrage Pricing Theory developed by Ross [1976]. In that model, all risk factors that could not be diversified away were referred to as "systematic risks". In our discussion here, risk factors that cannot be diversified away are classified as market risk and common factor risk. Residual risk can be diversified to a negligible level.

Active Risk Decomposition

Asset managers need to assess a portfolio's risk exposure and actual performance relative to a benchmark index is explained. The active risk decomposition approach is useful for that purpose. In this type of decomposition, shown in Figure 7, the total excess return is divided into benchmark risk and active risk. Benchmark risk is defined as the risk associated with the benchmark portfolio.

Active risk is the risk that results from the manager's attempt to generate a return that will outperform the benchmark. The active risk is further partitioned into common factor risk and specific risk.

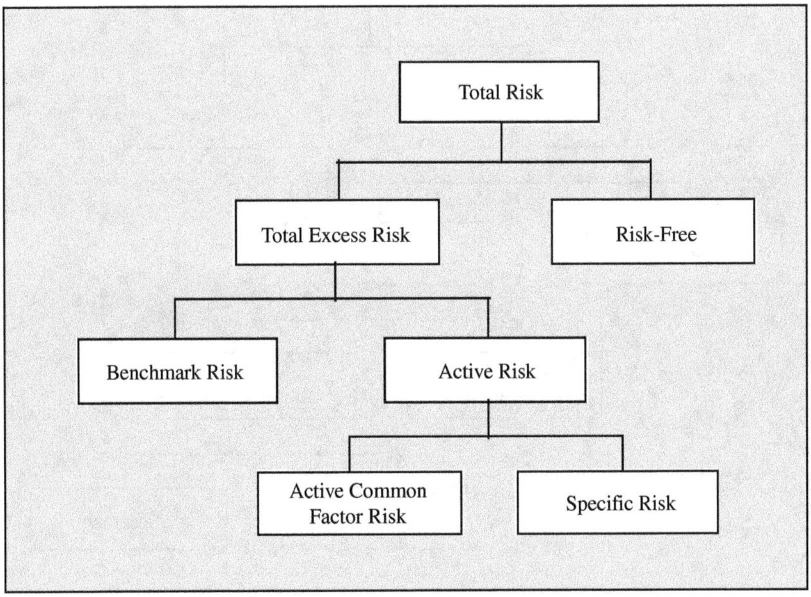

FIGURE 7: Active Risk Decomposition

Source: Barra [1998, p. 34, Figure 4.4]. Reprinted with permission.

Active Systematic-Active Residual Risk Decomposition

There are asset managers who overlay a market-timing strategy on their stock selection. That is, they not only try to select stocks they believe will outperform but also try to time the purchase of the acquisition. For an asset manager who pursues such a strategy, it will be important in evaluating performance to separate market risk from common factor risks. In the active risk decomposition approach just discussed, there is no market risk identified as one of the risk factors.

Since market risk (that is, systematic risk) is an element of active risk, its inclusion as a source of risk is preferred by managers. When market risk is included, we have the active systematic-active residual risk decomposition approach shown in Figure 8. Total excess risk is again divided into benchmark risk and active risk. However, active risk is further divided into active

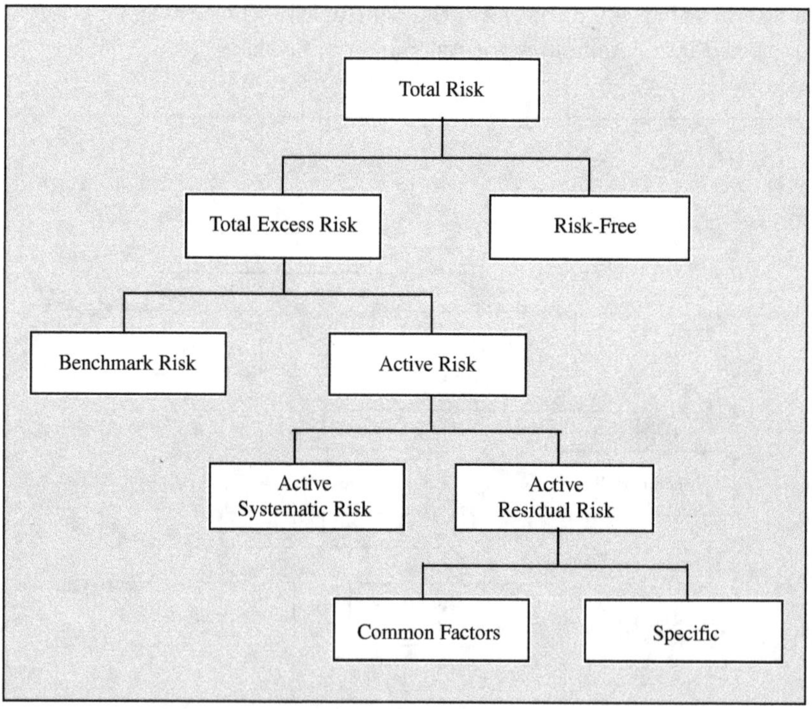

FIGURE 8: Active Systematic-Active Residual Risk Decomposition
Source: Barra [1998, p. 37, Figure 4.5]. Reprinted with permission.

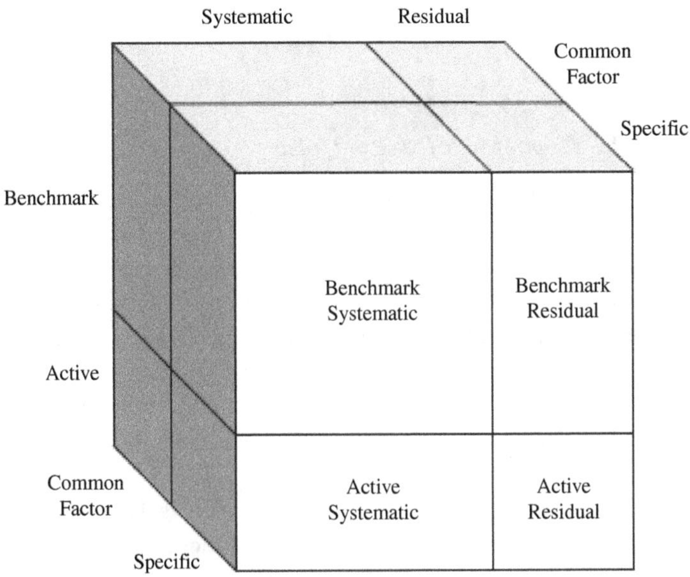

FIGURE 9: Risk Decomposition Overview
Source: Barra [1998, p. 38, Figure 4.6]. Reprinted with permission.

systematic risk (that is, active market risk) and active residual risk. Then active residual risk is divided into common factor risks and specific risk.

Summary of Risk Decomposition

The four approaches to risk decomposition are just different ways of slicing up risk to help a portfolio manager in constructing and controlling the risk of a portfolio and for a client to understand how the portfolio manager performed. Figure 9 provides an overview of the four approaches to carving up risk into specific and common factor, systematic and residual, and benchmark and active risks.

Applications in Portfolio Construction and Risk Control

The power of a fundamental factor model is that given the risk factors and the risk factor sensitivities, a portfolio's risk exposure profile can be quantified and controlled. The following three examples show how this can be done so that a portfolio manager can avoid making unintended bets by (1) assessing the exposure of a portfolio, (2) controlling risk against a stock market index, and (3) tilting a portfolio. In the examples, we use the Barra E3 factor model.[4]

Assessing the Exposure of a Portfolio

A fundamental multifactor risk model can be used to assess whether the current portfolio is consistent with a manager's strengths. Table 2 is a list of the top 15 holdings of Portfolio ABC as of September 30, 2000. Table 3 is a risk-return report for the same portfolio. The portfolio had a total market value of over $3.7 billion, 202 holdings, and a predicted beta of 1.20. The risk report also shows that the portfolio had an active risk of 9.83%. This is its tracking error with respect to the benchmark, the S&P 500. Note that over 80% of the active risk variance (which is 96.67) comes from the common factor risk variance (which is 81.34), and only a small proportion comes from the stock-specific risk variance (which is 15.33). Clearly, the manager of this portfolio has placed fairly large factor bets.

Panel A of Table 4 assesses the factor risk exposures of Portfolio ABC relative to those of the S&P 500, its benchmark. The first column shows the exposures of the portfolio (Mgd), and the second column shows the exposures for the benchmark (Bmk). The last column shows the active exposure (Act), which is the difference between the portfolio exposure and the benchmark exposure. The exposures to the risk index factors are measured in units of standard deviation, while the exposures to the industry factors are measured in percentages. The portfolio has a high active exposure to the momentum risk index factor. That is, the stocks held in the portfolio have significant momentum. The portfolio's stocks were smaller than the benchmark average in terms of market cap. The industry factor exposures reveal that the portfolio had an exceptionally high active exposure to the semiconductor industry and electronic equipment industry. Panel B of Table 4 combines the industry exposures to obtain sector exposures. It shows that Portfolio ABC had a very high active exposure to the technology sector. Such large bets can expose the portfolio to large swings in returns.

An important use of such risk reports is the identification of portfolio bets, both explicit and implicit. If, for example, the manager of Portfolio

[4]The illustrations were created by Varadharaj, Fabozzi, and Jones based on applications suggested by Barra [1998].

TABLE 2: Portfolio ABC's Holdings (Only the Top 15 Holdings Shown)

Portfolio:	**ABC Fund**		**Benchmark:**	**S&P500**		**Model date:**	**2000-10-02**
Report date:	**2000-10-15**		**Price date:**	**2000-09-29**		**Model:**	**US Equity 3**

Name	**Shares**	**Price ($)**	**Weight (%)**	**Beta**	**Main Industry Name**	**Sector**
General Elec. Co.	2,751,200	57.81	4.28	0.89	Financial Services	Financial
Citigroup, Inc.	2,554,666	54.06	3.72	0.98	Banks	Financial
Cisco Sys., Inc.	2,164,000	55.25	3.22	1.45	Computer Hardware	Technology
EMC Corp. Mass.	1,053,600	99.50	2.82	1.19	Computer Hardware	Technology
Intel Corp.	2,285,600	41.56	2.56	1.65	Semiconductors	Technology
Nortel Networks Corp. N	1,548,600	60.38	2.52	1.40	Electronic Equipment	Technology
Corning, Inc.	293,200	297.50	2.35	1.31	Electronic Equipment	Technology
International Business	739,000	112.50	2.24	1.05	Computer Software	Technology
Oracle Corp.	955,600	78.75	2.03	1.40	Computer Software	Technology
Sun Microsystems, Inc.	624,700	116.75	1.96	1.30	Computer Hardware	Technology
Lehman Bros. Hldgs. Inc.	394,700	148.63	1.58	1.51	Sec. & Asset Management	Financial
Morgan Stanley Dean Wi.	615,400	91.44	1.52	1.29	Sec. & Asset Management	Financial
Disney Walt Co.	1,276,700	38.25	1.32	0.85	Entertainment	Cnsmr. Services
Coca-Cola Co.	873,900	55.13	1.30	0.68	Food & Beverage	Cnsmr. (non-cyc.)
Microsoft Corp.	762,245	60.31	1.24	1.35	Computer Software	Technology

TABLE 3: Portfolio ABC's Risk-Return Decomposition

Risk-Return			
Number of assets	202	Total shares	$62,648,570
		Average share price	$59.27
Portfolio beta	1.20	Portfolio value	$3,713,372,229.96

Risk Decomposition	**Variance**	**Standard Deviation (%)**
Active specific risk	15.33	3.92
Active common factor		
Risk indexes	44.25	6.65
Industries	17.82	4.22
Covariance	19.27	
Total active common factor risk[a]	81.34	9.02
Total active[b]	96.67	9.83
Benchmark	247.65	15.74
Total risk	441.63	21.02

Notes: [a]Equal to risk indexes + Industries + Covariances.
[b]Equal to active specific risk + Total active common factor risk.

ABC did not want to place such a large technology sector bet or momentum risk index bet, then she can rebalance the portfolio to minimize any such bets.

Controlling Risk Against a Stock Market Index

The objective of equity indexing is to match the performance of some specified stock market index with little tracking error. To do this, the risk profile of the indexed portfolio must match the risk profile of the designated stock market index. Put in other terms, the factor risk exposure of the indexed portfolio must match as closely as possible the exposure of the designated stock market index to the same factors. Any differences in the factor risk exposures result in tracking error. Identification of any differences allows the indexer to rebalance the portfolio to reduce tracking error.

To illustrate this, suppose that an index manager has constructed a portfolio of 50 stocks to match the S&P 500. Table 5 shows output of the exposure to the Barra risk indexes and industry groups of the 50-stock portfolio and the S&P 500. The last column in the table shows the difference in the exposure. The differences are very small except for the

TABLE 4: Analysis of Portfolio ABC's Exposures

Factor Exposures

Risk Index Exposures (std. dev.)	Mgd	Bmk	Act
A. Analysis of Risk Exposures to S&P 500			
Volatility	0.220	−0.171	0.391
Momentum	0.665	−0.163	0.828
Size	−0.086	0.399	−0.485
Size Nonlinearity	0.031	0.097	−0.067
Trading Activity	0.552	−0.083	0.635
Growth	0.227	−0.167	0.395
Earnings Yield	−0.051	0.081	−0.132
Value	−0.169	−0.034	−0.136
Earnings Variation	0.058	−0.146	0.204
Leverage	0.178	−0.149	0.327
Currency Sensitivity	0.028	−0.049	−0.077
Yield	−0.279	0.059	−0.338
Non-EST Universe	0.032	0.000	0.032
Industry Weights (percent)			
Mining and Metals	0.013	0.375	−0.362
Gold	0.000	0.119	−0.119
Forestry and Paper	0.198	0.647	−0.449
Chemicals	0.439	2.386	−1.947
Energy Reserves	2.212	4.589	−2.377
Oil Refining	0.582	0.808	−0.226
Oil Services	2.996	0.592	2.404
Food & Beverages	2.475	3.073	−0.597
Alcohol	0.000	0.467	−0.467
Tobacco	0.000	0.403	−0.403
Home Products	0.000	1.821	−1.821
Grocery Stores	0.000	0.407	−0.407
Consumer Durables	0.165	0.125	0.039
Motor Vehicles and Parts	0.000	0.714	−0.714
Apparel and Textiles	0.000	0.191	−0.191
Clothing Stores	0.177	0.308	−0.131
Specialty Retail	0.445	2.127	−1.681
Department Stores	0.000	2.346	−2.346
Construction Real Property	0.569	0.204	0.364

(*Continued*)

TABLE 4: (*Continued*)

Industry Weights (percent)			
	Mgd	**Bmk**	**Act**
Publishing	0.014	0.508	−0.494
Media	1.460	2.077	−0.617
Hotels	0.090	0.112	−0.022
Restaurants	0.146	0.465	−0.319
Entertainment	1.179	1.277	−0.098
Leisure	0.000	0.247	−0.247
Environmental Services	0.000	0.117	−0.117
Heavy Electrical Equipment	1.438	1.922	−0.483
Heavy Machinery	0.000	0.062	−0.062
Industrial Parts	0.234	1.086	−0.852
Electric Utility	1.852	1.967	−0.115
Gas Utilities	0.370	0.272	0.098
Railroads	0.000	0.211	−0.211
Airlines	0.143	0.194	−0.051
Truck/Sea/Air Freight	0.000	0.130	−0.130
Medical Services	1.294	0.354	0.940
Medical Products	0.469	2.840	−2.370
Drugs	6.547	8.039	−1.492
Electronic Equipment	11.052	5.192	5.860
Semiconductors	17.622	6.058	11.564
Computer Hardware	12.057	9.417	2.640
Computer Software	9.374	6.766	2.608
Defense and Aerospace	0.014	0.923	−0.909
Telephone	0.907	4.635	−3.728
Wireless Telecom.	0.000	1.277	−1.277
Information Services	0.372	1.970	−1.598
Industrial Services	0.000	0.511	−0.511
Life/Health Insurance	0.062	1.105	−1.044
Property/Casualty Ins.	1.069	2.187	−1.118
Banks	5.633	6.262	−0.630
Thrifts	1.804	0.237	1.567
Securities and Asst. Mgmt.	6.132	2.243	3.888
Financial Services	5.050	5.907	−0.857
Internet	3.348	1.729	1.618
Equity REIT	0.000	0.000	0.000
B. Analysis of Sector Exposures Relative to S&P 500 Sector Weights (percent)			
Basic Materials	0.65	3.53	−2.88
Mining	0.01	0.38	−0.36
Gold	0.00	0.12	−0.12
Forest	0.20	0.65	−0.45
Chemical	0.44	2.39	−1.95

TABLE 4: (*Continued*)

	Mgd	Bmk	Act
Energy	5.79	5.99	−0.20
Energy Reserves	2.21	4.59	−2.38
Oil Refining	0.58	0.81	−0.23
Oil Services	3.00	0.59	2.40
Consumer (non-cyclical)	2.48	6.17	−3.70
Food/Beverage	2.48	3.07	−0.60
Alcohol	0.00	0.47	−0.47
Tobacco	0.00	0.40	−0.40
Home Prod.	0.00	1.82	−1.82
Grocery	0.00	0.41	−0.41
Consumer {cyclical}	1.36	6.01	−4.66
Consumer Durables	0.17	0.13	0.04
Motor Vehicles	0.00	0.71	−0.71
Apparel	0.00	0.19	−0.19
Clothing	0.18	0.31	−0.13
Specialty Retail	0.45	2.13	−1.68
Dept. Store	0.00	2.35	−2.35
Construction	0.57	0.20	0.36
Consumer Services	2.89	4.69	−1.80
Publishing	0.01	0.51	−0.49
Media	1.46	2.08	−0.62
Hotels	0.09	0.11	−0.02
Restaurants	0.15	0.47	−0.32
Entertainment	1.18	1.28	−0.10
Leisure	0.00	0.25	−0.25
Industrials	1.67	3.19	−1.51
Env. Services	0.00	0.12	−0.12
Heavy Electrical	1.44	1.92	−0.48
Heavy Machinery	0.00	0.06	−0.06
Industrial Parts	0.23	1.09	−0.85
C. Analysis of Sector Exposures Relative to S&P 500			
Utility	2.22	2.24	−0.02
Electric Utility	1.85	1.97	−0.12
Gas Utility	0.37	0.27	0.10
Transport	0.14	0.54	−0.39
Railroad	0.00	0.21	−0.21
Airlines	0.14	0.19	−0.05
Truck Freight	0.00	0.13	−0.13
HealthCare	8.31	11.23	−2.92
Medical Provider	1.29	0.35	0.94
Medical Products	0.47	2.84	−2.37
Drugs	6.55	8.04	−1.49

(*Continued*)

TABLE 4: (*Continued*)

	Mgd	Bmk	Act
Technology	53.47	30.09	23.38
Electronic Equipment	11.05	5.19	5.86
Semiconductors	17.62	6.06	11.56
Computer Hardware	12.06	9.42	2.64
Computer Software	9.37	6.77	2.61
Defense & Aerospace	0.01	0.92	−0.91
Internet	3.35	1.73	1.62
Telecommunications	0.91	5.91	−5.00
Telephone	0.91	4.63	−3.73
Wireless	0.00	1.28	−1.28
Commercial Services	0.37	2.48	−2.11
Information Services	0.37	1.97	−1.60
Industrial Services	0.00	0.51	−0.51
Financial	19.75	17.94	1.81
Life Insurance	0.06	1.11	−1.04
Property Insurance	1.07	2.19	−1.12
Banks	5.63	6.26	−0.63
Thrifts	1.80	0.24	1.57
Securities/Asst. Mgmt.	6.23	2.24	3.89
Financial Services	5.05	5.91	−0.86
Equity REIT	0.00	0.00	0.00

Note: Mgd = Managed; Bmk = Benchmark; Act = Active, which is Managed − Benchmark.

exposures to the size factor and one industry (equity REIT). That is, the 50-stock portfolio has more exposure to the size risk index and equity REIT industry.

The illustration in Table 5 uses price data as of December 31, 2001. It demonstrates how a fundamental factor model can be combined with an optimization model to construct an indexed portfolio when a given number of holdings are sought. Specifically, the portfolio analyzed in Table 4 is the result of an application in which the manager wants a portfolio constructed that matches the S&P 500 with only 50 stocks and that minimizes tracking error. Not only is the 50-stock portfolio constructed, but the optimization model combined with the factor model indicates that the tracking error is only 2.19%. Since this is the optimal 50-stock portfolio to replicate the S&P 500 that minimizes tracking error risk, this tells the index manager who seeks a lower tracking error that more stocks must be held. Note, however, that the optimal portfolio changes as time passes and prices move.

TABLE 5: Factor Exposures of a 50-Stock Portfolio that Optimally Matches the S&P 500

Risk Index Exposures (std. dev.)			
	Mgd	**Bmk**	**Act**
Volatility	−0.141	−0.084	−0.057
Momentum	−0.057	−0.064	0.007
Size	0.588	0.370	0.217
Size Nonlinearity	0.118	0.106	0.013
Trading Activity	−0.101	−0.005	−0.097
Growth	−0.008	−0.045	0.037
Earnings Yield	0.103	0.034	0.069
Value	−0.072	−0.070	−0.003
Earnings Variation	−0.058	−0.088	0.029
Leverage	−0.206	−0.106	−0.100
Currency Sensitivity	−0.001	−0.012	0.012
Yield	0.114	0.034	0.080
Non-EST Universe	0.000	0.000	0.000
Industry Weights (percent)			
Mining and Metals	0.000	0.606	−0.606
Gold	0.000	0.161	−0.161
Forestry and Paper	1.818	0.871	0.947
Chemicals	2.360	2.046	0.314
Energy Reserves	5.068	4.297	0.771
Oil Refining	1.985	1.417	0.568
Oil Services	1.164	0.620	0.544
Food and Beverages	2.518	3.780	−1.261
Alcohol	0.193	0.515	−0.322
Tobacco	1.372	0.732	0.641
Home Products	0.899	2.435	−1.536
Grocery Stores	0.000	0.511	−0.511
Consumer Durables	0.000	0.166	−0.166
Motor Vehicles and Parts	0.000	0.621	−0.621
Apparel and Textiles	0.000	0.373	−0.373
Clothing Stores	0.149	0.341	−0.191
Specialty Retail	1.965	2.721	−0.756
Department Stores	4.684	3.606	1.078
Construction and Real Property	0.542	0.288	0.254
Publishing	2.492	0.778	1.713
Media	1.822	1.498	0.323
Hotels	1.244	0.209	1.035
Restaurants	0.371	0.542	−0.171
Entertainment	2.540	1.630	0.910
Leisure	0.000	0.409	−0.409

(*Continued*)

TABLE 5: (*Continued*)

	Mgd	Bmk	Act
Environmental Services	0.000	0.220	−0.220
Heavy Electrical Equipment	1.966	1.949	0.017
Heavy Machinery	0.000	0.141	−0.141
Industrial Parts	1.124	1.469	−0.345
Electric Utility	0.000	1.956	−1.956
Gas Utilities	0.000	0.456	−0.456
Railroads	0.000	0.373	−0.373
Airlines	0.000	0.206	−0.206
Truck/Sea/Air Freight	0.061	0.162	−0.102
Medical Services	1.280	0.789	0.491
Medical Products	3.540	3.599	−0.059
Drugs	9.861	10.000	−0.140
Electronic Equipment	0.581	1.985	−1.404
Semiconductors	4.981	4.509	0.472
Computer Hardware	4.635	4.129	0.506
Computer Software	6.893	6.256	0.637
Defense and Aerospace	1.634	1.336	0.297
Telephone	3.859	3.680	0.180
Wireless Telecom	1.976	1.565	0.411
Information Services	0.802	2.698	−1.896
Industrial Services	0.806	0.670	0.136
Life/Health Insurance	0.403	0.938	−0.535
Property/Casualty Ins.	2.134	2.541	−0.407
Banks	8.369	7.580	0.788
Thrifts	0.000	0.362	−0.362
Securities and Asset Mgmt.	2.595	2.017	0.577
Financial Services	6.380	6.321	0.059
Internet	0.736	0.725	0.011
Equity REIT	2.199	0.193	2.006

Note: Mgd = Managed; Bmk = S&P 500 (the benchmark); Act = Active, which is Managed − Benchmark.

Tilting a Portfolio

Now let's look at how an active manager can construct a portfolio to make intentional bets. Suppose that an asset manager seeks to construct a portfolio that generates superior returns relative to the S&P 500 by tilting it toward low P/E stocks. At the same time, the manager does not want to increase tracking error significantly. An obvious approach may seem to be to identify all the stocks in the universe that have a lower than average P/E. The problem with this approach is that it introduces unintentional bets with respect to the other risk indexes.

Instead, an optimization method combined with a fundamental factor model can be used to construct the desired portfolio. The necessary inputs to this process are the tilt exposure sought and the benchmark stock market index. Additional constraints can be placed, for example, on the number of stocks to be included in the portfolio. An optimization model can handle additional specifications such as forecasts of expected returns or alphas on the individual stocks.

In our illustration, the tilt exposure sought is towards low P/E stocks, that is, towards high earnings yield stocks (since earnings yield is the inverse of P/E). The benchmark is the S&P 500. We seek a portfolio that has an average earnings yield that is at least 0.5 standard deviations more than that of the earnings yield of the benchmark. We do not place any limit on the number of stocks to be included in the portfolio. We also do not want the active exposure to any other risk index factor (other than earnings yield) to be more than 0.1 standard deviations in magnitude. This way we avoid placing unintended bets. While we do not report the holdings of the optimal portfolio here, Table 6 provides an analysis of that portfolio by comparing the risk exposure to that of the S&P 500.

Key Points

- Multifactor risk models fall into two categories: forecasting expected return models and forecasting risk models.
- In quantitative-oriented equity portfolio management, multifactor risk models are typically used to construct and rebalance a portfolio.
- A key measure used in portfolio construction is tracking error. Tracking error quantifies the variation of a portfolio's active return (i.e., the difference between the return on the portfolio and the return on the benchmark index).
- Tracking error is the standard deviation of the active returns.
- The five major factors that affect the level of tracking error are (1) number of stocks in the portfolio, (2) portfolio market capitalization and style difference relative to the benchmark, (3) sector deviation from the benchmark, (4) market volatility, and (5) portfolio beta.
- There are two types of tracking error: backward-looking and forward-looking tracking error.
- Backward-looking tracking is calculated from the actual returns realized from a portfolio.

TABLE 6: Factor Exposures of a Portfolio Tilted towards Earnings Yield

Risk Index Exposure (std. dev.)			
	Mgd	**Bmk**	**Act**
Volatility	−0.126	−0.084	−0.042
Momentum	0.013	−0.064	0.077
Size	0.270	0.370	−0.100
Size Nonlinearity	0.067	0.106	−0.038
Trading Activity	0.095	−0.005	0.100
Growth	−0.023	−0.045	0.022
Earnings Yield	0.534	0.034	0.500
Value	0.030	−0.070	0.100
Earnings Variation	−0.028	−0.088	0.060
Leverage	−0.006	−0.106	0.100
Currency Sensitivity	−0.105	−0.012	−0.093
Yield	0.134	0.034	0.100
Non-EST Universe	0.000	0.000	0.000

Industry Weights (percent)			
	Mgd	**Bmk**	**Act**
Mining and Metals	0.022	0.606	−0.585
Gold	0.000	0.161	−0.161
Forestry and Paper	0.000	0.871	−0.871
Chemicals	1.717	2.046	−0.329
Energy Reserves	4.490	4.297	0.193
Oil Refining	3.770	1.417	2.353
Oil Services	0.977	0.620	0.357
Food and Beverages	0.823	3.780	−2.956
Alcohol	0.365	0.515	−0.151
Tobacco	3.197	0.732	2.465
Home Products	0.648	2.435	−1.787
Grocery Stores	0.636	0.511	0.125
Consumer Durables	0.000	0.166	−0.166
Motor Vehicles and Parts	0.454	0.621	−0.167
Apparel and Textiles	0.141	0.373	−0.232
Clothing Stores	0.374	0.341	0.033
Specialty Retail	0.025	2.721	−2.696
Department Stores	3.375	3.606	−0.231
Construction and Real Property	9.813	0.288	9.526
Publishing	0.326	0.778	−0.452
Media	0.358	1.498	−1.140
Hotels	0.067	0.209	−0.141
Restaurants	0.000	0.542	−0.542
Entertainment	0.675	1.630	−0.955
Leisure	0.000	0.409	−0.409

TABLE 6: (*Continued*)

	Mgd	Bmk	Act
Environmental Services	0.000	0.220	−0.220
Heavy Electrical Equipment	1.303	1.949	−0.647
Heavy Machinery	0.000	0.141	−0.141
Industrial Parts	1.366	1.469	−0.103
Electric Utility	4.221	1.956	2.265
Gas Utilities	0.204	0.456	−0.252
Railroads	0.185	0.373	−0.189
Airlines	0.000	0.206	−0.206
Truck/sea/Air Freight	0.000	0.162	−0.162
Medical Services	0.000	0.789	−0.789
Medical Products	1.522	3.599	−2.077
Drugs	7.301	10.000	−2.699
Electronic Equipment	0.525	1.985	−1.460
Semiconductors	3.227	4.509	−1.282
Computer Hardware	2.904	4.129	−1.224
Computer Software	7.304	6.256	1.048
Defense and Aerospace	1.836	1.336	0.499
Telephone	6.290	3.680	2.610
Wireless Telecom	2.144	1.565	0.580
Information Services	0.921	2.698	−1.777
Industrial Services	0.230	0.670	−0.440
Life/Health Insurance	1.987	0.938	1.048
Property/Casualty Ins.	4.844	2.541	2.304
Banks	8.724	7.580	1.144
Thrifts	0.775	0.362	0.413
Securities and Asset Mgmt	3.988	2.017	1.971
Financial Services	5.510	6.321	−0.811
Internet	0.434	0.725	−0.291
Equity REIT	0.000	0.193	−0.193

Note: Mgd = Managed; Bmk = S&P 500 (the benchmark); Act = Active, which is Managed − Benchmark.

- A major drawback of backward-looking tracking error is that it does not reflect the effect of current decisions by the portfolio manager on the future active returns and hence may be misleading if the portfolio manager has significantly rebalanced the portfolio.
- Forward-looking tracking error is the estimated future tracking error of the current portfolio.
- There are four approaches that can be used to decompose a portfolio's risk: total risk decomposition, systematic-residual risk decomposition, active risk decomposition, and active systematic-active residual risk decomposition.

- In all of these approaches to risk decomposition, the total return is first divided into the risk-free return and the total excess return.
- Total excess return is the difference between the actual return realized by the portfolio and the risk-free return.
- The risk associated with the total excess return is called total excess risk and is further partitioned using four approaches.
- The four approaches to risk decomposition are just different ways of slicing up risk to help a portfolio manager in constructing and controlling the risk of a portfolio and for a client to understand how the portfolio manager performed.
- In a fundamental factor model, company and industry attributes and market data are used as "descriptors" to identify which are statistically significant in explaining stock returns.
- Examples of descriptors are earnings/price ratios, book/price ratios, estimated earnings growth, and trading activity.
- The descriptors that are found to be statistically significant are then grouped into "factors" or "risk indexes" so as to capture related company attributes.
- For example, descriptors such as market leverage, book leverage, debt-to-equity ratio, and company's debt rating are combined to obtain a factor referred to as "leverage".
- A fundamental multifactor risk model can be used to assess the exposure of a portfolio, control risk against a stock market index, and tilt a portfolio.

References

Barra, 1998. *Risk Model Handbook for United States Equity: Version 3.* Berkeley, CA.

Rosenberg, B., and J. Guy, 1976. "Prediction of beta from investment fundamentals," *Financial Analysts Journal*, July-August: 62–70.

Rosenberg, B., and V. Marathe, 1976. "Common factors in security returns: Microeconomic determinants and macroeconomic correlates," University of California Institute of Business and Economic Research, Research Program in Finance, Working paper No. 44.

Vardharaj, R., F. J. Fabozzi, and F. J. Jones, 2004. "Determinants of tracking error for equity portfolios," *Journal of Investing*, 13(2): 37–47.

Chapter 16

Managing a Bond Portfolio Using a Multifactor Risk Model

Learning Objectives

After reading this chapter, you will understand:

- how multifactor risk models can be used by bond portfolio managers to assess a portfolio's risk relative to a benchmark and reconstruct or rebalance a portfolio if the risk exposures are unacceptable;
- what is meant by the contribution to portfolio duration and contribution benchmark duration;
- what spread duration is;
- how optionality risk is handled in a multifactor risk model;
- the risk factors associated with investing in mortgage-backed securities;
- how multifactor risk models decompose a portfolio's systematic risk into term structure factor risk and non-term structure risk;
- why there is non-systematic risk in a bond portfolio;
- the use of an optimizer in a multifactor risk model; and
- how an optimizer can be used by an asset manager to structure a portfolio so as to incorporate a market view.

Introduction

In Chapter 15, we demonstrated how a fundamental multifactor risk model can be used in common stock portfolio management. In this chapter, we explain and illustrate how a multifactor risk model can be used in bond portfolio management. These models allow a bond portfolio manager to assess the portfolio's risk relative to a benchmark and reconstruct or rebalance a portfolio if the risk exposures are unacceptable.

Risk Characteristics of the Portfolio Relative to the Benchmark

In our illustration, we use an actual bond portfolio consisting of 40 bond issues. The bond issues are shown in Table 1. The last column of the table shows the percentage (weight) of each issue in terms of market value as of September 17, 2008. Table 2 provides the breakdown of the portfolio by sector. The benchmark used in this illustration is the Barclays US Aggregate Index (now called the Bloomberg Barclays US Aggregate Index). The last column of the table shows the difference by sector between the portfolio and the benchmark. A negative sign indicates an underweighting of the sector in the portfolio relative to the benchmark; a positive sign indicates an overweighting of the sector in the portfolio relative to the benchmark. As can be seen, this portfolio is underweighted in all sectors except for the financial sector and the mortgage sector (i.e., agency pass-through securities).

The allocation of the portfolio by credit quality is reported in Table 3, which also shows the credit quality of the benchmark. "MBS" credit means the exposure to agency MBS. The portfolio has only exposure to MBS issued by Fannie Mae and Freddie Mac, while the benchmark includes exposure to all three issuers in the mortgage sector: Ginnie Mae, Fannie Mae, and Freddie Mac. Because of the substantial exposure to the mortgage sector, it is important to understand the allocation within this sector compared to the benchmark. The MBS sectors are shown in terms of coupon rate and type.

The duration for the 40-bond portfolio and the benchmark is 5.56 and 4.84, respectively. Table 4 shows the duration by sector for the portfolio and the benchmark. Using the information about the weight of each sector and its duration, the contribution to portfolio duration and contribution duration can be computed. The contribution to portfolio duration is the amount that a bond holding in a portfolio adds to the duration of a portfolio. The contribution to benchmark duration is the amount that a bond in the index adds to the duration of a benchmark.

For example, consider the mortgage sector. This sector is 64.78% of the portfolio and 37.17% of the benchmark. The durations are 5.65 and 5.23 for the portfolio and benchmark, respectively. Therefore, the contributions

TABLE 1: 40-Bond Portfolio as of September 17, 2008

CUSIP	Issuer Name	Coupon	Maturity	Moody's	S&P	Sector	Market Value (%)
FGB06006	FHLM Gold Guar Single F.	6	3/1/2036	AAA	AAA	FHb	9.29
FNA05005	FNMA Conventional Long T.	5	2/1/2035	AAA	AAA	FNa	8.84
FNA05407	FNMA Conventional Long T.	5.5	5/1/2037	AAA	AAA	FNa	8.46
FNA05405	FNMA Conventional Long T.	5.5	3/1/2035	AAA	AAA	FNa	8.33
FGB05005	FHLM Gold Guar Single F.	5	2/1/2035	AAA	AAA	FHb	7.67
002824AT	ABBOTT LABORATORIES-GLOBA	5.875	5/15/2016	A1	AA	IND	6.18
FNA06006	FNMA Conventional Long T.	6	4/1/2036	AAA	AAA	FNa	6.15
912828CT	US TREASURY NOTES	4.25	8/15/2014	AAA	AAA	UST	6.11
FNA05403	FNMA Conventional Long T.	5.5	8/1/2032	AAA	AAA	FNa	6.03
060505DP	BANK OF AMERICA CORP	5.75	12/1/2017	AA2	AA	FIN	5.73
172967CQ	CITIGROUP INC-GLOBAL	5	9/15/2014	A1	A+	FIN	5.16
FNA06007	FNMA Conventional Long T.	6	6/1/2037	AAA	AAA	FNa	5.12
FNA05003	FNMA Conventional Long T.	5	9/1/2032	AAA	AAA	FNa	4.90
912828BH	US TREASURY NOTES	4.25	8/15/2013	AAA	AAA	UST	1.60
912828BR	US TREASURY NOTES	4.25	11/15/2013	AAA	AAA	UST	1.56
912828CA	US TREASURY NOTES	4	2/15/2014	AAA	AAA	UST	1.42
912828CJ	US TREASURY NOTES	4.75	5/15/2014	AAA	AAA	UST	1.39
912828DC	US TREASURY NOTES	4.25	11/15/2014	AAA	AAA	UST	1.27
912828DM	US TREASURY NOTES	4	2/15/2015	AAA	AAA	UST	1.24
912828DV	US TREASURY NOTES	4.125	5/15/2015	AAA	AAA	UST	1.22
31359MJH	FEDERAL NATL MTG ASSN-GLO	6	5/15/2011	AAA	AAA	USA	0.20
31359MFG	FEDERAL NATL MTG ASSN-GLO	7.25	1/15/2010	AAA	AAA	USA	0.19
31359MEY	FEDERAL NATL MTG ASSN	6.625	9/15/2009	AAA	AAA	USA	0.18
3134A35H	FEDERAL HOME LN MTG CORP-	6.875	9/15/2010	AAA	NR	USA	0.15
31359MEV	FEDERAL NATL MTG ASSN-GLO	6.375	6/15/2009	AAA	AAA	USA	0.15

(*Continued*)

TABLE 1: (*Continued*)

CUSIP	Issuer Name	Coupon	Maturity	Moody's	S&P	Sector	Market Value (%)
3137EAAT	FEDERAL HOME LN MTG CORP-	5	6/11/2009	AAA	AAA	USA	0.13
369604AY	GENERAL ELECTRIC CO-GLOBA	5	2/1/2013	AAA	AAA	IND	0.13
369604BC	GENERAL ELECTRIC CO-GLOBA	5.25	12/6/2017	AAA	AAA	IND	0.10
36962GYY	GENERAL ELECTRIC CAPITAL-	6	6/15/2012	AAA	AAA	FIN	0.09
17275RAC	CISCO SYSTEMS INC-GLOBAL	5.5	2/22/2016	A1	A+	IND	0.08
459200GJ	INTL BUSINESS MACHINES-GL	5.7	9/14/2017	A1	A+	IND	0.08
00209TAA	AT&T BROADBAND CORP - GLO	8.375	3/15/2013	BAA2	BBB+	IND	0.07
172967EM	CITIGROUP INC-GLOBAL	6.125	11/21/2017	AA3	AA−	FIN	0.07
22541LAB	CREDIT SUISSE FB USA INC	6.125	11/15/2011	AA1	AA−	FIN	0.07
437076AP	HOME DEPOT INC-GLOBAL	5.4	3/1/2016	BAA1	BBB+	IND	0.07
617446GM	MORGAN STANLEY DEAN WITTE	6.75	4/15/2011	A1	A+	FIN	0.07
61748AAE	MORGAN STANLEY DEAN WITTE	4.75	4/1/2014	A2	A	FIN	0.07
25152CMN	DEUTSCHE BANK AG	6	9/1/2017	AA1	AA−	FIN	0.06
78387GAP	SBC COMMUNICATIONS INC-GL	5.1	9/15/2014	A2	A	IND	0.06
233835AW	DAIMLER CHRYSLER NORTH AME	6.5	11/15/2013	A3	A−	IND	0.05
29078EAB	EMBARQ CORP	7.082	6/1/2016	BAA3	BBB−	IND	0.05
68402LAC	ORACLE CORP	5.25	1/15/2016	A2	A	IND	0.05
852061AD	SPRINT NEXTEL CORP	6	12/1/2016	BAA3	BB	IND	0.05
88732JAH	TIME WARNER CABLE INC-GLO	5.85	5/1/2017	BAA2	BBB+	IND	0.05
65332VBG	NEXTEL COMMUNICATIONS	7.375	8/1/2015	BAA3	BB	IND	0.04

TABLE 2: Sector Composition of Portfolio and Benchmark

Sector	% of Portfolio	% of Benchmark	Overweight (+)/ Underweight (−)
Treasury	15.81	22.66	−6.85
Agencies	1.00	10.12	−9.12
Financial institutions	11.27	7.83	3.44
Industrials	7.08	7.52	−0.44
Utilities	0.00	1.98	−1.98
Non-US credit	0.06	6.95	−6.89
Mortgage	64.78	37.17	27.61
Asset backed	0.00	0.79	−0.79
CMBS	0.00	4.98	−4.98
Totals	100.00	100.00	

TABLE 3: Credit Quality of the Portfolio and Benchmark

Credit Quality	% of Portfolio	% of Benchmark	Overweight (+)/ Underweight (−)
MBS	64.79	37.17	27.62
AAA	17.13	41.06	−23.93
AA	5.94	4.87	1.07
A	11.81	9.21	2.60
BAA	0.24	7.69	−7.45
BA	0.09	0.00	0.09
Totals	100.00	100.00	

TABLE 4: Duration and Contribution to Duration by Sector

	Portfolio			Benchmark			Difference	
Sector	% of Port.	Dur.	Cntrb. to Dur.	% of Port.	Dur.	Cntrb. to Dur.	% of Port.	Cntrb. to Dur.
Treasury	15.81	5.13	0.81	22.66	5.21	1.19	−6.85	−0.38
Agencies	1.00	1.40	0.01	10.12	3.98	0.35	−9.12	−0.34
Financial institutions	11.27	5.89	0.66	7.83	5.25	0.42	3.44	0.24
Industrials	7.08	6.00	0.42	7.52	6.48	0.49	−0.44	−0.07
Utilities	0.00	0.00	0.00	1.98	7.32	0.15	−1.98	−0.15
Non-US credit	0.06	6.88	0.00	6.95	5.90	0.41	−6.89	−0.41
Mortgage	64.78	5.65	3.66	37.17	5.23	1.58	27.61	2.08
Asset backed	0.00	0.00	0.00	0.79	3.15	0.02	−0.79	−0.02
CMBS	0.00	0.00	0.00	4.98	4.60	0.23	−4.98	−0.23
Totals	100.00		5.56	100.00		4.84		0.72

to durations are as follows:

$$\text{Contribution to portfolio duration} = 0.6478 \times 5.65 = 3.66,$$

and

$$\text{Contribution to benchmark duration} = 0.3717 \times 5.23 = 1.94.$$

Duration provides a measure of the exposure of a portfolio or a benchmark index to changes in the level of interest rates but fails to measure the exposure of a portfolio or a benchmark index to changes in the shape of the yield curve.[1] A simple way to get a feel for the yield curve risk exposure of a portfolio relative to a benchmark is by looking at the distribution of the present values of the cash flows for the portfolio and the benchmark index. Panel A of Table 5 shows the distribution of the difference in the present values of the cash flows for the 40-bond portfolio and for the Barclays US Aggregate Index. The difference seems to suggest that the portfolio is constructed like a bullet portfolio concentrated in the 5- to 10-year range.

A superior approach for assessing yield curve risk exposure is to determine the key rate durations of the portfolio and the benchmark. Key rate duration is the sensitivity of a portfolio's value to the change in a particular key spot rate. The specific maturities on the spot rate curve for which key rate durations are measured vary from vendor to vendor. The six key rate durations reported in panel B of Table 5 show the difference in key rate durations between the portfolio and the benchmark. It is clear that there is underweighting of the short and long end of the portfolio and overweighting of the 5-year and 10-year sectors.

The spread duration for a portfolio or a bond index is computed as a market weighted average of the spread duration for each sector. The difference in the spread duration by sector for the 40-bond portfolio and for the benchmark is shown in Table 6. Note that the spread duration is higher for the financial institutions and mortgage sectors and lower for every other sector.

Some corporate bonds and agency debentures have embedded options — call and put options. These options impact the performance of a portfolio and a benchmark. The adverse effect on performance resulting from these embedded options is referred to as optionality risk. The optionality risk exposure of a bond occurs because a change in interest rates changes the value of the embedded option, which, in turn changes the value of the bond.

[1] In Chapter 16 of the companion book, the various types of yield curve changes (i.e., shifts) are discussed.

TABLE 5: Estimating Yield Curve Risk Exposure Relative to Benchmark

A. Difference in Present Value of Cash Flow Structure (Portfolio — Benchmark)

Years	Difference (%)
0.00	0.181
0.25	0.569
0.50	0.363
0.75	0.849
1.00	−1.095
1.50	−3.958
2.00	−2.923
2.50	−2.343
3.00	−1.655
3.50	−1.518
4.00	−2.500
5.00	0.668
6.00	10.340
7.00	1.938
10.00	1.233
15.00	0.736
20.00	−0.013
25.00	−0.344
30.00	−0.505
40.00	−0.009

B. Difference in Key Rate Durations (Portfolio — Benchmark)

Years	Difference (%)
0.50	−0.003
2.00	−0.214
5.00	0.485
10.00	0.257
20.00	−0.185
30.00	−0.359

The same is true at the portfolio and benchmark levels. Optionality risk can be quantified using measures commonly used in option pricing. In option pricing theory, the delta of an option is an estimate of the sensitivity of the value of the option to changes in the price of the underlying instrument. For bonds, delta can be computed for each issue that has an embedded option and then these deltas can be aggregated to obtain an estimate of the delta for a portfolio or a benchmark.

Table 7 reports the delta of the 40-bond portfolio and the benchmark index, as well as the difference between the two. The percentage of the

TABLE 6: Difference in Contribution to Spread Duration by Sector

Sector	Difference
Treasury	−0.34
Agencies	−0.35
Financial institutions	0.36
Industrials	−0.04
Utilities	−0.14
Non-US credit	−0.38
Mortgage	0.98
Asset backed	−0.03
CMBS	−0.29

TABLE 7: Optionality Exposure for Benchmark

	Benchmark (excluding MBS)			Difference	
Option Delta	% of Port.	Delta	Cntrb. to Delta	% of Port.	Cntrb. to Delta
Bullet	41.48	0.0000	0.0000	−13.18	0.0000
Callable traded to maturity	14.62	0.0639	0.0093	−7.70	−0.0093
Callable traded to call	0.93	0.8354	0.0078	−0.93	−0.0078
Putable traded to maturity	0.02	0.2380	0.0000	−0.02	0.0000
Putable traded to put	0.02	0.4283	0.0001	−0.02	−0.0001
Totals	57.07		0.0172	−21.85	−0.0172

portfolio represents all holdings other than the mortgage sector. (Thus, the value of 35.22% for the portfolio is 100% minus the mortgage holdings of 64.78%.) Note that the holdings are partitioned in terms of the embedded option and how the securities trade. Bullet bonds do not have embedded options and, therefore, the delta for these bonds is zero. A security with an embedded call option is classified as trading either to its call date or to its maturity date, depending on its market price. In this context, "trading to" indicates that the price of the security is such that the market is pricing the security either as if it will be called or as if it will not be called. The same is true for securities with a put option — they are classified as either trading to the put date or trading to maturity.

The largest deviation of the hypothetical portfolio and the benchmark is in the mortgage sectors. The three major risks of investing in this sector are sector risk, prepayment risk, and convexity risk. The subsectors of the mortgage sector are generally based on the coupon rate. The motivation for using this classification is that the coupon rate relative to the prevailing mortgage rate has an impact on prepayments and therefore on the spread at which a pass-through security trades relative to Treasuries. In turn, prepayments impact how long the underlying mortgage pools have been outstanding. This characteristic is referred to as the seasoning of the underlying mortgage pool and can be classified as unseasoned, moderately seasoned, and seasoned. For the hypothetical portfolio, the difference in the contribution to duration between the 40-bond portfolio and the benchmark index is 1.31.

With respect to prepayment risk — the risk of an adverse price change due to changes in expected prepayments — the benchmark used for prepayments is the PSA prepayment benchmark.[2] One measure of prepayment risk is prepayment sensitivity which is the basis point change in the price of an MBS for a 1% increase in prepayments. For example, suppose that for some mortgage product at 300 PSA, the price is 110.08. A 1% increase in the PSA prepayment rate means that the PSA increases from 300 PSA to 303 PSA. Suppose that, at 303 PSA, the price is recomputed using a valuation model and found to be 110.00. Therefore, the price decline is −0.08, in terms of basis points, −8, so that the prepayment sensitivity is −8.

Some mortgage products increase in value when prepayments increase and some products decrease in value when prepayments increase. Examples of the former are pass-through securities trading at a discount (i.e., pass-through securities whose coupon rate is less than the prevailing mortgage rate) and principal-only mortgage strips. These securities have positive prepayment sensitivity. Examples of mortgage products that decrease in value when prepayments increase are pass-through securities trading at a premium (i.e., pass-through securities whose coupon rate is greater than the prevailing mortgage rate) and interest-only mortgage strips. These securities have negative prepayment sensitivity. A portfolio manager can compute the risk exposure in terms of the difference in the contribution to prepayment sensitivity for the 40-bond portfolio and the benchmark. For the 40-bond portfolio, it is 0.34.

Finally, let's look at the third risk by investing in the mortgage sector: convexity risk. The sector of the mortgage market that tends to exhibit negative convexity is pass-through securities. Consequently, a portfolio

[2]This benchmark for prepayments is discussed in Chapter 3.

manager should assess the convexity of a portfolio compared to the benchmark index. A portfolio manager's allocation to the mortgage sector might be the same as that of the benchmark index with the same effective duration, and yet performance can be quite different if the portfolio has different exposure to convexity. This concept is referred to as convexity risk. Exposure to convexity risk in the mortgage sector is measured by the difference between the convexity of a portfolio and the convexity of the benchmark index and for the 40-bond portfolio it is −0.54. This means that the portfolio has greater negative convexity than the index.

Tracking Error

As explained in the previous chapter, a factor model attempts to identify the specific risks that contribute to the forward-looking tracking error. All of the risks are quantified in terms of forward-looking tracking error as opposed to backward-looking tracking error. The tracking error for our hypothetical portfolio based on the multifactor risk model is 62 basis points. We can decompose the tracking error in order to understand where the risks are. The analysis begins with a decomposition of the risks into two general categories — systematic risk and non-systematic risk (also referred to as residual risk). For our hypothetical portfolio, the following was determined:

Forward-looking tracking error due to systematic risk = 58 basis points,
Forward-looking tracking error due to non-systematic risk = 20 basis points.

This may seem inconsistent with a 62-basis point tracking error for the portfolio given that the sum of these two risks exceeds 62 basis points. The reason for this is that tracking errors represent variances. Consequently, it is not the sum of these two risks that must sum to the portfolio's tracking error. Rather, it is the squares of these two tracking errors that when added equal the square of the portfolio's tracking error. Or equivalently, the square root of the sum of the square of the two tracking errors will equal the portfolio's tracking error; that is, $[(58)^2 + (20)^2]^{1/2} = 61.35$ or 62 basis points (rounded).

The adding of variances requires that an assumption be made. The assumption is that there is a zero correlation between the factors (i.e., the factors are statistically independent). If this is not the case, the correlation between the factors must be taken into account in estimating the tracking error.

Systematic risk can be decomposed into two risks: term structure factor risk and non-term structure factor risk. A portfolio's exposure to changes in the general level of interest rates is measured in terms of exposure to (1) a parallel shift in the yield curve and (2) a non-parallel shift in the yield curve. Taken together, this risk exposure is referred to as *term structure risk*. We know that the duration of the 40-bond portfolio is greater than the benchmark duration (5.56 versus 4.84). The difference between the yield curve risk for the portfolio and for the benchmark was shown in Table 5, based on the distribution of the present value of the cash flows and key rate durations. The factor model indicates that the forward-looking tracking error due to term structure risk is 52 basis points.

The other systematic risk that is not due to exposure to changes in the term structure is called *non-term structure risk*. These risk factors include sector risk, quality risk, optionality risk, coupon risk, and MBS risk (sector, prepayment, and convexity risks). For the 40-bond portfolio, the factor model indicates that the tracking error due to the non-term structure risk is 60 basis points. We now know that forward-looking tracking error due to systematic risk is 58 basis points, consisting of:

Forward-looking tracking error due to term structure risk = 52 basis points,
Forward-looking tracking error due to non-term structure risk = 60 basis points.

As noted, the predicted tracking error due to systematic risk is not equal to the sum of these two components of tracking error. If the term structure factor and the non-term structure factors are statistically independent, then the total forward-looking tracking error from all the systematic factors is 79 basis points. However, when the correlations are taken into account, the forward-looking tracking error due to systematic risk is 58 basis points.

In Table 8, the forward-looking tracking error subcomponents are reported for the systematic risk in two different ways. In the column labeled "Isolated Tracking Error", the tracking error was estimated considering only the effect of each risk factor in isolation. For example, the 9 basis points for the tracking error for quality considers only the mismatch between the portfolio exposure and benchmark exposure due to quality and taking into consideration the correlations only of quality exposure for the different quality ratings. The last two columns in the table with the headings "Cumulative Tracking Error" and "Change in Cumulative" report the second way in

TABLE 8: Decomposition of Systematic Tracking Error (in basis points)

	Isolated Tracking Error	Cumulative Tracking Error	Change in Cumulative
Tracking error term structure	52	52	52
Non-term structure	60		
Tracking error sector	18	59	8
Tracking error quality	9	64	5
Tracking error optionality	2	64	0
Tracking error coupon	3	65	0
Tracking error MBS sector	59	52	−13
Tracking error MBS volatility	33	53	1
Tracking error MBS prepayments	8	58	5
Total systematic tracking error			58

which the tracking error is decomposed. The cumulative tracking error is computed by incrementally introducing one group of risk factors at a time to the tracking error calculation. For example, in the first row the 52 basis points represent the tracking error due to term structure exposure. The third row shows the tracking error due to sector exposure. The cumulative tracking error of 59 basis points represents the combined tracking error due to both term structure exposure (52 basis points) and sector exposure taken together but ignoring all other systematic risk factors. Since the increase in tracking error by adding sector exposure to the term structure exposure is 7 basis points, the change in the cumulative tracking error is 7 basis points. A value of 8 is reported in the last column of the table only because there was rounding involved in the interim numbers.

Because of the way in which the calculations were performed, the cumulative tracking error shown for all the systematic risk factors in the next-to-the last column of 58 basis points and the same value reported in the last column for the "Total Systematic Tracking Error" take into consideration the correlations among the systematic risk factors. However, it should be remembered that while the total systematic tracking error will be the same regardless of the order in which the systematic risk factors are introduced, the interim values in the last two columns of the table will differ depending on the order in which the systematic risk factors are introduced.

Non-systematic risk is divided into those risks that are issuer specific and components that are issue specific. This risk is due to the fact that the portfolio has greater exposure to specific issues and issuers than the benchmark index. To understand these non-systematic risks, look at the last column of Table 1 which reports the percentage of the 40-bond portfolio's market value invested in each issue. Since there are only 40 issues in the portfolio, each issue makes up a non-trivial fraction of the portfolio. Specifically, look at the exposure to three corporate issuers, Abbott Laboratories, Bank of America, and Citicorp. They individually represent more than 5% of the portfolio. If any of these three issuers is downgraded, this would cause large losses in the 40-bond portfolio, but it would not have a significant effect on the benchmark which includes more than 5,000 issues. Consequently, a large exposure to a specific corporate issuer represents a material mismatch between the exposure of the portfolio and the exposure of a benchmark index that must be taken into account in assessing a portfolio's risk relative to a benchmark index. The non-systematic tracking error for the 40-bond portfolio is 21 basis points, consisting of issuer-specific tracking error of 20 basis points and issue-specific tracking error of 20 basis points.

Constructing and Rebalancing a Portfolio

So far we have seen how a factor model can be utilized by a portfolio manager to quantify the risk exposure of a portfolio to the factors that will impact the performance of a portfolio relative to a benchmark. We started with a 40-bond portfolio and then described the portfolio risks. However, in practice, the factor model is employed to construct the portfolio and then typically used to rebalance or restructure the portfolio.

The initial construction of the portfolio using a multifactor risk model involves using an optimizer. Portfolio optimizer software obtains the optimal value for an objective function subject to constraints. Although a discussion of the software is beyond the scope of this chapter, what is important to understand is that once a portfolio manager specifies an objective, the optimizer will compute the optimal portfolio. The two illustrations below using the 40-bond portfolio will illustrate how a portfolio can be rebalanced using a factor model and a portfolio optimizer.

In our first illustration, suppose that the portfolio manager wants to reduce the forward-looking tracking error significantly. For our 40-bond portfolio, the tracking error is 62 basis points. Assume that the portfolio manager wants to rebalance the portfolio in such a manner that its tracking error is 33 basis points. The goal is to rebalance the portfolio in a cost-efficient manner. A portfolio optimizer can be used to identify trades that reduce tracking error in a cost-efficient way. The portfolio optimizer begins with a universe of market prices for acceptable securities (i.e., those permitted by the investment guidelines). The portfolio optimizer is designed to select a trade that identifies a 1-for-1 bond swap with the greatest reduction in tracking error per unit of each bond acquired in the trade. In the case of our 40-bond portfolio, the portfolio optimizer identified the first trade in Table 9. This one trade reduced the tracking error from 62 basis points to 47 basis points. The five swaps in the table reduce in the most cost-efficient manner the tracking error to 33 basis points.

TABLE 9: Portfolio Optimizer Identified Swaps to Reduce Tracking Error from 62 to 33 Basis Points

Initial tracking error: 62 basis points
Targeted tracking error: 33 basis points

Swap #1:
Sell: $90,426,000 of FNMA Conventional Long T. 5.000 2035/02/01
Buy: $86,931,000 of Federal Home Ln Mtg Corp 5.375 2014/01/09
Cost of Trade: $443,392
New Tracking Error: 47 bps

Swap #2: New Tracking Error:
Sell: $31,199,000 of FNMA Conventional Long T. 6.000 2037/06/01
Buy: $32,186,000 of Unilever Capital Corp-Glo 5.900 2032/11/15
Cost of Trade: $158,462
New Tracking Error: 41 bps

Swap #3:
Sell: $44,621,000 of FNMA Conventional Long T. 5.500 2037/05/01
Buy: $32,186,000 of Unilever Capital Corp-Glo 5.900 2032/11/15
Cost of Trade: $219,553
New Tracking Error: 37 bps

Swap #4:
Sell: $19,337,000 of FNMA Conventional Long T. 6.000 2036/04/01
Buy: $17,278,000 of US Treasury Bonds 5.500 2028/08/15
Cost of Trade: $91,537
New Tracking Error: 34 bps

Swap #5:
Sell: $13,676,000 of Bank Of America Corp 5.750 2017/12/01
Buy: $12,233,000 of Federal Natl Mtg Assn-Glo 7.250 2010/01/15
Cost of Trade: $64,772
New Tracking Error: 33 bps

Cumulative cost of five swaps: $977,717

TABLE 10: Portfolio Optimizer Identified Swaps to Reduce Tracking Error but Maintain Tracking Error of Sector Risk

Initial tracking error: 62 basis points
Required tracking error for sector risk: 18 basis points

Swap #1:
Sell: $6,649,000 of Bank of America Corp 5.750 2017/12/01
Buy: $6,174,000 of Federal Home Ln Mtg Corp 5.250 2012/03/15
Cost of Trade: $32,057
New Tracking Error: 60 bps

Swap #2:
Sell: $4,659,000 of FNMA Conventional Long T. 5.000 2035/02/01
Buy: $6,174,000 of Federal Home Ln Mtg Corp 5.250 2012/03/15
Cost of Trade: $24,647
New Tracking Error: 59 bps

Swap #3:
Sell: $773,000 of Intl Business Machines-Gl 5.700 2017/09/14
Buy: $786,000 of Federal Home Ln Mtg Corp 5.250 2012/03/15
Cost of Trade: $3,898
New Tracking Error: 59 bps

Swap #4:
Sell: $773,000 of Cisco Systems Inc-Global 5.500 2016/02/22
Buy: $764,000 of Federal Home Ln Mtg Corp 5.250 2012/03/15
Cost of Trade: $3,842
New Tracking Error: 59 bps

Swap #5:
Sell: $515,000 of Oracle Corp 5.250 2016/01/15
Buy: $500,000 of Federal Home Ln Mtg Corp 5.250 2012/03/15
Cost of Trade: $2,537
New Tracking Error: 59 bps

Swap #6:
Sell: $11,560,000 of Abbott Laboratories-Globa 5.875 2016/05/15
Buy: $11,937,000 of Federal Home Ln Mtg Corp 5.450 2013/11/21
Cost of Trade: $58,743
New Tracking Error: 57 bps

Swap #7:
Sell: $7,176,000 of FNMA Conventional Long T. 5.000 2035/02/01
Buy: $8,026,000 of Travelers Cos Inc 6.250 2017/03/15
Cost of Trade: $38,005
New Tracking Error: 56 bps

Cumulative cost of swaps: $163,730

In our second illustration, we will see how a portfolio optimizer can also be used to structure a portfolio so as to incorporate a market view. Let's suppose that a portfolio manager follows a top-down approach to the selection of sectors. Consequently, the portfolio manager seeks exposure to sector risk, while at the same time seeking to minimize exposure to other risk factors such as term structure risk and non-sector, non-term structure systematic risk. A portfolio optimizer can be used to rebalance the current portfolio in a manner that maintains the current tracking error for sector risk but reduces the tracking error for the other systematic risks. The portfolio optimizer is set up so that there is a substantial penalty for reducing exposure to sector risk. For example, consider the 40-bond portfolio with a forward-looking tracking error of 62 basis points and the forward-looking tracking error due to sector risk of 18 basis points. The portfolio optimizer was run to keep the tracking error due to sector risk as close as possible to 18 basis points while reducing the tracking error due to the other risk factors. The seven bond swaps in Table 10 were identified by the portfolio optimizer. After these seven bond swaps, the predicted tracking error for the portfolio declines from 62 basis points to 56 basis points with the sector tracking error remaining the same and tracking error for the other systematic risks changing.

Key Points

- Multifactor risk models allow a bond portfolio manager to assess the portfolio's risk relative to a benchmark and reconstruct or rebalance a portfolio if the risk exposures are unacceptable.
- The contribution to portfolio duration is the amount that a bond holding in a portfolio adds to the duration of a portfolio.
- The contribution to benchmark duration is the amount that a bond in the benchmark index adds to the duration of a benchmark.
- Although duration provides a measure of the exposure of a portfolio or a benchmark to changes in the level of interest rates, this measure fails to measure the exposure of a portfolio or a benchmark index to changes in the shape of the yield curve.
- A measure for assessing yield curve risk exposure is the key rate durations of the portfolio and the benchmark.
- Key rate duration is the sensitivity of a portfolio's value to the change in a particular key spot rate.

- The spread duration for a portfolio or a benchmark index is computed as a market weighted average of the spread duration for each sector.
- Embedded options in bonds impact the performance of a portfolio and a benchmark.
- A bond's optionality risk exposure occurs because a change in interest rates changes the value of the embedded option, which, in turn changes the value of the bond.
- Optionality risk can be quantified using measures commonly used in option pricing.
- The delta of an option is an estimate of the sensitivity of the value of the option to changes in the price of the underlying instrument.
- The delta can be computed for each issue that has an embedded option and then these deltas can be aggregated to obtain an estimate of the delta for a portfolio or a benchmark.
- The largest deviation of the hypothetical portfolio and the benchmark is in the mortgage sectors.
- The three major risks of investing in this sector are (1) sector risk, (2) prepayment risk, and (3) convexity risk.
- One measure of prepayment risk is prepayment sensitivity, which is the basis point change in the price of an MBS for a 1% increase in prepayments.
- In a multifactor risk model, all of the bond portfolio risks are quantified in terms of forward-looking tracking error as opposed to backward-looking tracking error.
- Systematic risk can be decomposed into two risks: term structure factor risk and non-term structure factor risk.
- Term structure risk measures a portfolio's exposure to changes in the general level of interest rates measured in terms of exposure to (1) a parallel shift in the yield curve and (2) a non-parallel shift in the yield curve.
- Non-term structure risk is systematic risk that is not due to exposure to changes in the term structure.
- Non-term structure risk includes sector risk, quality risk, optionality risk, coupon risk, and mortgage-backed securities risk (sector, prepayment, and convexity risks).
- Non-systematic risk is divided into those risks that are issuer specific and components that are issue specific.
- Non-systematic risk is due to the fact that the portfolio has greater exposure to specific issues and issuers than the benchmark index.

- The initial construction of the portfolio using a multifactor risk model involves using a portfolio optimizer software to obtain the optimal value for an objective function subject to constraints.
- A bond portfolio manager can use a portfolio optimizer to structure a portfolio so as to incorporate a market view.

Chapter 17

Backtesting Investment Strategies

Learning Objectives

After reading this chapter, you will understand:

- what backtesting is and why it is a tool for asset managers;
- the three types of backtests (walk-forward, resampling, and Monte Carlo);
- the advantages and disadvantages of each type of backtesting;
- the reasons for backtesting;
- why backtesting is not a research tool;
- the pitfalls of using the walk-forward method for backtesting;
- the biases associated with backtesting: optimal period bias, time-period bias, survivorship bias, winner's bias, look-ahead bias, data-release timing bias, and selection bias;
- what overfitting is;
- the implementation issues associated with backtesting;
- the problem of selection bias under multiple testing;
- the information about backtesting that should be disclosed to a client; and
- questions that should be asked of a structurer of a backtest.

Introduction

Backtesting is an essential tool in an asset manager's arsenal. Unfortunately, it is probably one of the least understood tools, too. Although there are various definitions of what is meant by a backtest, a reasonable definition is that it is a simulation of how a proposed investment strategy would perform subject to certain conditions being true. In this chapter, we focus primarily on the pitfalls associated with historical backtesting, also known as the walk-forward method. The methodologies for conducting backtests require a strong background in probability theory and statistical analysis. Consequently, the details of backtesting will not be presented in this chapter. The objective of this chapter is to provide a non-technical description of backtesting methodologies focusing on the walk-forward method. In the next chapter, we focus on the use of another backtesting method: the Monte Carlo method.

Three Types of Backtests

There are three ways in which historical observations can be used for backtesting an investment strategy. We briefly describe these methods and explain the advantages and disadvantages of using them.

The Walk-Forward Method

The *walk-forward* (WF) *method* assesses the performance of an investment strategy under the assumption that history repeats itself *exactly*. Each investment strategy decision is based on observations that predate that decision. Carrying out a flawless WF analysis is challenging for the reasons that we discuss later in this chapter. There is no generic way for conducting a WF backtest. To be accurate and representative, each WF backtest must be customized to evaluate the assumptions of a proposed investment strategy.

The WF method has two major advantages. The main advantage of this method is that it has a clear historical interpretation. Its performance can be reconciled with paper trading.

There are four major drawbacks of the WF method. First, only a single scenario is tested (the historical path), which can be easily overfit. But history is but one realization of a stochastic process. If we were to take a time machine, history would have played out differently for a large number of events. Since WF backtests are not representative of the past, there is no reason to believe that they are representative of the future. Accordingly, WF is more likely to be a descriptive (or anecdotal) than an inferential statement.[1] Second, a WF's initial decisions are made on a smaller portion

[1]See Chapter 11 in López de Prado [2018]. For a further explanation, see Bailey, Borwein, López de Prado, and Zhu [2014a, 2014b].

of the total sample. Most of the information is used by only a small portion of the decisions. Third, a WF backtest does not tell us *why* the strategy makes money. The data-generating process (DGP) responsible for the success of the strategy is never stated. Should the DGP change, the researcher will not be able to decommission the strategy *before* it loses money. Fourth, the results are not necessarily representative of future performance because they can be biased by the particular sequence of datapoints.

Let's take a closer look at the fourth drawback. Proponents of the WF method typically argue that predicting the past would lead to overly optimistic performance estimates. And yet, very often fitting an outperforming model on the reversed sequence of observations (*a walk-backwards backtest*) will lead to an underperforming WF backtest. The truth is, it is as easy to overfit a backtest using the WF method as to overfit a walk-backwards backtest. Evidence of overfitting can be seen by how changing the sequence of observations yields inconsistent outcomes. If proponents of the WF method were correct, we should observe that walk-backwards backtests systematically outperform their WF method counterparts. That is not the case, hence the main argument in favor of the WF method is rather weak.

The Resampling Method

The second type of backtest is the *resampling method* (RS), which addresses WF's first disadvantage. RS assesses the performance of an investment strategy under the assumption that future paths can be simulated through the resampling of past observations. The resampling can be deterministic or random. An example of backtesting through deterministic resampling is cross-validation. In a *cross-validation backtest*, the researcher splits the dataset into k groups (called *folds*), and then uses $k-1$ for training the models, alternating the hold-out of the remaining group for testing the outcomes. An example of a backtest through random resampling is bootstrapping, whereby observations are drawn from the sample with replacement.

Clients who are pitched an investment strategy typically inquire as to how the strategy would perform if subjected to a stress scenario. Often the unforeseeable black swan scenario is the 2008 global financial crisis or the 2001 dot-com bubble. One way to deal with stress scenarios is to split the observations into two sets. The first set covers the period the client wants the asset manager to test and is called the *testing set*. The second set covers the rest of the dataset and is referred to as the *training set*. For example, in a machine learning (ML) developed strategy, a classifier would be trained on the period January 1, 2009–January 1, 2017, then tested on the period January 1, 2008–December 31, 2008. The performance obtained for 2008 is not historically accurate, since the classifier was trained on data that were only available after 2008. But historical accuracy was not the goal of the test. The objective of the test was to subject a strategy ignorant of 2008 to a stress scenario such as 2008.

The goal of backtesting employing the RS method is not to derive historically accurate performance. Instead, the goal of the RS method is to infer future performance from a number of out-of-sample scenarios. For each period of the backtest, we simulate the performance of a classifier that knew everything except for that period.

The RS method for backtesting has advantages and disadvantages. There are three advantages. The first advantage of the RS method for backtesting is that it is not the result of a particular (historical) scenario. The second advantage is that every decision is made on sets of equal size, making outcomes comparable across periods, in terms of the amount of information used to make those decisions. The third advantage is that RS can rely on many different paths, allowing the researcher to consider more general scenarios consistent with the DGP. For instance, through a RS backtest we can bootstrap the distribution of the strategy's Sharpe ratio, which is much more informative than the single-path Sharpe ratio derived by WF. Whereas it is trivial to overfit a WF backtest, it is very difficult to overfit a RS backtest.[2]

The Monte Carlo Method

The third type of backtest, the Monte Carlo method (MC method), addresses both of the disadvantages of WF. The MC method assesses the performance of an investment strategy under the assumption that future paths can be simulated via Monte Carlo. The MC method requires a deeper knowledge of the DGP, derived from the statistical analysis of the observations or theory (e.g., market microstructure, institutional processes, economic links, and the like). For instance, economic theory may suggest that two variables are cointegrated, and empirical studies may indicate the range of values that characterize the cointegration vector. Accordingly,

[2]See Chapter 12 in López de Prado [2018].

researchers can simulate millions of years of data, where the cointegration vector takes many different values within the estimated range. This is a much richer analysis than merely resampling observations from a finite (and likely unrepresentative) set of observations.[3]

Consider a researcher that wishes to design a market making strategy. Market microstructure theory tells us that uninformed traders cause short-term mean reversion as a result of temporary market impact, and informed traders cause permanent impact on market prices. Informed traders arrive at the market at a rate μ and uninformed traders arrive at the market at a rate ε. The statistical analysis of historical time series gives us a range of fluctuation of μ and ε, which can be used to simulate a long time series under various scenarios. For a given combination of μ and ε, MC allows us to derive the optimal market making strategy, that is, the set of profit taking and stop loss levels that maximize the Sharpe ratio in an MC backtest. In contrast, WF and RS would backtest the overall performance of the market making strategy, over all historical values of μ and ε, without allowing the researcher to estimate the performance at specific pairs of μ and ε, and without allowing the researcher to derive optimal market making strategies for each specific pair.

MC offers the following four critical advantages over WF and RS:

1. MC backtests help address the first epistemological limitation of finance because they allow researchers to conduct randomized controlled experiments. Admittedly, these experiments require the assumption of a particular DGP, but at least that DGP is explicitly stated (unlike in WF backtests published in financial journals). In MC backtests, the researcher declares the hypothesis underlying the findings. If the client believes that the true DGP is different, the researcher must be told an alternative DGP and then repeat the analysis.
2. MC backtests help address the second epistemological limitation of finance because the researcher does not need to assume that the DGP is immutable. Instead, the discovery is connected to a particular DGP, where realizations may be drawn from different DGPs over time. The probability that a particular DGP is producing the realizations can be evaluated statistically, which allows researchers to commission or decommission models as conditions evolve.

[3]See Chapter 13 in López de Prado [2018].

3. MC backtests allow the incorporation of priors, which inject information beyond what we could have learned from a finite set of observations. When these priors are motivated by theory, MC offers a powerful tool to simulate the most likely scenarios, even if some of those scenarios have not been observed in the past.
4. The length of MC backtests can be expanded for as long as needed to achieve a targeted degree of confidence. This is helpful, in that MC backtests avoid the indetermination inherent in working with finite datasets.

Of the three types of backtests, WF is by far the most common. For this reason, we will focus on studying the properties of WF throughout this chapter but will discuss the MC method for backtesting in the next chapter because it overcomes the major limitations of the WF method.

Reasons for Backtesting

The theory of knowledge or epistemology — the branch of philosophy dealing with the distinction between justified belief and opinion — provides guidance in evaluating backtesting. Two major epistemological limitations prevent finance from becoming a science, at par with physics, chemistry, or biology. First, finance does not comply with Popper's falsifiability criterion[4] because financial theories cannot be tested in a laboratory in controlled experiments. Claims such as "value and momentum factors explain the outperformance of stocks" cannot be proven wrong, even if they are. All researchers have is the outcome from a single realized path (a price time series) produced by an unknown DGP. We cannot draw millions of alternative paths from the same DGP and evaluate in how many instances value and momentum factors had explanatory power, while controlling for environmental conditions. Consequently, claims made by financial economists are based on anecdotal information, not scientific evidence. Unfortunately, this limitation has not prevented researchers from making a myriad of pseudo-scientific claims regarding presumed "factors".

The second epistemological limitation afflicting finance is non-stationarity. Financial systems are extremely dynamic and complex, with

[4] In the philosophy of science this criterion, proposed by the philosopher Sir Karl Popper, is used to distinguish between theories that are scientific and those that are unscientific.

conditions that quickly change over time. Financial cause-effect mechanisms are not invariant due to changes in regulation, expectations, economic cycles, market regimes, and other environmental variables. For instance, even if value and momentum factors truly explained the outperformance of stocks in the 20th century, that may no longer be the case as a result of recent technological and geopolitical changes. Perhaps value and momentum only worked under certain conditions that are no longer present. Consequently, financial researchers are unable to produce theories in the scientific meaning of the term.

Due to these epistemological limitations, researchers rely on backtesting for developing investment strategies. A backtest infers the performance of an investment strategy under the assumption that future observations will be drawn from the same DGP that produced past observations.

A WF Backtest is Not a Research Tool

One reason asset managers are interested in WF backtesting is that it provides a sanity check for a proposed investment strategy. Although a properly executed WF backtest can be extremely helpful in assessing the potential performance of a proposed investment strategy, performing WF backtests well is extremely difficult and an asset manager must be aware of the pitfalls in backtesting that we describe in this chapter. Unfortunately, too often in asset management backtesting is viewed as a research tool. That is not the correct use of backtests. As explained in the chapter, most backtests published in research-oriented academic journals are flawed, and there is reason to suspect that the same applies to many strategies proposed to clients of asset management firms.

A WF backtest is hypothetical. It is not what a scientist would refer to as an "experiment". In deducing from an experiment a precise cause–effect relationship, a scientist can repeat an experiment in a laboratory. In doing so, the scientist can control for environmental variables. Backtests cannot prove any cause–effect mechanism. They provide the asset manager with very little insight into the reason why a particular strategy resulted in a favorable performance metric. An asset manager can always provide some story once favorable results are found to explain why the strategy is successful. There are literally hundreds of investment strategies that are alleged successful in terms of some designated performance metric that are accompanied by some convoluted explanation. What is not disclosed is how many trials were conducted to find them, and under what conditions the strategy is likely to fail.

Too often, asset managers use backtests to improve the performance of their strategy. That misses the point of a backtest, which is to discard bad models, not to improve them. Adjusting an investment strategy based on the results of a backtest is a waste of time, and a way of misleading clients about the potential performance of the strategy. Asset management teams should allocate their time and effort to get all the components of the strategy right. A backtest should not be carried out until the model has been fully specified. If a backtest fails, the asset manager should fix the research process that led to testing a false strategy. When a factory produces defective cars, the solution is to fix the factory, not to fix every car that comes out of the chain.

Pitfalls of WF Backtesting

The pitfalls of WF backtesting are well known. Let's look at the pitfalls discussed by two financial institutions, Deutsche Bank and Citibank Derivatives Group.

Deutsche Bank's quantitative team referred to the pitfalls as the "Seven Sins of Quantitative Investing":[5]

- survivorship bias;
- look-ahead bias;
- storytelling;
- data mining and data snooping;
- transactions costs;
- outliers; and
- shorting.

The Citi Equity Derivative group in a presentation at the CBOE 2015 Risk Management Conference listed the following 10 pitfalls in backtesting:[6]

- focusing on expected value, ignoring other metrics;
- underestimating survivorship bias;
- confusing correlation and causation;

[5]Luo, Alvarez, Wang, Jussa, Wang, and Rohal [2014].
[6]For the presentation, see Sarfati [2015].

- selecting an unrepresentative time period;
- accounting for outliers improperly;
- overfitting and data mining;
- overlooking mark-to-market performance;
- failing to expect the unexpected;
- underestimating hidden exposures;
- forgetting practical aspects.

The above issues are just a few of the basic errors that most asset management firms make routinely, and they by no means constitute an exhaustive list. In what follows we discuss these pitfalls and a few more.

WF Backtesting Biases

In WF backtesting, the outcome is often influenced by *research bias* or *experimenter bias*. This takes place when the asset manager performing the backtest has the opportunity to deliberately bias the test for the purpose of obtaining a desired result. This can occur, for example, when the asset manager selects the time period over which the backtest is conducted and that time period is likely to produce the desired results. If an asset manager wants to test an investment strategy that involves one of the well-known factors that drives returns, the asset manager may select a period that includes a business cycle where the factor performs best. The reported backtesting results exclude the performance of time periods where the strategy performed poorly. This type of bias is referred to as *optimal period bias*. *Time-period bias* occurs when the time period for testing — when the backtest starts and stops — is such that the results are sensitive to different time periods with respect to volatility, economic growth periods, and interest rate levels.

Survivorship bias

Survivorship bias occurs when the backtest uses only surviving examples in assessing the performance of a strategy. By using only the current investment universe for backtesting, the investment strategy ignores the fact that some companies went bankrupt or securities were delisted along the way. Since survivorship bias results in only survivors or winners being in the data that is backtested, it is sometimes referred to as the *winner's bias*. It makes a proposed investment strategy appear better than it actually is.

To illustrate survivorship bias, consider that typically investment strategies involve the use of some market index as a benchmark. However, the constituent components change (i.e., companies are removed and replaced by other companies). So, the changing of the components of an index over the time period of the backtest must be accounted for. For example, the Dow Jones Industrial Average (DJIA) includes 30 blue-chip and important US industrial companies (i.e., the index excludes transportation and utility companies). Suppose that an investment strategy involving the DJIA is backtested by looking at its performance metric over a long time period. The performance metric used is the strategy's return. However, what would that information indicate? It is difficult to interpret the strategy's return because it ignores the fact that of the original 30 companies in the DJIA that were created in 1896, none are in the index now. General Electric, the last surviving member of the DJIA, was removed in 2018. Companies were removed for a variety of reasons, but it is typically due to financial considerations. General Electric, for example, had financial difficulties that led to a substantial decline in its stock price. Not only has the DJIA index changed, but the companies added are those that in the opinion of the selection committee reflect how the economy has changed. For example, when General Electric was removed, it was replaced by a drug store chain, Walgreens. Changes since 2010 have resulted in the DJIA not being represented by industrial companies but by prominent consumer, technology, health care, and financial companies.

Another example of survivorship bias is investing in early startup companies. A good data base for examining the performance of new ventures is from venture capital companies that invest in early startup companies. The organization that represents 450+ venture capitalist firms is the National Venture Capital Association (NVCA). According to *The Wall Street Journal*, venture capitalists suggest that a common rule of thumb is that 30–40% of start-ups fail completely, 30–40% return the original investment, and 10–20% produce substantial returns.[7] According to NVCA estimates, 25–30% of venture-backed businesses fail. In other words, 70–75% succeed. Sounds like the making of a potential profitable investment strategy. However, other studies do not give as rosy a picture about the probability of a new venture succeeding.

[7]Gage [2012].

A study by Ghosh [2011] suggests that no matter how failure is defined, the odds are not good that a new venture will succeed. He included in his study 2,000 companies that received venture funding (generally at least $1 million) from 2004 through 2010. The failure rate according to different definitions of failure is as follows: (1) liquidating all assets resulted in investors losing most or all their investment in the company for 30–40% of the sample, (2) falling short of the projected return on investment occurred for 70–80% of the sample, and (3) falling short of declared forecasted projections occurred for 90–95% of the sample. Ghosh proffers reasons for the discrepancy between his findings and that of the NCVA (as cited in Gage [2012]). Failure rates are biased downwards because many venture-backed companies are sold at a loss that is classified by venture capitalists as an "acquisition". That is, there is survivorship bias. A second reason for selection bias is that venture capitalists tend to emphasize the successes but avoid talking about the failures. As Ghosh points out, venture capitalists "bury their dead very quietly".

Look-ahead bias

Look-ahead bias occurs when information is used that was not public at the moment that the investment decision was made. Even a few minutes advantage in being able to use information before it actually becomes public could result in the false discovery of an investment strategy. Look-ahead bias occurs in at least two situations.

The first situation is when data that would be unavailable if the strategy is live is used in the backtest. For example, suppose an asset manager has formulated a strategy based on how quarterly earnings reports affect stock returns. Suppose the backtest involves using the quarterly earnings to forecast the return one week later. So, for example, the strategy might call for using third quarter earnings on say September 30 to forecast the return on the first week of October. The problem is that the third quarter earnings are not available on September 30. Rather, they are typically reported with a 1-month lag. Therefore, earnings information on September 30 is not known so the results of the backtest will be meaningless. This is the classic example of look-ahead bias. This form of look-ahead bias, also referred to as *data release timing bias*, can be avoided by making sure that the data used are actually available at the time the backtest simulates the decision. An example of this type of look-ahead bias is when price information is provided for different time zones and that is not recognized in using historical data.

A second way in which look ahead bias occurs is when financial statements filed with the Securities and Exchange Commission (SEC) are used without looking at subsequent revisions. One would think that the numbers reported in such reports are final numbers. That is not necessarily the case. Companies may revise their filings with the SEC and release a revised filing. This bias can be addressed by checking the timestamp for each data point and taking into account release dates, distribution delays, and backfill corrections.

Overfitting and selection bias

Backtest overfitting can be defined as *selection bias* on multiple backtests. This bias occurs when an investment strategy is designed to perform well on a backtest. This is fundamentally different from in-sample overfitting, which is associated with model complexity. In fact, backtest overfitting can occur on a very simple model.

Random patterns are unlikely to reoccur in the future, and when a backtest is overfit to profit from them, it leads to an exceedingly optimistic performance projection. The investment strategy designed for the purpose of performing well in backtests will fail as a result. Backtest overfitting is not entirely avoidable, and all backtests must be presumed to exhibit some degree of "selection bias". When asset managers share the results of their backtests for a proposed investment strategy, only those that portray supposedly profitable investment strategies are disclosed.

Overcoming the problem of backtest overfitting bias is arguably the most fundamental question in asset management. If there was a simple solution to this fundamental question, asset management firms would achieve high performance with certainty because they would invest only in winning strategies.

What makes backtest overfitting bias so hard to evaluate is that the probability of a backtest showing that a strategy being successful based on some performance metric when it is not — referred to as "false positive" — changes with every new test conducted on the same dataset. Moreover, the information about the results from all of the backtests is not shared with current or potential clients to whom the strategy is proposed. Although no simple solution exists to avoid overfitting bias, there are steps that can be taken by asset managers to mitigate this bias. These steps are described in López de Prado [2018, Chapter 12].

Studies on Biases

There have been a number of studies that have investigated the inherent biases in the design and backtesting of an investment strategy. Harvey and Liu [2016] look at the inherent biases attributable to data mining and multiple testing in the context of econometric analyses, as well as the propensity of researchers to publish only results that are positive. The specific area where they investigate this bias is in explaining the cross-section of returns, which began with the testing of the capital asset pricing model in 1967. Since then there have been tens of thousands of empirical studies in explaining the cross-section of stock returns, representing a great deal of data mining. This is a clear example of multiple testing. The question is then whether the usual statistical test with a Student t-value cutoff of 2.0 is appropriate given our discussion above regarding multiple testing? In the search for new factors that practitioners and academics data mine for and the proper dealing with statistical tests in a multiple testing setting, the authors question what the new cutoff for the t-value should be.

According to Harvey and Liu [2016], there have been 316 factors that have been used in 313 published studies to explain cross-section returns. In each study, the factors were tested using the usual 2.0 cutoff or the equivalent for the cutoff Sharpe ratio. The authors find that virtually all factors that were reported to be significant in the 313 studies, when adjusted for the estimated number of tests, fail to meet the significance criteria. Making an assumption about the number of tested factors that are known (316) and about how many additional factors that have been tried in non-published studies, they project what the appropriate t-value cutoff should be in the future (through the year 2032). They provide a time series of appropriate cutoffs from 1967 to 2032.

McLean and Pontiff [2016] focus on the post-publication performance of a strategy in predicting cross-section stock returns. Based on 97 variables tested in studies published in academic journals, they find that the returns are 26% lower out of sample and 58% lower post-publication. This indicates that there is both a data mining effect (as indicated by the lower out-of-sample performance) and a crowding effect as investors learn about stock mispricing from academic publications.

In recognition of the need to increase the cutoff t-value or the equivalent Sharpe ratio, Harvey and Liu [2016] discuss the common practice of applying a haircut of 50% to the Sharpe ratios of new strategies. They argue that in fact a nonlinear adjustment that takes into account the number of previous tests should be applied. In another study, Harvey and Liu [2014] suggest methods to account for multiple testing and consider a practical example using published quantitative trading strategies. Bailey and López de Prado [2014] also look at what adjustments must be made to the Sharpe ratio for multiple testing when there are non-normal distributions of strategy returns based on additional information of the strategy development process and statistical properties of strategy returns, under very general assumptions.

Implementation Issues

There are implementation issues associated with an investment strategy that may be overlooked in backtesting. Here are a few examples where the live trading of an investment strategy that passed the backtests may fail in practice because:

- Competitors or a dealer can front-run the strategy.[8]
- Transaction costs are higher than used in backtesting because of market impact cost.[9]
- Inability to buy a large amount of small companies that are part of the investment strategy.
- The capacity of the strategy is reached quickly as the strategy becomes known and used by competitors.
- The inability in taking a short position on cash products (to find in live trading a lender from which the security can be borrowed) at a cost assumed in the backtest.

Backtesting and Hypothesis Testing

In evaluating investment strategies, the null hypothesis (denoted by H_0) is that there is no profitable strategy. The alternative hypothesis (denoted H_1) is that the strategy is profitable. In separating profitable strategies from unprofitable ones, we can make two errors: A false discovery error and a missed discovery error. A *false discovery error* is an error made when an investment strategy is found to be profitable when in fact it is not. In

[8]Here, we define frontrunning in a general sense as the practice of trade ahead of other participants based on an informational advantage or on a faster implementation process.

[9]Market impact can be defined as the temporary or permanent effect that trading has on the price of a security.

statistics, this type of error is referred to as a Type I error, which occurs with probability α — the null hypothesis is rejected when it is in fact true. A *missed discovery error* results when an investment strategy is found to be unprofitable when in fact it is profitable. That is, the null hypothesis is not rejected when it is in fact false. This is referred to in statistics as a Type II error which occurs with probability β. The following table, referred to as a *confusion matrix*, summarizes the four scenarios:

Decision about Investment Strategy	**Investment Strategy is not Profitable (Null Hypothesis is True)**	**Investment Strategy is Profitable (Null Hypothesis is False)**
Accept the null hypothesis	True Negative	False Negative (Type II error)
Reject the null hypothesis	False Positive (Type I error)	True Positive

There is a tradeoff between a false discovery (Type I) error and a missed discovery (Type II) error. Let's make this tradeoff clearer with an example using the evaluation of an investment strategy via backtesting. We start by assuming that the investment strategy is false (the null hypothesis) until it can be proven otherwise by means of hypothesis testing. Using returns from a backtest, we can test whether the performance is statistically significant. How strong must the evidence be to reject the null hypothesis that the investment strategy is unprofitable? This is a function of the Type I error (false discovery error). The lower the significance level (α), the stronger the empirical evidence must be; hence a larger portion of actually profitable strategies is rejected (i.e., the probability of a missed discovery error rises).

The *power of the test* is defined as 1 minus the probability of not rejecting the null hypothesis when it is false. That is, the power of the test is 1 minus the Type II error (β). What would be ideal is to make the probability of both errors occurring as small as possible. However, the two errors cannot be set independently and as a result there is a tradeoff between the two.

The Problem of Selection Bias under Multiple Testing

Most of the empirical research in finance is likely false. To understand why, we need to review how hypothesis testing has been misused in the financial literature. In backtesting, practitioners and academics use statistical tests of hypothesis. In testing those investment strategies, they use the same historical datasets. The problem is, α and β do not remain constant as tests are conducted more than once on the same observations. Reporting the best backtest result out of many without accounting for the increased α leads to many more false positives than expected.

In its ethical guidelines, the American Statistical Association denounces the problem of *selection bias under multiple testing* in the following terms[10]:

> Recognize that any frequentist statistical test has a random chance of indicating significance when it is not really present. Running multiple tests on the same dataset at the same stage of an analysis increases the chance of obtaining at least one invalid result. Selecting the one "significant" result from a multiplicity of parallel tests poses a grave risk of an incorrect conclusion. Failure to disclose the full extent of tests and their results in such a case would be highly misleading.

The problem of selection bias under multiple testing cuts across all the sciences and the social sciences. Today, the large majority of journal articles in experimental sciences include a discussion of the impact of multiple testing on the findings. For example, Strasak, Zaman, Marinell, Pfeiffer, and Ulmer [2007] found that more than two-thirds of the papers published during 2004 in the top two journals in clinical science (the *New England Journal of Medicine* and *Nature Medicine*) included a thorough discussion of this problem.

Later in this chapter, we provide a template that can be used to assess the impact that selection bias under multiple testing has on evaluating a backtested investment strategy.

In 1933, two statisticians, Jerzy Neyman and Egon Pearson, proposed the framework used today for testing hypotheses.[11] However, they did not consider the possibility of conducting multiple tests and selecting the best outcome. When a test is repeated multiple times, the combined false positive probability increases. To see this, consider that we repeat for a second time a test with false positive probability α. At each trial, the probability of *not* making a Type I error is $(1 - \alpha)$. If the two trials are independent, the probability of not making a Type I error on the first *and* second tests

---

[10]This is from Guideline #8 in American Statistical Association [1997, p. 5].

[11]Neyman and Pearson [1933].

is $(1-\alpha)^2$. Assuming the commonly used 5% for α, the probability of not making a Type I error is 90.25%, which is less than with one test. The probability of making *at least one* Type I error is the complementary, $1-(1-\alpha)^2$. In our example, it is 9.75%, which is greater than the original 5%.

After a "family" of K independent tests, we would reject H_0 with confidence $(1-\alpha)^K$. The "family" false positive probability, known as the *familywise error rate* or FWER, is $\alpha_K = 1-(1-\alpha)^K$. This is the probability that *at least one* of the positives is false, which is the complement to the probability that none of the positives is false, $(1-\alpha)^K$. So, for example, if there are 100 tests and α is 5%, the FWER is 99.4%.

Suppose that we set a FWER over K independent tests at α_K. Then, the individual false positive probability can be derived from the above equation as $\alpha = 1-(1-\alpha_K)^{1/K}$. This is known as the Šidàk correction for multiple testing. From the first term of a Taylor expansion, it can be approximated as $\alpha \approx \frac{\alpha_K}{K}$, which is known as Bonferroni's approximation.[12]

Information about Backtest that Should be Disclosed

Because of the importance of the problem of selection bias under multiple testing, Fabozzi and López de Prado [2018] propose that developers of investment strategies provide a report when pitching clients about the strategy. They refer to this report as the "SBuMT report", which is an abbreviation for *s*election *b*ias *u*nder *m*ultiple *t*esting. The SBuMT report would be composed of the following sections: family of trials, family size, familywise error rate.

A *family of trials* is the collection of results among which the researcher selected the one result submitted for consideration by a client, potential client, or publication in a journal. They discuss two cases. In the first case, the researchers disclose the outcomes from a series of backtests computed on alternative investment strategies, with the purpose of choosing the best result according to some performance statistic (e.g., Sharpe ratio, information ratio, return to drawdown, and the like). In the second case, the researchers disclose the outcomes from a series of regressions computed

[12]FWER is a stringent procedure for multiple testing and is criticized as leading to making many Type II errors. Another procedure for multiple testing, which is less stringent, is the false discovery rate (FDR).

on alternative datasets or model specifications, with the purpose of selecting the most statistically significant outcome (e.g., effects with the lowest p-values, highest adjusted R-squared, etc.). The developer of the strategy should explain in the SBuMT report their precise definition of a family of trials. How they have recorded the trials. If the trials are not available to the public, they must explain why. What led them to execute those particular trials, and not others, etc.

The *family size* is the number of significantly different experiments conducted (K), where $K \leq N$. For example, a family of trials composed of two identical experiments has a size of one. In the SBuMT report, the strategy developer should explain the precise methodology used to determine the family size.

The strategy developer should report the FWER implied by their tests (α_K).[13] This can be expressed in terms of annualized Sharpe ratio cut-off levels based on the sample length, the number of trials, and a given α.

Given a single test significance level α and a family size K, the FWER can be estimated as

$$\alpha_K = 1 - (1 - \alpha)^K.$$

The above expression can be used in the case of regression studies. In the case of the Sharpe ratio, it is known that under the general assumption that returns are stationary and ergodic (not necessarily independent and identically normally distributed), if the true Sharpe ratio equals SR^*, then the statistic $\hat{z}[SR^*]$ is asymptotically distributed as a standard Normal,

$$\hat{z}[SR^*] = \frac{(\widehat{SR} - SR^*)\sqrt{T-1}}{\sqrt{1 - \hat{\gamma}_3\widehat{SR} + \frac{\hat{\gamma}_4 - 1}{4}\widehat{SR}^2}} \xrightarrow{a} Z.$$

The FWER can be derived directly from the Sharpe ratio estimate under the null hypothesis as

$$\alpha_K = 1 - Z[\hat{z}[0]]^K.$$

Panel A in Table 1 gives the Sharpe ratio cut-off associated with various combinations of sample length (T) and family sizes (K) for $\alpha_K = 0.05$ assuming that returns follow a standard Normal distribution

[13]Fabozzi and López de Prado [2018] propose determining the family size by clustering the correlation matrix of backtested returns and using the optimal number of clusters as a conservative measurement of the number of independent trials. The reason this measurement is conservative is that the number of independent trials cannot be larger than the number of low-correlated trials.

($\hat{\gamma}_3 = 0$, $\hat{\gamma}_4 = 3$). The Sharpe ratios in the table have been annualized by applying 250 observations per year. Notice that the cut-offs become smaller with higher α_K. Although not shown in the table (since only $\alpha_K = 0.05$ is shown), the multiple testing adjustment is more severe as α_K rises. For example, the cut-off increases by 57%, from 1.6526 ($K=1$) to 2.5902 ($K = 10$), when $\alpha_K = 0.05$ (see panel A). In contrast, when $\alpha_K = 0.2$ (not shown in the table), the cut-off raises 140%, from 0.8439 ($K = 1$) to 2.0251 ($K = 10$).

A more realistic assumption regarding returns as explained in Chapter 4 is that they are non-normal. Studies of hedge fund strategies suggest they are characterized by positive excess kurtosis.[14] Panel B of Table 1 shows the results of repeating the calculations of panel (A) for the non-normal case where $\hat{\gamma}_3 = -3$ and $\hat{\gamma}_4 = 10$ and $\alpha_K = 0.05$. These results indicate that ignoring the non-normality of returns can lead to a substantial underestimation of the FWER, thus a higher than expected number of false positives. For instance, at $\alpha_K = 0.05$, $T = 250$, and $K = 10$, taking non-normality into account raises the cut-off by 31%, from 2.5902 (panel A) to 3.4039. Also, under non-normality the multiple testing adjustment is much more pronounced: When $\alpha_K = 0.05$, the cut-off raises 74%, from 1.9536 ($K = 1$) to 3.4039 ($K=10$), instead of the 57% increase observed in the normal case (see panel A of Table 1).[15]

As an example, Table 1 shows these cut-off levels for $\alpha_K = 0.05$ for the normal case (panel A) and a specific non-normal case (panel B).

In addition, Fabozzi and López de Prado suggest two optional sections for the SBuMT report: power of the test and robustness analysis. Researchers should compute the power of the test and determine how multiple testing affects the test's true positive probability. Multiple testing also impacts the Type II error, to the point that the test could be rendered powerless. In other words, having a low false positive rate is meaningless if the cost is that we miss most of the true strategies. For this reason, researchers should report the power of the test, $1 - \beta_K$. The optional section of the SBuMT report would include an analysis of how the study's conclusions are susceptible to different family sizes.[16] In the context of backtesting, López de Prado and Lewis [2019] derive the false negative probability (β_K) as a

[14]For example, see Brooks and Kat [2002]; Ingersoll, Spiegel, Goetzmann, and Weich [2007].
[15]See López de Prado and Lewis [2018b] for additional details.
[16]For an example of robustness analysis, see López de Prado and Lewis [2019].

TABLE 1: Annualized Sharpe Ratio Cut-off Levels for Various Combinations of Sample Length (Rows) and Number of Trials (Columns) When $\alpha_K = 0.05$

Panel A: The Normal case ($\hat{\gamma}_3 = 0$, and $\hat{\gamma}_4 = 3$)

aSR	1	2	5	10	25	50	100	250	500	1000
250	1.6526	1.9660	2.3360	2.5902	2.9003	3.1189	3.3262	3.5857	3.7726	3.9525
500	1.1658	1.3861	1.6456	1.8236	2.0402	2.1925	2.3367	2.5168	2.6462	2.7705
750	0.9511	1.1306	1.3420	1.4868	1.6629	1.7867	1.9038	2.0499	2.1548	2.2555
1000	0.8234	0.9787	1.1615	1.2867	1.4389	1.5458	1.6470	1.7731	1.8637	1.9505
1250	0.7363	0.8751	1.0385	1.1504	1.2863	1.3818	1.4722	1.5848	1.6656	1.7431
1500	0.6720	0.7987	0.9478	1.0498	1.1738	1.2610	1.3433	1.4460	1.5197	1.5903
1750	0.6221	0.7393	0.8773	0.9718	1.0865	1.1671	1.2433	1.3383	1.4064	1.4718
2000	0.5819	0.6915	0.8205	0.9089	1.0161	1.0915	1.1627	1.2515	1.3152	1.3763
2250	0.5486	0.6519	0.7735	0.8568	0.9579	1.0289	1.0960	1.1797	1.2397	1.2973
2500	0.5204	0.6184	0.7338	0.8127	0.9086	0.9760	1.0396	1.1190	1.1759	1.2305

Panel B: Non-Normal case ($\hat{\gamma}_3 = -3$ and $\hat{\gamma}_4 = 10$)

aSR	1	2	5	10	25	50	100	250	500	1000
250	1.9536	2.4053	2.9802	3.4039	3.9555	4.3694	4.7828	5.3310	5.7489	6.1707
500	1.3088	1.5924	1.9438	2.1963	2.5168	2.7517	2.9814	3.2789	3.5005	3.7196
750	1.0445	1.2647	1.5346	1.7266	1.9680	2.1432	2.3132	2.5316	2.6928	2.8512
1000	0.8925	1.0777	1.3033	1.4629	1.6624	1.8065	1.9457	2.1237	2.2544	2.3823
1250	0.7911	0.9535	1.1506	1.2894	1.4624	1.5868	1.7068	1.8597	1.9717	2.0809
1500	0.7175	0.8636	1.0404	1.1645	1.3189	1.4297	1.5363	1.6718	1.7709	1.8673
1750	0.6609	0.7947	0.9561	1.0693	1.2098	1.3104	1.4071	1.5297	1.6192	1.7063
2000	0.6157	0.7397	0.8891	0.9937	1.1233	1.2160	1.3049	1.4176	1.4997	1.5795
2250	0.5785	0.6946	0.8342	0.9318	1.0526	1.1389	1.2216	1.3263	1.4025	1.4765
2500	0.5473	0.6567	0.7882	0.8800	0.9935	1.0744	1.1520	1.2501	1.3215	1.3907

function of FWER as

$$\beta_K = Z\left[Z^{-1}[(1-\alpha_K)^{1/K}] - \frac{SR^*\sqrt{T-1}}{\sqrt{1-\hat{\gamma}_3\widehat{SR}+\frac{\hat{\gamma}_4-1}{4}\widehat{SR}^2}}\right],$$

where $Z[\cdot]$ is the standard normal cumulative distribution function, $\widehat{SR}$ is the estimated Sharpe ratio (non-annualized), T is the number of observations, $\hat{\gamma}_3$ is the skewness of the returns, and $\hat{\gamma}_4$ is the kurtosis of the returns.

When returns are assumed to be normally distributed, the skewness of returns ($\hat{\gamma}_3$) is equal to zero for a standard normal distribution and the kurtosis of returns ($\hat{\gamma}_4$) is 3.

The value of the true Sharpe ratio used by the test as alternative hypothesis is SR^*.

Sample Questions by Clients

In addition to receiving the abovementioned disclosures, clients should ask specific questions regarding the particular backtests presented to them. The following lists a few questions that, with some adjustments depending on the strategy that is being presented, investors should keep in mind.

Looking Beyond the Mean

- Did you calculate metrics other than the mean, such as standard deviation, skewness, and Sharpe ratio?
- Can you show me a graph of the returns' distribution?

Survivorship Bias

- Did you check the backtest for survivorship bias?
- If looking at constituents of an index, did your account for membership change over time?

Correlation and Causation

- Does the alleged cause temporally precede the effect?
- Is predictive power strong?
- Did you test for biases that may be caused by a confounding variable?

Time Period

- What are the regimes included in your time period?
- Can I see the performance over each regime?
- Does the time period include a market environment similar to the current one?
- Does the time period include any extreme historical events?
- Does the strategy include a loss-cutting mechanism?
- Might the time period be too short/too long?

Outliers

- Did you identify possible outliers, and if so, what are they?
- Did you assess the influence of each outlier?
- Do the outliers tell a story, or should they be removed?

Overfitting and Data Mining

- How sensitive is performance to changes in the parameters?
- How many models did you try in addition to the one presented?
- Can I see some statistical tests (T-test, F-Test, etc.)?
- Was the model tested out of sample?

Mark-to-Market

- Did you assess the strategy's mark-to-market performance?
- Can I see the max drawdown, as well as the distribution of drawdowns?

Expecting the Unexpected

- What unexpected event or market environment could cause the strategy to blow up?
- How did you stress test the strategy?

Hidden Exposures

- Did you run the strategy through a risk attribution model in order to scan for unidentified risk exposures?

Practical Aspects

- Can this strategy be arbitraged or front run?
- Did you account for transaction costs?
- If the signal occurs close to trading, what is the basis risk of using an earlier signal?

Key Points

- A reasonable definition of a backtest is that it is a simulation of how a proposed investment strategy would perform subject to certain conditions being true.
- Walk-forward, resampling, and Monte Carlo methods are the three methods used for backtesting.
- The walk-forward method is the most common method used for backtesting.
- The walk-forward method assesses the performance of an investment strategy under the assumption that history repeats itself exactly and is challenging to carry out flawlessly.
- The main advantage of the walk-forward method is that it has a clear historical interpretation.
- An advantage of the walk-forward method is that its performance can be assessed with paper trading.
- The four major drawbacks of the WF method are (1) only a single scenario is tested (the historical path), which can be easily overfit, (2) the initial decisions are made on a smaller portion of the total sample, (3) the results do not tell us why the strategy is profitable, and (4) the results are not necessarily representative of future performance because they can be biased by the particular sequence of datapoints.
- The resampling method addresses WF's disadvantage of only assessing a single scenario because it assesses the performance of an investment strategy under the assumption that future paths can be simulated through the resampling of past observations.
- Clients are typically interested in how the strategy would perform if subjected to a stress scenario such as the 2008 global financial crisis or the 2001 dot-com bubble.
- The resampling method assesses stress scenarios by splitting the observations into a training set and a testing set.

- When using the resampling method, the goal of backtesting is not to derive historically accurate performance, but to infer future performance from a number of out-of-sample scenarios.
- There are three advantages of the resampling method: (1) it is not the result of a particular (historical) scenario, (2) every decision is made on sets of equal size, making outcomes comparable across periods, in terms of the amount of information used to make those decisions, and (3) it relies on many different paths, allowing the researcher to consider more general scenarios consistent with the data-generating process.
- The Monte Carlo method, which assesses the performance of an investment strategy under the assumption that future paths can be simulated via Monte Carlo, addresses the disadvantages of the walk-forward method and has several advantages relative to the walk-forward and resampling methods.
- The MC method requires a deeper knowledge of the DGP, derived from the statistical analysis of the observations or theory.
- The theory of knowledge or epistemology, which is the branch of philosophy dealing with the distinction between justified belief and opinion, offers guidance in evaluating backtesting.
- Two major epistemological limitations preventing finance from becoming a science are that (1) financial theories cannot be tested in a laboratory in controlled experiments and (2) financial systems are extremely dynamic and complex, with conditions that quickly change over time.
- As a consequence of the two epistemological limitations of finance, researchers rely on backtesting for developing investment strategies.
- Walk-forward backtesting offers a sanity check for a proposed investment strategy, but it should not be viewed as a research tool.
- Although an investment strategy may be attractive by looking at the initial investment and the terminal value attributable to the investment strategy and calculating profitability, a backtest is also useful in identifying market regimes when the strategy does not work as expected.
- It is a mistake for asset managers to use backtests to improve the performance of their strategy since the purpose of backtesting is to toss out poor models, not to improve them.
- There are good number of biases and implementation issues when backtesting a strategy.
- Research bias or experimenter bias occurs when the individual on the management team performing the backtesting has the opportunity to

deliberately bias the test for the purpose of obtaining a desired outcome for the investment strategy.

- Optimal period bias in reporting backtesting results occurs when the asset manager excludes the performance of time periods where the strategy performed poorly.
- Time-period bias occurs when the time period testing (start and stop dates) is such that the results are sensitive to different time periods with respect to volatility, economic growth periods, and interest rate levels.
- Survivorship bias occurs when the backtest uses only surviving examples in assessing the performance of a strategy.
- Look-ahead bias occurs when information is used that was not public at the moment that the investment decision was made.
- Selection bias occurs when an investment strategy is designed to perform well on a particular backtest.
- Backtest overfitting can be defined as selection bias on multiple backtests.
- Overcoming the problem of backtest overfitting bias is arguably the most fundamental question in asset management.
- Backtest overfitting bias is difficult to evaluate because the probability of a backtest showing that a strategy is successful based on some performance metric when it is not (i.e., false positive) changes with every new test conducted on the same dataset.
- Backtesting is basically hypothesis testing where the null hypothesis is that the investment strategy tested is not profitable.
- There are two types of errors in backtesting: a false discovery error and a missed discovery error.
- A false discovery error is an error made when an investment strategy is found to be profitable when in fact it is not, referred to as a "Type I" error (or an α error) in hypothesis testing.
- A missed discovery error results when an investment strategy is found to be unprofitable when in fact it is profitable and in hypothesis testing is referred to as a "Type II error" (or β error).
- There is a tradeoff between a false discovery (Type I) error and a missed discovery (Type II) error.
- In backtesting, hypothesis testing using statistical analysis is employed where the researcher uses the same historical database, without accounting for over-testing; this produces tests results that are false positive.
- The problem of selection bias under multiple testing cuts across all the sciences and the social sciences.

- Because of the importance of the problem of selection bias under multiple testing, in pitching clients a new investment strategy, asset managers should provide a report that allows a client to assess the backtests.

References

American Statistical Association, 1997. "Ethical guidelines for statistical practice." Committee on Professional Ethics of the American Statistical Association (April).

Bailey, D. H., J. Borwein, M. López de Prado, and O. J. Zhu, 2014a. "The deflated Sharpe ratio: Correcting for selection bias, backtest overfitting and non-normality," *Journal of Portfolio Management*, 40(5): 94–107.

Bailey, D. H., J. Borwein, M. López de Prado, and O. J. Zhu, 2014b. "Pseudo-mathematics and financial charlatanism: The effects of backtest overfitting on out-of-sample performance," *Notices of the American Mathematical Society*, 61(5): 458–471.

Brooks, C. and H. Kat, 2002. "The statistical properties of hedge fund index returns and their implications for investors," *Journal of Alternative Investments*, 5(2): 26–44.

Fabozzi, F.J. and M. López de Prado, 2018. "Being honest in backtest reporting: A template for disclosing multiple tests," *Journal of Portfolio Management*, 45(1): 141–147.

Gage, D., 2012. "The venture capital secret," *The Wall Street Journal*, September 20. Available at: http://online.wsj.com/news/articles/SB10000872396390443720204578004980476429190.

Ghosh, S., 2001. "Why companies fail—and how their founders can bounce back," Word Knowledge, Harvard Business School, March 2011. Available at: http://hbswk.hbs.edu/item/6591.html.

Harvey, C. and Y. Liu, 2014. "Evaluating trading strategies," *Journal of Portfolio Management*, 40(5): 108–118.

Harvey, C. and Y. Liu, 2016. "...and the cross-section of expected returns," *Review of Financial Studies*, 29(1): 5–68.

Ingersoll, J., M. Spiegel, W. Goetzmann, and I. Welch, 2007. "Portfolio performance manipulation and manipulation-proof performance measures," *Review of Financial Studies*, 20(5): 1504–1546.

Luo, Y., M. Alvarez, S. Wang, J. Jussa, A. Wang, and G. Rohal, 2014. "Seven sins of quantitative investing," White paper, Deutsche Bank Markets Research, September 8.

López de Prado, M. and M. Lewis, 2019. "Detection of false investment strategies using unsupervised learning methods," *Quantitative Finance*, 19(9): 1555–1565.

McLean, R. D. and J. Pontiff, 2016. "Does academic research destroy stock return predictability?" *Journal of Finance*, 71(1): 5–32.

Neyman, J. and E. Pearson, 1933. "IX. On the problem of the most efficient tests of statistical hypotheses," *Philosophical Transactions of the Royal Society. Series A*, 231: 289–337.

Strasak, A., Q. Zaman, G. Marinell, K. Pfeiffer, and H. Ulmer, 2007. "The use of statistics in medical research: A comparison of The New England Journal of Medicine and Nature Medicine," *The American Statistician*, 61(1): 47–55.

Sarfati, O., 2015. "Backtesting: A practitioner's guide to assessing strategies and avoiding pitfalls." Citi Equity Derivatives. Presented at the CBOE 2015 Risk Management Conference. Available at: https://www.cboe.com/rmc/2015/olivier-pdf-Backtesting-Full.pdf.

Chapter 18

Monte Carlo Backtesting Method

Learning Objectives

After reading this chapter, you will understand:

- what is meant by the all-weather hypothesis;
- the difference between strategic investment algorithms and tactical investment strategies;
- what is meant by the data-generating process (DGP);
- the practice of backtesting against synthetic datasets using the Monte Carlo method;
- how the Monte Carlo method for backtesting overcomes the problems associated with the walk-forward and resampling methods for backtesting;
- client concerns with the Monte Carlo method for backtesting and why they are misplaced; and
- a practical way of identifying the prevailing DGP.

Introduction

As explained in the previous chapter, there are two major limitations preventing finance from becoming a science, at par with physics, chemistry, or biology. First, because financial theories used in asset management cannot be tested in a laboratory in controlled experiments, claims such as "value and momentum factors explain the outperformance of stocks" cannot be proven wrong, even if they are. All asset managers have is the outcome from a single realized path (a price time series) produced by an unknown data-generating process (DGP). Investment professionals cannot draw millions of alternative paths from the same DGP and evaluate in how many instances value and momentum factors had explanatory power, while controlling for environmental conditions.

The second limitation afflicting finance is non-stationarity. Financial systems are extremely dynamic and complex, with conditions that quickly change over time. Financial cause-effect mechanisms are not invariant, due to changes in regulations, expectations, economic cycles, market regimes, and other environmental variables. For instance, even if value and momentum factors truly explained the outperformance of stocks in the 20th century, that may no longer be the case as a result of recent technological, behavioral, or policy changes. Perhaps value and momentum only worked under certain conditions that are no longer present. Consequently, claims made by financial economists, which asset managers rely upon in formulating investment algorithms, are typically based on anecdotal information, and do not rise to the standard of scientific theories.

Due to these limitations, in formulating investment algorithms asset managers rely on backtesting. As explained in the previous chapter, backtesting involves inferring the performance of an investment algorithm under the general assumption that future observations will be drawn from the same DGP that produced past observations. In that chapter, we explained two backtesting methods, walk-forward method and resampling method. By far the most common approach followed among practitioners as well as academics is the walk-forward method.

Implicit in that choice of backtesting method is the assumption that a given investment algorithm should be deployed throughout all market regimes. We refer to such assumption as the *all-weather hypothesis*, and the strategies based on that hypothesis are referred to as "strategic investment algorithms" (or "investment strategies"). The all-weather hypothesis is not necessarily true, as demonstrated by the fact that many investment strategies have floundered in the near-zero interest rate environment that has prevailed in recent years. This motivates the problem of identifying investment algorithms that are optimal for specific market regimes, which we denote by "tactical investment strategies".

In this chapter, we argue that backtesting against synthetic datasets should become standard practice for developing tactical investment algorithms. Here we look at how the Monte Carlo simulation method can be used in backtesting. This backtesting method can help address the two limitations mentioned above, thereby bringing financial theories closer to scientific standards. We begin with a discussion of what is meant by the DGP.

The Data-Generating Process

In data science and statistics, the term data generating process (or DGP) can mean different things. One meaning is that of the process or procedure by which the data are collected, entered into a database, and updated as new data become available. While the data collection process is important for creating an accurate database from which a researcher can use data to formulate models, test hypotheses of interest, and, in terms of our objective in this chapter, backtest strategies, that is not how we use the term DGP in this chapter. Instead, we use it in this chapter to define the stochastic process that generates the data under study. The DGP begins by identifying the random variables that are expected to be important in the DGP. These random variables will also include variables for which there are no observations.

The Three Types of Backtests

In general terms, we can differentiate between three types of backtests. First, the walk-forward (WF) method assesses the performance of a proposed investment algorithm under the assumption that history repeats itself *exactly*.[1] A first caveat of WF is that past time series merely reflect one possible path produced by the DGP. If we were to take a time machine, the stochastic nature of the DGP would produce a different path. Since WF backtests are not representative of the past DGP, there is no reason to believe that they are representative of the future DGP. Accordingly, WF is more likely to yield a descriptive (or anecdotal) than an inferential statement.[2] A second caveat of WF is that the DGP is never stated: should the DGP change, the asset manager will not be able to decommission the strategy before it loses money, because the manager never understood the conditions that made the strategy work.

The second type of backtest is the resampling method (RS), which addresses WF's first caveat. RS assesses the performance of an investment strategy under the assumption that future paths can be simulated through

[1]The main argument in favor of WF is that it prevents leakage from look-ahead information as described in the previous chapter. However, if a walk-backwards backtest does not exhibit significantly better performance than a WF, look-ahead leakage is not a concern, making the main argument for WF rather weak.

[2]See Chapter 11 in López de Prado [2018].

the resampling of past observations. The resampling can be deterministic (e.g., jackknife, cross-validation) or random (e.g., subsampling, bootstrap). Because RS can produce many different paths, where the historical path is just one possibility, it allows an asset manager to consider more general scenarios consistent with the DGP. For instance, through an RS backtest an asset manager can bootstrap the distribution of the strategy's Sharpe ratio, which is much more informative than the single-path Sharpe ratio derived by WF. Whereas it is trivial to overfit a WF backtest, it is more difficult to overfit an RS backtest. Still, resampling on a finite historical sample may not yield paths representative of the future.[3]

A backtesting method that we postponed discussion of until this chapter is the Monte Carlo simulation (or MC) method. An explanation of the MC method is provided in Chapter 5. In this chapter we explain how MC can be applied to backtesting, and how MC backtesting addresses both of WF's caveats. The MC backtesting method assesses the performance of an investment algorithm under the assumption that future paths can be simulated via MC. MC backtesting requires a deeper knowledge of the DGP, derived from the statistical analysis of the observations or theory (e.g., market microstructure, institutional processes, economic links, and the like). For instance, economic theory may suggest that two variables are cointegrated, and empirical studies may indicate the range of values that characterize the degree of cointegration. Accordingly, an analyst evaluating an investment algorithm can simulate millions of years of data, where the measure of cointegration used in the analysis takes many different values within the estimated range. This is a much richer analysis than merely resampling observations from a finite (and likely unrepresentative) set of observations.[4]

Four Unique Advantages of MC Backtests

MC backtests offer four critical advantages over WF and RS. First, MC backtests help address the first limitation of finance because they allow backtesting to be conducted based on randomized controlled experiments. Admittedly, these experiments require the assumption of a particular DGP,

[3]See Chapter 12 in López de Prado [2018].
[4]See Chapter 13 in López de Prado [2018].

but at least that DGP is explicitly stated (unlike in the WF backtests published in academic finance journals where empirical results of backtests are reported). In MC backtests, the hypothesis underlying the findings about performance is declared. If the asset manager believes that the true DGP is different, the manager just needs to propose an alternative DGP and repeat the analysis. MC backtests can be considered a particular case of Ersatz tests, where statistical methods are tested on computer-generated data from known models.[5]

Second, MC backtests help address the second limitation of finance because the asset manager does not need to assume that the DGP is immutable. Instead, the discovery is connected to a particular DGP, where realizations may be drawn from different DGPs over time. In other words, MC backtests allow us to develop *tactical investment algorithms* (i.e., investment strategies that are designed to perform optimally under a particular DGP), as opposed to the *strategic investment algorithms* (i.e., all-weather investment algorithms, that is, algorithms that are expected to perform well under all market regimes) developed with the help of WF or RS.[6] The probability that a particular DGP is producing the realizations can be evaluated statistically, which allows researchers to commission or decommission tactical strategies as conditions evolve.

Third, MC backtests enable the incorporation of the probability of an event before new data are collected,[7] which inject information beyond what we could have learned from a finite set of observations. When these priors are motivated by economic theory, MC offers a powerful tool to simulate the most likely scenarios, even if some of those scenarios have not been observed in the past. Unlike WF or RS, MC backtests can help us develop tactical strategies to be deployed in the presence of rare events (i.e., black swans events).

Fourth, the length of MC backtests can be expanded for as long as needed to achieve a targeted degree of confidence. This is helpful in that

[5]See Jarvis, Sharpe, and Smith [2017].

[6]In recent years, it has proven fashionable for some asset managers to promote certain investment factors through long WF backtests (in some cases, covering over a 100 years). Consider the validity of that work, for instance, in an environment of widespread negative interest rates which had never been experienced before. In contrast, it is possible to conduct an MC backtest on data simulated by a DGP with negative interest rates.

[7]In the terminology of Bayesian statistical inference, this probability is referred to as a prior probability.

MC backtests avoid the indetermination inherent in working with finite datasets.

Concerns with Monte Carlo Backtests

Clients are sometimes skeptical of MC backtests because they compute the performance of an investment algorithm based on synthetic data, which may not be representative of future realizations of the true DGP. This skepticism is largely misplaced for two reasons. First, estimating a DGP is not necessarily a harder problem than forecasting the markets. It is intellectually incoherent to assume that, on the one hand, statistical methods can lead to successful investment outcomes but, on the other hand, statistical methods cannot identify a DGP. Second, the observations used by WF and RS are unlikely to reoccur in the future exactly as simulated, and the paths generated by MC are not necessarily less likely.

Another concern is that the analyst performing the backtest may select a DGP that is particularly favorable to the investment algorithm. This concern is also misplaced: the MC method explicitly declares the assumptions underlying the performance simulations, so if the DGP is unrealistically favorable to the strategy, the client can object. In contrast, the WF and RS methods imply those assumptions through the selection of the historical dataset used by the simulations, obfuscating the dangers of selection bias and confirmation bias.

Examples of DGPs

The MC method randomly samples new (unobserved) datasets from an estimated population or DGP, rather than from an observed dataset (like a bootstrap would do). Monte Carlo experiments can be parametric or nonparametric. An instance of a parametric Monte Carlo is a regime-switching time series model,[8] where samples are drawn from alternative processes, $n = 1, \ldots, N$, and where the probability $p_{t,n}$ of drawing from process n at time t is a function of the process from which the previous observation was drawn (a Markov chain). Expectation-maximization algorithm can be used to estimate the probability of transitioning from one process to another at time t (the transition probability matrix). This parametric approach allows

[8]See, for example, Hamilton [1994].

the matching of the statistical properties of the observed dataset, which are then replicated in the unobserved dataset.[9]

One potential caveat of parametric Monte Carlo is that the DGP may be more complex than a finite set of algebraic functions can replicate. When that is the case, non-parametric Monte Carlo experiments may be of help by using various techniques. As explained in De Meer Pardo [2019], these techniques include variational autoencoders, self-organizing maps, and generative adversarial networks.[10]

An autoencoder is a neural network that learns how to represent high-dimensional observations in a low-dimensional space. Variational autoencoders have an additional property which makes their latent spaces continuous. This allows for successful random sampling and interpolation and, in turn, their use as a generative model. Once a variational autoencoder has learned the fundamental structure of the data, it can generate new observations that resemble the statistical properties of the original sample, within a given dispersion (hence the notion of "variational").

A self-organizing map differs from autoencoders in that it applies competitive learning (rather than error-correction), and it uses a neighborhood function to preserve the topological properties of the input space.

Generative adversarial networks train two competing neural networks, where one network (called a generator) is tasked with generating simulated observations from a distribution function, and the other network (called a discriminator) is tasked with predicting the probability that the simulated observations are false given the true observed data. The two neural networks compete until they converge to an equilibrium. The original sample on which the non-parametric Monte Carlo is trained must be representative enough to learn the general characteristics of the DGP, otherwise a parametric Monte Carlo approach should be preferred.[11]

The Tactical Investment Algorithm Factory

The WF and RS backtesting methods attempt to find "all-weather" investment algorithms, that is, strategic investment algorithms that are not

[9]See Franco-Pedroso, Gonzalez-Rodriguez, Cubero, Planas, Cobo, and Pablos [2019].
[10]These methods can be understood as non-parametric, nonlinear estimators of latent variables (similar to a nonlinear principal component analysis).
[11]For additional details, see López de Prado [2019].

associated with a particular DGP, and are deployed under all market conditions. The notion of strategic (all-weather) investment algorithms is inconsistent with the fact that markets go through regimes, during which some strategies are expected to work, and others expected to fail. Given that markets are adaptive and asset managers learn from mistakes, the likelihood that truly all-weather strategies exist is rather slim (an argument often wielded by discretionary portfolio managers). And even if all-weather strategies existed, they are likely to be a rather insignificant subset of the population of strategies that work across one or more regimes.

In contrast to WF and RS backtests, MC backtests help us define the precise sensitivity of an investment algorithm to the characteristics of each DGP. Once we understand what characteristics make the strategy work, we can deploy it tactically, while monitoring the appropriateness of market conditions, and deriving the appropriate ex-ante risk allocations. When used in this way, MC backtests allow us to trade the strategy rather than the markets. Under this investment paradigm, an asset management firm will develop as many tactical investment algorithms as possible,[12] and then deploy only those strategies that are certified to work under the prevalent market conditions. These strategies are DGP-specific, not instrument specific: the same strategy will be deployed tactically on different instruments over time, when those instruments temporarily follow the DGP associated with that strategy. The main difference between the tactical strategy factory (TSF) approach and the strategic strategy factory (SSF) approach is that TSF's objective is to develop DGP-specific strategies which are not required to work all the time. Instead, TSF's strategies only need to work during the DGP for which they have been certified.

DGP Identification

MC backtests allow researchers to pose the strategy selection problem in terms of a DGP identification problem. This is advantageous because finding a strategy that works well across all possible DGPs is much more challenging than estimating what is the current DGP (which in turn determines the strategy that should be run at a given point in time). Also, from a

[12]See Chapter 11 in López de Prado [2018].

mathematical perspective, identifying the optimal strategy associated with a particular DGP is a well-defined problem.[13]

One practical way of identifying the prevailing DGP is as follows. First, through MC backtests, develop many tactical investment algorithms for a wide range of DGPs. Second, select a sample of recent market performances. Third, evaluate the probability that the sample of recent market performances was drawn from each of the studied DGPs. This probability can be estimated through different methods.[14] The resulting distribution of probability can then be used to allocate risk across the strategies developed by the TSF. In other words, an ensemble of optimal strategies is deployed, and not only the most likely optimal strategy.

In practice, it takes only a few recent observations for the estimated distribution of probability to narrow down the likely DGPs. The reason is, we are comparing two samples, where the synthetic one comprises potentially millions of datapoints, and it typically does not take many observations to discard DGPs that are inconsistent with recent observations.

Another possibility is to create a basket of securities with a return distribution that matches the distribution of a given DGP. Under this alternative implementation, rather than estimating the probability that a security follows a DGP, we create a synthetic security (as a basket of securities) for which a given strategy is optimal.

One virtue of running an ensemble of optimal strategies is that the ensemble strategy does not correspond to any particular DGP. This allows the ensemble strategy to dynamically and smoothly transition from one DGP to another, and even profit from a never-seen-before DGP.

Closing Thoughts on the Backtesting with the Monte Carlo Method

Backtests using the MC method offer an asset management team the possibility of conducting the financial equivalent of randomized controlled

[13]Many journal articles promote investment algorithms without stating the DGP that those strategies supposedly exploit. Without knowing the DGP, a client and the management of an asset management firm cannot know the conditions under which that strategy is supposed to be run, or when to decommission it.

[14]The methods include the total variation distance, the Wasserstein distance, the Jensen–Shannon distance, some derivation of the Kullback–Leibler divergence, or the Kolmogorov–Smirnov test.

experiments. An MC backtest can be understood as a certification of the performance of an investment algorithm subject to certain declared environmental conditions, similar to how an engineer would certify the performance of a type of equipment. In contrast with the WF and RS methods, MC backtests inform us about the conditions under which the tactical investment strategy should be deployed. This information also helps an asset management team pinpoint the circumstances under which the strategy is most vulnerable, when the strategy should be decommissioned, and how much risk should be allocated to it.

Given that markets are adaptive, and asset managers learn from mistakes, the likelihood that truly all-weather strategies exist is rather slim (an argument often wielded by discretionary portfolio managers). And even if all-weather strategies existed, they are likely to be a rather insignificant subset of the population of strategies that work across one or more regimes. Accordingly, asset managers should embrace the TSF approach paradigm, hence developing as many tactical investment algorithms as possible, through MC backtesting.

Key Points

- Two major limitations prevent finance from becoming a science: (1) financial theories cannot be tested in a laboratory in controlled experiments and (2) financial systems are extremely dynamic and complex, with conditions that quickly change over time.
- Due to these limitations, in formulating investment algorithms asset managers rely on backtesting, which involves inferring the performance of an investment algorithm under the general assumption that future observations will be drawn from the same DGP that produced past observations.
- The DGP in backtesting is defined as the stochastic process that generates the data under study and begins by identifying the random variables that are expected to be important in the process.
- There are three backtesting methods: walk-forward, resampling, and Monte Carlo.
- The most common backtesting method used by practitioners as well as academics is the walk-forward method.
- Implicit in that choice of backtesting method is the assumption that a given investment algorithm should be deployed throughout all market regimes, an assumption which is referred to as the all-weather hypothesis.
- Strategies based on the all-weather hypothesis are referred to as strategic investment algorithms.

- Because the all-weather hypothesis is not necessarily true, this motivates the problem of identifying investment algorithms that are optimal for specific market regimes, which are referred to as tactical investment algorithms.
- The four advantages of the Monte Carlo method compared to the walk-forward and resampling methods are: (1) allows backtesting to be conducted based on randomized controlled experiments; (2) allows the development of tactical investment algorithms; (3) allows the incorporation of the probability of an event before new data are collected, and; (4) length of backtests can be expanded for as long as needed to achieve a targeted degree of confidence.
- Clients are sometimes skeptical of MC backtests because they compute the performance of an investment algorithm based on synthetic data, which may not be representative of future realizations of the true DGP.
- Some client concerns with MC backtests are misplaced because: (1) estimating a DGP is not necessarily a harder problem than forecasting the markets and (2) the observations used by the other two backtest methods (walk-forward and resampling) are unlikely to reoccur in the future exactly as simulated, and the paths generated by the MC method are not necessarily less likely.
- An advantage of MC backtests is that it allows researchers to pose the strategy selection problem in terms of a DGP identification problem.
- A practical way of identifying the prevailing DGP using the MC method is as follows: (1) develop many tactical investment algorithms for a wide range of DGPs; (2) select a sample of recent market performances; and (3) evaluate the probability that the sample of recent market performances was drawn from each of the studied DGPs.
- The distribution of probability generated by the MC method should be used to allocate risk across the strategies developed by the tactical strategy factory.

References

De Meer Pardo, F., 2019. "Enriching financial datasets with generative adversarial networks," Working paper. Available at: http://resolver.tudelft.nl/uuid:51d69925-fb7b-4e82-9ba6-f8295f96705c.

Franco-Pedroso, J., J. Gonzalez-Rodriguez, J. Cubero, M. Planas, R. Cobo, and F. Pablos, 2019. "Generating virtual scenarios of multivariate financial data for quantitative trading applications," *Journal of Financial Data Science*, 1(2): 55–77.

Hamilton, J., 1994. *Time Series Analysis.* Princeton, NJ: Princeton University Press.

Jarvis, S., J. Sharpe, and A. Smith, 2017. "Ersatz model tests," *British Actuarial Journal*, 22(3): 490–521.

López de Prado, M., 2018. *Advances in Financial Machine Learning.* Hoboken, NJ: Wiley.

López de Prado, M., 2019. *Systems and Methods for a Factory that produces Tactical Investment Algorithms through Monte Carlo Backtesting.* United States Patent and Trademark Office, Application No. 62/899,164.

López de Prado, M., 2020. *Machine Learning for Asset Managers.* Cambridge: Cambridge University Press.

Author Index

Subject Index

D

E

F

J

K

L

M

N

O

P

Q

R

S

T

www.ingramcontent.com/pod-product-compliance
Lightning Source LLC
LaVergne TN
LVHW011656200926
848484LV00004B/952